DATE DUE			

The Road to Redemption

White Democrats will not train in parti-colored regiments, and every attempt to enlist black recruits in our ranks, will drive more white soldiers away than gain black ones. . . . The road to redemption is under the white banner.
—Mobile *Register*, editorial, 13 January 1871

The Fred W. Morrison

Series in Southern Studies

The Road to Redemption
Southern Politics, 1869–1879

by Michael Perman

The University of North Carolina Press

Chapel Hill and London

© 1984 The University of North Carolina Press

All rights reserved

Manufactured in the United States of America

Library of Congress Cataloging in Publication Data
Perman, Michael.
  The road to redemption.

  (The Fred W. Morrison series in Southern studies)
  Bibliography: p.
  Includes index.
  1. Reconstruction. 2. Southern States—Politics and
government—1865–1950. I. Title. II. Series.
F216.P47 1984   973.8   83-12498
ISBN 0-8078-1526-8

*The publication of this work was made possible in part through a
grant from the National Endowment for the Humanities, a federal
agency whose mission is to award grants to support education,
scholarship, media programming, libraries, and museums, in order
to bring the results of cultural activities to a broad, general public.*

To Benjamin & Sarah

Contents

Acknowledgments

I have incurred numerous debts in the process of writing this book and it is very gratifying to me that I can now acknowledge them.

First, I would like to thank the staffs of the manuscript collections that I visited for their cooperation and their willingness to put up with my eagerness to cover as much ground as possible in the limited time available to me during my forays into the South. Most of my research, however, was carried out in Chicago and I am grateful both to the staff at my own university's library for their solicitousness and help and to the University of Chicago for providing such a wonderfully comfortable and well-equipped microfilm reading room where I spent so many days poring over the newspapers in its collection.

My research has been supported financially by several institutions and foundations and, without this aid, the project could not have been undertaken. I received grants-in-aid from the Research Board of the University of Illinois at Chicago in 1973–74 and from the American Council of Learned Societies in 1974–75. In addition, during the academic year 1979–80, I was awarded fellowships by the Guggenheim Foundation and by the Charles Warren Center at Harvard University. Because of these fellowships, I was able to spend a year on leave at the Warren Center where I wrote most of the first draft.

Several typists have had a hand in deciphering my handwriting and transforming it into typescript, and I would like to thank Gwendolyn St. Clair, Darlene Bakk, and especially Pat Denault of the Warren Center and Louise Alfini from my own department, for their patience and skill.

A number of historians have played a crucial role in encouraging me and offering valuable criticism of my work over the years. David Donald, John Hope Franklin, and Eric Foner have supported the project in many ways, and I am very indebted to them for what they have done and said. Les Benedict and Mills Thornton have been constant sources of advice, information, and encouragement in the many talks we have had, and I have benefited immensely from their friendship and insights. Mills Thornton has also read and criticized several chapters in draft, as have Eric Foner, George Fredrickson, and Otto Olsen. Their comments, both critical and approving, were of great importance, helping to improve the manuscript as well as encourage the author.

I want to thank my editors at the press, Iris Hill and Gwen Duffey, for their thoughtful cooperation in the preparation and production of this book. Also very helpful were the two readers who reviewed the manuscript; they spotted errors and made comments which were most useful.

Finally, I want to thank Bonnie, and Benjamin and Sarah. Bonnie offered valuable criticism and reassurance, particularly in the early stages of the project, while Benjamin and Sarah wondered how long it would be before the book was completed.

M. P.

Chicago, December 1983

Introduction

The history of southern Reconstruction is currently attracting a great deal of attention. After a period of comparative quiet following the excitement generated by the revisionism of the 1960s, the post-Civil War era in the South is experiencing a revival of interest. The reason for this renewed fascination is that the same kinds of concerns and techniques which have, in the past decade, been applied to slavery and the antebellum South are being transferred to the postwar situation. Econometricians are using quantitative methodology to discover the nature of the postbellum economy; historians employing Marxist analysis are investigating the system of class relations that prevailed after the planters had been defeated in war and deprived of their slaves; social and economic historians are examining the complexities and subtleties of the land and labor system of the late-nineteenth-century South; and, lastly, cultural historians are discovering the ethos and attitudes of the freedmen and their landlords in the world of the plantation after emancipation.[1]

While the social, economic, and cultural history of the Reconstruction South is being reexamined, the same cannot really be said for its politics. In fact, as it happens, politics both before the war as well as after it has received very little attention of late. Yet, the politics of the postwar South certainly does need reinvigoration, and it is my hope that *The Road to Redemption* may help make a start in this direction. But should it do so, it will not be because it is based on newly discovered sources of evidence. Nor will it be because it reintroduces topics previously overlooked or ignored. Rather, its contribution will lie in the perspectives and approaches that it brings to the study of southern politics in the postwar era.

These are essentially three in number. The first is that the entire South is covered here, not just a single state as has so often been the case in southern historical writing generally and in writing about the Reconstruction in particular. This has made it possible to discern patterns and trends across the region which might otherwise remain undetected. The second perspective has been to consider Reconstruction as an episode in southern political history, rather than as a discrete event cut out of the normal flow of the region's political development. Reconstruction was not imposed on the South and then later removed without leaving a trace. The formation of the Republican party and the creation of a vast new black electorate affected decisively the course of the South's politics. Indeed, both remained for several decades after Reconstruction had ended. But the process also worked in the other direction. For the existing political system in turn affected the Republican party and, to a large extent, shaped the way it functioned. Thus, there was a dynamic relationship between the Republican party and the political system in which it was forced to exist and operate. Reconstruction was not, therefore, played out against the background of the southern political system but was an essential part of it. What this means, in effect, is that the politics of southern Reconstruction cannot be understood without an appreciation of the role of Reconstruction in southern politics.

Because historians have usually conceived of Reconstruction as a discrete and self-contained occurrence, they have also fitted it into a rigid chronological mold marked out from 1868, when it began, to 1876, when it was effectively over. As a result, their studies have concluded with the overthrow of Reconstruction and so have not investigated the political universe that took its place. Because of this, Reconstruction and Redemption have been separated from each other, and whatever continuities and connections there were between these two worlds have been lost sight of. In addition, by compartmentalizing Reconstruction in this way, historians have focused their attention on what transpired during it without much consideration for what occurred beyond and after. This concentration on Reconstruction itself, without paying much attention to the context in which it took place, has resulted in a preoccupation with explaining its dramatic collapse. Since it was all over by 1876, the need to explain why it failed has been overwhelming, with the result that most of the history of the period has been written with this question in mind. And this leads directly to the third of the perspectives I have taken in this book. I have approached Reconstruction in the South, not in terms of why it failed but of how it worked, seeing it as a process to be described and analyzed rather than as a problem to be solved, a question to be answered.

Because Reconstruction was so anomalous and unsettling, it could be that the political process was likewise abnormal. To discover whether this was so has required me to examine the political parties to see what they were like and what they did. To this end, attention has been focused, in the first case, on the composition of both parties and on the images they projected and identities they assumed. To discover what they did, I have examined the way they formulated issues, mobilized voters, and conducted campaigns. Naturally enough, this kind of approach deals with both parties and the dynamics of their competitive relationship. It is not concerned only with the Republicans as is usually the case when the failure of Reconstruction is the focus of interest. Indeed, because the Democrats, unlike the Republicans, had already been in existence in the South for many decades and would, as events transpired, also outlive Reconstruction and later dominate the region's political life, more attention has been devoted to them than to their opponents. But their importance is greater than that, because, in effect, the Democrats embodied the continuities and the elements of persistence in southern politics with which the Republicans had to deal if they were to endure.

Interestingly enough, this focus on the two major parties has dramatized a development during the era which has often passed unnoticed but which was of great significance at the time. Despite the obvious contrast between the Republicans who were the agents of Reconstruction and their opponents who were committed to its defeat, there later developed, once the effort to prevent Reconstruction had failed by 1868, a tendency in which both parties deemphasized their formal differences and adopted policies and platforms that were similar. As both parties began to compete in this way for the political center, the differences between them became not only less evident but also of less significance in determining the course of southern politics. Of more importance were the internal divisions within the parties as they began to polarize into divergent factions that differed about the wisdom and expedience of the direction in which their parties were being led. The outcome of these contests affected, to a considerable extent, the way in which Redemption occurred and what its aftereffects were to be. These internal factions, or intraparty tendencies, were, in fact, the fulcrum on which southern politics turned in the 1870s. Furthermore, as we shall see, they were not without impact on the region's economic life as well.

During Reconstruction, an attempt was made in the South to return its politics to the two-party system that it had experienced during the Jacksonian era. *The Road to Redemption* is a study of that experiment in party formation. As such, it attempts to explain how this system operated, what brought about its collapse, and what took its place. After all, Reconstruction was not embarked upon solely to round out and settle the sectional conflict. Far more important was its purpose of establishing a new political order, even a new economic direction, for the South, and that is what this book is about.

Part I
The Politics of Convergence:
Reconstruction, 1869–1873

1. The Contest for the Political Center, 1869–1870

It will require a few years longer to wear away all the bitter memories of the great war of the Rebellion. But since the election of Grant a happy change has come over the spirit of their dreams. They are feeling better; they are looking forward to a bright and glorious future, and, indeed, evincing a little too much impatience for an overload of Northern men, with money and skill.
—Joseph Medill, reporting from the South, in Chicago *Tribune*, 9 April 1869

In the presidential election of 1868, the Republicans campaigned as the party of stability, peace, and sectional concord. By contrast, their Democratic opponents were identified with turmoil and disruption, even revolution. This was a surprising and sudden reversal of the roles assumed by the major parties, for during the previous few years, and even before the war as well, the voters had come to regard the new Republican party as the advocate and agent of change and the Democrats as a force for conservatism and continuity.

These public perceptions were not incorrect. The parties had not changed; it was just that the set of issues over which they had battled since the war were now placed in a different context. The changes that Republicans had been proposing for the South were no longer impending. Instead, the electorate was being asked to ratify them, and they constituted a postwar settlement in the South which was already in operation. The reconstruction of the southern states had preoccupied the Republicans since the final years of the war, and upon its successful formulation and execution the future both of the party and of the nation had depended. To withhold approval now that the Republicans' difficult and dangerous task had been completed would not only endanger the party itself but it would undermine the political and legal edifice that had been erected in the South, and this would constitute a repudiation of the status quo.

If in 1868, the Democrats had nominated Salmon P. Chase, the chief justice of the United States and Lincoln's opponent for the Union party presidential nomination in 1864, the Reconstruction settlement would not have been contested. But the selection of Horatio Seymour and Francis P. Blair, Jr., meant that the party was not acquiescent and would continue its opposition. Even though all the southern states—except Texas, Mississippi, and Virginia—had been reorganized and readmitted to the Union under the terms of the Reconstruction Acts, the party evidently regarded Reconstruction as still an open question. Evidence for this was abundant in the Democratic campaign whose keynote was provided by Blair's pronouncement that the Reconstruction laws were "usurpations and unconstitutional, revolutionary and void." Furthermore, if they were not resisted, Blair had added, "The peace to which Grant invites us is the peace of despotism and death."[1]

In the South, these avowals were perceived as offering a last desperate hope that Reconstruction might still be averted. So the opponents of the Republicans and of Reconstruction threw off their strategy of "masterly inactivity" and plunged feverishly into the campaign for a Democratic victory. Benjamin Hill's denunciation of Reconstruction as an "infamy" was followed by the violent eruption of the Ku Klux Klan.[2] Yet the effect on the Democrats' prospects of the South's active involvement and of the Klan's violence was catastrophic. To their image as disturbers of stability were added both a sectional identification with the South and complicity in political violence. The outcome was that, except in the South where the terrorism helped Seymour to win in Georgia and Louisiana and to come close in Alabama and Arkansas, the Democrats carried only

Oregon and New Jersey, the border states of Kentucky and Maryland, and Seymour's own state of New York.

Besides confirming and securing the Reconstruction settlement, the Republican victory in 1868 established the party's political credentials. In the first place, the Republicans were no longer a sectional party. They had a political base that was national in scope. Although they did not sweep the reconstructed South in the presidential vote, they did control state government and congressional delegations throughout the region, a significant contrast with 1860 when Lincoln had not even been a candidate there. A second gain from the 1868 election was the recognition that the party could win the presidency under normal peacetime circumstances. The Republicans had thus achieved legitimacy. This outcome had been achieved, in large measure, through the party's selection of General Grant, a nonpartisan national hero, who had then campaigned on the slogan of "Let Us Have Peace." If the Republicans could now turn the country away from sectional questions toward pressing and long-term issues of finance and economic development, not only would they outflank the Democrats who were still clinging to outworn sectional issues, but they would demonstrate their own fitness and ability to govern.

While the election of 1868 had bestowed legitimacy and nationalism on the Republicans, it had, at the same time, confirmed the Democrats in both their association with treason and irresponsibility and their status as the minority party. This outcome was alarming to southerners who had pinned their hopes for deliverance on a returning conservatism in the northern electorate, "the sober second thought" as they called it, which was expected to manifest itself politically through the Democratic party. Consequently, the 1868 election returns forced them to reassess their own strategic thinking. They had backed the wrong horse. Because of this, they had failed to prevent Reconstruction and now faced four years of Republican control of the national government as well as Republican domination of the southern states.[3] Consequently, their political assumptions and the calculations they based on them needed immediate reappraisal.

The southern search for an alternative strategy was initiated in the wake of the election, almost before Ulysses Grant had been inaugurated, and the focus of this search was the general himself. Ironically, it was those very qualities of national recognition and nonpartisanship that had been so significant to the Republicans when they nominated Grant which now suggested themselves as potential assets to the party's southern opponents as they sought release from their political quandary. The broadened appeal and diminished partisanship that his nomination had given the Republicans could be of advantage to the southern Democratic-Conservatives too.* Grant had, after all, no close identification with the Republican party; in fact he had usually voted Democratic before the war. Moreover, he had been sufficiently cautious and conservative in his political attitudes that the more radical members of the party had preferred Benjamin Wade over Grant in 1868. In fact, the general's availability as well as his obvious electoral assets and his past political record had even made him an attractive candidate for the Democrats to consider seriously.

The upshot of all this was that Grant was not beholden to the party's radical wing and even his ties with the Republican party as a whole were meager. This flexibility was evident in his letter to the Republican convention accepting its nomination. Impervious to party dogma and aware of the fluidity in the political situation, he announced that "in times like the present it is impossible, or at least eminently improper to lay down a policy to be adhered to, right or wrong, through an administration of four years."[4] With Grant's future course not fixed or clear and his past record and inclinations open to interpretation, there was reasonable hope that he might be receptive to southern overtures.

*From 1868 until about 1873 or 1874, the Republicans' opponents throughout the South referred to themselves as either the Conservative party or else as the Democratic and Conservative party. To generalize this trend, but yet to maintain the contemporary desire to be distinctive, in some way, from the Democratic party in the North, they will be referred to as Democratic-Conservatives.

This term is a little unwieldy, but it does embrace their ambivalence towards the Democracy. On the one hand, they naturally associated themselves with the northern party, which had opposed the Republicans during the secession crisis and the war as well as Reconstruction, and they did send delegates to the Democratic national convention in 1868. On the other hand, they did not describe themselves as Democrats in the South, since they wanted to retain as much flexibility and leverage as they could and they also hoped, by deemphasizing their Democratic affinity, to be able to capture the support of former Whigs.

The first person to take the initiative was Augustus H. Garland, a distinguished Arkansas politician who had been a Confederate senator and in 1874 would be governor of his state. Anxious that "something must be done quickly," he proposed that a delegation be assembled from the South to meet with the president-elect in the new year, in order to bring "some kind and considerate" influence to bear on him. The group could also inform him that those in the South "of social, pecuniary, and moral responsibility, desire peace earnestly, and are ready and willing to conform to rules under any one, if they can be protected in their rights as given them even in the general terms of the Constitution." Whether this protection would be provided depended ultimately on the president. He could either follow "the programme and the wishes of the party whose candidate he was," in which case "ruin, red ruin" would be the consequence. Or he could follow "his own judgement" and "administer the government according to the Constitution, and in justice to all." If he did the latter, he would "rescue us from destruction, and lay broad, deep, and permanent, the foundation for our future well being."[5]

The delegation, Garland suggested, should be composed of "*representative* men of the true conservatism," who were "neither active Democrats or republicans in the late contest," nor men "who stirred up strife and bitter feelings." In this category, Garland had in mind himself; his correspondent, Alexander Stephens, who had been vice-president of the Confederacy; William A. Graham of North Carolina who had been Winfield Scott's vice-presidential running-mate in 1852; James L. Orr, the outgoing governor of South Carolina; and Generals Robert E. Lee and Joseph E. Johnston. Regarded as possessing moderate and national views, both in the secession crisis and since the war, these southern statesmen and soldiers could demonstrate to Grant the evidence for southern conservatism and acquiescence and, in so doing, encourage him to adopt a conciliatory course toward the former Confederate states. In this way, the extremism of both section and party, which had erupted in the election campaign and been so disastrous, could be countered, and a conservative tone arise in its place. As Garland described the predicament: "During the last three months, ground in between the nether and upper mill-rocks, conservatism proper has been strangled, and bad men on both sides desiring trouble and commotion, have kept the country on fire, just as the late hell-born war originated in 1860–61."[6]

Garland was not alone in discerning the pivotal role that Grant might play in national politics now that Reconstruction was completed and the decisive presidential election of 1868 settled. Alexander Stephens himself, who, unlike Garland, had met Grant before when they had both been at the City Point peace negotiations during the war, announced publicly that he admired the general and expected him to resist pressures within his party to pursue a hostile southern policy. He was, Stephens wrote, "one of the most remarkable men I have ever met . . . a man of great generosity and magnanimity, neither selfish nor ambitious; and I believe he meant all that the words impart when he said: 'Let us have Peace.'"[7] This was an estimate of Grant that Stephens never relinquished; in 1873 and 1874, it would be the basis of his efforts to swing the southern Democrats behind a move to reelect the general to a third term. The strength of character and the conservatism that Stephens detected in Grant would lead, he hoped, to a split between the president and the more radical wing of the Republican party.

An even more dramatic transformation of American party politics was envisaged by Joseph E. Brown. A former secessionist who had turned against the Confederacy while he was wartime governor of Georgia, Brown, unlike the others, was currently affiliating with the Republicans, from whom he had received appointment as the state's chief justice. Despite his differing partisan associations, Brown shared the others' belief that existing party organizations were ephemeral and that, once the sectional issue was settled, the parties would undergo some kind of realignment. He explained his predictions to Alexander Stephens in December 1868. "When you counsel moderation and a generous confidence in Genl Grant I firmly believe he will deserve it," he wrote, "and that in a few months the extreme radicals of the North will join Toombs, Hill and others of the South in disowning him." In the presidential election, Robert Toombs and Benjamin Hill, both of Georgia, had been stridently sectional and anti-Republican. In view of this, Brown assumed that, with the southern and northern extremists joined in opposition to Grant, "the moderate conservative men of the Country will then rally to him without regard to past party associations and will sustain him." In the coalition that would thus occupy the middle of the political spectrum, even sectional loyalties would no longer be a major consideration, for Brown concluded with a quite remarkable suggestion. After congratulating the vice-president of the Confederacy on his "almost neutral" stance in 1868, he proposed: "I trust you will be looked to as the great southern leader of the party."[8]

Coming from Joseph Brown, one of the South's more hard-headed, even Machiavellian politicians, a man who could not be accused of political naivete or fanciful speculation, this was a most revealing comment. It suggested the extent to which a party realignment was anticipated and the lengths to which it was expected to proceed. The notion that a realignment of the parties was imminent and that the president would be the catalyst was not a new one for southern politicians to entertain. They had been convinced earlier that Andrew Johnson would split with the radical Republicans and, through the National Union movement that he launched in 1866, bring about a coalition of the conservative forces within the two major parties, thereby creating a new intersectional party of the center.[9] With Reconstruction seemingly completed, the prospects for party reorganization after 1868 appeared even stronger, giving rise to speculations as extreme as Brown's. Parties could no longer be aligned on the basis of irreconcilable stances toward Reconstruction as well as of mutually exclusive sectional identifications. The fateful cleavage in American party politics, evident since the late 1850s, had to be ended, and Grant's election brought resolution much closer.

Although there was extensive discussion of changes in the composition of the parties in the North after 1868, the major political breakthrough occurred in the southern states. This initiative was engineered, not by Grant's party, but by its Democratic-Conservative opponents, and it took place in Tennessee, Mississippi, Texas, and Virginia. The latter three states had been denied readmission to Congress in July 1868 because they had not ratified their new constitutions which had provided for, among other things, the black suffrage mandated by the Reconstruction Acts. So, in 1869, these constitutions had to be resubmitted. Simultaneously, new elections for state officials were to be held, because the refusal to adopt a constitution had invalidated the earlier election of 1868. Since Tennessee was also electing a successor to its Republican governor, William Brownlow, who had just resigned to fill a vacant seat in the U.S. Senate, there were four southern states holding elections in 1869, and these four inaugurated what was to be called the "new movement."

This initiative involved a major shift in political strategy on the part of the Democratic-Conservatives because it rejected confrontation and aimed instead at defusing the issues of Reconstruction and undermining the Republican party. The plan was that, in the ratification vote on the constitutions, the Democratic-Conservatives should approve them, thus acknowledging the provisions for black suffrage which they contained. Furthermore, in the accompanying state elections, the party was to back the more conservative group of Republicans whenever there was a split and the possibility of a separate and rival ticket. As a result of this tactical maneuver, it was hoped that the Republicans would not only be disarmed by their opponents' sudden conciliatory attitude but also be demoralized and further divided by it.

A change of this magnitude did not take place, however, without vigorous debate beforehand. In Texas, the argument for the "new movement" was presented most forcefully by former Confederate Postmaster-General John H. Reagan, and, in this, he was joined by Colonel W. M. Walton, the party chairman, and John Hancock, a leading moderate among the Democratic-Conservatives. Reagan argued that the proposed constitution containing universal suffrage should be adopted because it was "more liberal than any other we can expect will be submitted to us if we reject this." In fact, "Negro suffrage is now inevitable in any contingency. It cannot be averted without a change of national sentiment and of the federal government." Furthermore, ratification was not so disadvantageous after all because the constitution's imposition of black suffrage was offset by its provision of amnesty. Thus, numerous former Confederates who would most likely vote Democratic-Conservative would be re-enfranchised. Ratification would, therefore, "secure permanent civil government, in a few years at most, under our own laws to be made and administered by agents of our own choice." [10]

Cooperation with Republicans was not limited to the constitution. It was to be accompanied by a similar approach regarding party organization in the upcoming state election. Reagan advised, therefore, that party should be put "in abeyance" for the time being.

The basis for this advice was that "our most grievous political sin, the greatest impediment to our being allowed civil government and political rights now, therefore, is that we are democrats and conservatives." To avoid this trap, he suggested that "moderate democrats and moderate republicans . . . unite in the common object, for the common good." To this end, Reagan urged the leadership to "put forward candidates partly of both parties, but all eligible [to hold office] under the reconstruction laws and 14th amendment." All the same, a complete merger of the two party organizations was not envisaged. The Democratic-Conservatives intended to run on their own at the local level, while supporting the bolting Republican faction for state offices and for Congress. As Reagan explained: "We are going to do all we can here to elect conservatives to the legislature and the various county offices."[11] Evidently, he did not intend to surrender the local base of the party but rather expected to use it as the foundation for the Democratic-Conservatives' future resurgence.

This kind of maneuver would have been inconceivable if there had not developed within the Republican party two distinct factions that differed in their stance on the constitution. The conservatives, who favored ratification, were led by Jack Hamilton who had been provisional governor during 1865, and the radicals were headed by Edmund J. Davis and Hamilton's brother, Morgan. The latter group regarded the amnesty and liberal suffrage provisions, which had been included in the constitution, primarily at Jack Hamilton's insistence, as fatal to the future of the party in Texas. On the other hand, the strategy of forging a link with the conciliatory wing of the Democratic-Conservatives, through agreement on the desirability of amnesty, had been advanced quite purposely by Jack Hamilton. He believed that only by moving to the center could the Republicans be guaranteed longevity. And, as we have seen, Hamilton's overtures were reciprocated, Hancock and Walton both concluding that "in fighting this battle we must work through the Moderate Republicans" and elect Jack Hamilton governor "if we have strength to do it."[12] Meanwhile, Reagan put the issue rather more bluntly when he admitted that Hamilton "can do more than any other person I know to divide the Republican party" and defeat its "extreme radical" wing.[13]

The same outcome would transpire in the other three states,

but they would arrive at it by somewhat different routes. In Virginia, the emergence of a fusion ticket, coupled with Democratic-Conservative support for the previously rejected constitution, was accomplished through two parallel, though independent, moves within the ranks of the Democratic-Conservatives. The first was commenced by a group of prominent former Whigs, led by Alexander H. H. Stuart; his brother-in-law, John B. Baldwin; and the industrialist, William T. Sutherlin. Forming the Committee of Nine in January 1869, they negotiated directly and secretly with President Grant for relief from the proposed constitution's disfranchisement clause and office-holding test oath. The upshot was that Grant agreed to submit the two proscriptive clauses separately and, if defeated, they were to be entirely eliminated. Simultaneously, William Mahone, the railroad promoter who was attempting to consolidate Virginia's railroads under his own control, was engaged in a maneuver to develop a gubernatorial candidate sympathetic to those interests. Neither the Republican nominee, Henry Wells, whose railroad sympathies were too northern, nor Robert Withers, who was tied too closely to the interest of John Strode Barbour of the Baltimore and Ohio, was reliable. So Mahone and some aggrieved conservative Republicans created their own ticket of True Republicans, headed by Gilbert C. Walker. Fearing a divided vote, the Democratic-Conservative Executive Committee then decided to withdraw Withers and support Walker. This action committed the True Republicans to defeating the proscriptive clauses while ratifying the constitution and its provisions for black suffrage.[14]

This strategy succeeded in Virginia and it also worked in Tennessee. In the latter, the opportunity for a "new movement" developed because, quite unexpectedly, the Republican convention denied the acting governor, DeWitt Senter, its gubernatorial nomination in 1869. Feeling that he had lost the support of the bulk of the party and that the ensuing split had shattered its cohesion irrevocably, Senter tried to create a coalition of Republican conservatives and Democrats. To this end, he wielded his power to appoint registrars of election, perhaps to an illegal degree, and thereby enfranchised thousands of former Confederates who previously had been denied the vote by Tennessee's highly restrictive suffrage provision. As a result, Senter, a Republican, was elected primarily by

Democratic votes that, in actuality, had been created by his own executive action.[15]

In Mississippi, the outcome of the "new movement" was to be less satisfactory to the Democratic-Conservatives. After the constitution failed to be ratified in 1868, the Republican gubernatorial candidate, Benjamin Eggleston, and his Committee of Sixteen urged Grant to reject the election results and install both the Republican state ticket and the constitution. There were other, more conservative Republicans who also believed that the constitution should be resubmitted, but they differed with the Eggleston group because they felt that resubmission should take place only after the document had been purged of its proscriptive features. Concurring in this proposition were the Democratic-Conservatives, who then floated a fusion Republican ticket, headed by President Grant's brother-in-law, Louis Dent. The selection of Dent was obviously intended to secure the president's endorsement, but, instead, Grant supported the regular Republican nominee, James Alcorn, a prominent prewar politician who had been selected as U.S. senator in 1866. With Alcorn as standard-bearer for the regular Republicans, the dull, politically inexperienced Dent had no chance. Further undermining the Dent movement was the Alcorn Republicans' inclusion of amnesty in their platform. The result was that, as one of Dent's supporters put it, "we made a platform and the radicals adopted it and beat us on it." The constitution was therefore overwhelmingly ratified while the proscriptive clauses, which were submitted separately as in Virginia, were rejected.[16] Interestingly enough, the degree to which the Republicans and Democratic-Conservatives fused in the Dent campaign was quite extensive. One angry Democratic-Conservative regretted that "the Democracy instead of holding aloof from the movement until candidates were selected, and then taking hold of it only as a choice between men, have fused their incipient county meetings, become delegates to the State convention that nominated Dent, and put out a platform of principles Radical to the core."[17]

Although the "new movement" had been widely perceived as the first sign of an impending party realignment, its potential was not to be realized. In the first place, it was annihilated in Mississippi and, as it turned out, was also decisively beaten in Texas. A second problem was that many Democratic-Conservatives regarded the scheme as a piece of trickery, ultimately destructive of the party's integrity. Supporting a Republican ticket and endorsing both black suffrage and the Reconstruction constitution was too much to swallow so soon after the 1868 election and their party's unrelenting struggle to prevent Reconstruction. Even many of the protagonists regretted their participation in the "new movement." Wiley P. Harris, a leading Mississippi politician, admitted: "I am not altogether satisfied with what I did. . . . I conceived the idea of building up a party between the extremes; but I found I was too fast for one and too slow for the other. So that I and those who acted with me shared the fate of the Girondists."[18]

There were two further considerations that clinched the demise of the "new movement." The first and most important was that President Grant did not encourage it. He was noncommittal towards Walker, while, elsewhere, he gave his endorsement to the regular Republican candidates rather than to Hamilton, Dent, and Senter. Without Grant's cooperation, there could obviously be no national party realignment. His coolness was most surprising, but the clue to his refusal to promote a development that was widely believed to be in his interest was that Salmon P. Chase was already involved. In Virginia, it was observed, "From first to last Chief Justice Chase was consulted and for much of the time he was on the ground in person." Moreover, he was known to be actively fostering fusion efforts in New York and Maryland as well as Tennessee, Mississippi, and Texas.[19] With Chase trying to seize the middle ground in preparation for a bid for the Republican nomination in 1872, Grant would have forfeited his base of support in the Republican party if he had pursued a political scheme that could only aid Chase and might even fail to develop altogether. So, after an initial interest in Virginia, Grant backed off completely.

The second fatal consideration was that, in the rest of the South, most state Democratic-Conservative parties found a fusion initiative to be unnecessary, if not dangerous. Since all of the remaining states had been reorganized under Republican control in 1868, they did not have to resubmit their constitutions or hold new elections, so they were not faced with the situation that gave rise to the "new movement" in Mississippi, Texas, and Virginia. Moreover, their own organizations were often sufficiently strong that fusion would weaken them and lose more support than it would gain. In Alabama, the Democratic-Conservatives had abstained utterly in 1868 from the vote on the constitution and from the election for state and local offices. Although this strategy had been criticized at the time as imprudent, party leaders felt it had strengthened their hands for the future. As the Montgomery *Advertiser*, whose editor, Robert Tyler, was also the party chairman, put it: "The democratic party is united and sound, and we will elect our Governor and a majority of the Legislature, most probably by a powerful and combined party movement at the next election [in 1870]. We have not taken off our caps to Gesler, or bent the knee to Baal."[20]

Also confident that they could succeed without help from Republican dissidents or from deals parlaying amnesty for Negro suffrage were the parties in North Carolina and Georgia. In the former, the Democratic-Conservatives did not suffer from proscription because, as Josiah Turner of the Raleigh *Sentinel* commented, "Our Constitution does not disfranchise or disqualify."[21] Furthermore, the Republicans were sufficiently united and strong that there was little likelihood that a breakaway element would emerge with which fusion could be arranged. This was not the case in Georgia where the Republican party was lurching hopelessly towards defeat, unable to control the legislature and resorting to a postponement of the 1870 elections in hopes of delaying its eventual demise. Because of the opposition's weakness, the Democratic-Conservatives' wisest course was obviously to confront it vigorously rather than engage in any schemes of fusion.[22]

Thus, the "new movement" was not a strategy that Democratic-Conservatives throughout the southern states would find attractive. Instead, it had arisen in a specific context and under particular circumstances. Where new gubernatorial elections had had to be held and rejected Reconstruction constitutions needed to be resubmitted, the occasion had presented itself for breaking down party lines and using a Republican splinter group to revive the Democratic-Conservatives. But elsewhere, it would probably have been prejudicial to the party organization and to its electoral prospects to have emulated the experiment. Moreover, many party strategists calculated that endorsement of the Reconstruction policies of the Republican party was not a wise move in the context of national politics. As the Montgomery *Advertiser* warned, the "new movement" played directly "into the hands of the radical party leaders . . . [by] relieving the radical administration, from the immense difficulties . . . into which their tyrannies and follies had carried them."[23] The belief that the problems of the northern Republicans were more serious than their own was widely held and it necessitated firmness rather than appeasement. Accordingly, Alabama's new party chairman, James Clanton, advised against any reliance on the national Republicans for deliverance. "The Democratic party is the last hope of constitutional liberty on this continent" he asserted publicly in early 1869. "Nothing can render its success doubtful in the next election" because "the Republican party is on its last legs in the South, and wavering at the North. Gen. Grant will be forced in self defence to cut loose from the concern and come to us." Consequently, it was better to wait for his overtures rather than to move prematurely as had happened in the "new movement" in Mississippi and Texas, with unfortunate results.[24]

The "new movement" was therefore rejected as an electoral formula that could be applied throughout the region by the Democratic-Conservatives. In many quarters, it was even greeted with scorn and derision as not simply impolitic but a capitulation. Nevertheless, within a year or so, the Democratic-Conservatives found themselves moving very close to their opponents' position on the major issues of Reconstruction politics. Although they refused to merge organizationally and, in that sense, rejected the essential feature of the "new movement," they did nonetheless begin to acquiesce in the constitutional amendments and black suffrage that comprised the core of the Reconstruction settlement. Thus they merged with the principles of the party but not with its organization. The Democratic-Conservatives' own structure was to be maintained intact, while the issues that differentiated the parties were to be removed. The centripetal thrust of southern and national politics after 1868 could not, it seemed, be thwarted. It might not take the form of the "new movement," which was organizational in nature, but, that failing, the New Departure arose in its place to effect a merger on issues and policy instead.

The Democratic-Conservatives' susceptibility to this kind of development, after being convinced initially that it should be resisted, requires explanation. The answer is that continued resistance to black suffrage and the Reconstruction settlement began increasingly to seem inexpedient. Indeed, even the Montgomery *Advertiser* and the Alabama Democratic-Conservative party were soon to fall in line. For, by 1871, it was clear that black suffrage and the constitutional changes embodied in the Thirteenth, Fourteenth, and Fifteenth Amendments were ratified and irreversible. As the Jackson *Clarion* observed, "We must accept the inevitable and move onward to new fields. . . . The real question for sensible men to address themselves to, is not whether the negro will vote, but *how* he will vote."[25] By endorsing black suffrage and accepting it as a fixed feature of southern political life, the Democratic-Conservatives might reasonably expect to exert some degree of influence over the black electorate. But the partisan preference of black voters was not the only concern. Another anxiety was ventilated by W. P. Chilton, Jr., in a speech to a party meeting in Lee County, Alabama. He noted that "there is a political warfare between property and non-property holders; the latter comprising four-fifths of the radical party. The tendency of the age is to agrarianism; and a policy that would consolidate and embitter so large a voting element by refusing theoretically to accord to it political rights, which are already practically established—may well be thought of doubtful propriety." By refusing to recognize black suffrage and the changes brought about by Reconstruction, the Democratic-Conservatives would be contributing not only to the consolidation of the black vote in support of the Republicans but also to the radicalization of the party. With a warning that Democratic-Conservatives should "deceive [themselves] no longer" about "the strength of the *supposed* white vote," Chilton admitted, "The great defect all along in the management of the Democratic Party has been combatting, instead of using every effort to direct and control."[26]

The danger of abdicating their social and political influence through a refusal to acknowledge current realities was also evident beyond mere party considerations. John Reagan had worried about this in 1869, when he had pointed out, "The new State government, if it go into operation will have to inaugurate an enormous school system. . . . And it will have much to do in pressing forward our internal improvements."[27] Equally aware of the need for flexibility and openness to innovation was the Atlanta *Constitution*. "The present is no stagnant era," the newspaper observed, for "the human mind is rioting in its liberty and power." Consequently, if the Democratic-Conservatives were not to be swept away by these changes, "the proper policy [was] to mould and guide innovation, for good, and drop the defunct matter of worn out, settled and impracticable issues."[28]

To ensure the continued vitality and viability of the Democratic-Conservatives, the party leadership throughout the South therefore changed tack and endorsed black suffrage and the amendments. The party would not fuse with Republican splinter groups on an organizational basis, but it would maintain its independence by appropriating for its own use the opposition's main issues. Consequently, by early 1870, the stance that the party had adopted in North Carolina was quite representative. Reconstruction as well as black suffrage and civil rights, so its campaign address of that year pronounced, "are a finality. We accept them in good faith."[29] Unwise though they were, the Reconstruction measures had been sustained and established by "the American people as a whole," the Raleigh *Sentinel* observed, and there would be no further resistance in the South.[30] Indeed, acceptance of the Reconstruction measures had been viewed by many in the party as a prerequisite for Democratic revival. As E. G. Cabaniss, the Georgia party chairman, had once said, "It is reconstruction and the issues growing out of it which preserve the unity of the Republican party. Strip them of the support which this question gives them and their dissolution will speedily follow."[31]

This move might well achieve what Cabaniss anticipated. Yet, despite such high expectations, the party's reversal of its previous position was poised precariously between success and failure. Opposition to Reconstruction had, after all, been the reason for the Democratic-Conservatives' existence, so, by ending it, the party might be just as threatened as it was assumed the Republicans would be. Indeed compliance with these cardinal Republican policies could mean, as a gleeful Republican paper put it, that the party had "become Republican in fact, if not in name, by adopting, in some disguised form, the entire Platform of the National Party."[32]

The new strategy entailed high risks. All the same, to refuse to take them was felt to be even more dangerous. Even previously outspoken opponents of the Fifteenth Amendment were beginning to acknowledge the need to acquiesce. In 1869, Robert Tyler, the Alabama party chairman, had urged unremitting opposition to the Fifteenth Amendment providing for black suffrage. But, a year later, after the amendment had been ratified, Tyler was admitting that black suffrage was no longer a live political issue. "To attempt to rally a great party on an issue whose fruition depends on the happening of an improbable contingency at the end of six, eight or ten years, seems to us a sheer absurdity," he proclaimed. Universal suffrage was "as dead an issue as that of the right of peaceable secession."[33]

This change of direction was further confirmed by the decision of the northern Democrats to endorse the Reconstruction amendments. Even before the Fifteenth Amendment was ratified in March 1870, Senator Thomas Hendricks was in New Orleans giving a speech that clearly prepared the way for the party's future course.[34] This was revealed a year later in an address from the northern Democratic congressmen urging the South to accommodate to the Republican governments in their midst which had been chosen under universal suffrage and established under the Reconstruction Acts.[35] Gradually, these precursors would evolve into the New Departure, a strategy that the national party was to adopt in preparation for the 1872 election. Moreover, this developing trend seemed at the outset to be one that could be relied upon because it had been initiated by the Copperhead wing of the party, led by Clement Vallandigham, who had been the South's most thoroughgoing advocate during and after the war.[36]

Welcome though these developments in the North undoubtedly were, they served only to reassure the Democratic-Conservatives of the political wisdom of a course that they had already embarked upon. For the decision to recognize that "every issue upon which [the Republicans] rode into power is settled and dead" had been taken first by the southern branch of the party.[37] The southerners had assumed the initiative and they had done so in view of the political circumstances facing them in the South. Of course, the adoption of this policy had not been inevitable but, if the party were to continue to compete for control of the center of southern politics, it had to develop an alternative to the "new movement." The latter had evidently failed to present itself as an appropriate or viable strategy for taking advantage of the political fluidity in the reconstructed South. In its place, the New Departure offered the more likely possibility that the Republicans could be undermined, but it would be through the appropriation of their policies and not by organizational maneuvers.

The adoption of the New Departure by the Democratic-Conservatives indicated that the reorganization of the parties which had seemed possible after the 1868 election was, in all probability, unlikely to occur. This was because the party was now no longer as vulnerable as it had been during 1869 and 1870. In the first place, it did not need to hitch itself to bolting Republicans in order to obtain measures and identify with policies put forward by their opponents. For the party had effectively secured the reenfranchisement of the former Confederates and had now recognized black suffrage. Consequently, it was in a strong enough position to operate independently in its attempt to capture the support of blacks and wavering Republicans. This did not, however, preclude the future possibility of fusion with Republican dissidents, but if this were entered into, as it in fact would be, the coalitions that resulted would merely be temporary electoral expedients. They would not imply therefore that a longer range realignment was involved. A second consequence of the New Departure was that it prevented the Republicans from dividing the Democratic-Conservatives and siphoning off a major portion of their support. For, until the New Departure was espoused, the danger had always existed that the more conciliatory and flexible element in the party might respond favorably to Republican overtures.

That this might happen was very definitely the hope of the more conservative Republican leaders, and they worked assiduously to achieve it in the year or so after 1868. In the immediate aftermath of the 1868 election, Joseph E. Brown was warning Governor Rufus Bullock that "the negro vote will not do to rely on." As a result, "it is impossible to maintain the [Republican party in Georgia], or indeed in the South, without a division of the white vote. We must divide the Democratic party and unite with a strong wing of them who, if properly managed, will support Gen. Grant's administration."[38] A parallel move was initiated in Alabama by Alexander White who concocted a complex maneuver to draw into the Republican party a political group that he referred to as the "Old Union Men." This would be effected by splitting them off from the rest of the Democratic-Conservatives on the basis of "the old dividing line of Union & secession."[39] And variations on these Republican initiatives were being put into operation throughout the South prior to the adoption of the New Departure.

Nevertheless, an initial reaction to the Democratic-Conservatives' endorsement of black suffrage was to welcome it because it was thought likely to facilitate the desired split. The Atlanta *New Era*, for one, welcomed the opposition's acquiescence because it indicated that "the fight is no longer between Republicans and Democrats, as such, but rather between the Republican organization and that faction of the Democracy in Georgia and elsewhere, which seeks to reopen the issues of a past decade by their clamor for 'the constitution as it was.'"[40] But the *New Era* was quite wrong. Admittedly, the parties now agreed on the issues of suffrage and Reconstruction. But, rather than making it easier for moderates to leave, the convergence of the parties now made it unnecessary. Only if the Democratic-Conservative party had been led by its more stubborn and extreme wing would the moderates have felt thwarted and considered crossing over to the Republicans. Furthermore, the growing conservatism and conciliatoriness of the Republicans themselves, which was exemplified by the influence of Brown, White, and others, also made it less likely that they, in turn, would feel constrained to leave and join the Democratic-Conservatives. Since both parties were able to hold onto their more conciliatory wings, they were not so vulnerable to division and loss of support. The result was that, because both parties were simultaneously competing for control of the center in southern politics, the possibility of a significant realignment of the parties receded rapidly.

2. Republican Factionalism

I think the white people of South Carolina, by joining the republican party, might have placed the control of the State in the hands of the intelligent and educated population. And from my standpoint, I do not think it would have been any great sacrifice of principle, for I do not perceive any particular abandonment of principle in becoming a republican instead of a democrat.
—Former Governor James L. Orr of South Carolina, in testimony to the congressional Ku Klux Investigating Committee, 1871

Bryant Joshua Hill and all that sore head class . . . are seeking to make the Republican Party of Georgia Respectable *by Puting White Men in office. That cry of puting men forward who can command the confidence of the People is all Bosh. I understand it all.*
—Tunis Campbell to former Governor Benjamin Conley, 22 February 1872

By the end of 1868, the Republican party was at the pinnacle of power in the South. Although only eighteen months old, it had rewritten every state constitution and was in control of every state government, with the exception of Mississippi, Virginia, and Texas, though these too would be won within the following year. In addition, the Republicans had just elected U. S. Grant to the presidency. Consequently, through its domination of the federal government, the party would be able to protect its fledgling southern

branch and the Reconstruction political order that it had so ago-
nizingly created.

Nevertheless, despite initial appearances, Republican ascendancy
in the South was far from secure. At the very moment of their triumph, southern Republicans were aware of how extremely precarious was their hold on power. After all the party had, in effect,
been created by federal legislation; the elections through which it
had won power had been held under the Reconstruction Acts; and
it had all been supervised by federal civil and military officials. Furthermore, the composition of the electorate had been defined by the
strictures of the Reconstruction laws and, as a result, many potential opponents had been disfranchised, while others had simply refused to participate in what they regarded as a rigged election. The
party's electoral majorities were therefore anomalous. Thus, the Republicans had, in a sense, to overlook the reality of their current political ascendancy and act, instead, as if they were a minority party.

When a political party considers how it will function and what
electoral strategy it will pursue, it is faced with a choice between
two possible alternatives. Austin Ranney has called these the "competitive" and the "expressive" modes of party function and electoral
behavior.[1] A party can either emphasize its catholicity and its appeal to a broad segment of the electorate or it can, as Ranney puts it,
"express the nature and will of its members," relying on their devotion and satisfaction to sustain the organization. If the "competitive" approach is adopted, the party will stress its inclusiveness and
its flexibility, and it will seek electoral support from outside the
ranks of its existing constituency. Winning elections will be the primary consideration, with maximization of the vote the means of securing victory. Consequently, the party's focus will be on winning
over the marginal, independent, and swing vote, on the assumption
that the vote of the party faithful can be counted on anyway. Those
who opt for an "expressive" approach will have rather different priorities. Their preference is for a party of consistency and principle
whose strength lies not in broadening its support and increasing its
vote but in the devotion and enthusiasm of its membership. View-
ing the party in somewhat ideological terms, their electoral objective will be the security of the party rather than electoral success
achieved at a cost damaging to its integrity. Thus, their electoral
aim would be to forge the "minimal winning coalition," as William

Riker has described it, rather than to maximize their vote through nebulous appeals to floating voters and unaligned interests.

Very often these two approaches compete for influence within a particular party, and, as a consequence, factions or wings identify with one or the other of them. Joel Silbey has coined the terms Legitimist and Purist to categorize these two rival groups who adopt, respectively, the "competitive" and "expressive" modes of operation.[2] In his study of the northern Democrats during the Civil War, Silbey observed that it was the Legitimists, with their demand that the party broaden its appeal and pursue a "competitive" course, who were in control during the entire period when the Democrats were in the minority. It might have been supposed therefore that, since the Republicans were now in the majority in the South, the Legitimist ("competitive") approach would be in eclipse. This was especially likely since the southern Republicans were committed to a policy of change in the defeated South. But this was not to be the case, however. In fact, the very reverse occurred. After 1868, the Republicans gave scant consideration to the "expressive" option and pursued, instead, an expansive, "competitive" course.

Several factors in the existing political situation pushed the party in this direction. In the first place, as we have already observed, the Republicans were potentially a minority party and so they needed urgently to increase their vote. Some of those votes could be obtained by better canvassing and organization of the party's major source of support, its black constituency, but a far more productive method was to broaden its appeal so that it could develop a reliable base among white voters. To be viable outside South Carolina, Louisiana, and possibly Mississippi where blacks on their own provided the party with a majority, the Republicans had to have a considerable white constituency. Secondly, it was not only the votes of whites which the party wanted; Republicans also needed their respect and their acknowledgment that the Republican party was legitimate. Accordingly, each state Republican administration deemphasized partisanship and claimed that it was governing in the interest of the entire state. In this way, the party hoped to overcome its origins and acquire legitimacy. A final consideration that pushed the party towards a "competitive" strategy was the political risk involved in reliance on its black constituency. If an "expressive" approach were adopted, the Republicans would have to accentuate and give prominence to their cadres of black supporters. This would identify the party very closely with blacks and thus place obstacles in the way of whites recognizing or supporting it.

Although circumstances prodded the Republican party in the direction of a "competitive" strategy, aimed at conciliating whites and drawing many of them into its ranks, the outcome was neither foreordained nor was it, at any time, unopposed. Indeed, the factionalism that so permeated and bedeviled the Republican party during Reconstruction pivoted on the distinctions marked out by the "competitive" and "expressive" strategies. These rival factions also corresponded, in many respects, to the Legitimist-Purist dichotomy suggested by Joel Silbey. All the same, the precise form and content of these intraparty divisions varied according to time and location.

The alternative options open to the Republican party in the South were presented most sharply and irreconcilably in the party's formative years, from 1868 to 1870. During the constitutional conventions of 1868 and in the state elections that followed them, two distinctive wings developed within the party. The issue differentiating them was the question of whether to continue the political disabilities imposed on former Confederates by the Reconstruction Act and the Fourteenth Amendment. Upon this issue, two quite different views about the nature and purpose of the Republican party came to a focus. If the new state constitutions restricted white voting, and perhaps officeholding as well, the Republicans would probably be able to maintain their hegemony without having to rely on obtaining additional votes. In that case, their party's vigor and purity would be preserved and its original base of electoral support from blacks and a cadre of loyal whites would prove sufficient. This was the course chosen by the Radicals who were adhering to an "expressive" formula. Their opponents, the Centrists, believed, however, that the party had to seize the initiative and control the center of the political spectrum. Unless a conciliatory and inclusive approach were taken towards southern whites, the kind of Republican party that, in their view, was likely to result would be not simply uncongenial and undesirable but ineffectual as well.

Nevertheless, restrictions on Confederate voting were imposed in most of the 1868 constitutions, suggesting that, at this stage, the Radicals possessed considerable influence in the party. The initiative that the Radicals had seized in the conventions was, however, to slip rapidly from their grasp as, in the next two years, conservative forces within the party rallied to repudiate proscription. In three states—Texas, Virginia, and Mississippi—where the proposed constitutions had been rejected by the voters, in large measure because of their proscriptive features, new ratification elections were called in 1869. During these contests and in the accompanying state elections, the conservative element forced the issue, driving the party in a conciliatory direction and accomplishing the defeat of the proscriptive clauses. In this maneuver, they were, of course, abetted by the "new movement" that had been embarked upon by the Democratic-Conservatives and by Congress' lack of sympathy for proscription, made evident in its recommendation that the troublesome clauses be detached from the constitutions and submitted separately.[3] All the same, the Radicals' influence was clearly ebbing, for the party in Louisiana, without the need for resubmission, was moving anyway towards disavowing its severe restrictions on Confederate voting. In 1870, with encouragement from Governor Warmoth, Republican legislators voted overwhelmingly to eliminate Article 99 of the constitution and, a year later, the amendment was ratified.[4] Two years earlier, Alabama had also repealed the suffrage restrictions imposed by its Reconstruction constitution. Governor Smith had urged amnesty in his inaugural and, at its first session, the legislature complied.[5] Of course, limitations on officeholding still applied under the Fourteenth Amendment to every southern state. But, by the end of 1870, no state except Arkansas imposed restrictions on the right of former Confederates to vote.

The contest within each Republican party between 1868 and 1870 assumed different forms in different states. The alignment of forces was nowhere more clear than in Texas. There, the black vote was too small to rely on, so that the disfranchisement of whites was crucial to the Radical position. Indeed, some Radicals even felt that the party was so outnumbered and vulnerable that proscription alone would not be enough. To compensate for this weakness, they demanded that Texas be divided into three separate states. This would ensure that the Republicans would be guaranteed control in at least the southwestern division where they were concentrated and where the Radical wing had its base. While the constitutional convention was in session, one of the Radical leaders, Morgan

Hamilton, warned, "Unless we can secure a division of the state I have little hope of bringing this state into the Union, on a basis that will insure its continuance as a Republican state for a single year."[6] But the Centrists, led by Morgan's brother Jack and Governor Elisha Pease, had other ideas for the party's future development and, using their control of the constitutional convention, they defeated the Radicals' proposals for division and proscription.

Thus, the split between the two factions of the Republican party was about as complete and sharp in Texas as it was to be anywhere in the South. Indeed, both groups went so far as to organize their own nominating conventions in 1869 and to adopt irreconcilable stances on the ratification of the constitution. Fearing that this dissension would result in a Republican defeat in the state election, President Grant encouraged the formation of a compromise ticket headed by Edmund J. Davis, a Radical, and supported by George T. Ruby, another Radical and the most prominent black leader in the state. But Morgan Hamilton would not participate, nor would his brother and his Centrist allies, who by this time were affiliating with the Democratic-Conservatives. In addition, the compromise ticket could not be organized on a platform of opposition to the constitution. The result was that Davis, the Radical, was elected over Jack Hamilton, the Centrist, and the state was readmitted to the Union under Hamilton's conservative constitution.[7]

The Radical-Centrist cleavage was also very evident in Florida where, in 1868, the differences between the rival factions were embodied in two contrasting constitutions.[8] The Radical group, known as the "mule team," was led by William Saunders, a black from Maryland, and by two white U.S. Treasury agents, Daniel Richards and Liberty Billings. Before the convention met, they had already been active around Tallahassee organizing the freedmen on behalf of Salmon P. Chase's 1868 presidential ambitions. When the other members of the constitutional convention arrived in Tallahassee in January 1868, Richards presented them with a draft constitution that he intended to get the convention to adopt, but the Centrist Republicans resisted the "mule team's" pressure and withdrew to Monticello where they drew up their own version of a constitution. Then they claimed their right to sit in the Tallahassee convention hall and were joined in this request by many of the Democratic-Conservatives. General George G. Meade, the commander of the Third Military District, sympathized with their predicament, and the upshot was that their claim was recognized.

In the ensuing reorganization, the "mule team" faction was expelled. Because of this, the resulting constitution was more conservative than any other in the South. Not only was there no mention of the ban on Confederate voting and officeholding, which the "mule team" had insisted upon, but it rejected outright their attempt to maximize and consolidate the political power of the black electorate by providing that offices be filled by popular election and by apportioning state legislative districts according to population. Instead, officials were to be appointed by the governor and representation was arranged on a unitary basis, with a maximum of four per district. As a result, Charles Dyke, the editor of the Tallahassee *Floridian* and a leading light among the Democratic-Conservatives, was able to breathe a sigh of relief at the outcome. "We ought to feel grateful," he confided afterwards, "to [Harrison] Reed & Co. [the Centrist Republicans] for trying to break the power of such a dangerous faction headed by Billings and for forming a Constitution so much more liberal than was expected."[9] The meaning of its liberality was revealed by none other than Reed himself who observed, "Under our Constitution the Judiciary and State Officers will be appointed and apportionment will prevent a Negro Legislature." In this letter to David Yulee, Florida's most prominent secessionist in 1860 and now the president of the Florida Railroad, Reed indicated that the Radicals had also had different aims on economic matters and that these had thankfully been thwarted. "The conspirators," he told Yulee, "had a scheme to overthrow the railroads of the state—wipe out their charters and turn them over to [northern financiers like] Hoyt Sprague & Co. or some other villains."[10] As a result, Reed's plan for bipartisan harmony "on the basis of the material interests of the state" had been saved.[11] Thus, the elimination of the Radicals as a result of the maneuvers surrounding the constitutional convention ensured that Reed was elected governor in 1868 and that a Centrist approach would pervade the thinking of the party.

The Centrists' manipulations in Florida finessed the fifteen or so black votes in the convention and ruled out the political role envisaged for blacks by the "mule team" group. Likewise, in Georgia, during 1868 and 1869, the potential for a black presence in the Republican party was thwarted, as the Centrists gained the ascendancy.[12] The ease with which this was accomplished is explained, to a large degree, by the composition of the party in Georgia, for there was only a handful of northerners in it and, by contrast, an overwhelming number of natives, for whom a sizable black constituency and an active role in the party for blacks were respectively unnecessary and unpalatable. Accordingly, the emergence of a powerful Radical wing was unlikely. Indeed, it was virtually confined to the organizers of the Equal Rights League in Augusta and the coterie of federal officeholders around Foster Blodgett, the postmaster in the same town. The "Augusta Ring"—as Blodgett, Rufus Bullock, the Republican governor after 1868, and John E. Bryant, a Freedmen's Bureau official from Maine, were known—managed to dominate the party's executive committee in early 1868. But they did not have the votes in either the constitutional convention or in the party's nominating convention that year to impose a Radical perspective on the actions of those two bodies. Their demand for Confederate disfranchisement was defeated, as was their insistence that the right of blacks to hold office be specifically guaranteed. Orchestrated by Joseph E. Brown who was not actually a member of the convention, Centrists managed to vote down disfranchisement and leave the status of black officeholders undecided. At the same time, Centrists also opposed the Radicals' attempts to win the allegiance of white farmers by provisions for debtor relief and the exemption from taxation of their homesteads. This countermove, which was spearheaded by the future attorney general of the United States, Amos T. Akerman, but was discouraged by Joseph E. Brown, went down to defeat, however, and so debtor relief was provided. But, although the Radicals had secured relief, there was a large element opposed to their initiative towards developing a basis of white support among the small farmers of north Georgia. Nonetheless, the defeat of their attempt to give the party a Radical posture by disfranchising former Confederates and protecting its black electorate was decisive for it destroyed the foundations of Radicalism.[13]

The Radicals' problems were then compounded by the results of the 1868 election. Their candidate for governor, Rufus Bullock, was victorious, but he did not have undisputed control of the new legislature, since there was a solid bloc of Democratic-Conservatives and Centrist Republicans opposed to him. In alliance, they defeated

Bullock's slate for the U.S. Senate and expelled as ineligible about twenty-five black representatives. Faced with these setbacks, Governor Bullock sought the intervention of Congress in the hope that the process of reconstructing the state could be started all over again, thereby giving the party an opportunity to reconstitute its organization and its priorities along Radical lines. But the Democratic-Conservatives were too hostile both inside the assembly and out and the Centrists were too numerous and angry at Bullock's maneuverings. After trying to stave off the inevitable for two years, Bullock, the Radicals, and the party were finally defeated in the elections of early 1871.[14]

This trend was not confined to Texas, Florida, and Georgia; it was occurring everywhere in the South as the party's Centrists outmaneuvered its Radical wing. By rejecting those measures that were aimed either at limiting the white opposition vote or at maximizing the black vote, measures that alone could protect its essential constituency, the party was forced onto two possible paths. In 1870, Morgan Hamilton, the Texas Radical, pointed out what these were. On the one hand, the only hope for a viable Republican party was "in the action of the general government." "It is doubtful," Hamilton conceded, however, "whether it can be got to act, but it is the only chance in any of the old slave states except Missouri & Arkansas" where Confederate disfranchisement was still in effect.[15] The other alternative was the course the party was currently pursuing—the expansion of its base through the recruitment of native whites. The adoption of this remedy, Hamilton believed, "satisfies me more than ever that the party is already hopelessly broken down. It has recruited too many already, and the more it takes in the worse for the cause of Republicanism. All the southern states have been increasing the strength of the Republican party in the same way, and most of them have realized at the first election held under their respective constitutions a signal defeat. . . . North Carolina has just passed into the hands of the Democracy, and she contained the most numerous and most reliable material for permanent Republican government of any state in the south."[16] From a Radical perspective, therefore, the prospects for Republicanism looked gloomy indeed by 1870.

Also worried about the Radicals' decline were the party's black leaders. Because the Radicals had taken a more advanced position on issues affecting blacks than any other element, their eclipse left little hope that new initiatives would be taken or that the interests of blacks would be placed on the party's future agenda. Indeed, as Republicans became inevitably more and more committed to relying on white support and conservative policies, the prospects for blacks receded proportionately. Yet, even when the party's Radical wing had been influential, most notably in the 1868 constitutional conventions, matters that concerned blacks had still been treated with caution and circumspection. In their favor, however, it has to be conceded that Radicals did insist that there be no qualifications on the right of blacks to vote and hold office. Furthermore, they were vigorous in their demands for the protection of black civil rights. But when the question of race in the proposed public school system arose, Radicals, both black and white, did not demand integration. Instead, they voted against all attempts to require that schools be segregated, thus leaving the outcome moot on the assumption that at least blacks had obtained access, which was in itself a gain.[17]

Another question of importance to blacks was the acquisition of land. Although the provision of some kind of land to the landless freedmen was obviously essential to guarantee emancipation, Radicals and Centrists alike expressed little interest. Indeed, only on rare occasions was land distribution even discussed. A proposal to require that land forfeited by defaulting taxpayers be sold in small units to the landless was in fact discussed in the Louisiana convention.[18] Meanwhile, in the other convention with a black majority, South Carolina's, a petition asking Congress to loan $1 million so that land could be made available to the landless was adopted unanimously, and the convention then created a land commission to buy acreage for settlement by freedmen.[19] Beyond these attempts, however, little was said except for a few speeches from individual delegates. Far more attractive to the convention's members, however, were measures to relieve debtors. In the main, these comprised stay laws and homestead exemptions, and their purpose was not to deprive landholders of their acres and thereby upset property relationships but rather the reverse—to enable owners to keep their lands and protect them from both creditors and tax collectors. Instead of making land available to the deprived freedmen, policies like these would actually prevent land from changing hands and, for this reason, many Radicals were often opposed to relief measures.

With the props supporting the Radicals' position knocked away, the chances that policies would be forthcoming to placate blacks, who, after all, constituted the core of the party's constituency, became increasingly unlikely. Instead, the party turned away, deliberately and decisively, in order to obtain the votes of white men as well as the respect and gratitude of those of them who were the region's influential economic and political figures. Of course, electoral support from whites could have been secured by policies aimed at the small farmers whose economic interests had, for the most part, prompted the conventions' debtor relief proposals. But this was not to be the course the Republicans pursued. By contrast, they opted to make economic development the focus of their drive to dominate the political center and thus maintain control. Naturally, this decision precluded the option that the party might override racial distinctions to form a coalition based on common class interests.

To achieve the rather different objective sought by the party leadership after the conventions, railroad promotion was selected as the centerpiece of its strategy. Such a choice was not hard to arrive at, for, once the Centrists had turned back the Radicals, they could not ignore the railroad mania that was sweeping the region. As the party of progress that had been introduced into the South to revive its economy and make it prosperous like the North, the Republicans had to facilitate the building of railroads and also, by degrees, encourage manufacturing and economic diversification. For, not only was the party equipped for, and expected to play, the role of midwife to the region's transportation revolution, but, if it did not do so, it would very probably hand the Democratic-Conservatives a ready-made winning issue. As a North Carolinian once so aptly described the situation, "The party that first completes the Internal Improvement System of the state without regard to cost will hold the reins of power here for years to come."[20] Besides the evident external political advantages that a program of state railroad promotion would bring, there were also very clear benefits internally. Because internal improvements could be viewed as an impartial and necessary policy producing general prosperity and so benefiting all classes and races alike, the party's espousal of railroad aid would help to heal the divisions that had surfaced during 1868.[21]

Railroad building was thought to be a guaranteed proposition in economic terms as well, and this encouraged leading Republicans to cast aside all doubt. In the opinion of Governor Holden's *North Carolina Standard*, it was "an indisputable fact that the wealth of a State is in exact proportion to its number of miles of railroads."[22] Earlier that year, one of Holden's fellow Republicans, State Senator R. W. Lassiter, had proclaimed in the assembly: "Let a railroad be built through any country, and immediately the commercial prosperity of that section is increased an hundred fold," as towns spring up and trade booms.[23] During the fall of 1870, Governor Bullock, the leader of Georgia's Radical faction, toured the northern part of the state, speaking to railroad meetings. On each occasion, he cited the immense advantages that railroads brought to the state. Even if Georgia lost every dollar of the railroad bonds it endorsed, the governor assured his listeners that it would still have gained, because of "the increased value of taxable property by development and increase of population." Bullock even encouraged doubting freedmen that they would be benefited because "the enhanced price of land brings up with it the value of labor," and improved transportation would open up employment prospects and increase labor's mobility.[24] With the Republicans' leadership so convinced of the value and need for railroads, it was not surprising that the constitution of every state except Mississippi provided for state aid to internal improvements and that, in the first sessions of all the newly elected Republican state legislatures, railroad bills in profusion were introduced and invariably enacted. This would continue for three years or so.

Because railroad promotion was endorsed so widely within the party and because it appeared to be so universally beneficial, its impact on the alignment of forces and factions inside the Republican organization was not readily perceived. But, in fact, the importance given to a policy geared to supporting the interests of businessmen and promoters, and the energy devoted to its implementation, pulled the party in an overwhelmingly conservative direction and ensured that it could not realistically deviate from that stance. Propositions for redistributing wealth or for satisfying the needs of the poorest and weakest in the postemancipation South could hardly be embraced with enthusiasm by a party that was rapidly moving in the opposite direction. Reacting to this trend, Governor Davis's Austin *State Journal* urged the Texas legislature in 1870 to heed the complaint of "Many Colored Men" that, while railroad jobs went through with ease, "nothing is being done to provide home-steads" for blacks.[25] But far more common were sentiments like those of the Jackson *Pilot* which, in arguing for passage of a general railroad bill for Mississippi in 1871, asserted that it would "benefit the party more than any other measure that could be [presented] and will prove to the thinking people that the great Republican party is one of progress, of energy, of principles founded upon good, sound common sense."[26]

This overwhelming obsession with proving itself responsible and reasonable was also evident in the party leadership's reaction to the violence and disorder created by the Ku Klux Klan during 1870 and 1871. Although the state authorities were fully aware that outrages were being committed against Republicans and their supporters, they were reluctant to act. Instead, they hoped that the problem would soon go away or that officials in the particular localities where the disorders were occurring would take care of things. This was the response of Governor William H. Smith of Alabama. In a proclamation of April 1870 he announced that in Greene County, where the Republican county solicitor, Alexander Boyd, had just been killed, as well as in two neighboring counties, he, as governor, could raise a company of militia; but he would do so only after a group of responsible citizens requested it and after he had ascer-tained that there was at least one capable official under whose au-thority the militia could be organized.[27] Meanwhile in South Caro-lina, early in 1871, Governor Robert Scott was admitting that "there is no invasion which I am called upon to repel, and no insur-rection which I am called upon to suppress." Since he had taken action against the Klan in 1869 and 1870, when he had dispatched several state militia units to some of the Piedmont counties wracked by violence, Governor Scott was evidently backing down. He re-fused to declare martial law but instead conceded that he "dare not and will not assume that justice cannot be administered until the effort has been made and the failure evident."[28] Meanwhile, he heeded opposition calls to disband black militia units in Union,

York, and Chester counties and pleaded with seventeen Democratic-Conservative leaders in March to help him restore law and order.[29]

Because they were wedded to the strategy of winning approval and support from respectable whites, Centrists feared admitting that there was anything unusual about the situation or that the normal judicial and governmental processes could not cope with it. So they delayed action and took only minimal measures, like Governor James Alcorn's proposals for laws prohibiting the wearing of masks and disguises and providing for the creation of a secret service unit.[30] The Mississippi governor and his Centrist allies only acted forcefully in mid-1871 when, after Grant's message about southern outrages and the congressional hearings on the Klan, federal intervention seemed likely. Were this to occur, the authority of the state government and its ability to govern effectively would be seriously open to doubt, and this was the very concern that had dictated the course taken by Alcorn and some of the other governors in the first place. But what also worried Centrists like Alcorn and Smith was that federal action was now being called for by the more radical wing of the party. Under the leadership in Mississippi of Adelbert Ames, they were hoping to restore their own fortunes and policy priorities by the reintroduction of the nurturing presence and protection of the federal government. Accordingly, Alcorn began to take some belated measures for dealing with the Klan, which consisted of two bills, one to remove Klan trials from the county in which the offense had been committed and another to form a cavalry unit to detect and put down outrages. Both of these, the governor admitted, had been introduced "to avert Federal intervention," and, because of this, both were defeated with the help of votes from the rival Republican faction. "A combination of the carpetbagger proper with the fractious Democrat" was how Alcorn characterized the vote against his Klan proposals.[31]

In states like Mississippi and Alabama, the governor's cautious and irresolute response to Klan violence became the issue within the party around which its more radical element coalesced, demanding forceful action from the state as well as the involvement of the federal power. This opposition did not, however, constitute a real alternative to the general course of conciliation and accommodation upon which the party's leadership throughout the South had embarked. Rather, it was a check and a restraint on a Centrist strategy and a conservative set of priorities that had already been approved and were now being implemented. Therefore, proponents of a more resolute course might protest and dissent, but their alternative had been rejected. Because the foundations upon which it had been based had already been discarded with the rejection of disenfranchisement, it was no longer an option that the party could realistically pursue. Elements of the Radicals' agenda, such as, for example, their demand for greater protection against the intimidation of the party's black constituents and their invocation of federal authority, persisted of course, but they did not amount to a competing program. The party's basic options were now limited and so the differences among the intraparty factions amounted to little more than a matter of tactic and emphasis. Thus, they vied with each other for influence and recognition within a framework that had already been determined.

One group in the Republican coalition that might, at first glance, have been looked to as a significant force capable of stemming the party's rush to enter upon a conciliatory and conservative course was its black membership. Blacks had, after all, comprised a majority in the South Carolina and Louisiana constitutional conventions; they were the largest single bloc in Florida's convention; and they had had sizable delegations in Mississippi, Alabama, Virginia, and Georgia. Yet, at the crucial stage, during the 1868 conventions and in the eighteen months after when the suffrage had been a matter of urgent discussion, black delegates had rarely voted for proscription. "With few exceptions," Richard Hume, the authority on the Reconstruction conventions, has written recently, "Negro delegates showed limited interest in restricting ex-Confederates."[32] Instead, they conceived of suffrage as a right that was universal, tantamount virtually to citizenship. Consequently, it did not allow for any restriction. This claim was insisted upon, partly as an article of belief concerning the nature of democracy and also, no doubt, as a refutation of assertions that freedmen were not knowledgeable enough to exercise the franchise properly or that suffrage should be limited to those blacks who were literate or perhaps owned property. Equally, it was argued that to deprive whites of suffrage for any reason opened up the precedent and the justification for limitations on black voting.[33]

A further consideration was raised by James Lynch, one of Mississippi's leading black politicians. "The colored voters," he was reported as saying in 1869, "are inclined more strongly to the Radicals, but their leaders have long doubted [assumed?] the folly of proscription." This was because, unlike northerners who "can leave when it becomes too uncomfortable," blacks "must be in friendly relations with the great body of the whites in the state. Otherwise . . . peace can be maintained only by a standing army."[34] Thus, black delegates were firm in their support of unrestricted suffrage, and their ranks were broken only by a few who demanded that rebels be deprived of the vote and by some others, mainly elitist blacks, who wanted to maintain their own ascendancy and status within the black caste by depriving former slaves of the vote through literacy or property qualifications.

Not only were black Republicans unsympathetic to proscription, they were also not at all eager, initially, to assert themselves or pressure the party into giving them a conspicuous role. Since virtually all the blacks who aspired to office had not been active in politics before, and certainly not in southern politics, they moved with caution and uncertainty, letting natives and northerners take the initiative.[35] Needless to say, white Republicans did not need any encouragement to exclude blacks from office; the blacks' attitude meant simply that the whites would not be resisted when they did so. Of course, blacks also worried about the impression that would be created among southern white voters if the new and untried Republican party were to be permeated by Negroes. If it was perceived as a black man's party, then its prospects, along with those of the blacks whose hopes rested so much on its success, would be seriously damaged. Thus, James Harris, who had emerged as North Carolina's preeminent black politician, rejected the suggestion of a nomination for Congress in 1868 with the eloquent comment: "what fuel that would be to feed the flame of prejudice! I am not willing to sell out my race, for such a sale would my acceptance virtually be."[36] The prejudices that black politicians like Harris had to worry about were not only those existing outside the party, as white Republicans, who expected advancement from the new organization they had just joined, would also resent black competition for office and position. Then, of course, there were other black politicians, such as George T. Ruby from Galveston, Texas, whose districts included such a large number of whites that the encouragement of black officeholding would have been perilous.[37]

Ruby's situation was somewhat unusual because most black officials hailed from black districts. Nevertheless, to preserve their individual careers and protect the interests of their race, all black politicians found themselves accommodating reluctantly to the dominant trend within the party. Typical of this pattern was the political path taken by Josiah Walls, Florida's leading black Republican, who entered the 1868 convention as a "mule team" Radical and left it in alliance with the ruling faction headed by Governor Harrison Reed, which, at that point, was more sympathetic than its rival to the interests of Florida's blacks.[38]

In a party whose priority was now to recruit and reassure white voters, the options open to blacks became limited. Because of this, black politicians saw as their task not the promulgation of an alternative to the course the party was currently pursuing but the attainment, within that framework, of as much protection and advantage as possible for blacks as a group. Since they could neither leave the party nor control it, black Republicans began to operate as a pressure group within it. Through constantly emphasizing the importance to the party's electoral health of blacks as a voting bloc, they expected in return to be able to extract concessions and gain advantages. In this sense, they were practicing what later became known as ethnic politics. Operating as a group, they tried to barter votes for offices and benefits.[39]

Although there were exceptions of course, the essential ingredients and contours of black ethnic politics within the Republican party after 1870 can be readily described. In the first place, blacks used their power as a voting bloc to influence the factional alignments within the party. They rewarded their friends with their support, and they later punished them by withdrawing it if the initial commitment was not honored. Within a few years of entering office, Governors Reed of Florida, Warmoth of Louisiana, and Alcorn of Mississippi discovered that if they took black favor for granted, they would lose it. To all three, the loss of black support ensured the ascendancy of their factional rivals within a few years. On the other hand, this tactic was not so workable whenever blacks were split between the existing factions, as happened in Arkansas, or when there were factional divisions among blacks themselves, as occurred in Louisiana in the early 1870s.

Thus, by swinging their support between rival factions and by pressuring individual candidates, blacks were able to influence party politics in their direction. This was particularly important because they could not coax the party into responding to their demands by threatening to leave. Individual politicians who did run independent campaigns either were not supported by black voters, as William Saunders, the Florida Radical, discovered in 1869, or they were cold-shouldered by black party regulars, as Aaron A. Bradley found out in Savannah, Georgia, in 1870 and 1871.[40] There was a moment, however, when many black Republicans seriously considered bolting and that was in the Liberal-Republican split of 1872. Republican failure to promote blacks for office and to deliver on its pledge of equal rights made many vow to withdraw. Ultimately, after calculating the cost, few did so. The possibility was, however, vigorously debated at the Southern States Convention of Colored Men in 1871, but warnings like that of Frederick Douglass proved convincing. "To desert Grant now, to refuse to sustain him, to seek in any way to weaken his influence," Douglass had emphasized, "is the surest way to undo the work of the last ten years, and remand the Negro to a condition in some respects worse than that from which the Union delivered him."[41] Accordingly, blacks stayed with the party and became the most loyal and stalwart element within it. For their persistence, they expected recognition and reward. In some respects, with the ascendancy in most state parties after 1872 of the faction with which they were affiliated and in which they were an influential component, they obtained it.

Of course, the objectives of black interest-group politics were not confined to the acquisition of influence. There were specific benefits to be sought. To this end, black politicians, almost without exception, identified themselves with certain issues and were always to be found advocating them. The chief of these was civil rights. As soon as the first Republican legislatures met, black representatives were introducing proposals to give specificity to the general provisions for equal rights in the state constitutions. Sometimes these demands were presented in the form of civil rights bills. At others, they would appear as public accommodations clauses tacked onto railroad legislation or as provisions for equal access to public schools or public welfare institutions, such as asylums or hospitals. But, in whatever guise they appeared, black legislators lobbied unceasingly for civil rights. Education was another matter that blacks were continually fostering and promoting. Because it was so crucial to black advancement, Negro legislators voted overwhelmingly for measures that provided adequate funding for education and expanded its availability. Without education, blacks would also be vulnerable to literacy tests and other pressures concerning their ability to vote. As Josiah Walls told Congress in 1871, while arguing for a bill to create a national education fund, "can these people protect their liberties without education?"[42]

Also of fundamental concern to black legislators was the elimination of Klan violence. Not only were most of the Klan's victims black but the party's failure to act against terrorist organizations raised questions about its concern for blacks and its ability and willingness to protect them. Accordingly, it was imperative that the Republican party move firmly against the Klan and, invariably, black legislators were in the forefront of the demand for strong proposals, most often urging federal intervention. Closely allied to this issue was the general question of protecting the Republicans' black constituents through apportionment, registration, and election laws, and black representatives overwhelmingly backed proposals to increase and facilitate black voting while opposing measures that diminished or threatened it.[43]

But, even more important for ensuring a black role in politics was the demand for greater representation and officeholding. After initially assuming a low profile and not resisting white efforts to deny them office, black Republicans in 1870 and 1871 mobilized to increase their representation and obtain more influence and patronage. In South Carolina in 1870, the offensive was launched at a meeting in Charleston called by Robert C. DeLarge, and it resulted in the election of three blacks for Congress that year.[44] Alabama's blacks were also successful in 1870 because James T. Rapier was nominated for secretary of state and Benjamin S. Turner, a former slave, for congressman.[45] In Florida, the party selected Josiah Walls for the state's sole congressional seat in 1870, an outcome that caused Jonathan Gibbs, who was secretary of state and a black, to claim that "this was the great point sought after and gained."[46] Of course, in each case, black nominations had been made possible by the party's need to reassure and hold its black constituency. But, all the same, it had been black pressure that had made the discontent known and had demanded satisfaction, while often, as in Florida, it was blacks alone who had decided precisely who the nominee would be. In two other states, Mississippi and Texas, where in 1871 the party leadership had proven unresponsive to black concerns for state office, movements to control nominations arose at the local level in counties that were predominantly black. In Texas the most spectacular insurgency took place in the east-central sixteenth senatorial district of Matthew Gaines, and Mississippi's major black offensive occurred in Adams County (Natchez) where John R. Lynch was a leading figure.[47] Modest though these gains were, they constituted the opening salvo in a continuing campaign during the 1870s to have blacks nominated to elective office and appointed to patronage positions.

These were the issues that black spokesmen identified with and promoted in their effort to advance the interests of their race. Operating as an ethnic interest group within a larger coalition, they bargained and cajoled to obtain favor and influence. This kind of politics had been resorted to in order to take advantage of a situation blacks did not control. Yet, ironically, despite their party's preoccupation with obtaining support from whites and despite the disfavor with which most Republicans viewed blacks and their claims, blacks were nevertheless the fulcrum of Republican politics. In essence, the party's existence rotated around its black membership. Their presence in the party constituted its greatest problem and their role within it its liveliest issue. This was true even in states in which blacks were not particularly numerous. Texas had an overwhelmingly white population, yet race proved to be of critical importance to the Republican party there. Carl Moneyhon concluded his recent study of Texas Republicanism with the observation, "So long as the white Republicans were unable to go the full distance in recognizing the aspirations and political goals of blacks, however, they had to fight to keep blacks' votes from being drawn away. The result was a party of constant internal conflict that could never marshal its full strength against its opponents."[48] In Florida, the entire political order that the 1868 constitutional convention had created was constructed around the limitation of black political influence. Because it had been reduced drastically, the state's political system had been twisted out of shape and the Republicans had surrendered a valuable electoral asset. As a result, the rival white Republican factions struggled with each other over access to white votes and were constantly in fear that their opponents might decide to steal a march on them by mobilizing the party's blacks.[49]

If Republicans in Texas and Florida were so concerned about how to deal with the party's black element, then it can be readily assumed that elsewhere its relation to the party was a constant preoccupation. In fact, in every state, blacks were at the heart of the Republican party's division into factions. It was the refusal of Centrists to rely on blacks to sustain the party which had produced factional division in the first place, and it would be the refusal of blacks to support Centrists in their campaign to bring whites into the party that would frustrate their efforts and eventually force them into silence or drive them out of the party altogether.

Vital though the racial dimension was to the creation and shaping of the factions that bedeviled southern Republicanism, it was not the only characteristic affecting and determining them. A number of other related ingredients went into the making of the two factions that existed in each state Republican party. In the first place, the competing groups were sustained by two different sources of patronage. One of the factions invariably derived its strength from control of the state patronage, while the other was maintained by access to federal office. The latter was distributed through the state's congressional delegation, primarily its senators; state jobs, on the other hand, were in the hands of the governor. Thus, the factions tended to pivot on two patronage rings, one centered at the statehouse, the other at the U.S. customhouses located in the port cities of Savannah, Charleston, New Orleans, Mobile, and Galveston.[50]

A second distinguishing feature, and it was closely related to the first, was that the leadership of one of the factions was overwhelmingly native and local in origin, whereas the other was generally headed up by newcomers from the North. In contemporary pejorative terms, the white leadership consisted predominantly of either "scalawags" or "carpetbaggers." This connection was not unexpected because natives already possessed a record and a personal following and constituency, so that they would expect to build on that influence through the party's control of state government. By contrast, the northerners had no previous political roots in their adopted state but they did have federal contacts, through their work with the Freedmen's Bureau, through their positions as treasury or customs agents, or perhaps as a result of past political experience in the North. So they looked to congressional elective office and federal appointive positions as the object of their ambition and the source of their political strength. A corollary of the northerners' lack of a preexisting political base in the South was that they usually ran for office where the newly created black constituency was most numerous. As a result, they depended heavily on the support of blacks and would be more responsive to their concerns than the native element. Naturally enough, blacks generally affiliated with this wing of the party.

From this, a final and crucial distinguishing feature of the two factions arose—their approach to electoral strategy and the goals of the party. One group was overwhelmingly committed to the "competitive" approach. It sought to move the party's center of gravity to the middle of the political spectrum by competing with the Democratic-Conservatives for the unattached and influenceable white voters. By contrast, the other faction looked to the party's existing followers for the base of its support. It relied on their continuing enthusiasm and loyalty to the party and stressed consistency, stability, and regularity. Lest any misunderstanding arise, it must be emphasized that this "expressive" strategy was not as thoroughgoing as the version that had been espoused by the Radicals. This was because the institutional bulwarks behind which so exclusive a policy could be erected had been removed after 1868 by the rejection of disfranchisement and the failure to give strength and protection to the black voting base. Consequently, this faction's "expressive" approach was now qualified by the recognized need for the party to appeal to whites. All the same, it was anchored to the Republicans' black voting bloc and its small group of white loyalists. Unlike the Centrists, its members would not take for granted or cast aside the party's natural and more committed following.

The role of these various characteristics in determining the composition and goals of the two factions will become clearer once the factions themselves are analyzed. Of the two, the Centrists are more easily described because they had a distinct goal in mind and, after the 1868 conventions, they moved concertedly to attain it. They were the dynamic aggressive force in Republican politics and it was their attempt to alter the party's composition, shift its direction, and change its priorities which contributed more than anything else to the party's instability and internal strife. They would not allow the party to build its strength and consolidate its position gradually but instead opened up the unsettling possibility that it would be changed rapidly and decisively. Paradoxically, the Centrists' attempt to make Republicanism conservative generated turmoil and instability.

The Centrists were invariably southerners with considerable political experience and they affiliated with the Republican party in the hope that, and also on the condition that, they could reorganize and redirect it. Their intention was to fit the new party into a southern mold, incorporate it into the existing southern political system. Respectable and accepted, it would be led by traditional southern politicians like themselves and would rest on an electoral base consisting predominantly of native whites. Thus constituted, it would naturally serve as the instrument for conservative economic development and social improvement rather than as an engine for racial justice and social change. This was an agenda, therefore, not just an opportunistic electoral maneuver to bring in white votes for personal political advantage. The Centrist prospectus was never more concisely and accurately expounded than by Governor Elisha Pease of Texas in 1869. In a letter to another Centrist, James G. Tracy, editor of the Houston *Union*, he declared: "If we are to have a successful Republican party in Texas, it must act upon the broad principles of Republican liberty and equality, and must present a comprehensive system of State policy in regard to immigration and public improvements and education that will commend itself to the intelligence and business capacity of the whole people." In addition, Pease urged that the party "must show too by the course of its leading members that they have the intelligence and capacity to administer the affairs of the State government in such a manner as will advance the material interests of the whole people and give protection to the person and property of all alike."[51]

The party that the Centrists envisaged was to provide material improvements so as to regenerate the southern states and bring prosperity to everyone. The Republicans were particularly well placed to play this role because they had special access to northern interests and federal largesse. As Alexander White of Alabama was well aware, the party "brings into the State those elements of increase and growth which are *national*. It maintains the federal allegiance and its watchword is Union." And, through his organization of Alabama's prewar Unionists, White hoped to create the core for a reoriented Republican party, to be called the Union party, which would give Alabama access to northern benefits and aid.[52] Far less subtle than White about his hopes for his state if it were to repudiate Radicalism was Horatio Simrall, soon to be appointed to Mississippi's Supreme Court. "I am disposed to take my state from her isolation," he declared in a public speech in 1869, "and hitch her onto the car of progress; to place her in such condition that the rich streams that flow out from the national treasury may not float past her." Warming to his subject, Simrall discerned limitless economic horizons for his state. "Now that China is open to American commerce," he proclaimed, "Mississippi can become the focus for the trade of the Orient with the Eastern U.S. and Europe."[53]

Of course, if the party were to become the main agency for revitalizing the southern economy, it could not be partisan or combative. By spring 1870, William A. Smith, the director of the North Carolina Railroad, was gratified that this was rapidly transpiring. With great satisfaction, he was able to announce: "I belong to the party that wishes now to make party interest subservient to State interest and favors the sustaining of all good men regardless of party." Indeed, "What we want now is a North Carolina party—'A Liberal Party'—so that all good North Carolinians, both black and white, can sustain and be sustained in their rights and privileges."[54] Although they wanted the party to be inclusive and tolerant towards non-Republicans, the Centrists were quite willing, indeed eager, to fight some of their fellow partisans in order to obtain these goals. Indeed, their conciliatory approach was attainable only at the expense of dissenters within their own party. One group that would be pushed aside by the Centrists was obviously the blacks. As William B. Rodman of North Carolina explained: "If the Republican party could be made to believe that they might rely on the support of the white men of the South, there would be no reason to fear the undue influence of the negroes."[55] James L. Alcorn's priorities were even more explicit when he told a Radical, Robert Flournoy, that if the black man's advancement necessitated "arresting the Caucasian in his Heaven-inspired progress, then must negro liberty learn, so far as I am concerned, to take care of itself."[56]

Blacks were not, however, the only ones to be forced aside in the creation of a conservative and native-dominated Republican party. In order to focus the party's attention on developing its local white constituency, the influence of newcomers whose political base lay elsewhere, either with the party's black voters or with federal patronage, had to be curbed. Accordingly, Governor William H. Smith wasted no time in bringing pressure to bear on them. In March 1869, he complained to President Grant: "the condition of Alabama is Anomalous" because "with one exception," its congressional delegation was composed of "residents of the State only since the War & [who] consequently cannot be presumed to have a sufficient knowledge of the long resident population of the State to make that just distribution of the offices, which the public interest demands, without consultation with those who have."[57] Smith's allies constantly urged him to attack the northerners and instead "get the State into the hands or under the controul of our old or native union men" by appointing the latter to office whenever possible.[58] This same fight was also being waged in Mississippi where, as Senator Adelbert Ames told his wife in the fall of 1871, "The warfare [that] began on carpet-baggers when he [Alcorn] became Governor is raging more fiercely today than ever."[59]

The Centrists' campaign to make native whites the dominant element in the Republican coalition was not undertaken simply to increase the number of whites voting with the party nor was it intended just to recruit indiscriminately among the white population. Rather, their goal was to bring into the party men of influence and prestige. As Joseph E. Brown, Georgia's preeminent Centrist, saw the situation, "it is impossible to build up and maintain a party here on the reconstruction line without the aid of leading Southern men who know our people and sympathise with them."[60] Because of their interest and understanding, they would use their influence to put a brake on the radical tendencies in the party and steer it instead onto a conservative and accommodationist course. The role they were to play was exemplified by the action of William B. Rodman in North Carolina's constitutional convention. Arguing that his affiliation with the Republican party had been a "fortunate thing," he claimed that he had "done a good deal to soften the animosity of some of the Republican hot heads, against the Southern people."[61] If this moderating influence were applied effectively, the party would then become safe and acceptable so that an increasing number of prestigious and conservative politicians would begin to affiliate with it. By 1870, Governor Smith of Alabama was becoming convinced that his party was sufficiently tamed that influential conservative whites would join it, for he assured them proudly that "radicalism no longer exists in the Republican party of Alabama."[62]

Because the party had been brought into existence at a moment of great ferment in the South and was in fact an outgrowth of that revolutionary situation, its radical potential was both recognized by the Centrists and feared. This danger was particularly apparent because the Republicans' main constituency was the recently freed black population. Therefore, it was imperative, so Centrists calculated, that they move in quickly to check the party's propensity towards radicalism. James L. Alcorn was not alone in deciding to join the Republican party in order, as he put it, "to pluck our common liberty and our common prosperity out of the jaws of inevitable ruin."[63] Who was better equipped for this task than the freedmen's former masters, the large planters and slaveholders like Alcorn himself? But there were other social groups in the South which might begin to affiliate with the Republicans if the party's radicalism were not muted. Whites who were poor and exploited like blacks might reasonably conclude that a Republican party that was committed to agitating for social justice and economic opportunity was acting in their interest too. The formation of an alliance between aggrieved whites and blacks was an eventuality Centrists dreaded. It would mean that race had been subordinated to class and the Republican party converted into an instrument of class protest, threatening to the South's political and social order. This was the ultimate disaster that Republicanism posed to the region, in the Centrists' view, and they affiliated with the party to make sure it would not occur. Richmond Pearson, a former Whig who would later become the Republican chief justice of North Carolina, saw this only too clearly and urged conservative whites not to stand aloof in the 1868 elections and leave the Republicans to their own devices. He believed that an antagonistic posture would be "an open declaration of war, and [the freedmen] will stand firm in solid column against us, supported by what has been called in derision

'The mean white men', but supported by enough to give them a majority of 20,000 votes. What is to be the result? Agitation, of course. . . ."[64]

Although the Republican party had been born amid the tumult of emancipation and Reconstruction and had won power with the votes of dispossessed freedmen, the Centrists intended to make it into a bulwark against social change and political extremism. Politicians with this perspective on the Republican party were active in each southern state. They were most successful in Alabama and Mississippi where both governors were Centrists and thus controlled the machinery of the state as well as the party. The faction in Alabama was headed by a group of influential politicians from the northern part of the state—David C. Humphreys, Thomas Peters, David P. Lewis—and from Talladega county in the Piedmont by men such as Alexander White, Lewis E. Parsons, and Samuel Rice. The governor, William H. Smith, and the senior U.S. senator, Willard Warner, who was actually a northerner, were the faction's most conspicuous figures.[65] Meanwhile, in Mississippi the Centrists were headed by James L. Alcorn, and they numbered among their leading lights Joshua Morris, the attorney general; Horatio Simrall, a justice on the state's highest court; and a northerner, Henry B. Musgrove, who was the state auditor.[66]

Centrist factions were also powerful in Texas and Georgia, but in neither state were they able to dominate the party or control state government. Instead, they functioned as dissenters constantly pressing the party to open its lines to conservative white recruits. The culmination of this approach was reached in Georgia after the 1868 elections when Joseph E. Brown urged Governor Bullock to make overtures to the conciliatory element in the Democratic-Conservative party. Noting how divided the latter was, Brown advised that "we should make terms with the moderate wing and that the new administration should treat them with such consideration as to gratify them. If this is done, we can easily unite and carry the State in the next elections."[67] That kind of merger would have transformed the party and engulfed Bullock's wing of it, and so it was resisted vigorously. Although checked, the Centrists, nevertheless, remained with the Republicans, but that was not the case in Texas where the Centrists were in constant negotiation with the Democratic-Conservatives. They had broken with their own party over the 1869 constitution and they remained on its margins thereafter. This group was led by Jack Hamilton, Elisha Pease, John L. Haynes, and newspaper editor Ferdinand Flake. All of these men were natives, as were the Centrist leaders in Georgia, namely Joseph E. Brown, Amos T. Akerman, Joshua Hill, and Samuel Bard of the Atlanta *New Era*.[68]

Although the Centrist position was based on a view of what the Republican party ideally should be like, there was inevitably a more tactical and opportunistic facet to it. Since the recruitment of more whites into the party was at the crux of Centrism, Republican politicians often adopted a Centrist posture simply in order to increase their personal support within the party. This was the option available to influential Republicans who found their way to success blocked by rivals who were in control of the lion's share of the party's patronage and of its existing constituency. In late 1869, Governor Henry Warmoth realized that his domination of Louisiana Republicanism was seriously threatened by a rival faction—led by James Casey, the U.S. collector of customs in New Orleans—which had corralled the federal offices and could rely on the bulk of the black vote. Warmoth then proceeded to shift his political priorities dramatically. Very overtly, he vetoed major pieces of civil rights legislation, thereby signalling that blacks were no longer of primary importance to him, and began instead to court the support of respectable whites.[69] In Florida, at the same time, Governor Harrison Reed found himself at a similar disadvantage because his political rivals were in charge of the federal patronage. Consequently, he also vetoed civil rights bills and maneuvered for white votes.[70] In Reed's case, this move was reversed a year later, only to be changed back again in 1872; Warmoth's decision to pursue a Centrist course was, by contrast, to prove irreversible as well as unsuccessful.

The availability of a potential white vote encouraged other Republican aspirants to see it as a means of defeating rivals whose current position within the party seemed to be secure. In Arkansas, the Reverend Joseph Brooks—because of his past record with the Freedmen's Bureau and his earlier leadership of the Radicals—saw that he was being squeezed out by the dominant faction led by Governor Powell Clayton. By 1871, Brooks, like Warmoth earlier, began to see that his own and his supporters' only hope of preferment lay in the creation of a new base of support. By focussing his gubernatorial campaign on the issue of amnesty, he intended to win the numerous white voters who were still disfranchised by the state's ban on former Confederate voting. So effective was his newly espoused Centrism that Brooks very nearly won election as governor in 1872.[71] Meanwhile, in South Carolina, the faction led by the senior U.S. senator, Frederick Sawyer, and his allies, Congressman Christopher C. Bowen and Alexander G. Mackey, continually pursued a Centrist course. Secure in possession of the U.S. Custom House in Charleston, they nevertheless were shut out of control by the faction of Governor Robert Scott and Senator John Patterson which had a lock on the state patronage and the black vote. Accordingly, in 1870, 1872, and 1874, the Charleston faction sought white votes through an electoral alliance with the Democratic-Conservatives in an attempt to win control of the state, and thus outmaneuver their rivals. But their persistent party irregularity was not rewarded, for the bolters suffered defeat each time.[72]

By late 1871, the Centrists in every state were experiencing similar difficulties and were having to reassess their future prospects in the Republican party. At first, they had often been extremely influential and were confident that their influence on southern Republicanism was certain to increase. Their optimism was based on the assumption that whites could be brought into the party and that, as the numbers of them increased, so would their own position and influence. But these projections and hopes were not being realized and the Centrists found themselves tied to a strategy that was visibly failing. Undermined by the refusal of whites to cross over to the Republicans and pressured from within the party by opponents of their initiative, the Centrists became increasingly marginal and began to look for ways out of their quandary. With the appearance during 1872 of the Liberal-Republican movement, a vehicle was thought to have emerged by which they could obtain access to the uncommitted white votes they had sought all along. Moreover, it could be done through an organization concerned to reform the party and still calling itself Republican, but it did not work out that way. Because the Liberals moved increasingly into the Democratic-Conservative orbit as 1872 progressed, the Centrists were forced to acknowledge that they could obtain the support of white southerners only by going outside the Republican party. Thus, their only recourse was to leave altogether. This meant that they had lost in the struggle to determine the direction and priorities of southern Republicanism.

The faction that had repulsed the Centrists had been able to do so through its hold on the Republican rank-and-file and through its closer ties with the national party and with the federal government, which the latter controlled. Rather than risking its chances, as the Centrists had done, on the possibility that the party could be re-organized around a white constituency that it had not as yet ac-quired, this faction had made sure that the Republicans' present supporters were first organized and taken care of. The Regulars, as the rival faction can appropriately be described, did not defect in 1872 but stood behind the party's nominee, President Grant, just like their namesakes in the North. Consequently, with the evapora-tion of the possibility of drawing white voters into the Republican ranks, the Centrists were eclipsed by 1872 or else seceded from the party altogether. The result was that in those states where the Republicans still held power, the Regulars were in control. They had repulsed the Centrist challenge in Arkansas, South Carolina, Texas, Louisiana, and Alabama, and they gained the ascendancy in Mississippi.

With the exception of Texas, where the party's whites were over-whelmingly native, the Regular factions were headed by northern-ers. In Arkansas, northerners monopolized the upper reaches of the faction, since Powell Clayton, the governor, was a newcomer and so was his successor, Ozra Hadley. In addition, other leading Regu-lars, such as John McClure, the chief justice, and Benjamin F. Rice, Alexander McDonald, and S. W. Dorsey, who all served as U.S. senators, were also northerners.[73] South Carolina's leading Regu-lars were Robert Scott, the governor, and Senator John J. Patter-son, both of whom were from the North. Finally, the faction in Lou-isiana was headed by northerners like the New Orleans customs collector, James Casey, as well as by William P. Kellogg and Stephen B. Packard.

A second characteristic of the Regulars was that they invariably derived their political viability from the control they possessed over federal patronage. Their northern origins and experience gave them preferment in obtaining nomination to Congress as well as in being selected as the federal government's agents and officeholders in its southern outposts. Consequently, with this as their base of influence, Regulars used their access to the northern wing of the party and their patronage power to restrain the drive of the Centrists towards a rather different orientation for southern Republicanism. In Alabama and Florida, the Regulars, led by U.S. Senators George E. Spencer and Thomas W. Osborn respectively, had the federal offices in their hands. Their counterparts in Louisiana were James Casey, the customs collector in New Orleans, and Stephen Packard, the U.S. marshal, whose control of federal patronage was so firm that Warmoth had been forced to embrace Centrism. Arkansas' Regulars controlled not only the federal patronage but also the immense appointive power of the governorship, thus forcing any opponent to rely on outside support if, as Brooks did, he chose to pick a fight. An exception to this general rule was provided by South Carolina. There, the federal officeholders were confronted by a Regular faction so well entrenched behind its black support and its control of the state government that they, not their opponents, pursued a Centrist policy.

The most important feature of the Regulars which distinguished them from their Centrist competitors was, however, their position in the party's organizational structure and their resultant perspective on its electoral priorities. Unlike their rivals, the Regulars did not want to change the existing composition of the Republican party. They had no intention of opening it up to an influx of new recruits who would automatically unbalance its existing components, nor did they envisage forming alliances with the more conciliatory wing of the Democratic-Conservatives. Rather, the Regulars were the party loyalists and they strove to sustain and protect the institution as it was. Since, for the most part, Regulars were either in control of the party machinery or were trying to save it from being undermined by the Centrists, they saw themselves as the guardians of the Republican organization against its Centrist detractors and destroyers. As such, they could claim a kind of legitimacy and party orthodoxy, which, for their rivals, was quite unimaginable and therefore unattainable.

This meant that, on the question of patronage and party loyalty, for instance, Regulars would always be found urging that the party faithful be given preference in appointments and nominations. The party's gifts were to be offered as rewards for commitment and service and not as lures to entice potential recruits. What Regulars wished to avoid was the kind of disaffection among party activists and the rank-and-file which the selection of marginal Republicans or non-Republicans provoked. An example of this was an appointment to assessor in Alamance and Randolph counties in North Carolina. Party supporters there, it was reported in December 1871, "want fire-tried Republicans, men who have given evidence of the faith in them by their works. They say, if men at least doubtful and certainly inactive in politics, who appoint democrats under them, are continued in the best offices in the gift of the Administration, they will work no more & go to no more elections."[74] Although Regular factions did undoubtedly appoint men whose party allegiance was less evident than their respectability or their influence among Democratic-Conservatives, the tendency was nevertheless for them to use patronage to consolidate and build up the party rather than, as their Centrist rivals preferred, to expand it.

Because the Regulars placed so much emphasis on strengthening the Republicans' existing base of support, it followed that they relied considerably on the party's blacks. Indeed, without them, the Regulars knew that their position in the party as well as the survival of the party itself were precarious. They therefore had to have the cooperation and backing of black Republicans. To confirm the ties between the Regular faction and its black affiliates, black demands were heeded and responded to. But there were limits to the Regulars' commitment. First of all, the faction's white leaders worried about the effect on the party's image if blacks and their concerns became too visible. Second, they had to contend with the competition for office, particularly in overwhelmingly black areas, between northerners, who lacked a constituency of their own yet wanted to be guaranteed a position in a safe Republican district, and black officeseekers, who naturally felt they were entitled to office in a black district.

The Regulars' commitment to their black constituency and their ability to preserve the party organization were tested concurrently when the violence of the Klan threatened both priorities between 1869 and 1871. But the problem assumed even greater significance than this when it became the critical issue in the Regulars' struggle to stem the Centrists' attempt to reorient and redefine southern Republicanism. The Regulars demanded ceaselessly that tougher measures be taken to restore order, but, in Mississippi and Alabama where Centrists had the machinery of the state in their hands and where Regulars were out of power, the issues in the conflict were significantly sharpened and the protagonists' positions, particularly that of the Regulars, were presented with greater clarity. The contest in Mississippi was even argued on the floor of the U.S. Senate by the leaders of the two rival factions, Senators James Alcorn and Adelbert Ames, and a more decisive and dramatic confrontation could hardly be imagined. Indeed, in Ames's speech of 20 May 1872, the ultimate significance and impact of the issue were starkly revealed. He first arraigned Governor Alcorn for his claim that "peace reigns in Mississippi" and for his opinion that a federal Ku Klux law was unnecessary and "a menace to the people" of the state. But then Ames went on to explain why Alcorn adopted that course. Essentially it was because the leader of the Centrist faction had a totally different conception of the nature and composition of the Republican party from that of Ames and the Regulars.

Alcorn, so Ames reminded his listeners, always talked of "my people" and "my state" when referring to Mississippi. Furthermore, only a short while ago, he had told the Senate with great pride that, in 1871 when he had been reelected governor, "the Democrats and Republicans had [both] voted for him." Evidently, Alcorn saw no great difference between the two parties and was trying, so Ames suggested, to ride both horses at once. The trouble was that, while a circus performer's "horses are always going in the same direction," Alcorn's were not and, "in his circus effort, he gave over the state almost entirely in many counties to the opposing party." His appointees in this fusion scheme may have called themselves "Alcorn men," not Democrats, but, all the same, they had never been identified with Republicanism and so had not strengthened the party at all.[75]

At the root of the difference were two distinctive views of the party. On one hand, the Centrists regarded Ames as "a carpetbagger . . . with no right to be in the state . . . the representative of the extreme radical wing of the party." On the other, the Regulars contended that "the carpet-baggers and the colored men are the controlling element of the Republican party" of Mississippi. "They controlled it when [Alcorn] was nominated and when he was elected to the Senate," Ames contended, "and they control it now, as the action of the late [party] convention [which demanded a state civil rights bill] shows."[76]

While the thrust of Ames's depiction of the two factions and their differing conceptions of the party was accurate, it would be a mistake to assume that the protagonists had little in common. Instead, they both endorsed the conservative and conciliatory cast that their party had assumed since the defeat of the Radicals. As a result, Regulars, including of course Ames himself, did not eschew efforts to satisfy and reconcile, even recruit, respectable white support. They knew that the survival of Republicanism necessitated it. But the distinction between them and the Centrists, and it was of critical importance, was that the Regulars did not intend to reorganize the party around the infusion of whites nor did they consider coalescence with any segment of the opposition party as the means for establishing an enduring Republicanism. Instead, their appeal for white support was not to be made at the expense of the party's rank-and-file and its more committed members. Rather, it was to act as a supplement to the basic Republican constituency. Thus, the difference was over the decisive tactical question of priority and sequence. It was not over the adaptive role that the party would ultimately play in southern politics.

A corollary to that qualification was that both factions approved of the most important element in the Republican appeal for white approval and recognition—its policy of state subsidy for railroads. Except for Texas, where the incumbent Regulars led by Governor Edmund Davis generally opposed state aid, factional differences over state aid were never so fundamental.[77] Everywhere else, factions might differ in their preferences for particular lines over others, as occurred in Arkansas where the Minstrels backed the Little Rock and Fort Smith road while Brooks's Brindletails supported the Midland. Or they might disagree over particular railroad measures. But the factions were not so rigidly differentiated that they divided into principled supporters or opponents of railroad subsidization altogether.[78] Instead, the desirability of building railroads, as well as of publicly promoting them, was virtually consensual in the Republican party. Not until later, when the excesses and problems in the policy began to appear, did the harmony break down.

Ultimately, the differences between the Republican party's factions arose over the lengths to which the party should go in order to recruit those whites who would give it prestige and electoral support. The Centrists were the dynamic element in the situation, demanding that the Republicans shift priorities, reconstitute their party, and bring in large numbers of respectable whites. To this challenge the Regulars countered by mobilizing the party's black vote and entrenching themselves within the party machinery. This amounted to little more than a holding action, however, an attempt simply to maintain and preserve their position in the Republican party. In effect, the Centrists had seized the initiative and the Regulars had been forced to devote their energies to restraining them, but without the opportunity to offer a real alternative course for the party such as their Radical predecessors had provided. As a result, the Republicans were plunged into a state of constant turmoil and instability. Yet, once this ended with the failure of the attempt at recruiting white voters and with the defection of the Centrists in 1872 and 1873, the party simply drifted without focus.

3. The Democratic-Conservatives and the New Departure

I hope all the good people of the state may work together not only for our redemption from misrule & oppression, but also for our recuperation in wealth & permanent prosperity. To do this effectively, we ought to cooperate, by countenance at least, in all works of internal improvement calculated to benefit any part of the state.
—Levi W. Lawler to Robert McKee,
　Talladega, 23 July 1869

Keep the thing hot through the news papers and we will get the party up to the proper standard, the weak and sickly ones will fall into line easily when they see we intend to run on straight out principles.
—Dudley M. DuBose to Alexander Stephens,
　U.S. House of Representatives, 22 March 1871

N ow it seems to me that when a party loses its doctrines, it ought to dissolve."[1] Samuel Phillips, North Carolina's Republican attorney general, was convinced in July 1870 that the Democratic-Conservative party could not survive much longer. By renouncing the issues that had brought it into existence and justified it, he felt that the party was consigning itself to oblivion. The *North Carolina Standard* agreed, observing, "Only the hope of public plunder, and a desire for revenge, coupled with a certain pride of consistency and the memories of former sufferings and trials, hold the concern together."[2]

For Phillips and the editors of the *Standard*, the function of political parties was to embody and implement ideas about government and society. This was their understanding and it was derived from their knowledge and experience of the party battles of the antebellum decades when, as Phillips put it, "The old Whig and Democratic parties fought over great and important issues for twenty years and did not give them up."[3] The life of the issue and of the party were bound indissolubly together, and in the ideologically charged and passionate era of the sectional crisis and Reconstruction, there was no reason whatsoever to doubt that party politics was still all about major issues and questions of principle.

Nevertheless, despite warnings that the party's demise would be the certain consequence, the Democratic-Conservative leadership decided to end its opposition to Reconstruction as well as to black suffrage. The assumption was that, rather than destroying the party, abandonment of its previous position might actually regenerate it. Indeed, the party's decline was believed to be imminent if it did not change course. By acknowledging the new political situation in the South, the party might terminate its minority status and instead obtain considerable advantages. It would become not simply a participant in the political system of the reconstructed South but would also acquire legitimacy and put itself in a favorable position to gain access to the newly enfranchised black voters.

The New Departure, as this change of policy was called, was such a dramatic move for the party to make that a large segment of its membership was unable to accept it.[4] Like Phillips and the *Standard*, they were convinced that the party was committing suicide, or at least embarking on a course that was extremely unwise and likely to be regretted later. So the New Departure strategy encountered resistance. In North Carolina, the party was so split over the question of whether or not to endorse the Fifteenth Amendment that no statewide party meeting could be held in 1870.[5] Dissension was also rife and threatening that year in Alabama, where the party chairman, James Clanton, told Robert McKee, the editor of the Selma *Times and Argus*, that he had taken no position "in the Controversy which has been going on between our own friends as to our future *policy*, farther than to harmonize the discordant elements" as far as possible. "Under the circumstances," he added, "I believe the least said (in our convention) the soonest mended—"[6]

Although a formal acceptance of Reconstruction and black suffrage would produce dissension, it was thought likely to be offset by considerable electoral gains. In the first place, it would reassure northern Republicans that the edifice they had created in the postwar South was no longer in jeopardy and an item of contention. But more important perhaps was its impact on black voters who would be encouraged that the civil and political rights they had acquired from Reconstruction were not going to be endangered. Although the effect of the New Departure was to reassure both the northern Republicans and the southern blacks, those who urged its adoption intended to go further than mere propitiation in the case of the blacks. They were determined, by means of this policy, to compete with the Republicans for black votes. Not content with embracing the fundamental policies of their opponents, the Democratic-Conservatives now contemplated the appropriation of the Republicans' main source of electoral support, their black constituency. That this was no accident, but a presumptuous and flagrant attempt to finesse the Republicans was evident in a boastful remark of the Montgomery *Advertiser* in 1870 when it proclaimed proudly: "There is no 'white man's party' as such South of the Potomac."[7]

Politically astute though this policy was, it was not merely a cynical maneuver to get votes wherever they could be found or to deprive their opponents of "the negro question," which the New York *World* regarded as "their only principle of cohesion."[8] There were also broader considerations involved and to many, if not most, New Departurists these were very important. What they amounted to was a deep concern about the future of the region's government and politics if the two parties were divided along racial lines and, by implication, on the basis of class as well. As James B. Kershaw, South Carolina's most prominent New Departurist, explained angrily to an unconvinced Mississippi newspaper editor, "There can be no good government in your State until you adopt a policy which will unite to some extent the two classes composing your voting population."[9] The same preoccupation was in the mind of Kershaw's fellow South Carolinian, William L. Trenholm, who in 1870 produced a pamphlet explaining that there was more than mere partisan advantage in the New Departure. "Local political parties resting on distinctions of race and class," he wrote, "produce incessant jarring and tend invariably to violence and disorder; they are as powerless for good and as mischievous in their effects as national parties founded on sectional differences."[10] To ensure that the social and political order in the region was stable and tranquil, the New Departure was thought to be essential.

When, to all of these arguments for the New Departure, there was added the northern Democrats' decision to espouse it in 1870, the grounds for continued resistance seemed to have evaporated. All the same, the opposition, although outmaneuvered and unsettled, did possess a powerful argument and an alternative strategy. These dissenters, who are most aptly described by the term, "Bourbon," believed that the party's salvation was most likely to be obtained by refusing to recognize the political and constitutional changes of Reconstruction. In particular, they believed that, as an electoral strategy, the New Departure was mistaken. Democratic-Conservatives had a natural constituency that was sufficient and so they did not need to seek other sources of support. The party's electoral base was large enough that it could become the majority without having to extend its appeal or dilute its principles. After all, whites had stayed away in droves in the elections of 1868 and 1869 to ratify the Reconstruction constitutions and elect state officials. But, once the political situation normalized, they would return and participate. This assertion was far more cogent even than the equivalent argument put forth by the Bourbons' "expressive" counterparts in the Republican party, because white voters were a registered majority in every state, except South Carolina and Louisiana. Provided that these whites voted and that defections were stemmed, the "expressive" policy advocated by the Bourbons could transform the Democratic-Conservatives' minority status into a majority more surely and easily than the New Departure, its "competitive" alternative. Consequently, the latter was superfluous and, in its effect on the party, quite possibly subversive and damaging as well.

Nevertheless, the Bourbons' warnings about the dangers in the New Departure were dismissed. Instead, the policy seemed to hold out the promise that black votes could be won in such large numbers that the party would soon be able to return to power. The kind of optimism and conviction with which New Departurists viewed this prospect was conveyed by the comments in 1870 of Albert Elmore of Alabama who was urging the policy on his Bourbon friend, John W. A. Sanford, the party's nominee for attorney general that year. "It is important," he told Sanford, "that the vote of the colored man be governed by men to the 'manner born'. If the democratic party acknowledges that the suffrage question is settled, which it must do, or take issue with the party in N.Y., then they can carry Ala., because the negroes will divide as soon as that is known to them. They are anxious now to go with the old citizens, but cannot until suffrage is yielded by the democracy, which the sooner, the better."[11] The assumption that the black vote was susceptible to Democratic-Conservative influence was also shared by many Republicans, particularly those who were natives. One of the most distinguished among them, Joseph E. Brown, explained as early as December 1868 that "so soon as the Democrats admit the right of the freedmen to vote, and make no farther issue upon it, they will carry a large proportion of them in every election." "Indeed," he noted, "they did so in the [recent] Presidential election," even though "the mass of the party denied their right to vote." In Brown's view, this simply confirmed the dire predictions he had been giving to "Republicans North and South" about the unreliability of their black support.[12]

By the time the New Departure had undergone its first test in the 1870 elections, the Democratic-Conservative leadership was expressing its pleasure at the success of the strategy. After winning the legislative elections in North Carolina that year, the party's Central Executive Committee observed gleefully, "Even the colored race, controlled as it hitherto has been by evil counsels and gross misrepresentation of our motives and purposes as to them, in many portions of the State, in very considerable numbers, broke away from the trammels in which they were bound." The explanation for this switch was, in the committee's view, quite obvious, since "the interests of the white and colored races . . . are the same" and it was only the interference of the "carpetbaggers" which prevented racial harmony. To prove this, the committee then pledged that the party would protect the rights of black citizens.[13] A similar evaluation of the effect of the party's endorsement of black suffrage came from Alabama where the Democratic-Conservatives had just won control of the state. The victorious governor, Robert B. Lindsay, explained elatedly, "The Democratic party is beginning to electioneer pretty strongly with the colored people."[14]

The potential for the party in the black vote impressed few as much as Zebulon B. Vance, North Carolina's wartime governor and its most important and most flamboyant Democratic-Conservative. To the party in Georgia he brought the lesson of his own state's success in the summer of 1870. He assured the Georgians that blacks "will not suffer themselves to be fooled again" by the "glittering promises" offered by the newcomers from the North. Consequently, all that the party needed to do in the campaign was to "act so as to make them sick of the yankees, and show them that their old masters and themselves are natural allies." The spirit in which this was to be done was, however, to be far from solicitous and friendly. "Make no false promises to them," Vance stressed, and tell them that the Democratic-Conservative party gave up its opposition to black suffrage only because it was "useless" to continue any longer. In other words, "We acquiesced in what we could not prevent."[15] The drift of Vance's remarks was that influence and persuasion, rather than appeals and solicitude, were to be the means of winning black votes. As the Raleigh *Sentinel* once put it: "Heretofore to argue with the negro was to waste your time. . . . Those who work daily with the negro can exercise great influence over him" and this "will count more in the campaign than political speeches from the stump."[16]

Indeed, it was through the pressure that an employer could exert upon his black workers and plantation hands that the anticipated votes were thought most likely to be secured. A North Carolinian, W. H. Avera of Selma, reported to the party chairman in 1872: "I carried some 40 to 60 Colored Votes part of them for the whole ticket. Most of them however, I only succeeded in getting their vote for myself. This latter Class were mostly those that I had employed either at this time or at some time since the war. I allway try to get the Confidence of those I have employed."[17] The power of an employer's personal influence was often rather less effective, however, as David H. Hemphill of a prestigious South Carolina family from Chester found out. "I have been very busy for the past two months," he wrote during the 1870 campaign, "not only in my office—but electioneering among the infernal negroes." The result was that

> After all my trouble—and all the humiliation which I had to undergo—and the concessions made, I am defeated by over Thirteen Hundred Majority—now if that is what you call encouraging—I am off for another country pretty soon—where a man's abilities will be properly appreciated—I made it my business to pay my respects to the "colored friends" at Uncle Robert's [R. R. Hemphill's plantation] and got the promise of a few votes, but I understand that they all marched to the polls by sunrise and voted the full Radical ticket.[18]

Despite the optimism that had accompanied the Democratic-Conservative drive to obtain black votes, the results, as David Hemphill and countless others discovered, were meager. What had seemed to be an appeal for black support turned out to be in fact an attempt to cajole blacks either into acknowledging the personal influence of local grandees or into submitting to the economic pressure of their employers. Thus, the harmony of interests so often referred to was in reality little more than a hierarchy of influence. Accordingly, blacks demonstrated their scepticism about Democratic-Conservative intentions. The contrast between the appeal for black votes and the spirit and means employed in seeking those votes was, however, nowhere more blatant than in the rise to prominence of the Ku Klux Klan while the party was simultaneously embarking on the New Departure.

The Klan came into being before the Democratic-Conservative leadership adopted its conciliatory posture. Thus it was already in place and its persistence testified to the powerful residue of opposition to the New Departure which existed within the party. Nevertheless, the New Departurists who were at the head of the state parties did not proceed against the Klan despite the threat that its violence and intimidation posed towards the success of their electoral strategy. Partly, this was because they were no doubt fearful of the consequences if they tried. This was the view of Charles Hays, the Republican congressman from Alabama's western Black Belt, who said in mid-1871 that "in the beginning [leading men] winked at it, because they thought it would ultimately result in the breaking down of the republican party; but the thing has got too big for them now, and they cannot control it."[19] But, more likely, their own ambivalence about the New Departure was of considerable importance. Since, as we have seen, they had few illusions about the likelihood that blacks would join the Democratic-Conservatives willingly, they had to concede that coercion of some kind would have to be involved, and the line between intimidation by personal pressure and intimidation by violence was not at all precise. Thus, it was easy for them to delude themselves into thinking that Klan violence was not contradictory to their enunciated policy. Evidence to this effect was provided by two politicians from Greene County, Alabama, which was the center of Klan activity in 1870. In testimony to the congressional committee investigating the Klan in 1871, one of them, John G. Pierce, explained that blacks in the county were shifting their partisan allegiance because "we take the side of the negro now."[20] The other, J. J. Jolly, who was a leading political figure and probably involved with the Klan, explained that blacks were gaining confidence in local whites "as men, and I think they are rapidly getting to have confidence in them politically" as well.[21]

Notwithstanding efforts at self-delusion such as these, there was a good deal of concern within the New Departure faction about the repercussions of Klan terror. Indeed, unless checked, it could utterly wreck their entire policy. In 1871, Benjamin Hill revealed his fears to the Klan committee: "If we don't enforce the law ourselves it will be done for us. The Ku Klux business is the worst thing that ever afflicted the South. Every day that we let it continue we cut our throats."[22] The danger was so great that another New Departurist, Albert Elmore, wrote privately in the spring of 1871: "It is of the utmost importance to the democracy, & the country, that lawlessness and outrage, be put down. Let the democratic party move heavily in that direction." Unless "the disorder is put down by the people of the south, & not by the Prest.," it was feared that the anticipated Democratic victory in the following year's presidential election would be forfeited.[23] In fact, under the pressure of the Ku Klux Acts of 1871 and spurred by the action of Republican officials in their states to end the violence, the New Departurists did, by mid-1871, find the will and the means to help bring the Klan to heel.[24]

Naturally enough, however, this belated firmness was not likely to impress black voters. In fact, the attempt to lure blacks into affiliation with the Democratic-Conservatives through their conciliatory stance on the issues was already proving ineffective. Far more fruitful had been the party's less direct approach to the black vote by means of its electoral alliances with breakaway Republican factions. Fusion with dissident Republicans had begun with the "new movement" of 1869, and it was to play a major role in the party's electoral strategy under the New Departure. Through cooperation with bolting Republicans, the Democratic-Conservatives were able to increase their vote and broaden their support. Thus, fusion was not an alternative to the direct solicitation of black votes but was an adjunct to it, another way to draw off Republican support and break the party down.

This strategy of encouraging and then exploiting Republican dissension produced many benefits for the Democratic-Conservatives. The first was that a bolt, in itself, inflicted serious damage on the Republican organization and diminished its electoral prospects. If this setback were further exploited, the Democratic-Conservatives could increase the political gain that the bolt had already given them. A second advantage was that, through electoral collaboration, the votes of blacks, which Democratic-Conservatives acting on their own might have difficulty obtaining, could be brought in by their Republican allies. In fact, virtually every Republican bolter would bring some element of black support. And this would be especially likely in black districts, just the places in which Democratic-Conservatives were most in need of support from blacks. Naturally, these black votes would supplement the white support that the bolters already brought with them. A final consideration was that cooperation with Republicans was obviously an indication of a conciliatory and accommodating attitude on the part of the opposition, even of a willingness to abandon combative partisanship. Belief that this was so would help legitimize the party in the North as well as the South.

Fusion was not, however, a tactic that was appropriate everywhere in the South. Although the New Departure was party policy in every state, it was not necessarily accompanied by fusion. At the state level, the Democratic-Conservatives were often able to mount winning campaigns without having to consort with bolting Republicans. In 1870, the party won statewide in Georgia, Alabama, and North Carolina, and three years later in Texas as well, without reliance on any fusion arrangements. Meanwhile, at the county and local level, fusion was unnecessary wherever the Democratic-Conservatives were in a clear majority, usually in constituencies where whites predominated or where, for some other reason, the Republican organization was weak. Fusion, on the other hand, could be adopted only in those situations where a section of the Republican party was actually running a separate campaign or was threatening to do so if assured of Democratic-Conservative backing. Usually, a bolt would occur after a faction within the party failed to gain control and it was forced, therefore, either to play second fiddle or try to win power in the ensuing campaign by pursuing a Centrist strategy and seeking the support of the Democratic-Conservatives. This aid would be available only when the latter were in a minority and needed a coalition with breakaway Republicans to come within striking distance of securing an electoral majority.

Thus, the prerequisites for fusion were: the Democratic-Conservatives must find themselves in a minority; to compensate for this, they must seek an electoral coalition; and the Republicans had to be polarized and splintering. At the state level, the Democratic-Conservatives backed a bolting Republican ticket in Mississippi in 1873 and in Arkansas, Louisiana, and South Carolina in 1872. Of course, 1872 was the year of the Liberal-Republican split when fusion was being negotiated on the national level and it was often duplicated in the southern states where the seceding Republicans were strong enough to mount their own campaign. Below the state level, fusion was most frequent in races for the state legislature and for local office in those localities where, prior to the anticipated bolt, the Republicans were in the ascendant because of an overwhelming preponderance of blacks. Outnumbered in these black areas, Democratic-Conservatives had no hope of political success unless they could coalesce with breakaway Republicans.[25]

The importance of some kind of fusion to the viability of the party in these areas explains why the core of support for the conciliatory New Departure lay in the black belt. To Democratic-Conservatives in the regions of heaviest black population, refusal to accommodate to black voters was politically suicidal. Moreover, an

unyielding stance towards the party that the blacks were supporting would serve only to solidify its ranks. In addition to the sheer
partisan calculation, Democratic-Conservative landowners and
propertyholders feared a rigid political division along racial lines
because, as Kershaw and Trenholm had pointed out, such a cleavage was fraught with danger. Confirming them in their espousal of
the New Departure and of the electoral fusion that invariably accompanied it was the conviction of the black-belt whites that they
would be able to influence their black neighbors and workers politically just as, in the past, they had been able to control them eco-
nomically and socially. Whether it was a notion of paternalism or
simply an assumption that blacks were, in the end, dependent on
them did not matter; their political necessity and their racial assumptions reinforced each other and thus supported them in their
convictions about the likely success of the New Departure.

The tendency within the Democratic-Conservative party after
1868 towards adoption of a policy that deemphasized the differences between itself and the Republicans was not confined to the
sphere of electoral policy. On substantive issues, too, there was convergence. This was particularly true with regard to the vital question of the South's future prosperity and economic revival. Next to
political reconstruction, economic rehabilitation was undoubtedly
the most important matter confronting the region after the war. Indeed, there was a close connection between the two, because a sympathetic political climate was deemed essential to the regeneration
of the southern economy. The Republican party was intended to
create that atmosphere and thereby encourage economic development, and this it began to do as soon as it entered office. Consequently, those Democratic-Conservatives who also wanted the internal improvements that the Republicans were promoting could
not risk endangering the program's success by threatening the stability and survival of the party sponsoring it. So it was not surprising that the pressure to acknowledge the political order created by
Reconstruction was closely related to the desire for internal improvements and the development they would stimulate. Indeed, advocates of the New Departure and proponents of the New South
were, if not interchangeable, certainly operating in parallel, and
both were in the ascendant within the Democratic-Conservative
party in the late 1860s and early 1870s.

The practicality and expediency that had pervaded the party's thinking about politics also characterized its concern about the material resources and the economy of the region. In the past, the South had overlooked and ignored economic development. This had to change, it was felt, and Democratic-Conservatives were among the first to realize it. "Wealth is power, among nations as among individuals. After all, that is really what the world is seeking," declared the Raleigh *Sentinel*, a few mornings after the presidential election of 1868. The South, however, had so far failed to develop its wealth and become self-sufficient. Instead, the region had wasted "its strength in a contest at large odds for political power," winding up as "a hewer of wood and a drawer of water for the North."[26] In contrast to the South's emphasis on the theoretical and political, the North had stressed practicality and material interests, with results that proved unmistakably which priority was preferable. Learning from its indifferent stewardship and missed opportunities, southerners were exhorted "to go to work to build up our own fortunes, and get possession of our own affairs," for "a new era" was dawning and "our material prosperity must now begin."[27]

Admonitions and aspirations like these were not confined to Benjamin H. Hill, the man who had uttered them. Nor were they restricted to the Republican party, which, as its official organ in North Carolina put it, had already identified itself with "the improvements of the age" and was at work introducing programs of "state aid in building railroads that will develop [southern] resources, give life to trade, and build up hundreds of new cities and villages."[28] Instead, the leading newspapers and politicians of the Democratic-Conservative party were also alive to the need and the possibility of a New South.

Newspaper readers could not have failed to be cognizant of, although not perhaps imbued with, the New South enthusiasm that pervaded the editorial columns in 1869 and thereafter. A few samples will reveal the tenor of this sentiment. On 25 March 1869, the Jackson *Clarion* urged Mississippi to develop its "bountiful resources" by improving the productivity of agriculture, by encouraging skilled immigration, and by expanding its railroad system "until each county will be bound to the other by iron ties." In its next issue, the paper warned the city of Jackson that, if it did not become "a seat of manufacturing and commercial industry, it will be for the reason that her citizens will not take the tide which leads to fortune."[29] Similar exhortations came from the Atlanta *Constitution* a month later. "The lethargy and inertness of the past, seems superceded by a spirit of industry and enterprise," its new editor, Isaac W. Avery, observed. "The people are brimming with railroad and other material enterprise . . . it is all stuff that our Southern people do not possess enterprise. We do need capital; and we need more people to populate our vast country, and redeem our wild lands." If this development were set in motion, Avery was convinced, the state's economic independence was assured because "everything sought elsewhere can be obtained in the comprehensive limits of Georgia."[30]

A prerequisite for economic independence was, of course, the introduction of manufacturing, and one New South promoter, J. Withers Clay, editor of the Huntsville *Democrat*, noted in April 1869, "Nearly everywhere in the South we observe a disposition manifested to engage in manufactures. We seldom pick up an exchange without seeing some new enterprise of this sort suggested or in progress."[31] Equally eager for manufacturing was the Montgomery *Advertiser*. "Let Us Have Cotton Factories," Robert Tyler wrote in October 1869, coining a slogan similar to the Charleston *News and Courier*'s later and often repeated injunctions to "Bring New England down South" and "Bring the Mills to the Cotton." It was actually quite simple, Tyler believed, because a "good factory" cost only $200,000, and so "what is to prevent the planters of each county in this State from having a factory at their county seat, or some other eligible point?"[32] Furthermore, as the *Advertiser* pointed out, the means for financing these mills had become available as a result of emancipation since "the money formerly invested in negroes and lands will now go towards building up extensive cotton and other manufactories all over this favored section."[33]

In the late 1860s, there erupted an unprecedented outpouring of propositions and exhortations, almost amounting to a public campaign, to rouse southerners into diverting their energies away from politics and towards the creation of a prosperous New South. Furthermore, there was an urgency in the appeal, not simply because the section had already delayed too long in diversifying its economy, but because the Republicans were just embarking on a program of internal improvements aimed at dramatically expanding the South's railroad system. Democratic-Conservatives could not remain indifferent to this development; they had to shape and influence it, since they would be vitally affected by it. So railroads quickly became the focus of the New South campaign and the tangible form it assumed. Indeed, between 1868 and 1870, a mania of railroad promotion swept the entire section. "The changed order of affairs, since the late war, makes railroads a necessity in the South," the *Advertiser* concluded. In response to these altered circumstances, every hamlet and town began to contemplate visions of greatness in the coming of the iron horse or disaster if it did not.[34] Consequently, "Every State or District line has its thousands of claquers, lobbyists, and idol-worshippers," the same paper observed, "and there is scarcely a County where a number of good citizens have not resolved themselves into a Railroad corporation and are bent on building a Railroad from some point or other to their Court House, within twelve months or two years at farthest."[35] The frenzy swept through the southern legislative assemblies too. In Georgia, it had gone so far by the summer of 1870 that a black Republican, Edwin Belcher, introduced a sarcastic motion proposing that, since the legislature was so fanatical about railroad building and since there was "no more territory for the construction of railroads," it should be resolved that "we ask the United States government for permission to construct railroads in Alaska, and that we be allowed to extend State aid to the same."[36]

Excessive and incautious though the schemes of publicly assisted railroad promotion often turned out to be, the Republican party was by no means exclusively responsible. Democratic-Conservatives were thoroughly implicated. Later, they would criticize the policy for its extravagance, its corruption, and its haste, and they would make their opponents' railroad program the touchstone of their condemnation of Republican rule. But, at the time, a sizable portion of the party and its representatives in the state legislatures were actively supporting Republican measures of state aid. Perceiving this, Republican newspapers often rejoiced that, as the Atlanta *New Era* observed in 1870, "Such is the disposition to ignore politics in business that Republicans and Democrats now unite upon a common platform in advocacy of new railroad enterprises, and this is the case not only in Georgia, but throughout the South and the entire Union."[37] Although it was clear that the Democratic-Conservatives were not as uninvolved as they often claimed, their participation was nonetheless far from unequivocal. The party's approach to the issue was circumspect and somewhat devious. It never endorsed the state-aid program in a campaign platform nor were the party's legislative representatives given instructions to vote in favor of aid measures. In fact, the matter was never made a party issue at all, either in favor or against. Instead, legislators and party spokesmen acted on their own initiative.

There were basically four explanations for this caution and indirection on the major question facing southern legislators from 1868 until the early 1870s. The first was that there were many Democratic-Conservatives who were ideologically opposed to the use of state credit or public aid of any kind in the promotion of internal improvements. In addition, some opposed particular policies and grants if they thought them too expensive. Also thwarting a united front on the railroad question were the diverse and often antagonistic interests representing rival railroads or competing communities that vied for access to state aid. Finally, of course, Democratic-Conservatives were aware that supporting Republican measures did not hasten the party's downfall but merely contributed to its viability. This was especially true of the railroad program because its success was regarded as a major ingredient of the Republican party's effort to acquire respectability and elicit gratitude.[38] As the Republican Vicksburg *Times* once put it, "Railroad building is strictly a matter of business, affecting the interests of all alike, and here at least is one common ground upon which all can meet and be friends. If we attempt to make a political question of it, we shall very likely spoil everything."[39] On the other hand, while wanting to frustrate the *Times*'s aspirations, influential Democratic-Conservatives as well as many of their constituents were eager to have railroads developed and wanted very much to take advantage of the Republican initiative. Thus, the party's attitude was ambivalent and beset by cross-pressures.

A possible exit from the dilemma was provided by the fortuitous circumstance that the Republicans were in a substantial majority in the southern legislatures and thus always able to outvote their opponents. Consequently, as Morgan Hamilton pointed out, the Democratic-Conservatives "know they will not be held responsible for any of the schemes of plunder or the extravagance of the government."⁴⁰ This enabled them to obtain railroads without voting for them, leaving their stance ambiguous and unresolved. This posture also placed the party in a strong political position, should the state aid program begin to encounter serious difficulties or incur criticism and unpopularity. Having no substantial past record of support, they could then denounce the program with impunity. The position of the Democratic-Conservatives on state aid was also obscured by their casting votes that concealed their real intentions. Thomas P. Conner, a Mississippi legislator, complained that his Democratic-Conservative colleagues had voted against the omnibus railroad bill in June 1870 only because it had included a public accommodations section of which they disapproved. Otherwise, Conner revealed, "There would have been practically no opposition to the bill."⁴¹ Confirmation of this remark was offered by the Jackson *Weekly Pilot* when it observed: "The Democrats are we believe, as much identified with it in proportion to their number, as the Republicans."⁴² With the Democratic-Conservative party's support for railroads disguised and obfuscated by its voting record, the program of state aid to railroads was to remain thoroughly identified with the Republicans. They initiated it, legislatures that they dominated enacted it, and administrations that they controlled implemented it.

This was very misleading because Democratic-Conservative support was considerable. Indeed, the foundation of postwar state aid had been laid by the state legislatures that had sat during 1866 and 1867, before the southern Republican party had even been created. In fact, it could be argued that this introduction of state aid in the immediate postwar years was simply a continuation of the railroad policies that had been pursued by most southern governments in the 1850s but had then been interrupted by the war.⁴³ With the return of peace, they, in effect, picked up where they had left off. Accordingly, state-aid bills were introduced in most states. For instance, the Arkansas legislature did so in 1866. So intent were the legislators on its passage that they passed it over the veto of Governor Isaac Murphy who had warned, in vain, that the state's credit was too vulnerable to bear the additional burden of financing railroads. The law provided for the granting of aid in the form of state bonds at the rate of $10,000 for every mile of road already built, and this was accompanied by a five-year tax exemption for new roads.[44] As final proof that the inauguration of a state railroad program was not the concern of Republicans alone, the leading Democratic-Conservative paper, the *Arkansas Gazette*, served notice on the Republicans as they entered office in 1868, saying, "Our great and overwhelming present need, upon which all other interests depend, is a wise and beneficent system of internal improvement. The people demand that our railroad interests shall be trifled with no longer."[45] Alabama's law of 1867 bestowed aid a little more generously, at $12,000 per mile after the first twenty. Even though the Republicans later increased the rate yet further to $16,000, the scheme "was inaugurated," as Levi Lawler—who was one of the commissioners appointed in 1875 to investigate the state debt— conceded, "by a legislature composed of white men, and before the Radicals in this State, as a party, had any existence."[46]

North Carolina's legislature of 1866-1867 renewed the state's two-thirds responsibility for building the Western Division of the North Carolina Railroad and aided a couple of other roads. In addition, the Democratic-Conservative minority in the 1868 constitutional convention voted heavily for three measures of railroad aid. Even though the party's delegation was split on two others, Charles Price, the historian of the state's railroad policies during Reconstruction, concluded that there was "almost no political partisanship" in the convention on railroad votes.[47] In Georgia, the state's prewar commitment to the development of the Western and Atlantic Railroad, which was actually owned by the state, was confirmed in 1866 with the appropriation of funds to repair the line. But for the veto of Governor Charles Jenkins, a number of measures granting aid to specific railroads would have been enacted by the 1866 legislature. As it was, only the Macon and Brunswick was benefited.[48] Finally, the Texas constitutional convention of 1866 provided for state aid by guaranteeing a company's bonds up to the amount of $15,000 per mile.[49] Thus, the pattern of support was clear and incontrovertible. Indeed, it had been initiated throughout the region in the year or so before the Republicans came to power and, as such, laid the groundwork for the expansion that followed.

It might have been expected that Democratic-Conservative support for public aid to railroads would have been least in evidence in North Carolina, because the Republicans were embarking upon an extensive program of state aid that could be enacted without requiring Democratic-Conservative approval, and also, by 1870, the party had exploited the deficiencies and excesses of the program so effectively that the Republicans were ousted from control of the legislature that year. Nevertheless, Democratic-Conservative complicity and support were pervasive. In June 1870, the *North Carolina Standard* looked back over the legislative sessions of 1868 and 1869 and noted that one out of every three Democratic-Conservatives had supported the appropriations for which they were currently assailing the Republicans. At the same time, there was a bloc of Republicans, about a third, who voted against the railroad proposals, leading the *Standard* to conclude that the legislature's actions possessed "little of a party nature, internal improvement measures and cognate matters having engrossed nearly all the time."[50] Consequently, when the Democratic-Conservative party reversed itself entirely in late 1869 and, "acting according to a preconcerted plan" and with "perfect" organization, attacked the Republican record on state aid, the *Standard* exposed its contradictory and hypocritical course.[51] Under the leadership of "Argo & Co. who were committed . . . on internal improvements," the Democratic-Conservatives had made such a record that, so the *Standard* claimed, "when they charge the Republican party with extravagance, they but hold up the mirror to their own faces."[52]

Although only a third of the Democratic-Conservatives voted for railroad measures, it would be misleading to conclude, as Allen Trelease has done, that this tally was evidence that the parties assumed quite distinctive attitudes regarding state aid to railroads.[53] Until the excesses of state aid offered the Democratic-Conservatives a winning issue, the policy was, in fact, nonpartisan. Indeed, the Democratic-Conservative vote might have been greater than it actually was had it not been apparent to the party's legislators at an early stage that the policy's extravagance would create a highly favorable political issue, thus encouraging them to withhold their support. Legislative support was, however, only one of the ways in which Democratic-Conservatives were involved. They were active in public railroad policy at all levels and in all manner of ways. As Charles Price has pointed out, party members who were railroad directors frequently originated state-aid bills, while others who were attorneys drafted them. In addition, seven of the eleven lines that received state aid were owned and run by Democratic-

Conservatives and the stockholders' meetings that were dominated by the party's supporters never once considered rejecting the proffered aid.[54] The extent of the party membership's involvement was perhaps best revealed by a remark of William A. Graham, its elder statesman. He complained to his son, in April 1870, of the listlessness that characterized Democratic-Conservative leadership in the state election campaign. This had occurred, he admitted, because "the bar at Raleigh [from which much of the party's executive committee was selected] has been so entangled in the legislature and railroad frauds, that they are embarrassed, and shorn of influence."[55]

The early years of Republican ascendancy had afforded the opportunity for state-assisted promotion of internal improvements that the Democratic-Conservatives' New South advocates had been denied for so long and that their legislation during the period of presidential Reconstruction had envisaged. Consequently, they had been active in every state in the promotional ventures of the time and only a discretion prompted by partisan considerations had constrained them. More often than not, however, their support for aid to internal improvements was considerable. The former Republican governor of Louisiana, Henry C. Warmoth, described the norm when he once pointed out how involved Democratic-Conservatives had been in his state. "An almost unanimous vote of the legislature," he recalled, had approved the North Carolina and Texas Railroad bonds, while the state's other major railroad project, the building of a connection with Texas by means of the New Orleans, Mobile, and Texas line, was favored by "everybody."[56] Consequently, the dramatic shift in Democratic-Conservative tactics from passive acquiescence in the granting of state aid to a forceful attack on the policy's outcome was not a welcome switch as far as the New South group was concerned. It meant that their moment of triumph and opportunity had been distressingly brief. After receiving only a spasmodic trial, the active involvement of the public sector in fostering and shaping economic development through the provision of state aid was to be discontinued.[57]

The collapse, after 1873, of the Republicans' experiment in state aid for internal improvements had repercussions within the ranks of the opposing party. Not only had the hopes and the reputations of those Democratic-Conservatives who had supported the policies been undermined, but a reaction had been set off against governmental activism in general. As a result, forces within the Democratic-Conservative party were propelled forward which demanded the repudiation of those very debts that had been incurred by the state to benefit railroads. Gradually, this attack broadened to include demands for both repeal of the statutory right to provide state aid as well as for the reduction of the costs and scope of government. As the decade progressed, this emerging current of opposition would gather force and velocity, until it reached a culmination just when the New Departure disintegrated and the party began to search for an alternative electoral strategy. In view of this, an examination of the outcome of these developments is more appropriate at a later point in this study. In the meantime, it is necessary to consider the opposition to the party's overall political strategy that was emerging at an earlier stage between 1869 and 1873 while the New Departure and the convergent economic policies accompanying it were in operation.

The alternative approach was based upon a conviction that the New Departure was undermining the party's essential nature and operating contrary to its best interests. These critics believed, furthermore, that, as an electoral strategy, the New Departure was a delusion and quite incapable of guaranteeing electoral success. In other words, the party leadership's assumption that the "competitive" mode was likely to be the most rewarding and viable course to pursue was challenged frontally. In its place, the dissenters proposed that an "expressive" approach to party function and goals be adopted instead.

Since these dissenters stood in opposition to a change in policy and preferred instead that the party remain true to itself and resist new and previously untried ways, it is not inappropriate to describe this group as the Bourbons. Indeed, such a label was also reasonably accurate because that was how they were described at the time, though with different connotations, by both themselves and their critics. Within each southern state, a significant element inside the Democratic-Conservative party existed which could be regarded as Bourbon. In Georgia, the opponents of the New Departure were concentrated in the Seventh Congressional District where the Augusta *Constitutionalist* was their major newspaper and Alexander Stephens, Robert Toombs, Dudley M. DuBose, and Herschel Johnson were the leading figures. The Mobile *Register*, edited by

John Forsyth, was the main opponent of the New Departure in Alabama, and Robert McKee and his Selma *Times and Argus* agitated unceasingly for the party to return to its pure Democratic principles. Opposition in Texas to the collaborationist proclivities of the majority of Democratic-Conservatives was waged by the Austin *State Gazette* and that wing of the party calling itself the John Ireland Democracy. Meanwhile, Democratic-Conservatives in Mississippi who opposed the fusion strategies of the controlling "Jackson clique" looked to George W. Harper's *Hinds County Gazette*, William H. McCardle's Vicksburg *Democrat*, and J. Z. Landrum's Columbus *Index*, among many, for inspiration and encouragement. The Bourbon critique of party policy articulated the restlessness and the uneasiness evident throughout the South over the party's decision to embark on the New Departure. Although unable to get control of the party at the state level except in Alabama in 1872, the Bourbons nevertheless maintained a running barrage of criticism against the party's leaders, reminding them that there was nothing inevitable about the direction in which they were steering the party or about its guarantee of success.

The Bourbons' attack on the New Departure strategy consisted essentially of three indictments. The first and most serious criticism was that the New Departure would not produce the electoral gains it had promised. Thus, the premise upon which its adoption had been urged was false. This was because, so the Bourbons argued, blacks would not respond to the appeals of the Democratic-Conservatives and vote in large numbers for them. The writer of an 1870 broadside criticizing the party leadership in South Carolina explained that there was absolutely no reason for blacks to shift their partisan allegiance because the Democratic-Conservatives were able to offer them nothing they had not already obtained from the Republicans. The appeal to blacks was bound to fail because it ran counter to the flow of political power; therefore, "Can we, knowing his nature, expect to tempt him, by such promises in the future, from the party already in power, to the party who asks his assistance to regain it?"[58] John Forsyth of the Mobile *Register* concurred. Blacks could not be won over by appeals and conciliation; that approach was bound to be pointless. "It is *power* that attaches them to Radicalism; once break that spell and show that it has been transferred to the Democratic-Conservative white party, and you have done what was needful to detach them from your enemies, for *power* is something they understand—something they were brought up to regard."[59] By appealing for black votes, Democratic-Conservatives were operating from a position of weakness and Forsyth considered it to be a posture as degrading as it was ineffective. The remedy was to stop squandering the party's strength and instead to arouse its own supporters and rally them in a show of electoral force against the black Republicans. Only after being confronted by "the power of independent white influence" would blacks begin to desert their current allies. The New Departure was therefore based upon a grievous political error; the electoral sequence it proposed had to be reversed. "The road to redemption is under the white banner," Forsyth announced; black votes would never save the party.[60]

In many parts of the South, if not most, black voters were just not numerous enough to warrant the adoption throughout the region of a policy that counted upon them for success. A number of states had majorities that were white, and in others there were political subunits at the county and local levels whose composition was overwhelmingly white. To insist on the New Departure approach as a norm was therefore inappropriate and impracticable. Accordingly, in Alabama in 1870, John Forsyth met with twenty or so newspaper editors who were from white sections of the state, and they agreed to ignore the party's state-wide policy during the current gubernatorial campaign. The result, so Forsyth claimed, was that Mobile County was won for the Democratic-Conservatives, as was the entire state because of the additional white votes the dissenting strategy had generated.[61] Although Forsyth may have exaggerated his claims, there was still no doubt that an appeal for black support offered only minimal electoral advantages. But most Bourbons were prepared to go even farther in their denunciation of the New Departure. Alabama's Democratic governor during the 1850s, John A. Winston, was one of them. He was convinced that, though "the negroes may make promises of cooperation with us . . . they will never perform them"; the reason for this was that "the natural affinities of race create an identity of sympathies and interest." "Local advantages might result from a mongrel ticket" in some areas, but ultimately, Winston asserted, Democratic-Conservatives had to recognize the enduring division between the races. To refuse to do so was to ignore the underlying realities of southern politics which no mere political maneuver, such as the New Departure, could modify or obliterate. The assertion of the party's strength required "an open out-and-out White Man's Ticket," for "the gray-eyed, straight-haired men of destiny must govern the earth among civilized nations," and "any entanglement with the negro must but result in embarrassing us."[62] White supremacy was not merely an asset the party was foolish to squander, it was a reality most unwise to overlook.

Governor Winston's ruthless and unashamed depiction of the sinister forces percolating irresistibly through southern political life suggested that there was an additional disadvantage in the New Departure which went beyond its inability to expand the party's support. By espousing its priorities and assumptions, the Democratic-Conservatives were not merely seeking a benefit that was unattainable but were actually inflicting harm on their party. The rush to accept the Reconstruction amendments, declare them "dead issues," and then compete with the Republicans for control of the political center encouraged party members to disregard the principles that had brought the Democratic-Conservatives into existence as the opposition party. Not surprisingly, loss of confidence and a feeling of demoralization were the inevitable result. As ever, John Forsyth expressed most clearly the problem that the New Departure presented to the party when he wrote that, in the struggle to regain power, "our Southern stake is so enormous that it begets timidity. We walk fearfully, as if treading on eggs; and long suffering and adversity have taught us to be distrustful of the very principles in which alone we can find our political redemption and salvation." Under the New Departure, the survival of the party and its ability to obtain power depended upon opportunism and the seizure of immediate advantage. What was overlooked in this approach was the realization that "great parties are founded on great ideas, and are not to be patched together with the putty of expediency." Principles were not therefore liabilities, nor were they luxuries to be discarded when the pressures on the party were intense. Rather, a time of difficulty was the very moment when principle had to be asserted most strongly in order to keep the party together and restore the confidence of its constituents. "Principles rally a party," Forsyth claimed. By enthusing and stimulating the voters, the party could obtain the victory that expediency and opportunism were incapable of providing.[63]

The Bourbons complained that the Democratic-Conservatives were squandering their ideological strength by functioning as a pale reflection of Republicanism. Instead, the party should recognize that it was the heir to the antebellum Democratic party with which the Bourbons themselves had overwhelmingly been identified. As old-line Democrats, they argued that the Democratic party had, after all, had a long existence and its persistence was attributable to the importance voters had attached to the values it espoused. It "was based on deep substrata of ideas and principles dear to the great masses of the American people"; by abandoning these enduring beliefs the party in the South was risking political suicide.[64] The principles that Bourbons like John Forsyth considered the essence of the Democracy were local self-government or home rule as it was often called; decentralization of power within the federal system; noninterference by government in matters of individual behavior and belief; and laissez-faire in the relations among economic interests as well as nations, that is, free trade. By contrast, the values and ideology of the Republicans were regarded as homogenizing and centralizing in thrust, aimed at curbing and restraining local and individual autonomy.[65] Yielding the ground to which the Democrats had prior claim rather than employing it as the foundation for the revival of the party was foolish. Indeed, if the party could harness these values and claim exclusive guardianship over them, the prospect was not remote or unrealistic that the Democratic-Conservative party could capture the support beyond its existing constituency which it coveted so eagerly.

For many Bourbons, the most important of the Democratic doctrines, and the most relevant one in the situation they faced during Reconstruction, was opposition to the centralization of power. This was what Alexander Stephens had in mind when he commented, "The country must be redeemed, if ever it is redeemed, by the old line Democratic Jefferson ideas & principles." Stephens explained what these ideas were when he urged his friend, Herschel V. Johnson, to become the party's gubernatorial nominee in 1870. For Johnson had been Stephen Douglas's running mate in 1860 and was therefore "the surviving standard bearer of the great National Democratic Party at its last great conflict with Centralism."[66]

Phrased more specifically and more positively, resistance to central-ism involved the restoration of "the states in their rights of absolute equality and the constitution in its original purity and power," as John Forsyth once stated it.[67]

This was a cardinal Democratic doctrine, but it became in-creasingly difficult to give it practical application and make it the centerpiece of the Bourbon creed. Initially it had derived specificity and focus from the party's disposition to oppose the Reconstruction amendments. But as the New Departure began to dominate Demo-cratic thinking, at the national level as well as in the South, and as the presidential candidacy of Horace Greeley seemed likely to con-firm the party's acceptance of the amendments, opposition to cen-tralism became less and less viable as a significant issue between the parties. Indeed, Dudley M. DuBose, the Georgia congressman who was a friend of Stephens and a relative of Toombs, complained in 1871 that there was only minimal interest among fellow Demo-crats in asserting this principle. When he voted against a resolution calling for a committee to investigate the Ku Klux outrages in the South on the grounds that Congress had no "right to appoint a committee to investigate acts done in any state in the Union that has all the machinery of a state government in full operation," he was distressed to discover "very few democrats" voting with him.[68]

In the early 1870s, a more effective context for the advocacy of a distinctive position based on traditional Democratic principles was the arena of state politics. Resistance to the encroachment of federal power was not in any way renounced by this preference—it was still an article of faith—but it was to be set aside temporarily. In-stead, the general principle it embodied, opposition to the consoli-dation of power, was focussed on the state level, where the scope of government had increased significantly under the Republicans. The public sector had assumed responsibilities for social welfare through the funding of asylums, penitentiaries, and hospitals; for public education by means of government provision for the building and administration of a system of schools; and for economic devel-opment, as a result of its promotion of railroads and other internal improvements. A principled opposition to these costly and dan-gerous innovations was likely to resonate well with voters whose ire had been provoked by the increased taxation, the public indebted-ness, and the corruption that had accompanied them. Consequently, a frontal assault on the growth of state government, particularly its costly economic activities, began to be mounted by the Bourbons. Its ingredients and spirit were perhaps best exemplified by John W. A. Sanford's remarks when complimenting an acquaintance in Opelika, Alabama, who had just commenced publishing a newspaper that was obviously Bourbon in sentiment. "I infer from the prospectus that you will advocate the principles of the party as you did years ago," he wrote: "that you are opposed to 'departures,' new or old, from the ancient creed: and that the fraudulent issue of bonds: the illegal payment of interest upon them: the combination of monopolists of every description for the purpose of public plunder will receive your unqualified condemnation." After adding that "the Federal government has usurped such powers that even men who are opposed to the usurpation see nothing nearer than Washington," he concluded with a paean to the politics of principle: "There are many better things than mere success. Truth, honor, manhood, devotion to principle all are infinitely preferable to success destitute of those qualities."[69]

In this letter, Sanford also made mention of the third component of the critique the Bourbons leveled at the politics of the New Departure. He referred during it to "servile men," men "utterly unfit for high office, and who prize success beyond reason."[70] The implicit suggestion was that the party's decision to compete with the Republicans on their own terms and to abandon principle for expediency and short-term advantage had pushed to the fore politicians with qualities appropriate to the circumstances. In a word, the New Departure had legitimized opportunism. Once principle was abandoned, observed Henderson M. Somerville, a future Alabama Supreme Court justice, it was "followed by the disgusting tergiversations of party leaders, and the Judas-like betrayals of party spoilsmen."[71] "Trimmers," "policy men," "time-servers" were consequently at a premium as the party tried desperately to get its nominess elected by appealing to Republican voters and by downplaying its distinctive Democratic identity.

The demoralization into which the New Departure policy had plunged the party was never more apparent to Bourbons than in Georgia. In February 1870, James Randall, editor of the Augusta *Constitutionalist*, told Alexander Stephens he was disgusted with the party. Its current deliberations over which of the Republican choices for the two contested U.S. Senate seats the party should back revealed its bankruptcy. "We ought to triumph on principle or not at all," he avowed. "I think the time is not distant when the true Democracy should have a Convention of their own, lay down square principles, make square contests and drum the traitors and time-servers out of camp. There has been too much trickery of late."[72] Later, in July, Randall reported that he, like Stephens, feared that "the democracy [was] sold out," a remark that seemed to be confirmed by Richard H. Clark's assessment that "The radicals are compact & about 33⅓ pr. ct. of our own members [of the legislature] are [Governor] Bullock's bought & paid for subservient tools. Our News papers are in the same condition."[73] It was this state of affairs that had earlier prompted Alexander Stephens's attempt to place Herschel Johnson at the head of the party and take it out of the hands of trimmers with little stature such "as [E. G.] Cabaniss, or [Thomas] Hardeman, [?] Ridley or A. W. Ridding," who dominated its councils.[74]

Besides increasing the influence of trimmers who dampened the party's ideological intensity, the New Departure also weakened it organizationally. In its attempt to encourage Republicans to cross over and vote for the Democratic-Conservatives, the New Departure strategy necessitated a loosening of party lines and a depreciation of the importance of party regularity. As a result, the discipline of the organization had been considerably impaired. On the one hand, men whose hold on the party's supporters or whose service in its ranks was limited were frequently nominated for office. On the other, those who failed to obtain a Democratic-Conservative nomination could easily bolt and run as independents. Lacking the ability to censure and prevent it, Democratic-Conservatives discovered that independency was, to their dismay, a constant occurrence, threatening both to weaken the party internally as well as to deprive it of the electoral majority it sought so desperately. Independency was particularly rife because the party was out of power and did not possess sufficient offices to satisfy the innumerable aspirants. "This tarantula of desire for office," as one party leader in Georgia described it, was therefore easy to explain, but the remedy he recommended for the resulting independency—treating "independent candidates as enemies to the party . . . to be whipped out by party disapproval"—was less easy to impose because the party's inability to censure and discipline its membership had made the bolt possible in the first place.[75]

The reliance of the Democratic-Conservatives on attracting support from Republicans not only undermined party discipline but this impotence, in turn, made the party susceptible to influence by its opponents. One of the most dramatic examples of this was presented by the balloting for U.S. senator in North Carolina during the winter of 1872-73. In that contest, the selection of Augustus S. Merrimon over Zebulon B. Vance was secured by the votes of Republican legislators. Whether or not Merrimon had obtained this support through a deal, as was charged, did not really matter, for the unpalatable fact was that Republicans had chosen a Democratic senator. The lesson to be learned from this episode, which opponents of the New Departure continually pointed out, was that, without organizational discipline, the party's autonomy was in jeopardy. This dependence and lack of mastery was most evident, however, in the fusion tactic that, much to the Bourbons' distress, was so often a component of the New Departure. Fusion, in fact, epitomized the fallacy and danger of the New Departure. By supporting Republican candidates, even though they were dissidents in opposition to the regular nominees, the Democratic-Conservatives were losing far more than could ever be offset by the few votes they might gain. For fusion prevented the party from establishing its own organization and conducting its own autonomous and self-interested campaign. Because of this, it perpetuated the party's organizational disarray and its ideological confusion. John Sanford noted how devastating even the talk of fusion was. He commented, with sarcasm, "Already a newspaper of some influence writes 'We Democrats and Conservative Republicans'! How long before we shall have the 'Democratic and Conservative Republican Party'?"[76]

Demoralization and a loss of confidence in the Democratic-Conservative organization were inevitable if the party tangled with fusion. This was also Alexander Stephens's confirmed opinion. He welcomed "all cooperation with us with joy" but the idea of "a *fusion* of the Democracy with the Conservatives so-called" he "utterly opposed" since it entailed "the abandoning of the true principles & name of the party."[77] Despite their vehemence, these objections did not actually confront the *raison d'être* of the New Departure strategy which was that winning the election was the primary consideration and fusion would help attain it. The ultimate rebuttal, however, was quite simple and John Winston provided it when he declared that, "Were we to be able to carry every Southern State on a mongrel ticket, we would be only a tender to the Radical party, and ready to do their bidding."[78] Even though it might achieve victory, fusion consigned the Democratic-Conservatives to a position of subordination and dependence. Therefore, fusion, and the New Departure that gave birth to it, were delusions.

The shortcomings of the New Departure as well as its likely ineffectiveness were pointed out continually during the years when it was party policy. All the same, it had a potency that its critics were unable to destroy. Consequently, the Bourbons remained a minority, advocating an alternative but invariably yielding to the dominant impulses and elements in the party. Indeed, by the 1872 election, only a handful of Bourbons would leave the party rather than support Greeley. For the most part, they consisted of the Georgia group led by Alexander Stephens and a bloc of Virginia irreconcilables, among whom were former Governor Henry Wise and John S. Mosby who actually voted for Grant. Elsewhere, they either took no part or simply concurred. There was, however, one major exception to this pattern and that was in Alabama where, because of Governor Lindsay's inept course towards the Alabama and Chattanooga Railroad, the New Departure and state-aid wing of the party was discredited. As a result, the Bourbons succeeded in controlling the state convention and its slate of nominees. Yet this soon proved to be an aberration, for the state ticket headed by Thomas H. Herndon went down to a resounding defeat. Meanwhile, Greeley carried Alabama.

A year or so later, however, when the assumptions of the New Departure had proven to be inapplicable, the Bourbon antidote of an "expressive" policy based on partisan exclusiveness would possess cogency and appeal. Furthermore, despite the risks it entailed, which had earlier seemed too great to overcome, the Bourbon approach now enabled Democratic-Conservative strategy to acknowledge those deeper realities of southern politics which the New Departure had hoped to counteract. The evident failure of this attempt to reshape the party and the political system was supplemented by the collapse of the parallel effort to encourage economic development and diversification through governmental intervention. Thus, the public sector experimentation of the late 1860s and early 1870s, which had had both political and economic dimensions, was in disarray. Naturally, therefore, as the Democratic-Conservatives abandoned their short-lived and somewhat ambivalent attempt to rearrange the political and economic policies of both their party and their region, the Bourbons and their views began to assume increasing importance.

4. The Whigs: Fulcrum of Faction and Party

It is a favorite theory with some that a successful republican party can be organized in the south by uniting the old line whigs with colored voters. No proposition could be more chimerical.
—Charleston *Republican*, 30 November 1875

The Reconstruction episode brought to the surface all the undercurrents and residual forces of southern political life, but none was stranger or more anomalous than the resurgence of the former Whigs and the endless speculation that ensued about what political course they would follow. Their salience, almost twenty years after the party itself ceased to function in the South, was not, however, an indication of the timelessness of Whig policies or of the historical necessity of the Whig party. Rather, it revealed how fluid southern politics was during Reconstruction and the extent to which politicians, as a response to that uncertainty, sought stability in familiar, and often outmoded, notions. Thus, the political persistence of Whiggery was important, both in itself as a feature of Reconstruction politics and also as an indication of what that same politics was like.

In 1870 a statewide gathering of former Whigs was summoned to meet in Canton, Mississippi. When he heard about it, the editor of the Jackson *Pilot* was both amused and incredulous. "Just think," he expostulated, "a meeting of Whigs, eighteen years after the party was defeated, dead and buried."[1] Nevertheless, although the party was as dead as the Age of Jackson that had spawned it, most of the men who had been its members were still alive. What was more, these former Whigs had, for the most part, never really given up their partisan identity. They had neither been absorbed into the rival Democratic party nor had they reorganized and re-named themselves as an alternative party of opposition to the Demo-crats. Instead, during the 1850s some had flirted with the nativist parties, while later, during the secession crisis, many of them had tried to revive the Whigs by organizing the Constitutional Union party. Although evidently acting as a force of opposition ever since their own party disbanded in 1852, former Whigs had functioned as a political grouping without ever tying themselves permanently to an established party. Consequently, their possible party affiliation was a matter of conjecture. In the years after 1868, when the Republicans were in process of formation and the Democratic-Conservatives were struggling to regroup, the former Whigs were an unpredictable element in a volatile political situation. As such, they became the fulcrum on which a party realignment or a major shift in party composition might occur. Consequently, they were viewed with anxiety and interest—virtually a third force hovering between the two parties in the emergent Reconstruction political system.

Besides their strategic importance as the swing vote between the two parties, the former Whigs possessed attributes that were highly prized and much sought after in the political atmosphere of the late 1860s and early 1870s. The Whigs were thought to be a force for moderation and harmony in a region whose politics in the previous decade or so had been frenetic and disruptive. While they had been loyal to the South and the Confederacy before and during the war, the Whigs were thought to have acted as a conservative restraining influence on the section during its great crisis. They had warned of the turmoil and destruction that would ensue and they had urged that the South instead be more national in its outlook and actions. Upon reflection, contemporaries concluded that the conservatism and nationalism with which the Whigs were identified was what the South might have benefited from earlier, and it was certainly what many believed the region needed now in the throes of Reconstruction.

Since the former Whigs were regarded as an unattached political group embodying attributes that were politically valuable, they acquired immense significance and leverage in southern politics during Reconstruction. Indeed, they became so crucial that historians of the period have often lavished a lot of attention on them, even going so far as to attribute to the phenomenon of a resurgent Whiggery a pivotal role in the political history of the era. Two historians in particular have formulated interpretations of southern politics during the Civil War and Reconstruction decades which revolve around the former Whigs. The first to propose the idea of a residual and enduring Whiggery was C. Vann Woodward in 1951. He argued that, after being submerged and rejected from the 1850s on, the Whigs reasserted themselves as Reconstruction came to an end in the mid-1870s. The result of that resurgence was that they became the dominant influence in the ruling Democratic party as well as a major force in the redirection of the economic life of the region, which became known as the "New South." The return of the Whigs and their final vindication Woodward described as "the Rejuvenation of Whiggery." A decade later, Thomas B. Alexander found that the former Whigs were extremely influential throughout the 1860s and 1870s and not just in the closing stages and the aftermath of Reconstruction. Their role, he argued, was significant at all times, as they rose to power during the years of presidential Reconstruction from 1865 to 1867 and thereafter were influential as well as numerous within the Democratic-Conservative party. But their presence was not confined to one party alone, for they were also to be found wielding power in the Republican party. In fact, so ubiquitous were the former Whigs that Alexander concluded that Whiggery was "persistent" throughout Reconstruction and played a formative role in postwar southern politics.[2]

Although both historians had unearthed an enduring Whig element in the postbellum South and had attached great significance to their discovery, that was the extent of their agreement. Their evaluation and definition of resurgent Whiggery were, in three respects, quite distinctive. In the first place, the content of the Whiggery they were both describing differed markedly. In Woodward's analysis, it was primarily economic in thrust and was understood as an approach to economic issues, a "New South" orientation that favored the development of railroads and manufacturing, urbanization, and political alignment with the industrial Northeast. Alexander, on the other hand, conceived of Whiggery in political terms and construed it more narrowly to refer to a particular party identification. A second point of difference was that, for Woodward, the rise of the Whigs to power in the Democratic party after 1876 represented a fundamental breach in the continuity of southern history. By contrast, in Alexander's interpretation, the persistence of Whiggery underscored the continuity of the region's history despite the cataclysm of disunion and war. Moreover, the appearance of Whigs in both parties suggested a degree of consensus in Reconstruction politics which Woodward would probably not accept. The final source of disagreement was over the timing of the Whig resurgence. Vann Woodward's Whigs achieved power only after Reconstruction, which meant that their earlier position must have been one of subordination or, at least, of only limited influence within the Democratic party. On the other hand, the Whigs to whom Thomas Alexander was referring were highly visible and influential within whichever of the two parties was in power after the war, whether it was the opponents of Reconstruction from 1865 to 1868, the Republicans between 1868 and 1876, or the Democrats thereafter.

Clearly, the thesis of an enduring Whiggery presents problems. The existence of the phenomenon and its significance is admitted, but its meaning and content are disputed. To unravel this problem, two facets of it which both authors overlooked need to be investigated. The first is the importance of the former Whigs to the Democratic party during Reconstruction itself, a phase which Woodward did not examine and Alexander overlooked. The other aspect is the significance of the former Whigs as a dynamic element in the political system as a whole during Reconstruction. Because Thomas Alexander was mainly concerned with their incidence and size, that is with their quantitative aspects, he did not emphasize the volatility of Whiggery, its function in the developing political structure of Reconstruction as the decisive element determining its final shape. In a sense, the former Whigs represented the unknown in an extremely fluid and critical situation.

The political significance attributed to the former Whigs as a floating detachable bloc of voters was revealed dramatically on two occasions in particular after the war. Both occurred at the highest levels in the national government, and, symbolically, one was at the very beginning of Reconstruction, the other at its close. As they contemplated the political prospects of the defeated South in 1865, Abraham Lincoln and William H. Seward, both of whom had been Whigs before joining the Republican party, thought that the South's former Whigs would be a primary source of support around which political forces sustaining federal policies of reorganization and reconstruction could be gathered.[3] Exactly twelve years later, in the winter of 1876-77 when Reconstruction was disintegrating, another Republican president, Rutherford B. Hayes, reintroduced the prospect of the Whig element acting in concert with the president's party in an attempt to shape the course of southern politics.[4] Both efforts failed, but, coming as they did at the outset and very end of Reconstruction, they testify to the remarkable tenacity of the belief in and wish for a persistent and distinctive Whiggery.

This search for allies among southern Whigs was a constant preoccupation throughout Reconstruction and was not restricted to its beginning and end. In fact, neither of those two initiatives had much chance of success because they were either too early, before a Republican organization existed in the South, or too late, after Republicanism was all but destroyed. Far more likely to succeed than these or any other attempts to corral the former Whigs was the initiative taken after the establishment of the Republican party in 1868. At that point, and for several years thereafter, the situation was ripe for the nascent Whigs to assert themselves. For the first time in years, there existed in the South a party that represented a solid alternative to the Democrats. Moreover, if this meant that a political structure based on two parties was reemerging in the region, the Whigs might well regard this moment as an auspicious one to commit themselves firmly to the new anti-Democratic party.

Since the Republican party in most states needed to broaden its base of support among whites, there was little hesitancy in moving to pry loose uncommitted former Whigs who were associating temporarily with the Democratic-Conservatives. To an increasingly influential segment of the Republican leadership, those whom we have styled the Centrists, the former Whigs, with their qualities of conservatism and nationalism and their reputation for moderation and responsibility, were precisely the element they wanted to bring into the party. The task of obtaining the adhesion of the former Whigs was, however, to be full of difficulty and disappointment. The Democratic-Conservatives were not about to let the Whigs go. They, too, needed every bit of support they could get. Furthermore, they needed the Whigs for their attributes and reputation as much as did the Republicans. As a result, the former Whigs became a bone of contention between the parties and they assumed a decisive importance in the politics of southern Reconstruction. Not until the contest for the favors of the former Whigs was decided would the region's politics lose its evanescence and volatility.

The possibility that the Republicans could win the fight for the former Whigs appeared quite hopeful in the wake of the 1868 elections, since the Democratic-Conservatives were demoralized and in disarray after their failure to prevent the imposition of Reconstruction. At that point, so the Atlanta *Constitution* believed, "The seduction of old Whigs into the Republican ranks by flattery and the exciting of their prejudices against the Democracy" seemed to be distinctly more viable than the alternative method of achieving success, that is, "by *dividing* the Democratic party."[5] So the party pursued the former tack, knowing that in 1852 on the eve of its demise, the Whig vote had been not less than 295,500 and that the Whigs' support of the Democratic-Conservatives constituted the weakest link in the latter's armor.[6] Indeed, immediately after the 1868 elections, there was a noticeable loosening of the Whigs' ties with their current political partners. They did not necessarily join the Republicans right away, but often they did assume a stance of independence. This caused concern among many Democratic-Conservatives. The Montgomery *Advertiser*, for one, noted with alarm the evident dissatisfaction that Whigs expressed about the anti-Republican forces being organized under the aegis and name of the old Democratic party. Accordingly, the paper's editor, Robert Tyler, criticized leading Whig organs, such as the Richmond *Whig* and the Nashville *Banner*, that were encouraging this disaffection and demanded instead that former Whigs "take their chances in the general party, instead of merely appealing to old prejudices respecting defunct parties and issues." And, to help stem this discontent, Tyler then published a long list of prominent Whigs who were currently influential in the Democratic-Conservative party.[7]

Earlier in the same year and in the same state, the party had acted more concretely. To counter the "secret and most insidious appeal to the old party prejudices of the old Union men of this State" which Alexander White had launched, a meeting of Unionists whose loyalty to the Democratic-Conservatives remained unaltered was held in Montgomery on 26 January; and it was led by Whigs like B. S. Bibb, P. Tucker Sayre, Joseph Hodgson, Bolling Hall, and W. W. Screws. The purpose of the gathering was to reveal not only the limits of the response among Union Whigs to White's scheme but also the deficiency of courage and political sophistication of those who considered it seriously. The only motive for even considering it was thought to be self-interest and self-advancement. This was duly pointed out by the *Advertiser*, which accused the defectors of "all expecting the very highest places" that a "Radical party," desperate for respectability and stature, "can possibly bestow on them." To this indictment were added charges of treason to party and section. As a result the "11th-Hour Scalawag Party" in Alabama consisted of fewer adherents than at first feared. Besides White himself, there were only Sam Rice, former Provisional Governor Lewis Parsons, John A. Minnis, and several others, causing Robert Tyler to congratulate the state's Democratic-Conservative editors on having "crushed this conspiracy as soon as it developed itself."[8] In Alabama, those politicians who ignored such pressures and proceeded nonetheless to shift their allegiance were more prominent than elsewhere but, all the same, a massive flight of the state's Union Whigs had been forestalled.

Nevertheless, there was to be no relaxation in the party's campaign to dissuade former Whigs from considering affiliation with the Republicans. To this end, the Democratic-Conservatives first stressed how unattractive to Whigs such an alliance would be. Few were more convinced of this than Zeb Vance, a former Whig and wartime governor of North Carolina who was the state's leading Democratic-Conservative in the 1870s. Addressing former Whigs in Iredell County during the 1872 campaign, Vance asserted, "Some men pretend to find a great similarity between the doctrines of the old whig party and radicalism. There never was a greater

mistake. There is no whiggery in any of these violations of the constitution and outrages upon civil liberty that I have mentioned." To
further emphasize the incompatibility of Whiggery with a party
that had, in Vance's view, perverted government through its encouragement of corruption and its suspension of habeas corpus
rights in the 1870 campaign against the Klan, he suggested: "Just
imagine, if you can, Henry Clay wallowing in the same bed with
Billy Holden, the Hon. Cuffy Mayo, and Windy Billy Henderson,
and Daniel Webster stirring them with a stick." So outrageous was
the comparison of Clay and Webster with North Carolina's current
Republican leaders that Vance concluded by ridiculing the only
possible motive a Whig might have for affiliating with the party: "I
repeat, if you have any inkling [inclination?] for the flesh pots of
Egypt, say so, and be done with it."[9] The essential characteristic of
the antebellum Whig party had been its conservatism, both in policy and constitutional interpretation. By contrast, as the Jackson
Clarion once pointed out, the hallmarks of Republicanism were
radicalism and willful tampering with constitutional protection,
even to the extent of setting aside civil supremacy in favor of military rule.[10] Those constitutional guarantees that Whigs had looked
to as a protection against centralized power and the destruction of
southern rights had now been overriden by the Republicans. Their
aim, so "Old Line Whig" in the Jackson *Clarion* claimed, seemed to
be to carry this even further, and "to overthrow the government as
established, to substitute equality for liberty, and the will of the
mob for a written Constitution."[11]

"Old Line Whig's" distaste for "the mob" was evidence that
Whiggery's conservatism was social as well as political in nature.
Vance had told the Iredell Whigs, no doubt with a good deal of
acerbity, "The old Whig party was at least a decent party. The democrats in olden times used to call it *aristocratic*, and to some extent it
was," since it was composed of stereotypical gentlemen, wearing
starched collars, shined boots, and fastidious dress.[12] This facet of
Whiggery's conservatism was emphasized by the editor of the Meridian *Mercury* in Mississippi, Colonel Alexander Horn, when, in
the spring of 1870, he joined the Whig editors of the Brandon *Republican*, Natchez *Courier*, Iuka *Gazette*, and Holly Springs *Reporter* in rejecting Governor Alcorn's invitation to his fellow Whigs
to join the Republicans. The Whigs, Horn said in his reply, ap-

proved of strong government, "but it wanted a decent one. . . . Its tendency was to check and to hedge in the profane rabble, and not to turn it loose in the spirit of a wild fanatical howling of democracy, to trample intelligence and decency and honesty in public affairs out of sight—as has been done by the Radical party of this day."[13]

Whig conservatism may have been at odds with Democratic bluster and precipitancy in the secession crisis, but, in the 1870s, to disengage from the Democratic-Conservatives was regarded as an abandonment of both political principle and class loyalty. To even consider such a course of action was, it was believed, attributable only to an unyielding and impermeable hostility to association with any party that called itself Democratic. The irony of this was that, if affiliation with the Republicans were motivated by loathing for the Democratic party, Whigs who followed that path were often in for a surprise. During the 1872 election campaign, Josiah Turner, Jr., himself a former Whig who became the editor of the Raleigh *Sentinel* after the war, explained to the "old whigs" in the mountains east of the Blue Ridge who had been "voting the negro ticket because they would not be called democrats," that "If you vote for Grant you vote for an old democrat, with such signers of the ordinance of secession as Judge [Robert] Dick, Billy Smith, Billy Holden, etc. . . ." On the other hand, by voting for Greeley, former Whigs would be endorsing one of their own kind and doing so in conjunction with other ex-Whigs, among them such Democratic-Conservative luminaries as "[William A.] Graham, W. N. H. Smith, [John Motley] Morehead, [Edward] Warren, [Thomas] Sparrow," and others.[14]

That was not, however, the only irony in the situation, for the fundamental assumption in the scenario of an enduring Whiggery was that the issues that preoccupied and distinguished the antebellum parties were still vital and relevant. Yet, as Democratic-Conservatives tried to demonstrate, that was no longer true. Instead, as Ethelbert Barksdale of the Jackson *Clarion* protested, those measures "are as dead as the men who lived before the flood."[15] To suggest the contrary, thought the Atlanta *Constitution*, was "only intended to sow distrust and suspicion in the Democratic ranks." The paper concurred with the Augusta *Constitutionalist*'s view that it was the "vain device of an enemy" to claim that antebellum differences persisted, for "the issues that divided Whigs and

Democrats in the South have long passed away" and been "buried out of sight by the tremendous struggle in which the Southern people vainly fought for independence."[16]

Ironically it was a former Democrat, Joseph E. Brown who had joined the Republican party in 1868, who pointed out most graphically the anachronism of forcing the Whig-Democrat rivalry into the context of the two-party competition emerging during Reconstruction. Refuting accusations that he had betrayed his party by leaving it for the Republicans, Brown charged, in an 1868 campaign speech, that the organization he had quit was Democratic only in name. One by one, he cited the distinctive policy-positions of the antebellum Democrats—the right of secession, opposition to a high tariff, resistance to "internal improvements by the general government," and opposition to "a National Bank" as well as to the distribution of the proceeds of the public lands among the states. Probably, these were more rigid stances, in any case, than the prewar Democracy had generally adhered to, but thirty years later, they were quite outmoded and irrelevant. Consequently, Brown asserted, "the present so-called Democracy does not even profess to stand upon a single principle of the old State Rights Democracy."[17]

So both parties were competing for the Whigs, but the Democratic-Conservatives' task was quite different from that of the Republicans, and a good deal easier. They had to retain the Whig support they already possessed, whereas the Republicans had to lure it away from their opponents. Judging by the numbers of Whigs in the former party as well as their prominence, it was evident that there was really little reason to complain and even less for them to consider leaving. As a result, when the New York *Herald* suggested, during the 1872 presidential campaign, that the nomination of a leading former Whig, Horace Greeley, as their presidential candidate would lose the Democrats a lot of their support in the South, the Jackson *Clarion* retorted quickly that the *Herald* was apparently unaware that the southern Democrats were "largely composed of Old Line Whigs." A few months earlier, in March 1872, the Louisville *Courier-Journal* had dispelled similar speculation about a Whig defection with this observation: "We can not but recognize the fact that a great many of the most efficient and faithful members of the Democratic party are men who were once opposed to it."[18]

The Whig influence within the Democratic-Conservative party was built on a foundation laid immediately after the war. In the wake of defeat, the South turned to the men who had advised against secession and who, in the main, had been Whigs. As Thomas Alexander commented, it was not surprising that "the Democratic party was shattered by the debacle for which it bore chief responsibility." At the time, this had been the expectation of the Whigs themselves. One of them, Benjamin H. Hill, concluded that since "all the evils of secession which we prophesied became true, now we suppose the people will believe us, and not believe the old secession Democrats." Later he recalled, "Frankly . . . after the war ended, we, the old Whigs and the Union men expected to take control of affairs down here."[19] The upshot was that the Whigs, with a smattering of Douglas Democrats, completely dominated the constitutional conventions and the state legislatures that were elected throughout the Confederacy in 1865. In addition they obtained the lion's share of the congressional seats; nine out of ten, if Texas and South Carolina, where the Whigs had never established much of a party organization, were excluded.[20]

This early ascendancy the Whigs never relinquished. They played a leading role in southern politics during the fight against federal Reconstruction policy and then, in 1868, when the Republican party was created and the Democratic-Conservatives organized formally, the Whigs maintained their considerable influence within the reconstituted party. Indeed, its very name, Democratic-Conservative, or Democratic and Conservative, or sometimes, as in Virginia, just Conservative, was an index of how significant non-Democrats were within the party and how important it was to attract the remainder who balked at joining a simon-pure Democratic organization.

In every state, therefore, Whigs were conspicuous among the Democratic-Conservatives, invariably controlling the party's apparatus and, with only a few exceptions, monopolizing the important elective offices. By the end of 1869, the Republican *North Carolina Standard* was announcing, "The present party is *not* the Democratic party nor has it the slightest right to the name," for William A. Graham, Zeb Vance, and Thomas Ashe, all widely-respected Whig grandees, were at the helm, while Thomas Jarvis, Plato Durham, and the younger William A. Graham were the leaders of the party's delegation in the legislature. By 1871, William A. Hearne, the editor of the Charlotte *Carolinian* was threatening that "if the old Whig politicians are longer permitted to control [the party] . . . there are several thousand democrats . . . who will seek shelter, protection and justice in the republican party."[21]

Similar assertions about Whig dominance were made, and with good reason, in Alabama, Mississippi, Virginia, Arkansas, and elsewhere, for in all those states former Whigs were conspicuous and influential.[22] In another state, Georgia, Joseph E. Brown was claiming that, in addition to having abandoned the principles of the antebellum Democracy, the Democratic-Conservatives now could not even claim the allegiance of its leading members. With scorn, Brown asked rhetorically: "Except Howell Cobb, what old Democratic leader in Georgia now leads the democracy?" There was, of course, Robert Toombs who "furnishes the brains to [the party], and it follows his bidding," but he had actually been a Whig until just before secession. So Brown concluded triumphantly that its leaders were, almost without exception, Whigs, and he then proceeded with great relish to list them: "Ben Hill, John B. Gordon, David Irwin, Augustus Reese, E. G. Cabaniss [chairman of the state central committee], poor old Snead [who was secretary of the committee], Ranse Wright, Gus Wright, E. A. Nisbet, P. W. Alexander and Cincinattus Peeples. I beg your pardon. I had forgotten Warren Aiken." These were the leaders when the party emerged in 1868, yet previously they had been the Democrats' "bitterest revilers . . . its most determined political enemies."[23]

The ease with which former Whigs had been able to affiliate with the party they had opposed for so long was perhaps explained, Brown speculated, by their knowledge that "the so-called Democracy is not the true Democracy." Whatever their initial reasons, Whigs soon pervaded the party's leadership and shaped its policy. Consequently, when, in early 1872, Benjamin Hill urged his fellow Whigs to cooperate fully with the Democratic-Conservative party and to help determine is policies and principles, he was not recommending a novel course of action. His admonition to "whigize the democracy" was descriptive of what was already taking place and not a prescription for the future.[24] The Democratic-Conservatives, a new party, "organized under new conditions and upon new issues," as Hill noted, had never been antipathetic to former Whigs. In fact,

Whigs had been influential from the beginning and of immense strategic importance to the party in its formative years after 1868.

When Hill had enumerated those qualities that the Whigs could offer the Democratic-Conservatives, he had stressed their constitutional principles, for "the old theories of the democracy," with their emphasis on the primacy of the states, "will not do now." By contrast, Hill believed that the "domestic policy" usually associated with the Whigs and Henry Clay was not merely irrelevant but also quite unlikely to benefit the Democratic-Conservatives. The American system and all its specifics were indeed of little value now.[25] But there was a facet of Whig economic policy that was greatly in demand. On one occasion, Joseph E. Brown explained to Alexander Stephens what it was. "Under the old state of things, when you and I first fought on different sides in politics, the Democratic party went against internal improvements by the general government. The Whig party favored them, under proper circumstances. The result generally was, that the North got all the money while [we] accepted the honors."[26] Brown was now determined that Democratic scruples were not to interfere with southern economic growth any more. The greater sympathy of the Whigs for public promotion of economic development was generally recognized throughout the South. Moreover, it was thought to be a major factor in the prediction that former Whigs would gravitate naturally towards the Republicans since the latter were enthusiastically in favor of stimulating railroad building and other internal improvements assisted by federal and state aid. On this assumption, James Alcorn had based his appeal to the Whigs in Mississippi. He had observed that "internal improvements, by the general government, is as much as ever a subject of Democratic hostility," but the extent of that antipathy was far less than Alcorn had assumed.[27] Rather than being rebuffed, Whig support for internal improvements was acknowledged and reciprocated in the Democratic-Conservative party. So, along with their constitutional conservatism and political moderation, Whig sympathy towards internal improvements was part of the process whereby the Democracy of the Reconstruction South was "whigized."

Republican maneuvers to siphon off the Whigs were thus, for the most part, resisted. Even so, the struggle had serious ramifications for the successful Democratic-Conservatives. Although they had countered the attempt to inject old party rivalries into their internal affairs by the rejoinder that those issues were as dead as Henry Clay, the party had nevertheless been forced to recognize that their organization consisted fundamentally of two groups—former Whigs and former Democrats. The result was that, ironically, the focus of factional disputes within the party centered, to a large extent, on the distinctions between Whig and Democrat whose existence the party was otherwise vigorously denying. The reason for this seeming inconsistency was that, because Whiggery was at a premium, the Democratic-Conservatives had constantly to appease and pander to it. Accordingly, Whigs gained advantage and influence, with a resultant loss to former Democrats in the party. Seeing themselves pushed aside, the Democrats, in turn, began to search for ways of exerting greater leverage to compensate for their declining influence and exclusion.

In North Carolina, as was noted earlier, the former Democrats contemplated leaving the party during the spring of 1870 when confronted by Whig ascendancy. Their diminished influence reflected a serious imbalance in the party, for in the county conventions, so the Democrats claimed, "about eighty per cent of the chosen are old line Whigs, whereas the voting proportions to sustain these nominations are as eight Democrats to two Whigs."[28] The intensity of old partisan rivalries was unmistakable, and it was dramatized most clearly in the confrontation between William A. Graham, Jr., and David Schenck for a state Senate nomination in North Carolina in 1871. Schenck complained that Graham's friends did not scruple to "use any argument to defeat me and especially to organize a partizan Whig Ring against me; in this he most signally failed. My old Democratic friends rallied en masse for me to his utter ruin."[29] Graham's father was, for his part, equally angry at the virulence of party animosity. "I was aware of very strong political prejudices on the part of some of the population of the district, arising from a feeling I thought, of envy, but supposed it has died out in a good measure with the war." If, however, the Schenck coterie persisted in their partisanship, Graham warned that he "would have Mr. S & all like him to know, that if they expect to proscribe men this early for being Whigs, it will be some time before they are installed in power. They should know that, but for the cooperation they have had from the Whigs, they could do but little in organizing a party in 9 Counties in 10, of this State."[30]

Thus, far from being anachronistic, antebellum party identifications had become devices for organizing and differentiating the elements vying for control within the Democratic-Conservative party. Fitness and availability for a party nomination or for a post in the party apparatus were being judged on the grounds of previous party loyalty. Furthermore, factions were organizing around these party labels that in turn were then used to disqualify or exclude rival contenders.

Frequently, party identifications were broadened and the stand that a politician had taken in the secession crisis became a further means of differentiation and identification. Since antisecessionists and Unionists were invariably Whigs, the distinction did not add much to the partisan delineation. All the same, resuscitation of yet another feature of prewar southern politics confirmed still further the importance of past records and differences for current political purposes. Yet many among the Democratic-Conservatives regretted this fixation, believing it to be productive of strife within the party as well as tending to distract the party from more compelling and contemporary concerns. One of the critics was John Kirkwood, an active Democratic-Conservative in Arkansas' Third Congressional District. He complained in 1870 that, since there were currently no major differences between or within the two parties, "why, then, the necessity of inquiring whether this man was a whig or democrat, or that man a unionist or secessionist?"[31] Earlier that same year, the leading party newspaper in Alabama had endorsed an editorial from the Tuscumbia *Times* asserting, "The time has come when the question should not be asked, whether a man was in favor of or opposed to, secession."[32] Two years later, however, the party's former Democrats and former secessionists revealed that they did not share this toleration but demanded, instead, that the party's current favoritism towards Whigs and Unionists be reversed. Instead of renominating Governor Robert Lindsay who had been selected two years earlier as the standard-bearer of the ascendant Whig-Unionist wing, the rival faction lambasted his record of excessive support for Republican railroad interests and for the state's program of railroad aid, and nominated their own slate instead. The ticket was so self-consciously factional that "Henry Clay Whig" complained publicly: "At least one half of the Democratic vote of Alabama is notoriously composed of Whigs. The Democratic secession convention proscribed these men . . . this is notorious and palpable. The old Whigs will never be treated as equal by the secession Democrats, when offices are to be filled."[33] This Democratic resurgence harmed, not only its former Whig component but the party as a whole, for Thomas Herndon and the ticket he headed suffered an ignominious defeat that enabled the Republicans to return to power. After that reversal, which was unprecedented during Reconstruction, the Mobile *Register* announced angrily: "As long as the Democratic party permits itself to be divided as to the antecedents of a man in *ante bellum* days, just so long will defeat be encountered."[34]

The salience of antebellum antecedents in southern politics after 1868 was not causing difficulties for the Democratic-Conservatives alone. In fact, their problems were slight compared with those of the Republicans, who were running into numerous obstacles in their attempt to win the support of the former Whigs. In the first place, they were unable to counter Democratic-Conservative assertions that their own party was the natural heir to the conservative and respectable Whig party. Furthermore, the extremely favorable treatment that former Whigs had received at the hands of the Democratic-Conservatives made it very difficult to pry them loose.

Beset with troubles though it was, the Republican courting of former Whigs was further complicated by the lack of agreement within the party about how important Whig support should be considered and even how much emphasis was to be given to obtaining the support of whites at all. Just as the Democratic-Conservatives were split over the role in the party of the rival former Whig and former Democratic elements, those Republicans who urged the expansion of its white constituency, that is the Centrists, were arrayed against a faction, invariably federal officeholders and the black leadership, that feared an infusion of whites into the party which would threaten their own political base and influence within the organization. Fears such as these were evidently in the mind of J. Clarke Swayze, a Georgia Centrist and former editor of the Atlanta *Era*, when in 1872 he noted with alarm that a powerful opposition had arisen to "prevent the element we so much need in our party from coming in, viz: the old Whigs and Union men." He swore that, rather than "get down on our knees to these Hungry, never-satisfied carpet-baggers, who are held in their places by the Grant [admin-istration]," he "would rather fight, and if necessary carry the fight against [Grant]" in the 1872 presidential election.[35]

Despite the turmoil that the advocacy of an opening towards the former Whigs generated, thousands of them did, nevertheless, affili-ate with the Republicans during Reconstruction. They voted for the party and many held office in it. Indeed, in North Carolina where the native white element was probably more numerous, more prestigious, and more experienced than anywhere else in the South, it consisted overwhelmingly of former Whigs. One party paper, the Wilmington *Post*, went so far as to claim in 1876 that "the old whig element in the Republican party gave . . . success to that party, and but for that element now in [it], the State would be largely Democratic." As evidence, the *Post* compiled a list of seventy-two of the leading Republicans, of whom just twenty were former Democrats. Furthermore, well-known Whig counties, like Randolph, Rutherford, Wilkes, Forsythe, Montgomery, and David-son, were strongholds of Republicanism.[36] This contemporary ob-servation was remarkably insightful and accurate, for a recent study of the state's "scalawags" concluded that about three in every four native white Republicans had been Whigs.[37] The same Whig pre-dominance held true for Alabama. Of those active Republicans whose prewar affiliation could be ascertained, Whigs, at the outset, "greatly outnumbered" the others by a three-to-one margin.[38] In yet a third state, Mississippi, the native white Republicans have been identified as former Whigs and this judgment applied not simply to the activists and officials but also to the voters as well. The author of the latest study has determined that the native white's "apparent importance and prominence in areas which had been strongly Whiggish before the war and his relative weakness outside those areas indicate that the Republican party drew its southern white voters in Mississippi from the antebellum Whigs."[39]

Impressive though the evidence is that native white Republicans were overwhelmingly Whig, their Whig identity could not alone have accounted for their decision to affiliate with the new party. As we have seen, the course taken by most former Whigs would sug-gest that their Whiggery disposed them towards not joining the Republicans. Instead, they either withdrew from political activity altogether or else associated with the Democratic-Conservatives. Indeed, in the case of North Carolina it was found that three of every five identified as Whigs stayed with the Democratic-Conservatives.[40] But if their Whiggery was not decisive, then perhaps it was their opposition to secession which prompted them to switch. In both Alabama and North Carolina, support of the anti-secession candidates in 1860, Bell and Douglas, was even more striking than Whig affiliation as a "scalawag" characteristic. About 90 percent were antisecessionist in Alabama and 93 percent in North Carolina. Although undeniable as an attribute, Unionism was still not determinative because Unionists were abundant within the rival party as well.[41] In North Carolina, for example, as much as 99 percent of the Whigs in the profile developed by James Lancaster were opposed to secession and most of these stayed with the Democratic-Conservatives. Thus, it was reasonable to conclude that Unionism was not exclusively Republican.[42] In fact, the incidence of both Whiggery and Unionism was statistically high in both parties, leading to the conclusion that Whig Unionists were preponderant and of critical importance, not just in one party but in the political life of the entire region.[43]

This focus on Whigs and Unionists as the categories of white support that the party aimed to attract inevitably gave the strategy a basically conservative thrust. The Centrists who advocated this approach did so quite purposefully, since they wanted to bring into the Republican party political elements that would give it a cautious and respectable tone. Moreover, by pitching their appeal on the basis of a potential recruit's past record, that is, the position he took on an earlier issue and the identification he made with an extinct party, the Centrists were making sure that those who might come to the party with an agenda for the future would not be attracted. The influence of the Centrists over party strategy thus precluded an appeal to another source of white recruits who would be drawn to a Republican party that promised a more radical and programmatic course of action.

Rather than seek out white allies from among former Whigs and Unionists, the Republican party could have presented itself as the champion of the interests of those who saw themselves as disadvantaged and who would welcome the support and sympathy of a party that espoused egalitarian principles and was prepared to improve their condition. Since the Republican party was already on record in the South as the emancipator and spokesman of the former slaves, it would have been simply an extension of that stance to spread its concern for the welfare of one disadvantaged group to include another. After all, if, as the Charleston *Republican* once put it, "The Republican party [was] emphatically the poor man's party," then poor whites as well as poor blacks were its natural constituency.[44]

From time to time, southern Republicans did emphasize this feature of their party. In 1872, the Columbia *Daily Union* of South Carolina reminded "the poor whites of this State, the laboring classes, [that they] have no other hope for the education of their children but in the continued success of this party."[45] Two years earlier, Governor Holden's *North Carolina Standard* had appealed to "working-men" to "remember the oppressions of the past" and support the Republicans.[46] But these were usually desperate appeals made at election time and were not backed by a sustained effort to win the confidence and allegiance of the white masses through a series of measures or programs geared to their needs. In 1868 and 1869 the party had enacted legislation in most states which provided for the exemption of homestead property from seizure for debt, guaranteed the laborer's lien for wages, and, of course, democratized the political system.[47] But there was rarely much follow-up. In the same way, Georgia Republicans who had enacted relief for debtors in 1868, and thereby probably secured their margin of victory later that year, did not pursue the matter further once they were in power.[48] Even the school systems that the Republicans had introduced were unlikely to elicit an outpouring of support from the white masses because they had not been created exclusively with poorer whites in mind. If anything, they had been provided mainly for the black population. Moreover, when in the 1871 election Texas Republicans tried to make education the centerpiece of an appeal for the support of the white masses, they had undercut their pledge of commitment by urging that the schools be sustained only "at the smallest cost possible to the people."[49]

The Republicans did not therefore focus their quest for white support on the disadvantaged and the poor.[50] In essence, southern Republicanism was unwilling to depict itself as a class party. To have done so would have required the party to adopt a quite different image and posture from what the two existing blocs within the organization already wanted. The first of these was that group of politicians, the Regulars, whose influence in the party derived from the black constituency they represented. Naturally, they resisted any shift of the party's axis towards developing a rival base among the whites. The other was, of course, the Centrists who saw a different segment of white support as essential to the future success of the party and they saw themselves as a leading element in it.

The likelihood that a third competing perspective could be included in the Republicans' already divisive search for a secure electoral base was thus quite out of the question; but there was yet another obstacle to such an initiative. The strategy for eliciting support from the white population that had already been activated by the Centrists was quite different from the kind of approach an appeal to the white masses would have necessitated. The Centrists' appeal to Whigs and Unionists was aimed at individual politicians and activists, who, by their influence, could then pull in votes. An appeal on the basis of previous party affiliation or on a stand taken on the secession issue was not likely to produce a significant response from voters themselves since considerations like these were of little importance to them. To politicians, on the other hand, party ties were primary attachments and crucial to their careers, and publicly declared stands on controversial issues were the essence of the political records they strove to compile. Thus, the Centrist approach rested on the assumption that parties consisted of alliances among leaders and notables rather than of coalitions of interests within the electorate. If enough influential politicians could be attracted with office and patronage, a corresponding expansion of the Republican vote among the white population was expected to follow. This was an elitist conception of politics and its espousal meant that grass-roots electoral mobilization around issues of mass appeal was ignored. White voters would rally to the party once those who had been their recognized leaders in the past were identified as Republicans; there was no need to enlist them by direct methods.

The attempt by the Republican party to reach out and capture a segment of the white vote was the most absorbing and volatile feature of southern party politics after 1868. It was the pivot around which oscillated the contest between the parties as well as the alignment of forces within each of them. Moreover, upon the outcome of the Republicans' search for support among the whites, the course of Reconstruction largely depended. Since the direction that it took was conservative, however, it would restrain rather than foster the political changes initiated at the founding of the party during 1867-1868. Leaders and officeholders, as opposed to voters, were the target of the appeal, and the political antecedents of individuals, not current issues or the interests of groups in the electorate, were its focus. In effect, it amounted to little more than "trading with disaffected Democrats," which was the way one Texas politician described the process.[51] Not only was this kind of approach unlikely to succeed in consolidating the dynamic new Republican party, but it challenged the Democratic-Conservatives to a contest on ground where they already possessed the advantage.

5. Climax of Convergence: The Election of 1872

The [New Departure] movement secures the reelection of Grant.
For it will bring not strength, but scism, at the North, while it
destroys the sympathy and zealous cooperation of the South.
—Herschel V. Johnson to Herbert Fielder, 26 June 1871

The fusion of the Liberal-Republicans and the Democrats in the national election of 1872 marked the culmination of the politics of convergence. The intention of the New Departure strategy, which had initially been inaugurated in the South and then later adopted by the Democratic party as a whole, had been to defuse the issue of Reconstruction and thus clear the way for lukewarm Republicans to join with the Democrats. To this end, a split and subsequent secession from the ranks of the Republicans was exactly what the party in the South had been trying to engineer by means of the New Departure lure. The developments at the national level in 1872 were therefore most welcome and reassuring to the Democratic-Conservatives. But their party was not alone in the South in attempting to draw off the support of an opponent. The Republicans were also pursuing a parallel strategy in their attempt to entice the former Whigs away from their uneasy affiliation with the Democratic-Conservatives. Yet the tide was turning against the Republicans in the South; and now, on the national level, too, the Liberal-Republican exodus seemed to indicate that, everywhere, the contest for dominance through control of the political center was being won by the Democrats.

The Liberal-Republican movement and the nomination of Horace Greeley as its presidential candidate opened up immense possibilities for the Democrats in both the North and the South. Although it was accompanied by risks, the Democrats now had the opportunity to forego making their own nominations and to endorse instead the Liberal ticket. Were it to do this, the party would become part of a broad-based coalition that was opposed to the Grant administration and organized around the nonpartisan and nonsectional issue of reform. Thus, divested of its partisan animus and exclusiveness and of its identification with the South, the Democratic party's prospects of victory were substantially increased.

This optimistic assessment was, for the most part, embraced by the leaders of the party's southern branch. All the same, there were considerable misgivings about the desirability of alliance with bolting Republicans headed by, of all people, Horace Greeley. John S. Mosby, the Virginia general, was dismayed. "Why should the South array itself on the side of Greeley, her unrepentant life-long enemy, against General Grant," when Greeley "justified and approved" every one of the president's acts that was "odious to us?"[1] Mosby was a Bourbon, and it was from that source within the party that most of the opposition arose. Another of them, Alexander Stephens, based his objections not so much on Greeley himself as on the Liberals' "ideas of Constitutionalism," embodied in their pledge to oppose "any reopening of the questions settled" by the Thirteenth, Fourteenth, and Fifteenth Amendments.[2] Nevertheless, the Bourbons' vociferous and angry objections were overwhelmed by a tide of enthusiasm for the Greeley candidacy. As early as May, only a month after the Liberals' convention at Cincinnati, the party's executive committee in South Carolina was claiming publicly, "The South prefers, almost unanimously, [the Liberal nominees]."[3] By late May, even John Forsyth, the leading Alabama Bourbon, who had initially been guarded about Greeley, was enthusiastically urging his endorsement by the national Democrats.[4]

The explanation for the Democratic-Conservatives' eagerness was that the political advantages seemed to be irresistible. Besides increasing the vote of the Democrats nationally, endorsement of Greeley was certain to improve the South's own political prospects. In the first place, a sympathetic response to Greeley's invitation to "join hands over the bloody chasm" would help change northern assumptions that southern whites were still hostile and unrepentant. Indeed, not only did the South obtain an amnesty act during the campaign itself as evidence of northern reassurance, but several years later, Senator John B. Gordon of Georgia reckoned that the impact of southern conciliatoriness had been so far-reaching that cooperation with Greeley was "the wisest political movement in our history."[5] The other major gain was that, by becoming part of a coalition pledged to reform, Democratic-Conservatives were setting aside "the bitter memories of the past, the effete issues of old [party] organizations, and in the spirit of noble brotherhood and patriotic liberality combining to save the government from overthrow and the people from the tyrannies of a centralized despotism."[6] That was how the party in Georgia depicted itself in the campaign. Meanwhile, its equivalent in North Carolina ran on the unexceptionable and obviously virtuous slogan: "Reform Retrenchment Reconciliation: Purity Patriotism Peace."[7] Because of its alignment with the forces favoring good government against the corruption and self-aggrandizement of the Grant regime, southerners no longer felt apologetic and defensive but were convinced of the superiority and justice of their position.

Seemingly, the only problem facing them had been the possibility that the national Democratic party might make a separate nomination at its convention in Baltimore. That would have split the party irrevocably and destroyed Southern hopes that Democratic fusion with the Liberals could bring victory. But, when this danger was averted, all problems and difficulties seemed to have been removed. Indeed, the manner in which the issues had been shaped and the political forces aligned seemed to guarantee that this broad coalition of reform was bound to win. The vote told a different story, however, as Horace Greeley crashed to defeat, winning only 68 electoral votes to Grant's 268. His rout cannot be attributed solely to the candidate's own shortcomings, though they helped, nor to the issues he raised, for they were evocative and potent. Rather, the difficulty lay with the mechanics of the campaign, its organizational machinery. This was revealed most clearly in the South, where the alliance with the Liberals was thought to be most likely to develop strength. The difficulties that the southerners encountered laid bare not simply the obstacles to party realignment but also the deficiencies in the Democratic-Conservatives' entire strategy of convergence.

The Liberal-Republican party within each southern state originated in meetings that were convened during April and May 1872 to choose delegates for the Cincinnati convention. Once the party was established nationally and its presidential ticket selected, the state organizations were expected to act as the focal point to which increasing numbers of the dissident and dissatisfied from both major parties would be drawn, eventually burgeoning into a powerful movement that was independent of party ties and committed to achieving political and governmental reform.

Before the Cincinnati gathering had assembled, Senator Lyman Trumbull was fearful about the composition and tenor of the convention, for he noted that there would be "several delegations present from N. Eastern & Southern States, who will be controlled by N.Y. influence, through which they have been got up." If this were pervasive, he worried about the party's prospects, for "a reform movement cannot succeed which starts off under the auspices of trading politicians."[8] Unhappily, these premonitions were soon to be realized with the selection of Greeley and in the course of events at the state level. John Forsyth too detected in the precipitate rush for Greeley "the old Rings in [New York] which, being out of office, have jumped at the Cincinnati movement, for there are traders who hastened to put themselves into position because it appeared that Greeley was the winning card." The Alabama editor thought that there was a distinctly Whiggish flavor to these knots of office-seekers, but, whatever their party antecedents, his surmise was quite correct that their lack of power and office was the motivation for their joining up with the Liberals.[9]

When he returned home, Forsyth soon discovered similar developments unfolding in his own state and throughout the South. For, by and large, there congregated at the core of the Liberal organization a cluster of men who possessed little influence in the regular Republican party structure. Because of their political marginality, they had often been active in earlier efforts to realign the parties so as to form a new party of the center. In North Carolina, the leading spirits in the Liberal initiative were Daniel R. Goodloe and Hinton Rowan Helper's brother, Hardie Hogan Helper.[10] Two years before, in February 1870, when the Republicans had been in turmoil, Goodloe had tried to act as midwife to a "new movement" consisting of anti-Holden Republicans and "the most intelligent"—that is, moderate—Democrats, to form "a new and respectable Republican party." For encouragement and aid in his scheme, he had looked to the Hedrick-Battle family network in Orange County, but they themselves were a group without access to political power and so could provide little substantive support.[11] Goodloe's current effort in 1872 appeared to be far more auspicious, but even so the personnel of the Liberal-Republican executive committee revealed that only politicos who were marginal were associated with it. William S. Mason was the chairman, and Lewis Hanes, the newspaper editor from Salisbury, as well as Dossy Battle, E. W. Pou, J. R. Thompson, S. B. Craven, L. C. Johnson, along with Goodloe and Helper, comprised the lackluster committee.[12]

The situation in Mississippi was similar. The prime mover was Jefferson L. Wofford, editor of the Corinth *News*, who had initiated the Dent movement in 1869.[13] Also active in the 1869 move as well as in that of 1872 was Elza Jeffords, and he and Wofford, along with Governor Alcorn's cousin, Robert, Joseph Bennett, William M. Hancock, Joseph L. Morphis, and W. H. Vasser were the most prominent Republicans at the Liberals' statewide meeting in Jackson during August. All were either loosely tied to the party or else, like Bennett, were so conservative as to have very little influence on the bulk of its membership. Indeed, it seems that Bennett, Hancock, and Alcorn affiliated with the Liberals because they had already been shunted aside by the Regulars, and thus it was the very fact that they lacked personal influence which prompted them to join the Liberal camp.[14]

It was to be expected that many of the Liberals would be officials without office and politicians without a party. What was not anticipated was that the party often did not expand beyond this knot of disaffected and marginal men. What was true of North Carolina and Mississippi also applied to Georgia, Texas, and Alabama. In all these states, the Liberals failed to lure away from the regular party the considerable numbers of dissatisfied Centrists who had been counted upon to join them. The explanation for this was to be found in the tone and proclivity of the Republican party itself. In all three states, the Centrist wing remained influential and the party was moderating its policy positions and seeking to attract support from among the whites. A New York *Herald* correspondent, reporting from Atlanta in August 1871, noted this pattern and urged his readers to "Observe how conservative the Republicans are in every Southern State." As evidence, he pointed out how their conciliatory tendencies often put them at odds with the "principal planks" in northern party platforms and that a further indicator of their conservatism was their extensive wooing of former Whigs.[15] Perhaps he should have qualified his remarks somewhat in the case of Louisiana, Arkansas, and South Carolina, but, for the most part, the observation was accurate in the summer of 1871 and it was increasingly confirmed during the ensuing year. Because the party had moved in a "liberal" direction, there was therefore no necessity for that element to cut itself loose, jeopardizing thereby both personal prestige and party power. Thus, recruits for the Liberals might be generated from the losers in local feuds or personal quarrels, but no widespread bolt was likely.

On occasion, however, the possibility did arise that a large contingent of Republicans might bolt to the Liberals. In Alabama, the dispute between the Warner-Smith segment of the party and the Regular wing, led by Senator George Spencer, which had been so destructive in 1870, was still active. But the party managed to head off the possible clash. Because "there are now, at least upon the surface, no antagonised policies presenting their respective claims" and because there was "nothing connected with the political issues of the present campaign which should cause men's blood to become hot," the official Republican newspaper, the *Alabama State Journal*, warned the party's convention to choose a ticket satisfactory to the many "conservative and patriotic" men who "might, but for the names of Republican and Democrat be classed together."[16] Wisely, the party chose a slate of natives with moderate or nonpartisan reputations. This contrasted most favorably with their opponents' folly of "adopting the Cincinnati platform, embodying Republican principles," while simultaneously nominating "a State ticket composed mainly of secessionists of the strictest sect, [which] not only ignored

the Greeley Republicans, but . . . even ignored the old Union portion of the State, North Alabama."[17] As a result, the prospects for
Willard Warner's Liberal party and for its coalition with the Democrats were critically damaged. Of the leading Centrists, only Sam
Rice and Frederick Bromberg, as well as the Huntsville clique of
Nicholas Davis, Joseph C. Bradley, and William B. Figures, accompanied Warner into the Greeley ranks.[18]

Because the Liberals failed to develop strength, Democratic-
Conservative fears that coalition with them would be threatening to
their own organization were soon put to rest. In May, the Atlanta
Constitution had reassured doubters by suggesting that "if we preserve our organization intact, the Democracy must necessarily
absorb the Liberal Republicans—the greater the weaker body."
Moreover, "cut off from their old allegiance," the Liberals "will have
nowhere to go except to the Democrats."[19] By August, this prediction was proving accurate and John Forsyth in Alabama was dis-
missing the Liberals with contempt. It was absurd, he mocked, to
"bind the elements of a great combat for free government to the
whimmdiddle hitched to less than a score of needy and seedy office-
mendicants."[20]

Consequently when formulae were being devised for coordinat-
ing the two parties in the fall campaign, the Liberals were treated
high-handedly. In Texas, the Democratic-Conservatives' convention at Corsicana in June endorsed Greeley but refused to negotiate
a share of the offices with the Liberals, who were led by two former
governors, Elisha Pease and Jack Hamilton. As a result, Pease and
Hamilton scurried back into the Republican party. This provoked
the Galveston *News* to comment scornfully, "The Liberal Republicans of Texas are not well pleased with the manner in which the
Democrats have treated them." If "they want a share of the offices,"
then "let them join the Democrats," was the *News*'s patronizing advice.[21] The Liberals in Mississippi were fobbed off with only those
presidential electors who were chosen at large and from the Fifth
Congressional District, though a tacit equality was accorded them
with the offer of a half share of the ten members of the Board of
Control that was to coordinate the canvass.[22] Even in Georgia, the
Liberals were spurned. A delegation consisting of Joseph E. Brown,
R. L. Mott, John D. Pope, R. L. McWhorter, and John Harris
went to the Democratic-Conservative convention to suggest that

the two parties produce a joint presidential ticket, with a fair and proportionate distribution of the electors. The convention ignored their request, however, causing Brown and his colleagues to withdraw angrily and retract their offer to support the party's state ticket.[23]

The confidence, amounting to arrogance, with which the proposals of the Liberals were rejected testified to the Democratic-Conservatives' overwhelming superiority in the coalition. Gratifying and reassuring as that might have been, it was, at the same time, convincing proof that the Liberals unfortunately had little to offer to their allies. Some extra support would be brought to the state ticket, but it was so limited that it did not justify any further concessions. Accordingly, as the Huntsville *Democrat* observed, the Liberals and Democrats did not really fuse at all. They merely formed an alliance. For the most part, they operated independently, but, in those localities in which there was cooperation, they would generally agree that a Liberal would run in a Republican area and a Democrat in Democratic strongholds.[24] That was the method employed in Georgia and North Carolina as well as Alabama. Of course, despite its apparent equity, the arrangement obviously benefited the Democratic-Conservatives at the Liberals' expense.

The Liberals' weakness was not so evident in Louisiana, South Carolina, and Arkansas, however. In those states, the Republican party was seriously divided and a large segment of its membership was splintering off into various kinds of collusion with the Democratic-Conservatives. The explanation for this divergence from the general pattern of Liberal marginality was to be found in the strength of the Regulars in these three states. In Louisiana and South Carolina, the size of the black electorate gave them the upper hand. This grip was further consolidated in the case of Louisiana by the president's support of his brother-in-law, James F. Casey, who was the customs collector in New Orleans and head of the Custom House faction. The potency of the Regulars in Arkansas was attributable to the state's retention of its prohibition against voting by former Confederates. This measure gave electoral security to the Republicans and viability to the Regulars' perspective. Paradoxically, it also provided the issue of amnesty and enfranchisement around which a competing faction could easily organize, as in fact occurred.

Although the size of the Republican split was determined in all three states by the ascendancy of the Regulars and their organizational and electoral priorities, the shape which each assumed varied. A close look at developments in Louisiana and Arkansas reveals how this happened. In Louisiana, the bolting Republicans were potentially a highly significant force, for the adroit and energetic governor, Henry C. Warmoth, had initiated the split. Indeed, he had separated completely from the Republican campaign by refusing even to endorse Grant for president, a course that his counterparts in South Carolina rejected. By contrast, Warmoth threw his support to Greeley and gave his organization the distinctive label of Liberal-Republicans. But the Republican party was not the only one to split; there was also in the field a splinter group of Democratic-Conservatives styling themselves the Reform party which was based mainly in New Orleans and derived its support chiefly from among former Whigs and business elements.[25] The only consolation that Democratic-Conservatives could derive from this situation was that the Republicans themselves were utterly disorganized, the party dividing still further into two factions, one allied with the Custom House group and the other with the black leadership, headed by Pinckney B. S. Pinchback. Party lines and party discipline that, in Reconstruction Louisiana, had been even less firmly established than elsewhere were being thrown into utter disarray by the solvent of the 1872 campaign and the Greeley movement.

Warmoth's defection from the party of which he was titular head had been provoked by the Custom House faction's unrelenting efforts to use its patronage and its special relationship with President Grant to clip Governor Warmoth's wings and ultimately break him down. The latter's difficulties had been aggravated by his veto of a civil rights bill in 1869, which provoked anger and disappointment from the blacks in the party.[26] In an effort to reestablish his influence with Republican blacks and undermine the Custom House group's influence among them, Warmoth had maneuvered to have Pinchback appointed lieutenant governor upon the death of the incumbent, Oscar Dunn, who had been the instrument for cementing the alliance between blacks and the Custom House. The trouble was that if this move to give blacks the lieutenant governorship failed to restore Warmoth's influence within his own party, it was also guaranteed to provoke the opposition of the Democratic-Conservatives, to whom he would, of necessity, then have to turn. Assessing the impact of Warmoth's scheme, the leader of the Custom House faction, Senator William P. Kellogg, concluded: "It strikes me it was a bad move for Warmoth. This, I take it, settles the question of the Democracy or any considerable portion of the Conservative element, uniting with him in any contingency, and leaves it a fight [within the Republican party] for the 'black element.'" Moreover, Kellogg was dubious that "Pinchback and his friends can control any considerable number of blacks."[27] Even if they could, it soon became apparent that Pinchback was not about to commit them to Warmoth, and this left the governor cut off from the bulk of both major parties.[28]

In the spring of 1872, when Warmoth had headed the Louisiana delegation to the Cincinnati convention and had thereby seized control of the Liberal-Republican movement, matters had looked far more threatening to the state's Democratic-Conservatives.[29] They could not ally with Warmoth, because, as two of their prominent leaders, William M. Levy and P. A. Morse, explained in November 1871, "We do not expect nor do we wish Gov. Warmoth to throw himself into the embraces of the Democratic party. Such a movement would ruin him so far as any power to benefit our people is concerned."[30] All the same, he had to be contained and prevented from forming a coalition with the Reformers. The way to outmaneuver Warmoth and the Liberals was outlined during May by a leading Democratic-Conservative strategist, John Ellis. The essence of the plan was for the party's upcoming convention to reverse the decision it had made in April and, instead, to run a party ticket in the election. "This is right, square and honest," argued Ellis. "If we fail to nominate, the Reformers *will* & then more time is given for coqueting with the arch enemy [that is, Warmoth]. This will tend to divide and destroy us. My judgement tells me it is best to accept or rather vote for Greeley. This will be done I think by the Baltimore Convention. Then our electoral ticket, *the Greeley* electoral ticket is in the field & what becomes of Liberal Republicanism. Voting with *us*, for *our* electoral ticket, too weak to nominate for themselves they can but vote and work with us."[31]

Ellis's expectations were realized almost to the letter, for, in July, the Democrats and the Reformers combined their tickets. Off-

setting this gain, however, were two less encouraging developments: the Liberals exhibited more strength than anticipated and
the feuding Republican factions agreed to unite their campaigns.
Thus, a deal with the troublesome Liberals became imperative to
the Democratic-Conservatives in order to defeat the Republicans.
In the arrangement that ensued during August, the Democrats' gubernatorial choice, John McEnery of New Orleans, was retained
over the Liberals' Davison B. Penn, who had proven to be very
popular in the countryside. In exchange, Penn became the Fusionist choice for lieutenant governor and the Liberals took two other
cabinet slots as well as congressman-at-large.[32] Sensing that the
Democratic-Conservatives needed the Liberals more than the Liberals needed them, Governor Warmoth, who had already recognized his own political liability by withholding his name from consideration as the Liberals' gubernatorial choice, now exerted his
considerable personal influence to wring further concessions from
the Democrats in return for supporting fusion. Although the Democrats had coalesced with the Liberals and the Reformers, the
agreement was obviously not what they had wanted. They had
hoped to emasculate the Liberals and Warmoth, rather than be
forced to conclude a truce with them.

The quandary and ultimate failure of the Democratic-Conservatives' handling of the Liberals in Louisiana was nothing compared
to the disaster in Arkansas. For several years prior to the 1872 election, the Republicans had been wracked by a crippling internal
feud between one faction led by Joseph Brooks and another representing Governor Powell Clayton and his administration. The formation of the Liberal-Republican party at Cincinnati provided the
occasion and pretext for Brooks finally to launch his own dissenting
organization.[33] Called the Reform party, its convention in late May
was attended by delegates from all but six counties in the state and
almost half of these were black. After nominating a state ticket
headed by Brooks himself and containing two blacks as candidates,
the convention proceeded to arraign the Clayton administration as
"the most corrupt and oppressive government ever tolerated by a
free people."[34] Because of its substantial support among Republicans, constituting a cross-section of blacks and whites as well as
Regulars and Centrists, the Reformers cut the ground from under
the fledgling Liberal-Republican organization that had been formed

in March.[35] To complete their subversion of the Liberals, the Reformers not only endorsed Greeley and attacked Clayton but also threatened, as Brooks put it, to "make war upon any party" that opposed the Republican administration—a clear admonition to the Democratic-Conservatives to forego nominating their own ticket and to consider, instead, some sort of collaboration with the Reform party.[36]

Unlike the hopelessly outflanked and overwhelmed Liberals, the Democratic-Conservatives were a significant force in Arkansas politics. As a result, their convention was bitterly divided over the question of whether to select their own ticket. A delegate, who called himself "Proctor," later told the *Arkansas Gazette* that the gathering consisted of four distinct groups. The first urged a separate Democratic ticket, the assumption being that the party might win in a three-way race and that Brooks's record and reputation precluded Democratic-Conservative support. In fact, one proponent of this course warned the convention not to equate Greeley with Brooks because, although both were Republicans, they were as different as "daylight and dark." Another group, which "Proctor" identified with Little Rock and with unrelenting hostility to the Democracy, proposed a straightforward endorsement of the Reform ticket. Meanwhile, a third element wanted to keep Brooks but to achieve a compromise on the rest of the state ticket. A final possibility was to keep the Reform ticket but to put a Democratic-Conservative at the top instead of Brooks, who was to be pacified with the position of congressman-at-large.[37] Ultimately, the welter of possibilities so overwhelmed the convention that it ended up making no nominations at all. It also failed to arrange any kind of division of the offices with the Reformers. The only departure from this inertia and indecisiveness was the recommendation that, in the state's three congressional districts, the party should make separate nominations and that the central committee should enter into discussions with the Reformers and Liberals.[38]

By delaying its convention until June, a month after the Reformers nominated their ticket, the Democratic-Conservatives had enabled Brooks to upstage them and claim the Greeley mantle. Already outmaneuvered, the party's discomfiture was then aggravated by the bewilderment and indecision of its own nominating convention. The deluge of criticism that was poured on the party leaders throughout the summer was not, therefore, surprising. Because the convention had rejected Brooks and his slate, yet simultaneously endorsed the Reform platform, advocates of coalition with the Reformers ridiculed their fellow Democratic-Conservatives, deriding them as "a party without a ticket and with a Republican platform."[39] Meanwhile, the proponents of separate nominations, located mainly in the white counties of northwest Arkansas, regarded the party's passivity "as a virtual disbandment of the Democratic party as it leaves them without a leader and without an organization."[40] Assailed by these recriminations, party leaders wisely resisted the call for a new convention and instead sought actively to harmonize the three anti-Clayton parties. By late August, a state central committee of the Reform parties had been created and it recommended acceptance of the Brooks ticket, except for several alterations favoring the Democratic-Conservatives.[41]

By waiving their claims to the governorship whose powers had been considerably increased under the Reconstruction constitution, the Democratic-Conservatives had actually made a major concession. In return, however, there was an unspoken assumption that the Reformers would allow them to control the legislature.[42] Nonetheless, convinced of their superior strength, the Reformers proceeded to run legislative candidates in Democratic districts. When the Brooks forces refused to desist, the aggrieved and desperate Democratic-Conservatives withdrew from the agreement altogether. Instead, they decided to support the ticket that the Liberal-Republicans had recently selected after they too had rejected cooperation in August when the Reform parties' conclave had given them the cold shoulder by denying them representation on the state ticket.[43] The embarrassment and disarray of the Democratic-Conservatives had not yet reached its nadir, however, for, a few days later, Andrew Hunter, who headed the Liberal ticket, rejected their endorsement. It was by now the middle of October, with the election only a few weeks away. Yet the Democratic-Conservatives were all at sea without a ticket or organization and, what was worse, the Republican party had cannily selected a gubernatorial nominee, Elisha Baxter, who was a native Arkansan and far more palatable than the frequently radical northerner, Joseph Brooks. Already disenchanted by Brooks's untrustworthiness and partisanship, many

Democratic-Conservatives voted for Baxter and thus probably provided his margin of victory.

This was the crowning ignominy in a campaign that had rendered the Democratic-Conservatives impotent and foolish. They had not only failed to seize control of the state from their divided opponent, but their own internal affairs were ultimately reduced to a shambles. Surveying the wreckage, the party's central committee observed that party operations and morale were permeated by "demoralization, disorganization and, worse than all, cold, ruinous apathy."[44] The extremism of that verdict was most appropriate in Arkansas, but, to a lesser degree, it was also applicable throughout the South. The mechanics of fusion had produced obstacles that precluded its ultimate realization.

The defection of the Liberal-Republicans had presented the Democratic-Conservatives with a political gift. They would not only gain the support of the Liberals but their Republican opponents would be hurt by the turmoil that the Liberal defection produced. The outcome, however, turned out to be quite different. Instead of stimulating and increasing support for the party, the addition of the Liberals had, in all probability, diminished its vote. In some contests, the anti-Republican vote actually decreased, while in others, it increased only marginally. At all events, both at the national and state level, Democratic-Conservatives looked on aghast as their candidates went down to defeat. "The rout of the Greeley coalition was even greater than I anticipated," was Herschel Johnson's comment after it was all over.[45] The very same word was used to describe the election result by former Governor James W. Throckmorton, who told his fellow Texas Democrat, Ashbel Smith: "We have been so badly routed in the Presidential contest" that perhaps the Democratic-Conservatives should take a respite from party politics for a while.[46]

Little solace could be derived from the returns. Greeley had reduced the Democrats' share of the national vote by three percentage points from 47 percent in 1868 to 44 percent in 1872, and his count in the electoral college had dropped to 66 from Seymour's 80. Meanwhile, in the South, the Democratic nominee had been unable to add to the party's limited tally of two states in 1868.[47] He retained Georgia, but he lost Louisiana while picking up Texas. Yet

even those victories were tarnished by his polling 26,000 fewer
votes in Georgia than Seymour in 1868 and by his running 7,000
votes behind the combined statewide totals of the party's four congressional nominees in Texas a year earlier.[48] In addition, the party's
presidential vote in both Carolinas fell significantly in 1872, the
Democrats' share of the poll in South Carolina collapsing to less
than half its 1868 total.[49] The Greeley candidacy's inability to
arouse the southern electorate was further demonstrated by his defeat in two states where there were no statewide elections to compensate for his own deficiencies. In Virginia, he should have been
able to win because the Democratic-Conservatives were in control
of the state and, in Mississippi, he mustered only a little over half of
Grant's vote.[50]

Even where state campaigns were carried on simultaneously,
Greeley consistently ran behind the head of the fusion ticket at the
state level. Only in Georgia, where the Democratic-Conservatives
were already dominant, did the party chalk up a victory. It lost control of the state in Alabama; it failed to consolidate the gains made
in North Carolina in 1870 when the party had captured the legislature; and in Louisiana, it could not capitalize on its alliance with
Governor Warmoth who controlled the election machinery. Over
and above these disappointments, however, there hung the realization that the Democratic-Conservatives had fared badly because
their supporters had simply not bothered to vote. They had stayed
away in droves. Abstention had been a factor in previous elections
since the war, but it seemed to be getting even worse. This meant
that in Alabama, the total Democratic-Conservative vote actually
decreased by about 1,000 votes compared with 1870, and the
party's choice for attorney-general in the off-year election of 1870 in
North Carolina had generated 1,641 more votes than its gubernatorial nominee in 1872.[51] Admittedly, the Republicans in both
states had increased their vote by 10,000 to 16,000 and would have
been difficult to overtake. Still the truth was unavoidable and it was
very disturbing; among Democratic-Conservative voters, apathy
and lack of interest were rampant. Nowhere was it more evident
than in South Carolina where the combined gubernatorial vote
of the Democratic-Conservatives and the bolting Republicans
amounted to a mere 36,533, about 15,000 fewer than in 1870 in
the disastrous Union Reform campaign.[52]

During the canvass itself, this lack of voter interest had provoked alarm among the leaders of the party. "A great deal of Democratic apathy prevails" in Georgia, the Atlanta *Constitution* had observed with dismay during September. To remedy this, the editors appealed to the voters' wives and sweethearts to urge their menfolk to pay their $2.00 poll tax and register.[53] Three weeks later, in neighboring North Carolina, the Raleigh *Sentinel* detected that "there is a fearful apathy at present"; moreover, it was not even being countered by active campaigning.[54] The prevalence of inertia was not surprising or unforeseen in the Old North State, for it had already revealed itself most dramatically in the state election held during August. On that occasion, the *Sentinel* had concluded that about 56,000 registered voters had failed to appear on election day and another 41,000, most of whom were probably white, had not even registered. "All over the state there was an unaccountable and inexcusable indifference manifested," the paper complained. "In Granville, Johnston, and other counties, we hear hundreds of white men refused to vote."[55] And in the general election, the outcome was the same. Grant won by a plurality of 20,000, yet there were, the *Sentinel* calculated, 30,000 opposed to him who failed to vote.[56] About the same number of anti-Grant voters failed to manifest their disapproval at the ballot box in Mississippi, according to estimates made by the Jackson *Clarion*.[57] The amount of abstention in Virginia was also very high. Colonel Robert E. Withers, the Democratic-Conservative gubernatorial nominee in 1868, reflected: "I thought . . . that we could carry the State as I did not suppose 35 or 40,000 conservatives would stay at home."[58]

These estimates of the potential Democratic-Conservative vote were, in all likelihood, somewhat inflated. After all, they were based only upon favorable assumptions about the voting behavior and party preferences of people who had in fact not voted. Some of them may not even have registered, while others may not have cast a ballot since the end of the war, yet it was predicted that they would have voted Democratic-Conservative. Nevertheless, the very fact that party spokesmen and editors were beginning to emphasize the potential of their own vote for transforming their minority status into a winning majority was highly significant, for this represented a fundamental shift of perspective. Party leaders no longer assumed that they could obtain a majority only by winning support away from the Republicans. Instead, the remedy lay not outside party lines or in the hands of marginal Republicans and their followers but within their own ranks, and its emergence was solely dependent upon the leaders' own action. Moreover, if the potential were as large as was now being imagined, the overthrow of the Republicans was eminently achievable in virtually all the southern states.

If apathy was the problem, how could the party's inert masses be aroused from their supineness? After the election, James Throckmorton discussed the difficulties in Texas. "The people did not turn out in this upper country [of Texas] more than one third of their strength. They seem dead to the future of free government," he complained. The antidote was a dramatic one. "Only live coals can bring them out of their shells," he suggested.[59] The need for fiery, stimulating campaigns was also stressed by a local correspondent of the Jackson *Clarion* called "William." He observed that not since 1868 had there been a movement in Mississippi "calculated to arouse the enthusiasm of the masses."[60] Along these lines, Charles C. Langdon of Alabama concluded that, in 1872, "There was no great excitement in this campaign as in old times." This, he believed, was on account of "the reason and judgement of the people, not their passions being enlisted."[61] Quite obviously, the issues and appeal of future campaigns had to be more emotive, more personal, in effect, more exciting.

Rousing rhetoric and stirring speeches alone were not enough. One of the primary causes of nonvoting was the bewilderment voters had experienced when faced with the complex and confusing electoral arrangements that had accompanied the attempts at electoral fusion. Coalition and fusion had been essential to the New Departure strategy, but they had required Democratic-Conservatives to vote for tickets that included Republican candidates and to support platforms written by Republican conventions. Furthermore, in local races, the terms of fusion had sometimes required the withdrawal of the Democratic-Conservative nominees in favor of the candidates of their allies. But whatever the exact stipulations, they invariably diluted the appeal to Democratic-Conservative voters, and what was more, the ingredients and composition of the fusion agreement itself took time to work out and often were later changed or, as in the Arkansas parody, were later changed often. All of this left voters bemused, and certainly uninvolved.

Besides the impact on the voter, fusion affected the party's campaign organization adversely. The leadership cadres were so tied up in negotiations with their potential allies that they overlooked the voters whose mobilization was essential for electing the ticket under consideration. A corollary was that, because the whole purpose of forming fusion tickets was to generate crucial additional support from the bolting Republicans, the electoral contribution of the Democratic-Conservatives was taken for granted. Yet another explanation for the insufficient mobilization of the Democratic-Conservative vote lay in the fusionists' joint campaign committees, which were usually established at the state and local levels, for they ensured that the party's campaign effort would be restricted by the needs of its allies.

Indeed, it seemed that the more the party pursued fusion and courted deviating Republicans, the less it actually gained. Herschel Johnson had predicted in early June that fusion with the Liberals would result in thousands of Democrats staying away from the polls and that considerably fewer Republicans would switch to the fusionists.[62] By November, the accuracy of his forecast was confirmed. One Democratic-Conservative editor in North Carolina admitted that "we lost fifty Conservatives where we gained one Liberal."[63] Hard though it was to acknowledge, fusion with the Liberals had not only confused and ignored the voters but had also crippled the party's campaign effort.

The harm to the party's campaign organization which was most noticed at the time was the encouragement that fusion gave to independency and bolting. By opening party lines to facilitate and encourage the entry of outsiders, the Democratic-Conservatives had weakened their ability to discipline their own members. Yet, at the same time, the need for authority was more pressing than usual. Because the prospects of victory were brightening in the wake of the Liberal-Republican split, innumerable Democratic-Conservatives saw 1872 as offering the chance at last of obtaining office after so many lean years. Gleefully, the Republican *Alabama State Journal* reported in September, "Twelve or fifteen men in a county are aspiring for a position," and in Georgia it was estimated that as many as forty members of the state legislature were competing for congressional nominations.[64] I. G. Harris told Robert McKee that, in his own west Alabama district, there was "a wild hunt after office.

Parties and their friends are filling the columns of all our journals with complimentary notices of this man or that." The ensuing "'scramble' after office" was intended, Harris was convinced, to force candidates on the upcoming conventions and to "forestall if possible [their] free deliberate action."[65]

With the thirst for office so keen and the party able to satisfy only a few of the aspirants, it was not surprising that many of them persisted in the attempt even after failing to receive a nomination. With party discipline lax and the courting of non-Democratic voters thoroughly legitimate, there was little to prevent or discourage disappointed contenders from running on their own and looking for votes wherever they could be found, just as the party itself was doing.[66] The incidence of independency was accordingly rife, causing the Atlanta *Constitution* to plead with bolters to reconsider and try to settle their complaints inside the party rather than weaken it by running on their own.[67] That same month, September, saw the situation in Alabama reach such alarming proportions that the *Register* was compelled to threaten, in bold type, that "IN UNION ALONE IS SAFETY—IN DIVISION DEFEAT." Furthermore, the paper warned, like an army, a political party could not expect to win, let alone survive, "without discipline or obedience to the word of command from its officers."[68]

Not the least of the party's obstacles in exerting authority over its activists was the widely held view that it had outlived its usefulness. To many in the party, the endorsement of Greeley and the alliance with the Liberals was evidence that the party was on its deathbed. The coalition of 1872 was thought to be not simply a short-term electoral expedient that might propel the party to victory but the catalyst for a possible new political combination. This was the conclusion reached by Alexander Stephens in Georgia. He thought the party leadership in his state was betraying Democratic principles by endorsing the Cincinnati platform. When, in August, the executive committee refused to meet with him to reconcile differences before the upcoming campaign, his suspicion that the creation of a new party was their overriding purpose turned to conviction.[69] Furthermore, he was hardly reassured by the sentiments expressed by the state chairman, Thomas Hardeman, who stated publicly that, "as it widens and spreads," the reform movement behind Greeley's candidacy "will shake party organizations to their foundations, because it is a contest of the *people* independent of party association or requirements."[70] As a result, Stephens refused to support the Greeley coalition and endorsed instead the Straight Democratic ticket, headed by Charles O'Connor.

Organizationally, the Democratic-Conservatives throughout the South had received a battering in 1872. Party distinctions had been blurred, party loyalty unrewarded, and party discipline undermined. This breakdown did not, however, go unnoticed by the leadership. Before the returns were even in, they were frighteningly aware of the impending disaster, for, in the campaign's final weeks, frenzied appeals were issued urging better organization and renewed effort. Casting about for ways of injecting their lethargic supporters with new energy, party leaders began to focus on styles of electioneering that had not been considered seriously and systematically before. Towards the end of the campaign, the state chairmen of the fusion parties in North Carolina called for intense activity on election day itself and in the days remaining. To achieve this, they suggested that, without further delay, every neighborhood be intensively canvassed by five or six activists.[71] Meanwhile, in Georgia, the head of the Democratic-Conservative party, Thomas Hardeman, impressed upon the party the importance of "subelectors," or canvassers, who "should visit the people and urge them to action and to duty."[72] In the neighboring state of Alabama, just before polling day, the Mobile *Register* reprinted an article from the New York *Tribune* entitled "Advice to Alabama." Horace Greeley's paper recommended, "Barbecues and mass-meetings will not suffice now, as they did in old times. There must be a personal canvass of every district, with local clubs and committees in all parts of the State." Such a shift of focus was particularly needful as "the negroes have what is equivalent to this in a secret system of communication." As a result, the Republicans were often able to deliver their anticipated vote without appearing to engage in any obvious canvassing, thereby frequently surprising the opposition and catching it off guard.[73]

Although ineffective in the election itself, these admonitions were symptomatic of a profound change taking place among the Democratic-Conservatives. Their views of how parties were structured and how successful election campaigns had to be conducted were undergoing transformation. Nevertheless, the organizational priorities and electoral techniques that they were about to embrace were not unique to the South but were being adopted increasingly throughout American politics in the 1870s.[74] In this modulation of electioneering practice, it was not organization as such that was the new ingredient. Parties in the United States had been fully aware of the importance of organization in conducting an election and in communicating with the broadly based and extensive electorate with which they had to contend since the 1820s. During the 1870s, it was, however, the focus and purpose of campaign organization which shifted decisively. The new emphasis was directed towards getting out the vote rather than making the candidate and his views known to the voters through public appearances. Far more effective now than the public campaign was what the Raleigh *Sentinel* described as "the personal canvass." "Have every township thoroughly canvassed and let every man's name be entered in a book," the *Sentinel* explained, and then, after local operatives and neighbors had contacted the voter and impressed him with the need to vote for the party, those who expressed support were to be contacted on election day and hustled to the polls.[75]

Nothing better illustrated the changing perception of party function than the list of prohibitions and recommendations published by the Mobile *Register* in August 1872. Fearful that the party leadership had relied too much on a spontaneous "popular uprising" in favor of Greeley, the editor, John Forsyth, wrote, "It is in politics as it is in war; the battle is not always to the biggest army, but rather to the best drilled." In order to produce a military apparatus, he proceeded to instruct party activists:

1. *Don't waste all your strength on parades . . .*
2. *Don't rely too much on public meetings.*
3. *Don't rely too much on circulars . . .*
4. *Don't waste your money on Campaign Chowder Clubs/or barbecues outside the seaport of Mobile!*
5. *Organize the party thoroughly by districts . . .*
6. *As soon as a Club is formed* [in each ward] *appoint active canvassers to visit every home . . .*
7. *Have district meetings at regular times . . .* "Never mind gatherings for buncombe, but meet often for business."
8. *Do these things at once.*[76]

Apathy had been unavoidable in a campaign strategy that had rested on the assumption that voters were inert until appealed to by the party's candidates and instructed by its policymakers. The antidote was grass-roots organization that would involve local party supporters as canvassers who, in turn, would mobilize others by direct personal contact. The philosophy behind this mass mobilization was explained by Robert J. Powell, a prominent figure in North Carolina politics who was himself running for the state Senate in 1872: "Man with no particular work to do, and no responsibility resting upon his [sic] is apt to be indifferently inactive. Give him a special duty to perform, and make him [realize?] fully his personal responsibility, and he not only becomes active, but enthusiastic." Having explained the theory behind the new campaign style, Powell proceeded to outline the mechanics of electoral mobilization. "A few friends in each township [should] quietly get together, and organize a club," he wrote. The membership was then to be divided into three sections—one to call club meetings, correspond with other clubs, and arrange public campaign events; another "to look after such friends as may need attention" so as to ensure that doubters voted Democrat; and a third "to watch the enemy" on election day to prevent any kind of voting fraud. This "thorough organization, and systematic work," Powell reckoned, was far superior to the old-fashioned formulae of "mass meetings, stump speaking, and documents," all of which were actually "of but little real value" in stimulating voters and getting them to the polls.[77]

The increasing acceptance of these methods amounted to an innovation in the conduct of elections in the South.[78] It constituted a rejection of the political assumptions and electoral practices that had been predominant in the Democratic-Conservative party certainly since 1868, and most probably before as well. Rather than rely on attracting external sources of support, the party was in the process of deciding that a more effective approach was to identify its own supporters and make sure they voted. The thrust of the party's concern was therefore no longer to be directed outwards and horizontally, but inwards and vertically instead. Therefore, in effect, the inclusive, "competitive" mode of party operation was to be jettisoned in favor of the partisan, "expressive" approach. A political style that assumed a degree of deference and acceptance on the part of the party's base was to give way to one that was built upon the involvement and responsibility of the mass membership located in the constituencies. Thus, the organizational apparatus was to penetrate into the electorate; the party would be mobilized and rallied from its base rather than exclusively by the leadership cadres at the apex. Although this transfer by no means constituted a democratization of the party or a devolution of power within it, the new campaign style did increase participation. Furthermore, it mobilized the energy and interest that existed outside the closed world of the state and county committees but that had previously been excluded and therefore was dormant. Finally, the reversal of electoral priorities brought to the fore a set of politicians and operatives who had been on the sidelines during the New Departure. The changes were therefore far-reaching. Moreover, they provided the impetus and ingredients for the overthrow of Republicanism during the three or four years that followed Greeley's defeat.

This change of direction in the party's strategic thinking was complemented and corroborated by two other realizations arising from the experience with the Greeley maneuver. The first was that the Democratic-Conservatives' efforts to give a nonpartisan, disinterested reform tone to their campaign had evidently failed to convince. Throughout all their attempts at fusion, maintenance of the identity and priorities of their party had been the paramount concern. Therefore, despite all the speculation, the party was not about to die or be transformed into something else. "The two parties stand facing each other, grim, firm, hostile," proclaimed the Republican Columbia *Daily Union* as early as June.[79] Indeed, the existing parties were so tenacious and well-established that efforts to discount them or disguise partisan interests were doomed and foolish. "Party," the Atlanta *Constitution* asserted after the election, "is a necessary thing" and was nothing to be ashamed of or to regret; "it is the union of men who think alike to carry good public measures."[80] Party and partisanship were therefore normative, and they required not merely accommodation and acceptance, but, put more positively, they needed strengthening and development. "To try to win Republican votes by ignoring our true friends . . . is the veriest nonsense," Senator Samuel B. Maxey of Texas later told his wife. "We had better solidify our own ranks by turning out the best possible men to satisfy Democrats. This was my advice you know at

Corsicana [the party's 1872 convention], and it is just as wise now as then."[81]

The other lesson learned in 1872 was that sectionalism was still virulent and, like party, could not be wished away. Despite the South's acceptance of the New Departure and despite its endorsement of its old enemy, Horace Greeley, the conciliatory gesture was not reciprocated. No northern state went for Greeley. In view of this, the Raleigh *Sentinel* was forced to conclude that the sections were so irreconcilable that "any man who would be popular and acceptable at the South would not be popular at the North." In fact, the election revealed that the South was regarded not simply "with distrust, but with absolute dislike."[82] If this was the real and unvarnished northern sentiment, then it had to be accepted. Continued attempts to change these attitudes were futile, so that the lesson seemed obvious. The South "probably has made an error in taking any part in national politics," the Atlanta *Constitution* decided. "All of her efforts seem to have only put her more deeply in the mire." But still, the *Constitution* continued, a genuine attempt at cooperation had been made. Consequently, experiencing no feelings of shame and knowing that, after the South's conciliatory behavior in supporting Greeley, there was no justification for northern retribution, Democratic-Conservatives could safely ignore opinion in the North and, instead, concentrate on the "struggle for State control and State prosperity."[83]

Despite the *Constitution*'s disclaimer, "State control and State prosperity" had actually been the objective from the beginning. But, after the experience of 1872, there was no need to be covert about it. In fact, the attempt to disguise their self-interested intentions was now thought to have been a mistaken course for the Democratic-Conservatives to pursue. Equally misguided had been their assumption that sectional reconciliation and party realignment were essential prerequisites for regaining control of state government. With this realization, the party began to discover that, all along, it had possessed the political assets necessary for local self-determination. There was no need any longer to search for them elsewhere, either in Washington or within the ranks of the opposition party.

Part II

The Politics of Divergence:

Redemption, 1874–1879

6. The Collapse of the Center, 1873–1875

Turning and turning in the widening gyre
The falcon cannot hear the falconer;
Things fall apart, the center cannot hold
—Opening lines of "The Second Coming" by
  William Butler Yeats

The condition of all parties is now exceptional—they float upon
uncertain waters . . .
—*Arkansas Gazette*, 14 August 1874

The 1872 elections laid bare the essentials of politics in the Reconstruction South. Despite their persistent efforts to capture the middle ground and draw their party towards the political center, practitioners of the politics of convergence within both parties had sustained a fatal reverse.

On the Democratic-Conservative side, the evidence for the failure of the New Departurists was incontrovertible. On every level, their party had gone down to defeat. In the presidential election, Horace Greeley had been beaten handily in the South, losing even Louisiana, which Horatio Seymour had probably carried in 1868. The only compensation was that Greeley had carried Texas as well as four border states. The party's record at the state level was equally abysmal, for it made no gains while managing to lose control of

Alabama, which had gone Democratic in 1870. This debacle
prompted the Republican *Alabama State Journal* to conclude that
the "Democratic party . . . was so effectually defeated that it can
never rally again. Its career is ended."[1] The *Journal*'s verdict was
given broader application by South Carolina's Columbia *Daily
Union*, which, after the election, asserted confidently that "the
South is largely Republican," the exceptions being only Kentucky
and possibly Texas.[2]

The Republicans' success was, however, less certain than it
seemed, for, behind the victorious election-returns, there lurked another reality. The party's electoral margin was diminishing rapidly,
while its hold on state government in the South was often tenuous.
Its majority in North Carolina had slipped from Holden's twenty
thousand in 1868 to a slim one thousand for Tod Caldwell four
years later.[3] In Texas, the legislature had been lost in 1871 and,
after Greeley carried the state in 1872, continued retention of the
governorship seemed highly unlikely. Meanwhile, the results had
been so close in the gubernatorial races in Louisiana and Arkansas
and in the legislative election in Alabama that the opposition was
threatening to gain control by challenging the returns. Thus, on
closer examination, the Republicans' jubilation was premature.[4]

The narrowness of the Republicans' victories in 1872 revealed
that their grip on power was slipping, perhaps irretrievably. Their
attempts to broaden the party's base of support had produced no
discernible gains. Indeed, there had even been attrition. Meanwhile, the party's pursuit of the former Whigs had been successfully
countered by the Democratic-Conservatives and, to this setback
was added the defection of much of the Centrist wing of their own
party in the bolt of the Liberals during the 1872 campaign. Some
returned after the election, but their number was small. In fact,
there was really no compelling reason for them to rejoin, since the
Centrist electoral strategy, whose repudiation in 1872 had been the
occasion for their exodus in the first place, was now virtually out of
the question as a possible Republican option. With the Centrist formula seriously undermined, if not eliminated, the party was thrown
back onto its own resources. The trouble was that those resources
were known, in most states, to be insufficient in size and strength.
What was more, the essential Republican constituency was black,
and this identification, as it became more and more explicit, could

only confirm the accusations of an increasingly vociferous segment of the Democratic-Conservative party about the ultimate source and foundation of southern Republicanism.

The Republican party's growing reliance on its basic constituency of black voters coincided with the increasing salience of that very same group within the party structure. This rising influence was attributable partly to the departure of whites because some withdrew from politics to return to the North and others—natives for the most part—decided to cast their lot with the Democratic-Conservatives, a trend that the Liberal-Republican fusion had facilitated. The increasing influence of the party's blacks was also considerably accounted for by the persistent and increasingly successful efforts of black politicians to force the party's white leadership to yield its monopoly on place and power. After initially assuming a low profile because of political inexperience and uncertainty about how black participation in the political process would be received, leading black Republicans took action to remedy the imbalance between what blacks gave to the party with their votes and what they received in return in the form of beneficial legislation, influence within the party, and access to office.

In South Carolina, blacks had commenced their campaign for influence early in 1870 when a public meeting was called in Charleston to demand offices.[5] The upshot was that Alonzo J. Ransier was nominated for lieutenant governor, and three other blacks, Robert DeLarge, Robert Brown Elliott, and Joseph H. Rainey, were sent to Congress.[6] By 1872, blacks held four of the state's five congressional seats, a justiceship on the state Supreme Court, and four of the eight state-level executive posts. In addition, they controlled key positions in the legislature, either as officers or as committee chairmen, and this enabled them to affect the course and content of legislation as well as acquire influence within the party. Thus, by the 1874-76 session, blacks controlled 70 percent of the committee chairmen in the House and three-fourths in the Senate. Moreover, in terms of sheer numbers, they dominated the Republican delegation in the legislature.[7]

Although blacks were numerically powerful in Louisiana Republicanism, they did not translate their votes into proportionate influence within the party. P. B. S. Pinchback once told Governor Warmoth, "Political preferment can only be obtained in Louisiana by the votes of the Colored people," but, too often, the officials who were elected by black votes were not themselves black.[8] Primarily, this was because black politicians did not act as a cohesive unit but instead divided along the prevailing factional lines within the party. All the same, by 1873, four offices in the executive branch were held by blacks, and Pinchback had been chosen U.S. senator. Black representation in the legislature grew slightly in 1872 and again in 1874, but more important was an increase in the number of black committee chairmen and in the importance of the particular committees they controlled. Since these gains were made at a time when the total Republican representation in the legislature was diminishing, they signified that blacks were becoming a force in the party as a whole.[9]

As Reconstruction progressed, blacks were becoming more assertive and prominent elsewhere in the southern Republican party. In Texas, during the 1872 campaign, blacks in several of the black districts pressed for more party nominations for the legislature. In one instance, the Sixteenth District, the state senatorial incumbent, Matthew Gaines, who had earlier charged that "the black men of Texas are the real Republican party," was able to secure an entirely black slate.[10] In neighboring Arkansas, blacks had initially been squeezed out, but, in the evenly balanced assembly which had been elected in 1872, the *Arkansas Gazette* reported that the twenty black legislators (sixteen in the House and four in the Senate) were acting as a bloc and using their strategic position to become "masters of the situation," thereby controlling legislation and forcing white Republicans to recognize their reliance on black votes.[11] To the southeast, black Republicans in Mississippi were becoming extremely powerful. As early as the 1871 elections, they had organized to achieve a large degree of control over the black counties of Adams and Warren, where Natchez and Vicksburg were located. With an increase of the legislative seats blacks held—six or seven more in the Senate and a total of forty-two of the Republicans' delegation of sixty-four in the House—blacks were clearly a power within the party.[12] By 1874, Adelbert Ames recognized in his inaugural speech as governor that, because they comprised the largest single group of legislators, blacks were "greatly influencing, if not controlling legislation."[13] Many years later, Ames recalled that, in 1873, "The demands of the colored delegates for state offices seemed to be irresistible, especially that for Lieutenant Governor." In fact, blacks obtained the latter nomination and proceeded to secure in addition the selection of James Hill as secretary of state and T. W. Cardozo for superintendent of education.[14]

The salience of black politicians within the party and the awareness among party leaders of the need to satisfy and consolidate the Republicans' crucial black constituency were both growing, and in no way was this development more visible than in the sudden flurry of civil rights legislation that erupted after 1872. Black legislators had pressed unceasingly for additional civil rights guarantees, particularly in public accommodations and on common carriers, but, as regularly, their bills and proposals had been rebuffed. After the 1872 elections, however, the party's receptivity to them changed noticeably. Mississippi's black legislators lost no time. They immediately reintroduced a bill that had been defeated in the previous session and it passed both houses with alacrity.[15] Within a matter of months, the legislatures of Louisiana, Arkansas, and Florida had also enacted new civil rights laws.[16] Even in Alabama, where the party had been under the influence of native whites whose claim to favor had been partially vindicated by the party's successful capture of white votes in north Alabama during the 1872 campaign, an effort to pass a civil rights bill early in 1873 passed the Senate and failed narrowly in the House.[17] Because civil rights laws were a political symbol denoting the degree of the party's commitment to its black supporters, the passage of these measures in 1873 illustrated graphically the shift of priority and power that was occurring within the Republican party.

This need to reassure and strengthen the Republicans' essential black constituency was also apparent to the national leadership. In 1874, a civil rights measure was introduced into the U.S. Senate. Its emergence was, partially, a tribute to the late Charles Sumner who had tried persistently to pass a national public accommodations law extending civil rights protection beyond the 1866 act, but more instrumental in bringing it forward was pressure from blacks throughout the country and from many Republican politicos who regarded it as a party necessity. Foremost among the measure's proponents were Republicans from the South. Indeed, the president told some Alabama congressmen in September that they had "forced this question on the party" and would have to take the responsibility if it became law.[18] The bill's advocates argued that its passage would reaffirm the party's commitment to equal rights, rekindle the fervor of the party's more committed loyalists, and reestablish the influence of the party's Regulars after recent efforts during 1872 to steer it onto a Centrist course. To a large extent, therefore, the civil rights law was a symbolic issue in an internal struggle for influence and many, particularly from among its opponents, predicted a dire outcome in the 1874 elections if its supporters prevailed.[19]

By contrast, the prospect of a new federal civil rights law generally caused little concern in the South. This was because, as we have just seen, most states already possessed such laws and they were often more stringent and more likely to be enforced than a federal law. Nevertheless, in two states, Alabama and North Carolina, where the Republican party was dominated by native whites, the proposed federal law raised problems that the Democratic-Conservatives were not slow in exploiting. The first draft of the proposed bill contained a provision for mixed schooling and "A White Republican" informed the *Alabama State Journal* that the overthrow of the Republicans was "believed to be certain" unless the party, at its upcoming state convention, disavowed the proposition.[20] Even though it did, in fact, disclaim any intention of espousing what its opponents called social equality, the issue of race had been raised all the same, and not even the failure of Congress to pass the bill could defuse the issue. The upshot was that the bill had a devastating impact on the whites in north Alabama who had previously played a crucial role in enabling the party to "hold its place" and even win in 1872. This was the conclusion of H. V. Redfield of the Cincinnati *Gazette* who reported from Alabama during the 1874 election that the bill had "come down among [this element] like a tiger among a drove of sheep, and scattered them about as effectually." Furthermore, as he noted, "You may be sure the Democrats are not slow to play on this aroused prejudice."[21]

A similar uproar occurred in North Carolina, where the bill also drove a wedge between the party's blacks and its native white leadership. The day after he gave a speech to "an immense crowd at Rockingham" where he "found tremendous excitement on the Civil Rights Bill," Oliver H. Dockery, the party's state chairman, confided to Daniel Russell, another leading Republican and a future governor, his anxieties about the impact of the bill. He then informed Russell that he would "tomorrow write to Speaker [James G.] Blaine urging him to have the bill *killed* in the house, as no temporizing policy will now do." If the civil rights question were not removed from the canvass, Dockery feared defeat in both the legislative and congressional elections of 1874.[22] But the size of the eventual loss must have exceeded even his worst predictions, for, when the results were in, the Democrats had gained overwhelming control over the state assembly and virtually monopolized the state's eight-member congressional delegation.

These unanticipated setbacks were not confined to Alabama and North Carolina. The party suffered a sweeping defeat in Tennessee, another state with a sizable bloc of white Republicans, and this reversal was most distressing because the party had experienced something of a revival in the congressional elections of 1872.[23] The impact of the Civil Rights bill was disastrous within the South, but, outside the region, its repercussions were also far from beneficial. Although not exclusively to blame for the party's shattering reverses of 1874, when the Democrats regained control of the House of Representatives, the Civil Rights bill was certainly a major contributing factor in the electorate's repudiation of the Republicans and their scandal-ridden record during Grant's second term.

By 1874, the party's strength in the South was also declining precipitously. Besides the reverses in Tennessee and North Carolina, Alabama fell to the Democrats in 1874 and so did Arkansas. In addition, Texas, as expected, had been lost a year earlier. Although the Civil Rights bill had not been the cause of the Republicans' defeat in either of the latter two cases, the party found itself in control of only four southern states at the end of the tumultuous year in which the bill had been introduced. While the bill had been intended to reaffirm the party's commitment to its equal rights principles and to its most dedicated and loyal supporters, the Republican organization that the blacks and their allies were beginning to dominate in 1873 and 1874 was drastically diminished, almost evanescent. For only in South Carolina, Louisiana, Mississippi, and Florida was the party still in power.

Where the party remained in control, it was usually headed by the Regular faction, since the Centrists had been driven off by 1872 or shortly after. Florida, however, proved something of an exception, because the 1868 constitution had so curtailed the impact of black voting power that the Republicans had thereafter to court white support avidly, and both the Reed faction and its opponents, led by Thomas Osborn, negotiated with the Democratic-Conservatives. Thus, there was no real policy or philosophical difference between the factions except that Osborn controlled the federal patronage and used it as a base against Reed. After Reed and Osborn left politics in 1872, their places were taken by Governor Marcellus Stearns and Senator Simon Conover. The factional contest was at an impasse, with the Conover faction possessing the federal patronage and the allegiance of the party's blacks but unable to dominate the party itself.[24] Elsewhere, however, Regulars had gained the ascendancy. In Louisiana, the secession of Governor Warmoth to the Liberals in 1872 had drawn off the Centrists, and the party came securely under the control of the Custom House faction. This group's ascendancy was based on its control of federal patronage and the support of President Grant, whose brother-in-law, James Casey, was collector of customs in New Orleans and a central figure in the faction. Its power was also based on the support it elicited from blacks, who, although not united, backed the Custom House rather than Warmoth. One of the faction's leaders, William P. Kellogg, was currently governor, and another, Stephen B. Packard, U.S. marshal and the moving force within the group, would succeed him in 1876.[25]

The ascendancy of the Regulars was even more obvious in Mississippi where the new governor in 1874 was Adelbert Ames, head of the black wing of the party in its unceasing fight against James L. Alcorn's Centrist policies. Finally, in the state election of 1873, the Ames forces had defeated Alcorn after first driving him out of the party and into the arms of the Democratic-Conservatives.[26] By contrast, in South Carolina, the Republican party had possessed a sufficiently strong base of black voters so that the Centrist strategy had never posed a viable alternative. As a result, its advocates had always been forced to bolt whenever they persisted in pursuing that course. By 1874, the Regulars still predominated, and for governor they had nominated Daniel Chamberlain who, like Ames, Packard, and Kellogg, was a northerner. Chamberlain's selection had been engineered by Robert Brown Elliott, the state's leading black politician, and by its most powerful white Regular, Senator John J. Patterson. His opponent, John T. Green, was the defeated aspirant for the Republican nomination who, in the campaign, had solicited and obtained support from the opposition party.[27]

Ironically, the ascendancy of the Regulars came at a moment when the power of the party as a whole was ebbing. With the failure of the appeal for white support and the loss of many Centrists in the ensuing Liberal-Republican bolt, the party was forced to rely pretty exclusively on its black voters and, as in Louisiana, on a knot of federal officials and employees. But that was not the only irony in the situation. The policies they found themselves having to pursue bore the hallmarks of conciliation and apology characteristic of their Centrist rivals. During the mid-1870s, the demand for reform had begun to permeate southern politics. The cry became widespread and persistent that stringent curbs on governmental outlays be imposed through the reduction of expenditures, taxation, and public indebtedness. Also to be rooted out were corruption and favoritism. Faced with this pressure on the party to improve its performance and reputation, the Republican leadership had to respond. As early as 1872, the party in South Carolina espoused the cause of fiscal reform, its platform that year giving priority to reducing the financial liabilities incurred by previous administrations.[28] But, by 1874, these promises of reform had not amounted to much. Sensing the danger to the party if it failed to embark on a program of reform, Congressman Robert Brown Elliott had inveighed against the party's weaknesses and urged instead: "Honesty, economy, good government—in city, county, and in State—let this be our watchword and our firm resolve."[29] By July 1874, the Republican state executive committee was telling its supporters that "the pledges given to the people in our party platform of 1872 have not been fully redeemed, and that, in many instances, sound policy has been discarded and reckless extravagance manifested, we cannot deny."[30] The party had to improve its record. Accordingly, once elected, Daniel Chamberlain announced in his inaugural that "the practice and enforcement of economy and honesty in the administration of the Government" was "the paramount duty before us." And he proceeded to outline reforms in the operation of the tax system as well as cuts in the expenses of the legislature which would reduce appropriations below the level of anticipated revenues, and thus balance the budget.[31]

A similar preoccupation with retrenchment and reform was evident in Mississippi. Governor Ridgley Powers, who was Alcorn's successor as governor and a conciliationist by nature, first set out on the path of reform in 1872, but, two years later, the administration of Adelbert Ames, a Regular, was also committed to a policy of reducing expenditures and taxes. In his inaugural, Ames pledged "a rigid economy and a strict accountability" in the raising and disbursing of public funds; this was soon accompanied by separate messages proposing measures for cutting taxes and expenses, for returning state finances to a cash basis by eliminating the system of warrants, and for funding the state debt.[32]

Since the Kellogg administration in Louisiana was also preoccupied with fiscal and governmental reform, an equally anomalous situation arose there. Thus, the Regulars, who now possessed control of the executive branch in these three states, were enlisting in a cause that pandered to the objections of the Democratic-Conservatives. Naturally enough, many of the latter were delighted that Republican concern for retrenchment was not flagging with the increased influence of the Regulars but seemed instead to be quickening its pace. Francis Dawson of the Charleston *News and Courier* was convinced that, unlike his predecessor, Chamberlain was really in earnest. "We have an abiding faith," he wrote editorially, "that in carrying out the letter and spirit of his inaugural, the Governor will not flinch nor be moved the breadth of a hair."[33] Ames's course also gave satisfaction. Throughout February 1874, the Jackson *Clarion*, pleased with the new governor's financial messages, reprinted innumerable endorsements from the press and leading Democratic-Conservative politicians.[34]

Contrasting with the applause of the influential Democratic-Conservatives was the dismayed reaction of the Republican legislators to the economic measures proposed by the executive branch. For the espousal of retrenchment amounted to a decisive shift in party policy which in turn threatened the priorities and programs of the legislators as well as their own base of power. It meant, in all likelihood, that Republican governments could no longer pursue activist fiscal policies, while those programs that had already been implemented would probably be cut, perhaps even withdrawn. With this reduction of the cost and scope of legislation, a corresponding diminution of the influence and patronage of the legislative body and its members was also predictable. Consequently, the governor's financial reforms met with serious resistance in the state legislatures of South Carolina, Mississippi, and Louisiana. In the middle of the first legislative session of his administration, a session in which Chamberlain was to issue nineteen vetoes, the governor summed up the situation by saying: "The truth is there were very few men in my party last fall who *meant* reform." As a result, he mused, "My inaugural chilled them,—my special message [outlining specific measures to keep "expenditures within receipts"] enraged them,—and nothing keeps them from attacking me just as openly as they do Cardozo [the black state treasurer] except the power of my office and the support which the Conservatives and the Country at large give to me in all my efforts at reform."[35]

By persisting in his intended course of retrenchment, Chamberlain was inviting a confrontation with his party's legislative majority and this he incurred. All the same, he was remarkably successful. By pruning expenditures and defeating two measures to validate the floating indebtedness of the state, known as the "bonanza bills," Chamberlain saved the state $1.75 million, so Dawson's sympathetic *News and Courier* reported.[36] Kellogg's efforts in Louisiana also met with success. His great achievement was the Funding Act of the 1873-74 session. "The passage of this funding scheme has been an immensely popular measure here with the people," he informed the U.S. postmaster general, J. A. J. Cresswell. "It has relieved real estate and every material interest. Even the bondholders . . . are giving in their adhesion to the scheme with remarkable unanimity," an outcome hardly surprising, it should be added, in view of its highly favorable terms.[37] Kellogg was also able to reduce expenditures and taxes; appropriations dropped by a third, from over $2 million in 1873 to $1.3 million in 1876, and the millage rate of taxation fell from 21.5 to 14.5 over the same period.[38] More limited results, however, were obtained by Ames in Mississippi. In a state in which the budget was already lean and indebtedness minimal, Regulars in the legislature dug in their heels and refused to enact Ames's proposals for cutting expenditures. During that same session of 1874, state taxation was reduced but its impact was only superficial because the legislators had simply shifted the burden from the state to the counties.[39] This limited achievement caused the Vicksburg *Times* to lament that the "expectations" of retrenchment had "not been met."[40]

The reverberations of these economy drives were the same, whether or not they were successful. For they all provoked an intense and critical confrontation with Republican legislative majorities that were loath to repudiate existing programs and renounce prevailing practices. Increasingly dominated by Regulars and spokesmen for the black population, the Republican lawmakers were unwilling accomplices for any party leader embarking on a program of reform. Indeed, in the case of South Carolina, Governor Chamberlain's political course seemed to be predicated on the assumption that he would be opposed vigorously within his own party and that, out of the ensuing split, he could emerge as the architect of party realignment, pitting an interparty coalition of reformers against the Republican diehards.[41] This scenario was a repetition of Governor Baxter's maneuver in Arkansas in 1873, as he positioned himself to win support from moderate Democrats and Republicans who both favored reform and would see in Baxter's dramatic resistance to the railroad bond release bill, or "railroad steal" bill as it was known, the opening shot in a movement whose outcome was to be a realignment of the parties.[42] But where the Republican governor had no intention of employing reform to desert or divide his party, the end result was still unsatisfactory. It revealed, in Kellogg's case, how desperate he was to accomplish reform and, in Ames's, how powerful and unsympathetic to reform were the forces ascendant within the party. The fight for reform and retrenchment threw the Republicans into turmoil, as it challenged the priorities, values, and interests of its most faithful supporters and their representatives.

There was a second difficulty that arose from this preoccupation with economy. It elevated to a position of fundamental importance—in fact it became the central issue of the mid-1870s—a matter that the party's opponents had developed and then injected into political debate. Once acknowledged, the reform issue then locked the Republicans into a contest over cost cutting, which absorbed all of their energy and prevented them from developing other issues and strategies of their own. At a moment when the party had lost all reasonable hope of corralling white support, it was being forced to conciliate those very same whites, but without any real possibility of securing their votes. Simultaneously, as the party sought to reassure taxpayers and other critics of its past record, it abandoned those vital groups that had supported Republicanism because it had provided aid and services.

The direction that an offensive Republican strategy might have taken, had the party's leadership not been so preoccupied with retrenchment and with responding to the opposition's arraignment of its fiscal policies, was hinted at in the inaugural messages of Governors Moses and Ames in 1873 and 1874 respectively. Both men saw in the agricultural system, particularly the dependency of the tenants and croppers, a major cause of the South's economic and social difficulties. A bold move to reform the system would restore the faith and commitment of the party's basic constituency of black workers. At the same time, it would enable the party to renew its efforts to obtain white support through the benefits that agricultural reform would bring to suffering white tenants and laborers. This could provide the means and opportunity for establishing the Republicans as the party of the working people of both races. Accordingly, Governor Frank Moses of South Carolina devoted a considerable portion of his 1873 message to excoriating the sharecropping system, which was so "retrogressive" yet so widespread throughout the South. Likening it to "Italian peasantry," Moses urged the state legislature to eliminate the existing system and introduce instead the English model in which farm laborers were tenants paying a fixed annual rent to their landlords rather than giving them a share of the crop. Although Moses made some recommendations about how a tenant might be protected against his landlord and his supply merchant, both of whom were battening on his crop through the crop lien laws, nothing was done to implement this suggestion. Meanwhile, under Chamberlain, sympathy for the laborer would decline even farther.[43]

In Mississippi, a year later, Adelbert Ames told the legislature that the system of credit and dependence that was so ruinous to agriculture had to be abandoned. He recommended the adoption instead of "the system whereby [farmers] raise what they consume." Moreover, he added, "Large plantation planting . . . is hostile to the spirit of a free people," and, in words reminiscent of Moses, he said that such a system was similar to "monarchical countries where [cultivation] was done by a dependent peasantry." In contrast to the response in South Carolina, the Mississippi legislature came to the aid of its constituents. It enacted a stay law and a bill repealing the crop lien legislation, but Ames then backed off. Fearful of the turmoil likely to ensue from repeal and unwilling to stay the payment of debts, he vetoed both bills, and thus abandoned the fruitful initiative he himself had introduced.[44] Once again, the possibility of the Republicans embarking upon an independent course by redefining the issues and thus regaining the electoral initiative was dashed. Instead, they would compete with their opponents over financial retrenchment, a contest they could not win without yielding the core of the party's policies and support.

7. The Forked Road to Redemption, 1873–1876

The truth is, you may adopt as many color-line platforms as you please, but as soon as you put your candidates in the field, the first thing they will do will be to go for the colored voters.
—Jackson *Weekly Clarion*, 10 December 1874

The spirit of our people is roused to the highest pitch that will ad-mit of control—the negroes sink down before it as if stricken with awe—and the white men who have been using the negroes show by their conduct that they feel that "Othello's occupation is gone."
—Walter L. Bragg, Democratic party chairman, to
   E. H. Moren, Montgomery, 15 August 1874

The election of 1872 was a major setback for the Democratic-Conservatives. It seemed that the Republicans were proving far less easy to dislodge than many had thought and that, as a result, the return of their own party to power was far from inevitable, but behind the election returns, grim though they were, there lurked an even more significant and disturbing reality. The Democratic-Conservatives had reached a political dead end. Their endorsement of Greeley and their fusion with the Liberal-Republicans at the state level had been the culmination of the New Departure strategy that they had pursued for the four years since 1868. Yet it had failed mis-erably, leaving the party in a state of crisis. Its entire approach to electoral politics in the reconstructed South had now to be reassessed, and, perhaps, an alternative strategy found to replace it.

To many in the party, however, the potential for its revitalization had already become apparent. During the 1872 campaign, they had observed that the party's problem was not that it was failing to gain new adherents and broader support but simply that it was not capitalizing on the electoral assets it already possessed. Vast numbers of its supporters were just not being mobilized but, instead, were withdrawing and refusing to vote. This was widely remarked upon, as we saw at the end of chapter 5. Yet the antidote was obvious. If the leadership could stimulate the interest of these apathetic voters and organize them to get out and vote, the party's chances of success would be increased considerably. As the party chairman in Arkansas perceived in the 1873 campaign, "A closer and more thorough organization of the party" might make the difference.[1]

As the Democratic-Conservatives became increasingly aware of the latent internal strength of their party and thus of how little they needed to depend on attracting additional support from outside their own ranks, there soon emerged a more drastic and clear-cut version of this idea of partisan self-reliance. It was not a new formulation because, during the past four years, there had been a sizable contingent advocating it within each state. In the crisis confronting the party after the debacle of 1872, the strategy and its proponents began to grow in influence. This approach to electoral politics, which was earlier identified with the Bourbon wing of the party, was the exact antithesis of the New Departure. In contrast with the New Departure's emphasis on expanding the party's base through direct appeal to black voters or through fusion with dissident Republican factions, the alternative formula demanded that the party forego coalition and campaign with a separate and exclusive organization. Paralleling this change of direction towards organizing their party on what was called the "straight-out" basis, the Democratic-Conservatives were also to cease downplaying the differences between themselves and their opponents. Instead, they were to accentuate the contrasts and distinctions. This dramatic reorientation of the party's priorities and direction was to be given specificity, first, by throwing out its current mongrel sobriquet of Democratic-Conservative and unashamedly adopting instead the designation of Democratic. The second change was that the difference between the parties was to be defined by race, a distinction that was unmistakable and not open to challenge. In effect, the color line was to be politicized.

Adoption of the thoroughgoing straight-out, white-line formula was not necessary in a closely contested state like Texas. In the very next year, 1873, the Democratic-Conservatives gained control there simply by means of better electoral organization and closer attention to the party's loyal rank and file. But in the states of the lower South—Alabama, Louisiana, Mississippi, and South Carolina—where the party was confronted by an entrenched opposition, sustained by a majority or near-majority of dependable black voters, the alternative formula could be successful only if it were pursued with as much vigor and ruthlessness as possible. Even then, however, victory was far from certain because campaigns based on race were, on the face of it, unlikely to benefit the party identified with the white minority. In fact, many argued that the politicization of race would be suicidal for the Democratic-Conservatives in the black states. As the Charleston *Daily News* warned early in 1873, "Any policy which contemplates the arraying of whites against blacks at the polls, must fail, and will deserve to fail. Fortunately, there is little likelihood that so wild a project will be seriously submitted to the public."[2] Nonetheless, despite these predictions of disaster from a straight-out, white-line strategy, pressure was building throughout the Deep South for a complete reversal of the party's electoral priorities. As a result, there occurred within what was by the mid-1870s the stronghold of Republicanism, a decisive confrontation over the course the Democratic-Conservatives should pursue, and, naturally, this struggle also involved a contest for dominance within the party.

Faced with the challenge to their ascendancy, the New Departurists dug in and refused to yield. On grounds of both expediency and principle their position seemed unassailable. They argued that, as a practical matter, it was unlikely that a party which had for years been unable to win power with the help of support from outside its ranks could now expect to succeed on its own. More important still, a policy based on partisan and racial exclusiveness was in itself thoroughly undesirable. What the New Departurists feared most of all was a division of the parties along racial lines and the setting of whites against blacks in a contest for political dominance. It had been for the very purpose of precluding such an outcome that they had, in the first place, embraced the biracial and accommodationist approach that the New Departure had embodied. The function of political parties in the South, they argued, was to mask and temper the existing racial cleavage within the society. Therefore, if the Democratic-Conservatives adopted race as the key symbol of party differentiation, they would be confirming this perilous division and thereby inflicting on their state and region a dangerously turbulent politics that they would live to regret.

In the postemancipation South, this racial distinction almost certainly would be further compounded by a division on the basis of wealth and class, and New Departurists constantly warned of the fearful dangers it involved. Albert G. Brown, who was Mississippi's leading opponent of the white-liners, was troubled because "the capital of the state is mainly on one side of a political line and the labor on the other." Rather than accepting this as reality, Brown and the New Departurists denounced it as something "abnormal [that] must not be allowed to continue."[3] At the same time, James Chesnut, Brown's equivalent in South Carolina, was expressing concern that the "no property and no taxes" element was in one party aligned against the taxpaying property owners in the other.[4] The situation was extremely dangerous, they believed, and, now more than ever before, it required the antidote that the New Departure had always offered.

The foolishness of adopting a white-line policy in a situation that was so precarious was heightened, so the New Departurists judged, by the risk of committing the party to an overt and close identification with the national Democratic party. In view of its utter rout in the 1872 elections, the cultivation of ties with the Democratic party was hardly the essence of political wisdom. In addition to the weakness of the Democrats nationally, there was also the consideration that, during the year or so since the Greeley upset, the nation's politics had become extremely fluid and uncertain. There was a growing sense that the parties were about to undergo a significant rearrangement. By 1874, this perception was becoming widespread. In June, the New York *Tribune* was commenting, "Party lines no longer certify anything but past prejudices," and, a few months earlier, the New York *Herald* had been convinced that "disintegration . . . appears to be inevitable," even for the Republican party since it had "no fixed policy—no principles of policy."[5] New issues had to appear soon, it was believed, in order to breathe life into the political system. But, in the meantime, the *Arkansas Gazette* concluded, "The condition of all parties is now exceptional—they float upon uncertain waters . . . the disposition is and ought to be, rather to avoid trouble than to propagate opinions," and besides, the *Gazette* added, "In the past, national politics have occupied too great a share of [the South's] attention."[6]

Nevertheless, electoral trends during 1873 and 1874 did seem to reveal a discernible shift against the Republicans which the party's southern opponents could not but take seriously. After scandal rocked the Grant administration during 1873 and the panic of that fall produced widespread economic distress, the reverses suffered by the Republicans in the eighteen state elections held during the twelve months since the canvass of 1872 were being considered by many political observers as nothing short of remarkable; some even went so far as to believe it the most dramatic electoral shift in the country's political history.[7] All the same, the leading New Departure organ in South Carolina quickly warned that this was "a victory for the anti-administration party, not the Democracy pure and undefiled."[8] A year later, when the Democrats captured the United States House of Representatives, Alexander Horn, a prominent straight-out editor in Mississippi, hailed it as conclusive evidence that "the Democratic party of the whole country is coming to our relief and we must be in strict alignment with it."[9] Once again, the New Departure faction warned against jumping to conclusions concerning the strength of the national Democratic party that they were so eager to embrace. "The victories of last fall were not strictly Democratic victories," observed L. Q. C. Lamar, a leader of the Mississippi fusionists. "They were anti-administration victories."[10] By discounting the significance of the political shift away from the Republicans, the New Departurists were attempting two simultaneous maneuvers. In the first place, they were trying to undercut their intraparty rivals by refuting claims that an identification with the Democrats through the adoption of straight-outism on the state level was politically wise and necessary. Their second purpose derived more from principle than expediency. From the outset, the New Departurists had based their strategy on the premise that a policy of accommodation would appease and relax northern opinion. Therefore, if sentiment outside the South was now moving in the Democratic-Conservatives' direction as, despite their own disclaimers, it seemed to be, this development was a vindication of the effectiveness of conciliation, not proof that it should be abandoned. However, if a politics of race and extremism were embraced in the South, it might provoke federal intervention, and it would undoubtedly, as the Jackson *Clarion* warned, "check the rising sentiment in our favor at the North."[11]

Thus, armed with a quite different stance on the function of race and party in southern politics, the New Departure faction confronted its rivals in the struggle for party control in the Deep South. For the first year or so after the setback in 1872, the competing forces jostled for the advantage. There were a number of developments within the Democratic-Conservative party during 1873, but their contribution to the party's eventual decision about which approach it would pursue was often unclear. One of the first of these developments was the initiative taken in Louisiana during that summer.[12] Called the Unification Movement and launched in New Orleans under the auspices of P. G. T. Beauregard, the well-known Confederate general, its prime movers were Isaac N. Marks, an influential New Orleans businessman, and Louis Roudanez, a prominent black physician and founder of the New Orleans *Tribune*. They headed a Committee of One Hundred that was both bipartisan and interracial, consisting mainly of business and civic leaders who wanted to provide a political vehicle for harmonizing the races, displacing the existing parties, and reviving the economic prosperity of their city and state. In origin, the movement was a revitalization of the Reform party that had emerged in 1872 and later coalesced with the Liberal-Republicans. Its immediate aim was, as Beauregard described it in private, "Our carpetbaggers must be routed (bag and baggage) out of the state, or we shall be ruined."[13] To accomplish this, blacks were to be promised the "equal and impartial" enjoyment of civil and political rights; equal treatment in public accommodations; and even ownership of land through the creation of "small farms." But these concessions were far too propitiatory for most Democratic-Conservatives to tolerate. With the exception of the Jackson *Clarion*, the verdict from every quarter was a resounding rejection of the scheme. Even Francis Dawson's

Charleston *News and Courier* lambasted it, pronouncing "the Beauregard miscegenation movement . . . dead as a door nail."[14]

Far more gratifying, however, was the success of the New Departure strategy in Mississippi that same summer. There, the advocates of fusion turned back a bid to have the party nominate its own slate and run a separate campaign. By a vote of 101 to 45, the state convention decided to "disband" the party in the 1873 election.[15] As Hiram Cassedy, Sr., an influential New Departurist and prewar Democrat, stated the case, "Defeat [was] certain" if the party were to organize separately. Cassedy explained, "Old issues have become extinct, and party names have lost their prestige, the Democratic name serves no other purpose now than to arouse fears, North and South, by which alone the Republican party are enabled to keep up their organization."[16] Nevertheless, the New Departurists' victory in shaping the party's electoral strategy was not paralleled by the results of the election itself. Despite the influence of the head of the ticket, Senator James L. Alcorn, the party's coalition with the bolting Republicans went down to defeat.

There were two other state elections in 1873. In Texas, the Democratic-Conservatives overthrew the Republican administration of Edmund J. Davis, but, in terms of the emerging debate over party strategy, the meaning of this achievement was far from clear, since neither fusion nor an assertive white line approach had been adopted.[17] The same could not, however, be said of the party's campaign in Virginia. In that state, James L. Kemper, a well-known Democrat, ran on a straight-out ticket. Promising "Virginia for the Virginians" and forcing a break from the coalition with Centrist Republicans led by Gilbert C. Walker which had brought the party to power in 1869, the Kemper forces drew an indelible line between themselves and their Republican opponents. The strategy they adopted was explained by Nathaniel B. Meade, a leading Kemper activist. "To save the state," he revealed, "we must make the issue *White and Black* race against race and the canvass red hot—the position must be made so odious that no decent white man can support the radical ticket and look a gentleman in the face."[18] The color line maneuver succeeded. Nevertheless, even though the unthinkable had been broached, the white-liners could not really claim Virginia as evidence that their policy would work elsewhere.

In Virginia, the Democratic-Conservatives were already in power and therefore did not have to overthrow an entrenched Republican administration, backed by an electoral majority that was overwhelmingly black.

Nevertheless, during the course of the following year, 1874, the outcome of the contest within the Democratic-Conservative party became clearer, for in two states, Alabama and Louisiana, the white-liners achieved ascendancy, leaving just Mississippi and South Carolina still contested. Alabama was the first state to defeat the Republicans with the politics of the color line. Interestingly, however, there was no need, at the same time, to reject fusion and adopt the straight-out formula because Alabama's Democratic-Conservatives had never previously employed fusion in statewide campaigns. When they had won in 1870, they had operated as a separate and distinct organization, just like North Carolina and Georgia that same year. Nevertheless, even though they had rejected fusion, the Alabamians had endorsed the politics of the New Departure and had campaigned actively for black votes. Three years later, in 1873, those who had earlier advised against even the New Departure began to demand that the party renounce that policy as well. Led by John Forsyth, the prewar Douglas Democrat and earlier a leading opponent of the New Departure, a campaign was mounted, beginning in the summer of 1873, to convince the party leadership that Alabama could be won if all attempts to woo blacks and reassure white Republicans were abandoned. Instead, a vigorous appeal was to be made to the white voters of southern Alabama where Forsyth himself was based and, more importantly, to the same element in north Alabama whose apathy in 1872 was thought to have been pivotal in allowing the state to return to Republican control.

Although Forsyth had for long been confident that a campaign based on race was capable of arousing the apathetic and thus ensuring victory, others were not so enthusiastic. A powerful opposition arose which was concentrated in the Black Belt. The entire press of the area opposed the color line and one of these newspaper editors, Robert McKee of the Selma *Times and Argus*, was the chief spokesman and organizer. What they objected to was perhaps expressed most forcefully by Ben L. Herr of the Livingston *Journal*. He complained to McKee in August 1873 that "the aim of certain parties is to *coerce* acquiescence in what they may dictate. West Ala. is vitally interested and I am desirous of conferring with reference to her interests. A *race* alignment will involve serious consequences to the 'black' counties, and I trust they will not decide upon a line of action without counting the cost."[19] Besides losing the state through a course "being forced on us by men not reknowned for statesmanship," Herr feared that a white-line campaign would absolutely guarantee that the black counties would go to the Republicans and their local governments would certainly be remanded to Republican control. So objectionable was this prospect that, as late as June 1874, the Demopolis *News* was urging the Black Belt counties to secede from the party if it adopted the white-line.[20]

While much of the Black Belt opposition simply objected to race as the campaign issue, the group around McKee proposed a positive alternative instead. They wanted the contest with the Republicans to be based on an issue of substance and principle rather than the opportunistic and emotional rallying cry of race. As old-line Democrats who wanted the hybrid Democratic-Conservative organization with which they were currently affiliated to return to sound Democratic doctrine, renunciation of the public debt and of the state aid program that had been responsible for creating most of it was thought to be a far better issue. In Charles C. Langdon's view, the debt, not race, was "the great question of the day."[21] Unlike everywhere else in the Deep South, black-belt opponents of the white-line in Alabama could not propose as a substitute the continuation of the party's fusion policies because they had never taken root. Instead, Bourbon Democrats, like McKee, Langdon, Burwell B. Lewis, and Rufus K. Boyd, seized the opportunity to push the party towards embracing those enduring Democratic doctrines of minimal government and laissez-faire. As Boyd told McKee, "You do not now see and read so often the sneering allusions to Bourbonism, etc. The tide is changing and we may well hope [for] success in the immediate future upon the basis of Democratic principles as understood in the olden time modified somewhat by the changed condition of the country."[22] If this path were taken, then not only would the parties' distinctiveness become more apparent but so too would the differences among the Democratic-Conservatives themselves, and the Bourbons very much wanted to dramatize this cleavage.

Also objectionable to the McKee forces was the attempt by the white-liners headed by Forsyth and Walter Bragg, the party chairman, to place George S. Houston at the head of the ticket in 1874. A prewar congressman from north Alabama who had opposed secession, Houston was thought to be the ideal candidate to deliver the crucial, Unionist-inclined northern counties. Yet, to the McKee forces, he was anathema. It was not just that he was old and uninspiring when the party needed "some live strong man who has made his record during & since the war" to get out the vote, but, far more important, as Langdon insisted, Houston "is not with us on the bond question."[23] As a result, a fierce anti-Houston protest arose which was to continue up until the party's state convention assembled. Ultimately, however, the campaign for Houston and white supremacy triumphed. Partly, this was because its proponents conducted a well-organized preconvention strategy, but it was also attributable to the shortcomings of the debt issue. It was, first of all, less compelling and electrifying than race, but, in addition, once the specifics were broached, a wide range of divergence soon became apparent, even among its proponents. Questions about what parts of the debt were to be regarded as illegitimate and how much of it should be repudiated gave rise to unresolvable dispute. Nevertheless, the antidebt sentiment was so powerful that the convention inserted a plank in the party platform pledging drastic reduction.[24] Despite this concession, however, the white-liners controlled the party in 1874, and their victory was facilitated by their not having to challenge an entrenched fusionist element or to create a party organization *de novo* since straight-outism was already party practice in Alabama. The issue, therefore, was merely whether the New Departure was an effective platform and, if not, whether race was the best alternative. All the same, it still precipitated a vigorous contest for hegemony.

Although its outcome was similar, the sequence of events in Louisiana was quite different. The triumph there of straight-out white supremacy was surprising because there had been a powerful fusionist element among the Democratic-Conservatives in Louisiana which had forged an alliance with Governor Henry C. Warmoth's bolting Republicans in 1872. In addition, the Unification Movement of 1873 had promised a continuance, and perhaps expansion, of this approach. Behind these auspicious signs, there was, however, a deeper political reality, for the party was in the process of detaching itself from fusion. Rather than indicating that the New Departure was flourishing, the appearance of the Reform party in 1872 and of the Beauregard initiative the following year, both of which had originated outside the Democratic-Conservative organization, were evidence that the party had rejected it. The party's attention in the year or so after 1872 was not so much on deciding its electoral strategy at the state level as on discovering how the victory, which it claimed the Democratic-Fusion ticket headed by John McEnery had won in 1872, could be secured in the face of the objections and intervention of the federal government. By the end of 1873, when negotiation and remonstrance had failed to resolve the contested election in the party's favor, forces outside politics, increasingly impatient at the ineffectualness of this approach, began to mobilize on their own to overthrow the "Kellogg usurpation."[25]

During the spring and summer of 1874, the White League was organized throughout most of Louisiana's parishes. By means of public pressure and physical intimidation, it was to sap Republican morale in the local outposts of Governor William P. Kellogg's administration and force Republican officials to resign in Natchitoches, Avoyelles, Iberia, St. Martin, and many other parishes.[26] This undermining of the Kellogg government was climaxed by two military confrontations in September 1874, at Coushatta in Red River Parish and at Liberty Place in New Orleans.[27] So powerful had the league become that, during the summer, it threatened to take Democratic-Conservative politics into its own hands by preventing the party from holding its convention. To avert this disaster, the convention was moved from Alexandria, in the league's heartland, to Baton Rouge. This maneuver prompted E. John Ellis, a leader of the party in New Orleans and a high-ranking officer of the league, to comment knowingly, "I now feel the State is safe and that all opposition to the Democratic convention will be at once withdrawn."[28]

With the league able to undermine the Republicans' grip on power, a hold that was only secured by the federal government's imposition of the Wheeler Adjustment in late 1874 guaranteeing Kellogg's tenure, the Democratic-Conservatives' concern thereafter was to make sure that the paramilitary organization was held in check and that no occasion was offered for more extensive federal intervention. Unless that were done, the chances of defeating the

Republicans at the next state election in 1876 would be slim. Accordingly, the party in Louisiana, unlike everywhere else, was preoccupied not with the problem of how to arouse its constituents but rather with how best to restrain them. There was no need to debate whether to adopt a white-line strategy; that had already been decided by the actions of the White League. Instead, the party leadership had to devise a means to win the 1876 election without giving cause for federal interference and thereby firmly securing the redemption of the state which had been all but accomplished in 1874. To this end, they counselled their supporters to be patient and they developed a platform and ticket in the 1876 campaign which was unexceptionable, both to the federal government and to the party's accommodationist New Departure wing.[29] Thus, the platform was conciliatory, with its endorsement of black suffrage and public education as well as its vague commitment to retrenchment and reform. Furthermore, the head of the ticket was Francis T. Nicholls, a planter from Ascension Parish, with "well-known moderate views upon the issues of the day."[30] Nicholls had the additional asset of being a political neophyte, of whom it was said, "Neither Bourbon, nor Liberal, nor Reformer, nor Last Ditcher, nor White Leaguer can claim him as of their faction."[31] Rather than becoming more extreme and strident as the crucial election approached, the party leaders in Louisiana were proceeding in the reverse direction.

Before examining the vigorous fight put up by the New Departurists in Mississippi and South Carolina, another development in 1874 which was launched under the guiding assumptions of the New Departure needs to be introduced. This took place at the national level and it envisaged the possibility that relief might be obtained from that quarter, not by the return of the Democrats to power or by a major change in northern opinion, but by a split in the ranks of the Republicans. Ever since the end of the war, southerners had looked for a Republican schism at the national level to provide a way of escape from either the threat of Reconstruction or its actuality. The first occasion when this fatal split had been thought likely was during President Andrew Johnson's struggle with the Republican majority in Congress. Then, in 1872, great hopes had been placed on Horace Greeley. Even Ulysses Grant had had his backers, for, in 1869, as he commenced his presidency, Alexander Stephens, the former Confederate vice-president, and Augustus Garland of Arkansas had envisaged a scenario in which Grant, whose Republicanism was after all of very recent origin, might be the precipitator of a breakup within his party.[32] Now, at the beginning of 1874, Grant was once again, and more seriously this time, thought of as a possible ally and even savior. In the aftermath of his party's sobering electoral reverses in the previous fall, attributable partly to the deepening economic crisis and partly to the manner in which the government was being managed under Grant, it was thought likely that the president would be reassessing his political options. This likelihood was fueled by well-founded speculation that the president was considering a third term and was looking for sources of support outside the Republican party to promote it.[33] A speech by General Grant in late January seemed to confirm this rumor, for he announced on that occasion: "I begin to think it is time for the Republican party to unload. There has been too much dead weight carried by it." Furthermore, referring to the political and civil turmoil in Louisiana where his own southern policy had been at its most active and involved, Grant complained that "this nursing of monstrosities has nearly exhausted the life of the party. . . . I am done with them, and they will have to take care of themselves."[34] A Republican breakup, with a party realignment possibly resulting, seemed in the air, and the Democratic-Conservatives could only benefit.

Whatever President Grant's exact intentions and calculations were about how he might secure a third term, he nevertheless began immediately to seek support in the South. In fact, without a significant personal following there, another run for the presidency was probably impossible. If that support could not be obtained from the Republican party, and his "nursing of monstrosities" comment suggested that that was improbable, then he would have to approach the Democratic-Conservatives instead. This was in fact the course he was to pursue and, in doing so, he anticipated, by over two and a half years, Rutherford B. Hayes's overtures towards the South.

Offers of support from the Democratic-Conservatives were even in evidence before the president's "unload" speech, and they must have reassured him because they came from well-known southern politicians. The earliest and most active among them were Alexander Stephens and John S. Mosby, both of whom seemed, at first

sight, to be unlikely sources of aid since they had in the past opposed the New Departure and conciliation; but that actually caused
them to be more inclined to look outside their party for political allies. Their opposition to the New Departure and thus to Greeley as
well had put them at odds with the leadership of their own party.[35]
As a result, they had been excluded from influence and denied patronage. Furthermore, there was little chance that their fortunes
would improve in the foreseeable future because the Democratic-
Conservatives were already in power in their home states of Georgia
and Virginia where they had won control without having to rely on
the advice and votes of the anti-New Departure faction. Thus, overlooked and without leverage, the party's Bourbon wing in these
two states began to look elsewhere for ways of reviving their political prospects. In each case, this meant putting out feelers to Republicans, at both the local and national levels.

Beginning in their own districts, Mosby and Stephens cultivated
relations with the local Republicans who themselves were also out
of power and looking for outside support. Through these arrangements, they both managed to obtain a considerable share of the local federal patronage, while Stephens even negotiated a bipartisan
deal through which he was elected to Congress in 1873.[36] But there
was a far more grandiose scheme arising out of these local maneuverings. It emerged during the first week in January 1874, just before Grant's "unload" speech. The inaugural address of Governor
James C. Kemper of Virginia was the precipitant. In this speech,
Kemper noted that political parties seemed to be "in process of
transition and transformation." Because of this fluidity, Kemper
suggested that his own state of Virginia, which had been governed
since 1869 by a coalition of Republicans and Conservatives and
therefore was "not identified with any national party," was available
to support a national Republican administration if it performed
properly.[37] This was soon followed by a speech in the House from
Stephens, in which, after denouncing the pending Civil Rights bill,
he hailed Kemper's speech as heralding "the dawn of [a] new ep-
och," a time when "the elements of present party organizations"
would realign themselves. Stephens also detected in the inaugural
ideas about the nature of government—he referred to them as
"Jeffersonian principles"—which he was convinced were returning

to favor and would constitute the foundation of the victorious new party he envisaged.[38]

Grant may not have imagined himself as the high priest of Jeffersonianism, but he did perceive the political advantage he could derive from these developments in the redeemed states of Virginia and Georgia. They provided the basis upon which his southern following could be erected. To build on this beginning, he proceeded, during 1874, to wield his patronage power to appoint to federal office representatives of the kind of political groups that would be available for such a coalition. Mainly, they would be Democratic-Conservatives who were out of favor with their own party— Bourbons like Stephens and Mosby—or they would be Liberal-Republicans who were at the margins of their party or else unattached. In either case, they were politicians without firm party ties. So, in Georgia, General Lafayette McLaws, a political and personal friend of Stephens, was appointed collector of internal revenue in Savannah.[39] Federal offices in Mississippi went to Alcorn Republicans such as G. Wiley Wells and Captain J. H. Lake.[40] In South Carolina, bolters in 1872 like Frederick Sawyer received patronage, and in Texas, Elisha Pease, the former governor and Centrist Republican, was offered the customs collectorship at Galveston.[41] Along with his use of the patronage, Grant employed his executive authority to indicate how transient and limited was his commitment to the maintenance of the Republican governments in the South. His unwillingness to sustain Governor Davis in Texas in December 1873 was repeated six months later in Arkansas when, in a significant and well-publicized move, Grant supported Baxter and his allies over Brooks in the gubernatorial dispute known as the Brooks-Baxter war.[42] In addition, during July, he gave an interview to Senator Thomas Robertson of South Carolina in which he announced that, in the senator's state, "he would infinitely rather see the State Government pass into the hands of the Democratic party than to see it continued in the hands of the corrupt crew who have brought things to the present pass."[43] The emergence of what many believed were Grant's real feelings about Reconstruction provided Governor Ames of Mississippi with the explanation for Grant's refusal to supply troops: "He wants the support of the southern democrats for a third term."[44] Indeed, this general pattern was so evident

by the summer of 1874 that few doubted Grant's ambitions for a
third term or his awareness of the importance of a southern base to
the realization of this goal.

This conciliatory shift in the president's policy towards the South
during 1874 was widely applauded by Democratic-Conservatives,
but that did not, by any means, imply that they were enlisted in his
third-term campaign. In fact, the formation of a southern party for
Grant's reelection turned out to be just a mirage. However feasible
it may have looked on paper, the ingredients for actually developing
a powerful southern bloc were just not available. Those elements
that did gravitate towards it were marginal to both parties. In fact,
it was their powerlessness that induced them to seek affiliation with
Grant in the first place. Furthermore, the components of this
grouping were politically incompatible. On the one hand, there
were Bourbons like Stephens and Robert Toombs who, on the extreme wing of their party, were state rights Jeffersonians opposed to
the New Departure, and on the other were the Liberal-Republicans
and the nonpartisan reformers like Elisha Baxter who were New
Departurists and men of the political center. It was a ramshackle
coalition, more a collection of diverse individuals seeking personal
advantage from association with Grant than a viable and coherent
political force. Having little in common but the political marginality of its components, including Grant himself by late 1874,
the collapse of the third-term scheme was inescapable.[45]

By the time Grant's third-term initiative had disintegrated, the
forces of fusion and the New Departure had been beaten back in
both Alabama and Louisiana. The fight was, however, by no means
over in Mississippi and South Carolina, where the opponents of the
white-liners were so tenacious that they were able to present a clear-
cut and well-organized alternative. Their stance in these states was
less vulnerable because it was advocated and promoted by a group
of politicians who wielded considerable influence within the party.
Furthermore, fusion had been implemented in every state election
since 1868 and thus was a well-established strategy. As the confrontation with the straight-outs grew in intensity, the advocates of
fusion in South Carolina and Mississippi were able to consolidate
their forces and entrench their position. The basis of their support
was to be found in the black counties of both states. There, the
practice of biracial and fusion politics had been essential to the sur-

vival of the party locally, while, conversely, statewide adoption of an electoral strategy based on racial exclusiveness would be disastrous. In South Carolina, the center of cooperationism, as fusion was called there, was located in the tidewater, especially Charleston and adjacent districts. At the head of this wing of the party were James Chesnut, James Kershaw, John L. Manning, James Connor, and not least, Francis W. Dawson, the English-born editor of the Charleston *News and Courier*, who was the faction's spokesman and leading wire-puller. Further evidence about the source of cooperationist support was offered by Dawson himself, for, on one occasion, he wrote, "The up-country . . . must face the unpleasant truth, which is that, as long as radicalism preponderates in South Carolina, the middle and low country will rule the state. No combination among the white counties can prevent it."[46] He remarked at another time how important a fusion policy was to Charleston because "straight-outism, with its threat and bluster, with its possible disturbances and certain turmoil, is the foe of mercantile security and commercial prosperity" and also, he might have added, of good labor relations on the plantations of the tidewater.[47]

The fusionists' counterparts in Mississippi also derived their essential support from the Black Belt, particularly the western delta counties.[48] They also had considerable strength in Hinds County where the "Jackson clique," headed by Ethelbert Barksdale and Albert G. Brown, was located. Associated with this group were John W. C. Watson, Amos Johnston, L. Q. C. Lamar, former Governor Charles Clark, and Robert Lowry, a future governor. These men had been the guiding force behind the party since at least the fusion campaign of Louis Dent in 1869 and their sway was being contested by a white-line faction whose most prominent and vociferous leaders were, for the most part, newspaper editors, such as William McCardle of Vicksburg, Arthur J. Frantz of Brandon, C. L. Worthington of Columbus, and Alexander Horn of Meridian. Former Governors William L. Sharkey and Benjamin G. Humphreys were the leading politicians involved. Although the white-liners developed some support in the black counties, such as those containing Vicksburg and Meridian, their mainstay was in the northeastern and southern sections that were predominantly white.

Unlike their equivalents in Alabama and Louisiana, the fusionists in Mississippi and South Carolina were more firmly established within the party, and they were even able to develop a separate organizational apparatus with which they could wage their contest with the white-liners. This was the Taxpayers' Union, an institution that had appeared earlier in Reconstruction—in Texas and South Carolina during 1871 to be precise—but which, in the hands of the fusionists of 1874 and 1875, became the centerpiece of their effort to outflank the straight-outs.[49] Through the Taxpayers' Union, they could harness the widespread discontent with the burden of taxation and thereby broaden and strengthen the base of their appeal. In the first place, the union provided the organizational structure that had been so lacking under the New Departure that the Democratic-Conservatives had never run an independent statewide campaign. This intent was made evident by the remarks of James B. Kershaw, a leading South Carolina fusionist, who explained that "[James] Chesnut and his committee, at the first, expected that our tax union would be the Conservative machinery for political action."[50]

The Taxpayers' Union scheme offered two other benefits to the fusionists. Because aggrieved taxpayers were overwhelmingly white, the tax issue would appeal to white voters through their pocketbooks rather than on the grounds of race. Thus, the fusionists could hope to cut into the white support that the white-liners were trying to win over through the newly formed rifle clubs and White Leagues. Moreover, because taxation was a nonpartisan issue, discontented Republicans could be expected to join and, indeed, the taxpayers' protest in Mississippi was graced by such eminent Republicans as Henry Musgrove and Joshua Morris who had been state auditor and attorney-general respectively under Alcorn and Powers.[51] A final advantage provided by the Taxpayers' Union was that it enabled the fusionists to present themselves as men who were above party, reformers interested in good government rather than mere partisans seeking political gain. As Francis Dawson saw it, "The necessity of checking corruption and procuring honest officials is paramount to all questions of party politics or affiliation."[52] Consequently, "The only party needed in this state is the taxpayers' party, arrayed in solid opposition to the horde of non-taxpayers."[53] This kind of approach also accorded with the New Departurists' distaste for rigid partisanship and their fear about its impact on their state's political life. Indeed, they often hoped that party might be eliminated, a sentiment proclaimed publicly by the South Carolina Taxpayers' Convention of 1874 when it predicted that the movement would ultimately "sweep away party lines and destroy the trade of hungry political adventurers."[54] In their critique of party, the southern fusionists were expressing attitudes similar to the liberal reformers and mugwumps of the 1870s and 1880s in the North.[55]

The Taxpayers' Unions were therefore to operate both as a nonpartisan pressure group demanding retrenchment and reduced taxation from the incumbent Republicans and as the organizational structure for the fusionists' campaign to keep their party from falling into the hands of the white-liners. Despite the sophistication of the fusionists' approach, it nevertheless went down to defeat. As in the Republican party, the center collapsed, eliminating the possibility that a competitive two-party system might develop which was unhampered by racial exclusiveness and partisan rigidity. For, while the fusionists were holding taxpayers' conventions and encouraging the reform Republicans, even negotiating with them, their intraparty opponents were organizing with immense success at the grass-roots and demonstrating how effective race was in arousing whites who were their party's essential constituency. This was particularly true in Mississippi where the white-liners' success in getting control of Warren County, with its black majority, in 1874 enabled them to seize the initiative and even go so far as to usurp the jurisdiction of the party's executive committee and call a state convention for January 1875.[56] Thrown on the defensive, the fusionists tried to repulse this frontal attack by arguing that there was no need for a state convention in a year when there were no statewide elections. To outflank the white-liners, a committee of the party's legislators called a meeting in May to discuss the propriety of a state convention and, when it met, managed to defeat proposals to make race the issue of the canvass and to change the party's name to just Democratic.[57] Nevertheless, with the defeat of Ames's efforts at retrenchment during the legislative session, the fusionists' strategy of reform and realignment was dealt a fatal blow. By August, the fusionist-controlled state executive committee had to capitulate and summon a convention, which their opponents would almost certainly control.

Although they failed to prevent a convention, the fusionists

fought hard to restrain the white-liners once it met. They made
sure that the platform was conciliatory, especially on suffrage, education, and civil rights, and they prevented the party from adopting
the white-line as a mandatory statewide policy. Indeed, one of their
most prominent leaders, Congressman L. Q. C. Lamar, claimed
immediately afterwards that he had "just emerged from a struggle
to keep our people from a race conflict," which would have resulted
in "conflicts and race passions and collisions with the Federal
power."[58] But these remarks were either disingenuous or else an ex-
aggeration of the fusionist influence. More accurate was Adelbert
Ames's analysis, "The true sentiment of the assembly was 'color
line' though the platform said nothing about it. The understanding
evidently is that each locality can act as it chooses. But the state
convention shall put out a platform for Northern consumption."[59]
Or, as the Republican Jackson *Pilot* described it most succinctly,
"While the platform is peace, the canvass will be war."[60]

The denouement of the fusionist endeavor in South Carolina followed a similar pattern. Nevertheless, until mid-December 1875,
the collaboration between the cooperationists and Chamberlain was
proceeding sufficiently smoothly that the straight-outs were kept at
bay. Then, on 15 December, "Black Thursday" as it was to be
called, the Republican leadership in the assembly deliberately
broke with Chamberlain. The breach was made through the rejection of Chamberlain's nominees for trial justice and the selection instead of the notorious former governor, Frank Moses, and the
equally controversial William Whipper.[61]

Lamenting this "horrible disaster," Chamberlain predicted that
the straight-outs would seize on the event as conclusive evidence
that the Republican party was unreliable as an ally and incapable of
reform.[62] Dawson, too, was distressed: "Year after year we have argued and fought to prevent such an issue as this. We still hope and
pray that extreme measures may not be necessary."[63] To this end,
the cooperationists focused on reorganizing and tightening the
party's electoral machinery, while stopping short of making separate nominations. This goal was accomplished at the first state convention in May when it adjourned with a course of action mapped
out but with no ticket selected. The second tactic was to delay the
nominating convention until after the Republicans had held theirs
and, with luck, had chosen Chamberlain. The Republican could

then be presented as a ready-made moderate nominee whose endorsement by the Democratic-Conservatives would salvage fusion and cooperation.[64]

The straight-outs, however, captured the new state executive committee, thus enabling its incoming chairman, Alexander C. Haskell, who was an exponent of the white-line strategy of M. C. Butler and Martin Gary, to call a convention. To compound his success, Haskell had it meet on 15 August before the Republican convention and in Columbia, which was located in the Piedmont where the straight-outs were strong, rather than in Charleston. Furthermore, a delegate count by the *News and Courier* indicated that 89 out of 158 favored straight-out Democratic nominations.[65] But the cooperationists were still not daunted, and they hoped to force an adjournment without nominations. When that failed, however, they tried to defeat the straight-outs' gubernatorial choice, Wade Hampton, whom many regarded as insufficiently cautious and responsible. So vigorous was their opposition that the convention was compelled to meet in secret session and to forego a secret ballot to select him.[66] Even then, the fusionists' resistance was not over, for, as in Mississippi, they required that the party's platform be conciliatory in tone and uphold the civil rights and suffrage protections introduced by Reconstruction.

All the same, these concessions did not gainsay the fact that the cooperationists had been defeated. One of them, Richardson Miles of Charleston, confirmed this estimation when he observed that "the minority have yielded their views to the majority." A cooperationist himself, Miles had "preferred the plan which altho slower, promised to be more certain and lasting." Nevertheless, he conceded the issue by deciding: "Any policy however wanting in wisdom, foresight and breadth of view—but which commends itself to the instincts and feelings of the people—and which will *unite* them—and enlist their enthusiasm and earnest effort; is better for us than the wisest policy which statesmanship can suggest, but which the people are unwilling to accept, or would be lukewarm in carrying out."[67] This change of direction meant that the party was now embarking upon a line of policy entirely at odds with the priorities it had espoused under the New Departure and fusion. As a result, the campaigns that ensued in South Carolina as well as in Mississippi and in Alabama were quite different from the kind of canvass that had been characteristic of the earlier phase. They were highly organized and carefully coordinated operations. The campaign was under the exclusive control of the party chairman (Walter Bragg in Alabama, James Z. George in Mississippi, and Alexander Haskell in South Carolina), while the rifle clubs and White Leagues were the instrumentalities for stirring up and organizing the voters at the grass roots. In this way, the party's previous inability to discipline and mobilize its supporters was substantially counteracted. Furthermore, to arouse their constituents from their apathy and inertia, race was introduced as the focal point, the essence, of the canvass. Not only was race the identifying characteristic and symbol of the Democratic party, but, with party approval, racial violence was unleashed to satisfy the frustrations of whites and to intimidate blacks. Whereas during the Klan phase, violence had, for the most part, been covert, sporadic and uncoordinated, in the white supremacy campaigns, it was systematic and focused. First, the rifle clubs organized torchlight parades through the country towns to overawe local blacks. In addition, a racial affray, culminating in a massacre of blacks such as occurred at Clinton, Mississippi, and at Hamburg, South Carolina, was instigated at the outset of the campaign to set its tone and reveal its terrible possibilities. Finally, terroristic violence was inflicted on several targeted counties in the black belt, notably Greene, Choctaw, and Sumter in Alabama and Yazoo and "all the large Republican counties" in Mississippi, so as to illustrate white determination and power in the strongholds of black voting.

By means of campaigns like these, the last bastions of Republican rule were eliminated from the Deep South. Their success can be explained by their ability to arouse and mobilize the party's electoral resources in a way that the New Departure had utterly failed to do. The appeal to voters on the basis of old party loyalties and racial identities had resonated so strongly that the gains from so risky a course far outweighed its dangers. The benefit to be won from the affirmation of partisan, racial, and even sectional exclusiveness rather than from its denial was the great discovery that the Democratic-Conservatives made between 1874 and 1876. What it meant was that a profound change in the way southern politics was conducted occurred in those years, as the straight-outs uncovered and then fanned into flames the pervasive and immutable elements of southern political culture.

Since this decisive change occurred in the process of a struggle for ascendency within the Democratic party, what were its implications for the party's future? Because they were observing this shift in their opponents' demeanor at close quarters, Republicans were quick to offer explanations of what was involved. Mississippi's leading Republican newspaper, the *Pilot*, noted, "The fiery element is again at work in the State—the same leaders are again on the stump! Look at Lamar—Singleton—Hooker—Featherston, and others with all the great host of great and small sensation editors. They duped the people before. Will they do it again?"[68] From Alabama, "One Who Knows" answered that question resoundingly in the affirmative, claiming that the secessionists "have in truth, so far as the leadership of the party is concerned, usurped the banner of the old Democratic party. Like the parasite, they have smothered the old truth upon which it has grown." Because of this, George Houston, the well-known Unionist and Douglas Democrat from north Alabama, was really a foil behind which the secessionists were reinstalling themselves in control of the party.[69] This analysis of the transfer of power within the Democratic party in Alabama was reiterated in the Republican party's official campaign address. Pointing to a meeting in Blount Springs on 27 August at which James L. Pugh, William E. Clarke, John T. Morgan, and John W. A. Sanford were featured speakers, the address noted that these men were "the ablest and most prominent advocates of secession in 1861," and they now "give tone and spirit, purpose and direction to the democratic party of Alabama in 1874, as essentially as they did in 1861. States rights and centralization is their rallying cry, just as it was at that period."[70] The New York *Herald* drew a precise connection between the two campaigns, asserting that the straight-outs in South Carolina were the Rhett wing of the party.[71] Governor Chamberlain's paper, the Columbia *Union-Herald*, concurred, observing that "men having a thorough knowledge of the masses" were at the head of the straight-out movement, for, after all, "They had played upon them before and they knew what they could do."[72]

Although the parallels with the frenzied campaigns of the secession crisis often prompted observers to draw connections between the politicians involved in both, none went as far as Alexander White, the Republican congressman from Alabama's First District, in establishing the identity of the personnel involved on each occasion. In a speech to the U.S. House of Representatives on 4 February 1875, White provided specific instances showing an increasing secessionist influence in the state's Democratic party. In the organization of the victorious Democrats, he discovered that "of the executive committee of the Democratic party in Alabama, consisting of twenty-one members, there are none who were not active and conspicuous secessionists in 1861, several of them members of the secession convention; eight others equally pronounced as belonging to the extreme states-rights school but not old enough to have been conspicuous in 1861; while all over the State the old secession leaders entered into the canvass of last fall with a unanimity and ardor not approximated since the war, and not equaled by the fiery contest of 1860."[73] The trend that Alex White was documenting was really not all that surprising. After all, the meaning of the change in strategy was that a conciliatory, northern orientation had given way to a state-centered approach, while the Democratic-Conservatives' unequivocal identification with the Democracy reestablished the credentials of the party of secession and the politicians whose careers had been closely linked with it. Accordingly, the reappearance on the political stage of men who had in the past been prominent Democrats and secessionists accompanied the introduction and successful implementation of the straight-out campaigns.

Once the Democrats were in control, even in states that did not require a straight-out, white-supremacy campaign to achieve restoration, secessionists returned to influence and their presence was frequently noted. The New York *Times* correspondent in Little Rock during Arkansas' constitutional convention of 1874 reported that the secessionist former governor, Henry M. Rector, was selected as president, and ten others who had been members of the secession convention were the "leading spirits."[74] Another constitutional convention, meeting in North Carolina a year later, after persistent pressure from Joseph Engelhard and the Wilmington "Journal clique" in the Cape Fear plantation counties, was characterized by the Republican Wilmington *Post* as "the last effort of the broken-down, aristocratic, secession Democracy to replace itself in power in this State by riding over the conservative element in its own party."[75] The prominence in these conventions of men closely identified with secession was not confined to North Carolina or Arkansas. Leroy Pope Walker, the ultra who became Confederate secretary of war, was president of the Alabama convention in 1875, and Robert Toombs was the dominant figure in Georgia's convention in 1877.

This trend in southern politics during and after Redemption was confirmed by James W. Sloss, a north Alabama Democrat who was a dominant figure in the Louisville and Nashville Railroad. In 1877 he was asked by the congressional committee investigating recent elections in Alabama, "What especial element in the democratic party now has chief control of the democratic organization?" Sloss replied, "It is the extreme Bourbon element, we call it; the secessionists—radical secessionists—although they have quite a number of old Union men in their ranks now. They have been used to gain control of the State."[76] Either as the moving spirits behind the pressure for the adoption of straight-out electoral strategies organized around the color line or as the beneficiaries of their successful outcome, the secessionist element in the Democratic party seemed to have returned to positions of influence and regained respectability in the middle to late 1870s.

An abrupt change in the direction of Democratic politics had been ushered in with the shift to straight-outism as an organizational device and to white supremacy as a partisan issue. Sharply dramatized by the presence of, as well as the approval accorded to, the previously overlooked secessionists, this cleavage was characterized by three distinct features. Of these, two had been noted by Alexander White in his speech in Congress on 4 February 1875. The first was the apparent resurgence of the secessionists. Yet, despite the attention that White and others gave to this development, its meaning and implication was not so obvious as it seemed. White had graphically charted the secessionists' rise, but that occurrence in itself had little political significance since secession was no longer under consideration in the mid-70s. Furthermore, it was not a position that currently differentiated the factions and elements in the Democratic party. In other words, secession was no longer a live issue. Instead, what the secessionist resurgence signified was a change of tone and policy in the party.[77] In explaining the meaning behind the return of the secessionists, White noted, "Now, as in

1861, the violent and extreme lead the way, others follow in the whirl of excitement."[78] Conciliation was being replaced with confrontation as, under the pressure of the insurgents, the Democracy was setting aside the priorities that had governed it under the New Departure. Consequently, politicians whose current inclinations and past record suggested they were moderate and not rigidly partisan were no longer so necessary or so prominent, and, of course, the use of racial violence as an organized political instrument in the Redemption campaigns could not but help to stimulate the elevation of extreme men.

A second tendency stressed by Alexander White was the reintroduction into political discourse of the traditional principles and basic tenets of the Democracy. Drawing their inspiration and force from the idea of local autonomy and the right of particular political and social entities to pursue their own course without restraint or hindrance, Democratic dogma was reactivated by the rhetorical appeal of the straight-outers for home rule and self-determination. This facet of the straight-out movement Alexander White noticed with a good deal of alarm. "The danger to our country," he argued, "is not in centralization, but in decentralization," and, he continued, "The illusion of State rights which has been so fatal to our country . . . is now raising itself under the euphonious title of 'home rule,' in form more specious and dimensions more formidable than when it shook the nation to its center with the convulsions of war."[79] White was worried by this development, but Democrats who had been lamenting the betrayal of principle and the departure from basic party doctrine which had taken place since the war rejoiced that a return to the living fundamentals of the party was now possible. In the editorial columns of the Mobile *Register*, John Forsyth, an oldline Democrat who had supported Douglas in 1860, began to proclaim the Democratic credo of "Home Rule, Free Trade, and Hard Money" and to accompany this with a demand for its implementation. Evaluating the meaning of the victory of 1874 in his state, Forsyth offered a classic restatement of Democratic doctrine: "That revolution is farther-reaching than mere disgust at local outrages. It reaches to the foundations of the political economy and of government itself. It means that the reserved rights of the States, the Constitutional rights of home rule, shall be more scrupulously guarded. It means that monopolies shall give way to the natural law of open

harbors and free trade. It means that business shall revive and public confidence be restored by a return to a gold basis at the very
earliest moment."[80]

Although the hard money element in Forsyth's trinity of Democratic principles would not produce universal assent among the
party's politicians in the 1870s, home rule and free trade did. Party
policy therefore reflected this in its emphasis, first, on curbing government intervention in the private sector and attacking the monopolies it fostered and, second, on restricting the size and expense
of government. Democratic doctrines permeated the party in the
mid-70s, though few state organizations went as far as the Texas
convention in 1875 which avowed that Jefferson's inaugural and
Jackson's farewell address together comprised its articles of faith
and its guide for political action.[81] The decision to force the issue
with the Republicans and abandon fusion and conciliation had resulted in an agreement to call the Democratic-Conservative party
by its generic name of Democratic and it had also actually promoted
and legitimized all the essential elements of the party's constituency, of its identity, and of its principles and beliefs. Since they referred to themselves as Democrats and strove to draw sharply the
line between the two parties, the Democrats were reaching back beyond the eclectic trimming of latter days to the party's roots and
essentials. It was there that they were discovering the slogans and
philosophy that would shape their future approach to politics.

The third characteristic of the Democrats' change of direction
was not referred to directly by White but it was obvious enough.
The party had decided to call itself Democratic rather than Conservative partly, no doubt, because of pressure from former Democrats.
But, once the breach had occurred, there was no reason why politicians whose past allegiance had been to the Democrats should feel
constrained, either by pressure within the party or by their own political instincts, to remain in the shadows. The stigma of being an
old-line Democrat or even a secessionist was no longer so intense.
As a result, known Democrats, who previously had been denied
preferment or nomination, reentered the party's affairs and ran successfully for office. A couple of examples will suffice to demonstrate
this. In Alabama, the 1874 state convention produced a ticket that
was so solidly Democratic that U.S. Senator Francis W. Sykes implored the gathering to make some provision for a Whig. If this

were not done, he feared that Whig support would be lost to the party in the election. The result was that Robert S. Ligon, a well-known Whig, was nominated for lieutenant governor.[82] Confirmation of this was provided by the *Alabama State Journal*, which observed: "We noticed among the delegates nearly, if not all, the old political hacks of the Democratic party, who have been kept in the background for some time by the younger and more tolerant members of the party; but the race issue has been a sweet morsel, which they have rolled under their tongues until they have again succeeded in being brought to the front."[83]

A similar complaint in Mississippi was made by a correspondent who called himself "Marshall County." In a letter to the Jackson *Clarion* about the Democratic state ticket of 1875, he remarked angrily that the party had managed to elect five former Democrats to Congress and the only state office to be filled, that of treasurer, had gone to William Hemingway, the head of the state Grange and a supporter of Stephen Douglas in 1860.[84] What this meant for the party's composition and posture was explained by a correspondent of Alexander Stephens. "The old liners are the leading spirits of the [Democratic] party now," he wrote exultantly from the editorial offices of the simon-pure *Jeffersonian Democrat*, "and are pretty fully recognized by the people as the only true and safe guides in political affairs. The Democrats in the late Congress were the same set who got up the Greeley business and by no means truly represent the reconstituted Democratic party. The party has been made over."[85] No longer was preference given to former Whigs and denied to those who had an active Democratic record or a reputation for extremism in the secession crisis. Instead, Democrats became noticeably conspicuous, as might have been expected, when the Democratic-Conservatives changed strategy and, in the words of an Arkansas contemporary, learned that "there is not virtue in sham disguises."[86] Moreover, as Democrats reentered the party organization and became its nominees, their impact on the policies of the party correspondingly increased, making it less and less antipathetic to men and measures associated with the prewar Democracy.

The repudiation by the Democrats of their policies of electoral fusion and the New Departure marked a turning point in postwar southern politics. When the Republicans had failed to secure control of the political center by substantially increasing their white vote, their opponents accordingly discarded the parallel approach they had been pursuing. The realignment and reorganization of the parties which had been so widely anticipated was evidently not going to occur. Instead, both parties regrouped and consolidated around their loyal constituents and their original identities, a development that, as it happened, was also under way in the rest of the nation in the mid-1870s.[87] In the South, the reaffirmation of party identity resulted in the introduction of race as the primary characteristic distinguishing the Democrats from the Republicans. This politicization of race offered further evidence of how decisive was the shift in the region's political life after about 1873.

But although its identification as the white man's party established many of the priorities of the Democratic party as it assumed control of the southern states, it did not determine precisely what substantive policies it would then pursue and which interests it would respond to. Yet there were indications. Because the line between the parties was being drawn so sharply, not only were the Democrats' accommodationist, New Departure policies being rejected, but so too was their Whiggish approach to economic and fiscal questions. In their place, a different interest and a different set of priorities emerged in the struggle for ascendancy.

8. The Return of the Bourbons

The Present Constitution of Alabama was intended to make the negro the Political master of the white man. Let us frame a new one, which will do justice to the white counties.
—Mobile *Register*, 27 January 1875

Between 1873 and 1876, the Democrats had won a series of statewide elections in the South. But these electoral victories did not automatically ensure that their control over state government was secure, nor did it guarantee that the power the Democrats had won might not slip away from them if it were not carefully guarded and consolidated. After all, they had lost Alabama in 1872 after winning it two years earlier, and in all of the recent elections, their opponents' vote had actually increased. Accordingly, the party moved with determination and dispatch to control patronage, remove incumbents, and revise registration and election machinery in order to establish its domination. Nowhere was this more imperative than in Mississippi, where the Democrats had only won control of the legislature, thus necessitating the impeachment and removal of Republican state officials, and in South Carolina, where the opposition contested the results of the election and recognized rival versions of the executive and legislative branches.

The problems facing the victorious Democrats were not, however, confined to the mechanics of maintaining their ascendancy. Now that they were in office, they had to formulate policy and devise programs. Yet what these would be was not evident from the platforms on which they had campaigned in the Redemption elections. Indeed, the party had been purposefully vague and catholic about its intentions, Francis Nicholls promising, for example, to restore to his state of Louisiana "honesty, integrity and good government."[1] Furthermore, the debates within the party prior to these campaigns had been essentially over electoral strategy and its mechanics, not over matters and issues of substance. There was, therefore, no line of policy or set of proposals that the party would automatically pursue once in office.

Nevertheless, the Democrats were hardly confronted by either a policy void or a mass of confusion. The debate over election strategy had propelled to the forefront an element in the party which knew clearly what direction it wanted to take. The Bourbon insurgents believed that the position their party had just taken on election strategy was simply part of a similar approach it should adopt on broader, more substantive issues. Just as the Democrats had stressed in their campaign tactics how divergent and different the parties were electorally, so now they should apply these distinctions to policy and measures. To this end, the Bourbons called for a return to old landmarks and for the reintroduction of principle and doctrine into Democratic politics. It was their intention, therefore, that Redemption be accompanied by a return to the verities of the Democracy, that is, by restoration.

The debate over electoral strategy had therefore brought into focus a division of opinion on more basic matters of party identity and purpose. But the emergence of a more radical sentiment within the party, which wanted to stress the traditional Democratic doctrines, was occurring throughout the South, even in states where Redemption had not necessitated a major reappraisal of electoral strategy. In those states in which the Democrats had come to power earlier, the demand was now being made for an even sharper break with Republican practice than had been effected thus far. A vocal contingent existed in North Carolina, in Georgia, in Texas, and even in Virginia and Tennessee, which was calling upon Democrats to be far less respectful of the policies and concerns of the Republicans than they had been, and to march instead to a different drummer. The Republicans had been overthrown but, these more radical Democrats complained, their policies and the institutions they had created still lived. Yet the Democratic party was not protesting. Instead, a decisive break was required so that Democratic purity could replace the party's existing and somewhat ambivalent stance. In increasingly strident tones, purists demanded that the structure of Republican government be overturned and its priorities reversed. To this end, they questioned the legality of the state debts that the Republicans had created and demanded their repudiation. They also insisted that the power of the states to lend their credit be abolished, thus making it impossible for governments to assist manufacturing, railroads, or any other economic interest with subsidies or with the issue or endorsement of bonds. Finally, pressure was increased for the drastic retrenchment of public expenditures and for reduction of taxation. Not simply a demand for economy, the spirit of this movement could be discerned most clearly in Robert Toombs's insistence that Georgia "sweep the deck, sir,—sweep the deck."[2] Evidently, it was not sufficient to have redeemed the state. The momentum of that achievement had to be continued and expanded so as to accomplish, in addition, the redemption of the party.

While they had been out of power during the years of Republican domination, the Democrats had managed to submerge their differences. Once in office, however, these disagreements surfaced as the party pondered the course it should pursue. This struggle for influence over the party's future direction was visible, to some extent, in the legislative sphere as the insurgents introduced bills that would turn the party away from the interests it had earlier encouraged and from the priorities it had espoused. The challenge to prevailing policies was most clearly evident in the dispute over whether or not to hold a convention to rewrite the constitutions that had been introduced by the Republicans in 1868. The provisions of these constitutions, once they had been redesigned, demonstrated that it had been the Democratic party's more extreme and uncompromising elements that had taken the initiative in the movements for constitutional revision.

Surprisingly, historians of the Reconstruction period as well as historians of the South have paid very little attention to the consti-

tutional conventions that were called in most of the states after Redemption. The conventions of the 1890s and early twentieth century have, by contrast, attracted a great deal of interest. In those
assemblies, the limitation or elimination of black suffrage was the
central issue. For this reason, they have been viewed as marking the
inception of the South's twentieth-century political system, with its
single party and its electorate restricted only to whites.[3] These conventions also brought down the curtain on Reconstruction by removing black suffrage, the main pillar of the political edifice that it
had established. At the same time that they were disfranchised,
blacks were also being segregated by laws depriving them of the
civil rights guaranteed to them by state and federal law during Reconstruction. By comparison, the conventions that had been held
twenty years earlier were considered of no great significance. This
was essentially because they did not dismantle the equal rights provisions of Reconstruction. Indeed, they purposely disavowed any
intention of tampering with the legal and political rights of blacks.
To this generalization Georgia was the exception, but elsewhere,
both in the campaigns to call a convention as well as in the proceedings of the conventions themselves, all attempts to introduce such
measures were vigorously resisted.

One of the few historians to examine these conventions was
W. E. B. DuBois. He concluded that they demonstrated how real-
istic and responsible the Reconstruction constitution-makers had
been because their Democratic successors had not found it necessary to condemn their handiwork as inadequate: "They differ from
the negro constitutions in minor details, but very little in general
conception," DuBois wrote in his famous article "Reconstruction
and Its Benefits," published in 1910.[4] There was indeed little
change in the status of the civil and political rights of southern
blacks, and this was what DuBois and subsequent historians have
been primarily concerned about. But government in the Reconstruction period was not exclusively preoccupied with equal rights.
The Republicans had introduced policies in other areas and the
Democrats intended to reverse them. They were particularly eager
to reject the Republicans' principles of political economy and to replace them with a minimalist or laissez-faire philosophy of government. During Reconstruction, the Republican party had inaugurated a program of internal improvements stimulated and fostered

by government. Furthermore, the role of government and the burdens it assumed had been expanded immensely.[5] In view of this, it was not unlikely that the Democrats would want to restrict and retrench once they attained power. What was less expected was the emergence within the party of a vociferous element that insisted on the reversal or elimination of Republican policies and, to accomplish this more radical demand, it pressed relentlessly for a constitutional convention.

The process of constitution-making is complicated and lengthy. A bill has to be passed requiring that a convention be called. This is followed by an election to decide whether or not to have a convention as well as to select the delegates should the call be approved. Next, the convention itself meets. Finally, the new constitution is submitted to the electorate for ratification. Throughout this entire procedure, the Democrats could expect to be confronted by the opposition of the Republican party, which, it had to be assumed, would regard constitutional revision as a direct attack upon their accomplishments during Reconstruction and an attempt to reverse the priorities they had set for the postwar South. Moreover, in a region that had had a surfeit of conventions and elections just after the war and where, during Reconstruction, every election had been a passionate and significant matter, the agitation of constitutional revision was not likely to be greeted with enthusiasm. Particularly aggrieved at the prospect would be the Democrats' own supporters who had anticipated, as one of the major benefits of Redemption, a period of relief from elections and political turmoil. Nevertheless, ignoring the possibility of widespread resentment and resistance, the Democrats went ahead and called conventions in seven southern states during the 1870s. Tennessee held one in 1870; Arkansas in 1874; Texas, North Carolina, and Alabama in 1875; Georgia in 1877; and, lastly, Louisiana in 1879.

It would be a mistake to assume, however, that the frequent incidence of these constitutional conventions indicated that the party was united and enthusiastic about calling them, for that was certainly not the case. The advocates of a convention had to overcome substantial opposition, not only from within their own party, but from the Republicans as well. Therefore, the fight was often long and bitter. For instance, as early as the legislative session of 1871, the initiative for a convention was begun in North Carolina, but not until four years later was one actually convened.[6] Likewise, conventionists in Georgia were repulsed from 1873 until 1877, while Louisiana Democrats debated the issue for two years before a convention was finally called in 1879.

Although there was strong resistance, most opponents of a constitutional convention conceded that the existing fundamental law did need some alteration. Consequently, they proposed instead that amendments be introduced as a way of remedying the more glaring defects. Their purpose was of course to cut the ground from under the feet of the advocates of a convention by making it unnecessary. In North Carolina and Georgia, this meant that, from time to time, amendments would be produced and submitted, singly or in small groups, for ratification by the electorate. In neither case, however, was it sufficient to blunt the demand for a convention. Its proponents were vehement. In an effort to completely outmaneuver the conventionists within their party, Louisiana's Democrats went so far as to offer a package of no less than nineteen amendments in 1878; but the conventionists were not so easily diverted and they mobilized the electorate to defeat them. A convention was what they wanted and only when a convention proved unattainable might amendments be acceptable as the most that could be gained. That was the view of John Forsyth in early 1875 as he fought to obtain a convention in Alabama, and it was a viewpoint shared elsewhere.[7]

Forsyth's efforts to call a convention were countered by Governor Houston, who, as late as May 1875, was proposing that amendments alone would suffice.[8] He was supported in his opinion by the state executive committee of the victorious Democratic party which published an address during April suggesting that there were only a few items in need of revision, such as the elimination of unnecessary executive offices, abolition of the Board of Education, limits on the loaning of the state credit, and provisions for holding state elections in years different from federal ones. All of these, the committee argued, could be introduced by amendment, making a convention quite unnecessary. A month or two later, however, when the legislature voted for a convention anyway, the governor and the party leadership swung in behind the decision. They did so only after making sure that the Commission of Three, which Houston had appointed to settle the state debt, would not report until after the convention had adjourned. Behind this move was a fear that the sentiment for repudiation was so strong that the debt question had to be kept out of the convention's hands and adjudicated by the more cautious and controllable three-member commission.[9]

The line-up of forces on the convention issue in Alabama was replicated in other states. Interests that had a stake in the status quo, whether it was political or economic, tended to resist the pressure for a convention. They perceived, quite correctly, that, behind the convention movement, there surged concerns and ambitions that aimed to challenge both the fiscal priorities established previously by the Republicans as well as the existing alignment of political forces within the Democratic party. The New Orleans *Picayune*, itself an opponent of a convention, went to the heart of the matter when it observed that "a large majority of intelligent and thinking people, and especially a large majority of the great financial, commercial and trading classes" were arrayed against the convention. Consequently, the *Picayune's* editorial columns informed the conventionists that New Orleans, the commercial and urban center of the state, refused adamantly to accede to "the presumed demands of the people of Caddo and Natchitoches, or of any other parish."[10]

In Georgia, where the struggle for a convention was lengthy and intense, the Atlanta *Constitution* was in the forefront of the fight to defeat the proconvention insurgents. As the major organ of the Democratic party and of the commercial and financial interests in the growing city of Atlanta, the *Constitution* was fearful of the destabilizing effects a convention would produce. In December 1873, the paper warned: "It is well known that many extreme opinions have been entertained on diverse public matters, and the convention is to afford an opportunity of upheaving the whole aggregate of established institutions that are in conflict with individual prejudices."[11] What the *Constitution* feared was the reintroduction of a usury law, continued assault on the validity of the state bond issues of the Bullock era, reestablishment of imprisonment for debt, repeal of the homestead and relief laws and, perhaps most worrisome, the demand for removal of the state capital from Atlanta back to Milledgeville. A convention had to be prevented, therefore, because its whole thrust would be antithetical to the interests that had been promoted and encouraged under the Republicans.[12] The "Atlanta Spirit," the emergent New South, was under attack in the convention movement.

Equally disquieting in Georgia as well as elsewhere was the threat that the conventions posed to the Democratic party. The ceaseless agitation of the convention issue was preoccupying, sometimes paralyzing, the state legislatures, while it also heightened division within the party structure. Thus, the outcome might well be a fatal weakening of the party. Furthermore, the convention debate could uncover just the issue that the Republicans needed to revive their political prospects. This was exactly what was feared in Georgia, when word spread that the proposed convention intended to dismantle the state's homestead provisions. As the Gainesville *Eagle* anxiously observed, this would "give the Republicans the negro vote and those Democrats who favor our present Homestead laws, and [so] the Democratic party would be in danger of defeat at a general election."[13] The *Eagle*'s fears were not excessive. In 1871 when North Carolina's Democratic-Conservatives had tried to assemble a convention, the scheme had proven counter-productive, since the attempt had not only failed but the fortunes of the Republicans had also revived as a direct result. Even when, four years later, a convention was finally pushed through and delegates chosen, the prospects were still gloomy since, ironically, the Republicans had managed to secure a majority, albeit slim, in the Democrats' own convention. This unexpected outcome naturally delighted the Republican leadership. After telling Thomas Settle, "We are exceedingly happy here at the result," the former U.S. senator, Joseph C. Abbott, speculated that, with "the exercise of great caution and discretion," their party could quite possibly carry the state in 1876.[14] This was the worst development that David Schenck, a leading Democrat, had believed imaginable. In January 1875, he had written in his diary, "Nothing is settled in the South, every day presents some growing indication of revolution and turmoil. This Convention election will again bring about strife and contention, excitement and perhaps danger."[15]

Nevertheless, despite the obvious risks involved, the opposition ultimately caved in to the pressure of the conventionists. Often this occurred because, as a legislator from Atlanta's Fulton County complained, the demand for it was "so constant and on the part of a few gentlemen, so persistent."[16] This persistence often forced the anti-conventionists into the awkward position of seeming to be the obstacles to party unity. Gradually they, not those who had first raised the issue, were perceived as the cause of the agitation because of their stubborn refusal to yield and put the matter to rest. Nevertheless, when the opposition capitulated, it did so frequently on condition that the scope of the convention would be limited and specified, thereby precluding controversial and potentially damaging issues.

On occasion, the anticonventionists' objections were themselves reasonably limited and therefore were easily overcome. Their hesitation was sometimes based on little more than a disagreement over timing. Governor Richard Coke of Texas had resisted a convention in 1874 because he felt that, if it were held so soon after the Democrats had come to power, the electorate would be so excited and aroused that an orderly convention would be unattainable.[17] As he told Samuel Maxey, "Our people have become possessed of a feverish anxiety for change, have become revolutionary in their feelings, because broken from their old moorings" by postwar political and constitutional changes.[18] Despite Coke's opinion, excitement and passion were often, however, exactly what advocates of a constitution needed in order to push their measure through. Early in 1875, John Forsyth was arguing that delay could be fatal in Alabama. "The time to call a convention," he warned, had been immediately after the party's stunning victory in 1874. Later on, when urgency and momentum were dwindling, the party would find it difficult to rally its supporters. "Already," he complained, "we find that . . . there are enough Democrats, serenely satisfied as to their own infallibility, breaking away from the mass of the party on nearly every question, to delay and imperil every important measure." All the same, it was not yet too late and he urged the party to act decisively. "Now, while the whites are united on the Civil Rights question and opposition to military rule, and while there is [sic] no Federal elections to arouse questions of race and power," was the moment to strike.[19]

Forsyth's mention of federal elections referred to one of the major objections leveled against calling a convention. Even though it rarely constituted a fundamental obstacle, it was certainly a deterrent to any precipitate action. Governor Coke of Texas had raised it in 1874 because congressional elections were held that year.[20] Two years later, when the Atlanta *Constitution* finally collapsed in the face of conventionist pressure, the paper warned that it would, nonetheless, still oppose a call if it were made before the vital national elections of 1876.[21] The passage of a convention bill, which had been introduced at the beginning of the session in 1875, was purposely postponed by North Carolina's Democrats until after Congress had adjourned on 5 March.[22] The fear of repercussions in Washington was ever-present in the minds of the southern Democratic leadership and, on the occasion of Coke's and North Carolina's hesitation in the winter of 1874–75, there was the added pressure of leading southern politicians in Washington who urged them to resist calling a convention. John B. Gordon of Georgia, Matt W. Ransom of North Carolina, and the congressional delegations from Texas and Alabama all threw their weight decisively against any convention initiatives, even though they were aware that war-related and race matters were not likely to be involved.[23]

The proponents of conventions were clearly indomitable and persistent, and their opponents gave in only when they could no longer resist without inflicting greater harm on themselves and the party. Once they had capitulated, however, it was essential to try to contain the triumphant conventionists and limit the scope and extremism of their proposals. The forces that had resisted the convention call were convinced, and with good reason, that the convention movement was initiated for the purpose of reordering drastically the priorities of the Democratic party. Naturally enough, interests and individuals that had been downplayed by the party since the war would, in the process, be fostered and promoted. Thus the choice of a constitutional convention as the only acceptable instrument for effecting the changes desired by the movement's initiators seemed to suggest that the conventionists aimed at more than just the reforms themselves. Because most of the changes envisaged could be achieved by legislation or by amendment, the Atlanta *Constitution*, for one, was convinced that the conventionists had larger purposes in mind.[24] This perception was confirmed by the latter's constant rejection of any methods short of a convention. To them, the lobbying and logrolling of the legislative process tended to obscure and modify issues. Besides, legislatures were not suitable arenas for raising fundamental issues of government and politics; they were more concerned with day-to-day matters and with the practice of government, not its theory. A constitutional convention, on the other hand, was designed specifically to enunciate and codify the principles of government, to be a focusing event, unlike the episodic and intermittent passing of amendments. Consequently, a convention would accomplish, and simultaneously dramatize, the clear and decisive break with past practice which was sought by the insurgents.

Further evidence that the convention movement involved an alteration in the party's center of gravity was indicated by the critical role that the white counties were to play in it. In Georgia, Representative D. B. Hamilton of Floyd County told the legislature that his section demanded a convention, and since "in North Georgia we give two thirds of the vote of the Democratic party, we have a right to be heard. We have never failed you in the perils of the past" but have "rolled down the votes to your rescue" in middle and south Georgia.[25] Later, when the result of the election showed that "North Georgia secured the convention," the *Constitution* conceded that "their wishes in this matter should be respected."[26] The support of the northern white counties was also critical in Alabama, though there was some reluctance to endorse a convention call because of reservations about likely changes in local government which would be more beneficial to those areas with black majorities. Party leaders urged them to reconsider, assuring them, "We of the black belt will have little voice in the Convention, if called." The highland counties had given the party the victory in 1874; "Now it is to them holding the destinies of the State in their keeping, that we appeal!"[27] In Louisiana, however, the *Picayune* noted in August 1879 that "the white parishes favor action," while those along the Mississippi and in New Orleans did not.[28] After years of neglect, the white counties were becoming a force to be reckoned with in the Democratic party. Their votes had been crucial in the white-supremacy campaigns and they were aware of their importance.

Since the party's focus was changing toward stimulating its white supporters rather than trying to win over black voters, its electoral base had shifted. To take into account the increasing importance of the white counties, the party's structure was also being adjusted and changed. In the mid-1870s, the basis of representation in Democratic state conventions was frequently altered from an allocation determined by the size of a county's delegation in the lower house of the general assembly to one determined by the number of voters who had taken a Democratic ballot at the previous statewide election. In March 1874, Alabama Democrats established a ratio of one delegate to every two hundred Democratic voters.[29] Two years earlier Ethelbert Barksdale, the former party chair, had been urging the Mississippi Democratic-Conservatives to base county representation on the party's vote at the previous election.[30] The trend had set in so strongly that, by 1876, the Atlanta *Constitution* was commenting that this procedure, although not yet adopted by its fellow Georgians, was in operation "in most other states."[31]

Besides increasing the delegations of the white counties in the state convention, this change was also expected to stimulate and involve party supporters who lived there. Making sure that "a much larger body of citizens will be thus persuaded to actively participate in our party movements" had been the Alabama Democratic leaders' intention when they had adopted the reform. A similar result was envisaged in the introduction of the primary election method for choosing delegates which Mississippi had begun in its Redemption campaign back in 1875.[32] The net effect of these internal changes was that the white counties' role in the party was enhanced significantly. Their influence in party decisions had increased and so had the involvement of their cadres. Their role either in the initiative for a convention or else in the convention once it assembled was considerable. In this respect, the convention movement confirmed developments within the party which had been set in motion by the Redemption campaigns of 1874–76.

But whatever the implications of the convention calls on the alignment of forces within the Democratic party, there was one element that certainly expected to benefit from the agitation. As a Georgia legislator explained during debate on a convention bill in 1874, "The call for a convention does not come from the people. It is the old song of the politician laid on the shelf by his constituents."[33] Although this was obviously a contemptuous comment, it did nonetheless hit upon a crucial feature in the movement. It was obviously a struggle for power and influence within the Democratic party, but it involved primarily the party's active politicians rather than the public at large. As another Georgian, Representative Giles Hillyer, observed in 1877, "The politicians want a convention, but I have seen no stir among the people."[34] Evidence for these conclusions was provided most dramatically by the size of the popular vote on the convention question because the turnout was universally small.[35] This lack of voter interest was in sharp contrast to the excitement among party officials and activists who saw the convention as a decisive move in the struggle to change the party's direction. It was the trump card of politicians who wished to ride with the new political current that had set in with Redemption, for the convention and the changes it produced would confirm this trend and give recognition and renewed influence to those who had campaigned for it. This was precisely what the New Orleans *Picayune* had in mind when it concluded that the convention "was rather a political measure than a popular one."[36]

The fact that the convention provided a mechanism for obtaining influence and office for those currently lacking both was evident from the actions of the conventions themselves once they were in session. In Texas and Arkansas, the assembled delegates promptly demanded that offices under the old constitution be vacated and new elections held to fill them. When the Atlanta *Constitution* detected this, its editors quickly used it as ammunition to strengthen the resolve of the anticonventionists in Georgia. Because "it made a clean sweep of the offices and declared a 'new deal,'" the *Constitution*'s editors warned that the delegates in Texas had therefore "introduced a powerful element of discord" into the party. A direct result of this poor judgment was that ratification of the constitution was in jeopardy.[37] Warnings like these did not, however, deter Georgia Democrats from calling a convention. Nor did they dissuade the delegates in Louisiana from emulating those in Texas. New elections were required by the convention and, by means of them, Governor Nicholls was set aside and candidates nominated for all the state offices who were more congenial than Nicholls had been to the Bourbon and repudiationist elements ascendant in the convention.[38]

The likelihood of new elections made a convention a menacing proposition to current officeholders, but there were other indications that there was radicalism in the convention movement. Representative Turnbull of Georgia, describing himself as "one of the wool hat boys," announced to his fellow legislators, as they deliberated over whether to vote for a convention bill, "I am for a new deal. If it carries the democratic party under it ought to go under."[39] And, of course, Robert Toombs was calling for a convention that would "sweep the deck."[40] Yet, although it could be argued that the conventions would not necessarily wipe the slate clean by turning out incumbents or even by completely reversing party policy, enough was being said to worry the political and economic establishment. In the preconvention movements, demands were constantly made for repudiation of the state debt, for a "new deal," for ruthless reduction of offices and salaries. Furthermore, pressure was being exerted for the imposition of ceilings on the tax rate and state indebtedness, for prohibition of state aid to internal improvements, for curbs on monopolies, and for abolition of homestead and debtor relief provisions. Also in demand were the restoration of imprisonment for debt, reintroduction of the whipping post, and the removal of state capitals in Georgia and Louisiana from urban centers. In this catalog, not even the disfranchisement of blacks was overlooked. No one was more vociferous about this than Robert Toombs who threatened: "Give us a convention and I will fix it so that the people shall rule, and the negro shall never be heard from."[41] With immoderate and reactionary propositions like these surfacing throughout the campaign, it was small wonder that the defenders of orthodoxy and the existing order viewed the conventionists with alarm. Few of them would have disputed the judgment of the former U.S. attorney general, Amos Akerman, that the convention movement was instigated "by the more violent members of the Democratic party."[42]

Once the conventions assembled, the temper of the delegates was hardly reassuring. The interests that dominated the delegations and the beliefs they held were generally unsympathetic, leaving the defenders of the status quo little option but to try to curb and restrain the conventions they could not defeat. In state after state, Bourbons eager to prune the cost and power of government drastically were preponderant, and there was a powerful agrarian thrust to these delegations which put the New South in peril. In Alabama, "Bourbons with an agrarian outlook controlled the convention," concluded Malcom McMillan, the leading authority on that state's constitutional history. As a result, "a conservative agrarian-minded policy, which showed distrust of Republican interest in Alabama's railroads, mining and industrial resources dominated the work of the convention."[43] A similar description applied in Texas, where the delegates "represented primarily the views of an agriculture- and law-oriented Democratic majority," of whom "almost half acknowledged membership in the Grange."[44] Another Texas historian, who studied the state's 1875 constitution, considered it "a Granger product."[45] Georgia's convention was also dominated by farmers and the spirit that permeated it was the antimonopoly, anti-state aid animus of Robert Toombs and his followers who controlled the business of the convention through Toombs's chairmanship of the crucial Committee of Revision.[46] This agrarian, laissez-faire insurgency also characterized the composition and tendency of Louisiana's convention, for it was heavily influenced by debt repudiators from the white northwestern parishes. Accordingly, the *Picayune* warned these country delegations against fomenting "any violent party projects" or formulating proposals likely to "weaken the foundations on which the credit and the prosperity of this great commercial city repose." After all, the New Orleans delegates had not gone to the convention to "reinforce the views and wishes and the opinions of constituencies north of Red River, or west of the Atchafalaya."[47]

The resurgence of sectors and elements in the Democratic party which had been overlooked or set aside during Reconstruction was everywhere in evidence as the conventions assembled. The governmental activism and budgetary expansion inaugurated by the Republicans were under assault, and so were the urban, commercial, and railroad interests that had prospered under them. With the help of the Republican minority in the conventions, defenders of the Reconstruction order might be able to prevent developments which would be dislocating and threatening. But there were many who were less sanguine, like "Confederate," who told the Atlanta *Constitution* of his fears that "an effort will be made to re-open the measures of compromise and reconstruction . . . and to unsettle the rights of property and person as fixed and settled since the war."[48]

9. The Bourbon Constitutions

[Last year, the Georgia Senate] tried to rally the ignorant freed-
men; all the remnant of the Bullock gang both inside and outside of
the democratic party; all the friends of spurious bonds, all 'develop-
ers of resources' generally to defeat the convention.
—Robert Toombs to Leander N. Trammell, public letter in
  Atlanta *Constitution*, 3 May 1877

The Convention reposed no confidence in any manner of men or
officials thereafter. No willingness that any officer should possess
power, or any more money than would keep a shirt on his back.
—William P. Ballinger to Oran Roberts, Galveston, 19 August
  1878

Throughout the South during the 1870s, there was a preoccupation with constitutional revision. Since the writing of a
new constitution involves the recasting and reformulation of a
state's fundamental law, the decision to embark upon such a task
represented a break with existing priorities and practices in the
government and politics of the southern states. Indeed, this was the
intention of the Bourbon wing of the Democratic party as it strove
to accentuate the differences between its own party and the Republicans as well as between themselves and their party rivals, the ex-
ponents of the New Departure and the New South.

During this decade, every reconstructed state discussed seriously
the calling of a convention to rewrite its constitution. Some, like

Virginia, Florida, Mississippi, and South Carolina eventually abandoned the idea. Others managed to summon conventions that proceeded to discuss and incorporate substantive alterations which were indicative of the changes brought on by Redemption. These conventions will be discussed at length later. A third category comprised those states, Tennessee, Arkansas, and North Carolina, which called conventions during the Redemption process itself as a means of removing the Republicans from power, rather than as the culminating act in a sequence that included Redemption. Nevertheless, although the purpose of these conventions was procedural, policy questions were not ignored in the three states. It was just that they surfaced later in the legislatures rather than in the conventions themselves.

Because their purpose was to help return the Democrats to power, the scope of the three conventions in this third category was not intended to go beyond the party's immediate electoral needs. But, once they were in session, delegates found it difficult not to look into other facets of their state's fundamental law. The temptation proved too great for convention members in Arkansas and North Carolina, although, in Tennessee, they were considerably more restrained. The Tennessee convention had been called as early as 1869 by the acting Republican governor, DeWitt C. Senter. The reason for Senter's action was his need to remove all disfranchising restrictions from the state constitution in order to bring to fulfillment the coalition of Centrist Republicans and Democratic-Conservatives which, upon succeeding William Brownlow as governor, he had built around the issue of amnesty. Accordingly, the convention first removed all war-related restrictions on the franchise and then it declared all state offices vacant, thereby enabling the governor's supporters to fill most of them. Before it adjourned, the body did, however, proceed beyond these initial strictures by giving vent to its animus against the state's industrial interests and the encouragement given them in the prewar and postwar years. For the convention banned state aid to internal improvements (though county and local aid was permitted), levied a tax on income from stocks, and denied new manufacturing companies a proposed five-year tax exemption.[1]

Nevertheless, the convention did not proceed any further. It did not, for instance, take any action to reduce the state debt that had been incurred mainly for advancing New South policies. Instead, the debt was left intact and became the central issue in Tennessee politics for the rest of the decade and into the next. The struggle over the state debt commenced in earnest after passage of the Funding Act of 1873 which committed the state to repay a huge obligation of $39 million. This arrangement, which was so beneficial to the bondholders, provoked a powerful reaction in favor of extensive reduction, even repudiation. In a series of running battles, the Low Taxers, as they were called, forced concessions greater than had initially seemed possible. By 1879, they had succeeded in wringing from their opponents, the Funders, a proposition to pay only 60 percent of the debt at 4 percent interest. When even this was rejected by voters, the Low Taxers saw that they could get even more and, after persevering and winning control of their party and state by 1882, they obtained a final settlement to honor only 50 percent of the debt at 3 percent interest. In addition, the antipathy of Governor William Bate's administration towards the New South was so strong that, in 1883, it accompanied its debt settlement with a commission to regulate the railroads. The party's Bourbons had not been ascendant in the 1870 convention, but the debt issue, which other states meeting later in the 1870s would tackle in their conventions, had nevertheless given rise to a major internal struggle, and its outcome was nothing less than a victory for the insurgents.[2]

Arkansas' constitutional convention did not deal with the state-debt issue either. It was called in the midst of the Brooks-Baxter imbroglio to provide a means for ending the political stalemate and for releasing the Democratic-Conservatives from their reluctant dependence on Governor Elisha Baxter, who had been elected as a Republican but had later turned against his party. If a convention could be assembled, the Democratic-Conservatives calculated that it could effect a clean break by declaring the offices vacant and calling new elections. The *Arkansas Gazette* had this in mind when it urged: "If we are to commence purification, let us commence at the root."[3]

The summoning of the convention was carried out with alacrity and without the involvement of the voters. As a result, the Republicans denounced the entire procedure as illegal and revolutionary.

This radical spirit was not confined to the way it was called, for it also characterized many of the body's actions. The purpose of the convention had been primarily procedural—to call new state elections, to reapportion the legislature, and to reduce the gubernatorial term to two years. Yet what transpired was that forces in the party calling for a redirection of its economic and fiscal priorities used the opportunity to initiate their agenda. Accordingly, the convention introduced several measures of retrenchment. The offices of lieutenant governor and superintendent of public instruction were eliminated. The state tax rate was reduced to a maximum of 1 percent and the county levy to as little as .5 percent. Furthermore, the salaries of state officials were reduced substantially. Partly to reduce expenses and partly to undermine its operation, vigorous attempts were made to deny the school system adequate funding and to remove its central administrative apparatus. Although the convention did not attack the policy of state aid to internal improvements frontally, it did prohibit the state from ever being a defendant in a lawsuit, and thus opened up the possibility of repudiation of the public debt, most of which had been incurred for railroad and levee building.[4] Hostility to the New South also surfaced in the intense debate over tax incentives for manufacturing and mining firms. The issue became so heated that one of the opponents of a tax exemption, Jesse Cypert, accused its advocates of being opposed to the convention from the outset and of introducing the exemption in order to cause havoc and the eventual defeat of the constitution.[5] Ultimately, a seven-year exemption was allowed.

As in Tennessee, the state debt was left alone by the convention, only to become the battleground for a divisive factional fight that developed later. This struggle did not gain momentum until 1876, however, for the legislature scaled the debt by $15 million in 1874 with only a few such as William M. Fishback raising objections. Their complaint was that there was no distinction in the Loughborough scaling bill between those portions of the debt which they believed had been incurred legitimately and those that had not.[6] But, in 1876, a powerful faction developed that demanded complete repudiation of the invalid portion and did not cease its agitation until 1882 when it forced the party to endorse its position as party policy and to nominate for governor Judge James H. Berry, a well-known repudiator. After the election, the constitutional amendment nullifying the entire illegal state debt of $10.3 million, which had been narrowly defeated by the voters in 1879, was immediately re-submitted and ratified.[7] Before this, in 1877, the state's Supreme Court had disallowed the railroad and levee debt because of a technicality in the operation of the 1868 state aid act. Consequently, outright repudiation was accomplished in Arkansas and it constituted a triumph for the Bourbons and agrarians and a defeat for the more conservative elements in the party, such as former Governor A. H. Garland, Senator U. M. Rose, Attorney General W. R. Henderson, and the *Arkansas Gazette*.[8] A sharp cleavage from Reconstruction and its system of government finance was the outcome of the successful fight for repudiation. This was a contest of major proportions and, according to one historian, "Few questions in the history of the State ever agitated the public mind" so greatly.[9]

Like Tennessee and Arkansas, proponents of a convention in North Carolina planned to use it in order to clinch the overthrow of Reconstruction. One year after winning undisputed control of the legislature in 1870, a convention had been called, but the voters rejected the idea. The legislature then proceeded to pass eighteen constitutional amendments at its next session, and eight were submitted and ratified in 1873. But these changes did not solve the Democratic-Conservatives' initial problem, which was to obtain control of the executive branch and thus of the entire state. With only the legislature redeemed, the governorship remained in Republican hands and the Republican party continued to be a powerful competitive force in North Carolina politics. So, in 1875, the party again embarked on the risky venture of calling a convention. A powerful opposition arose, however, and even after concessions limiting the convention's agenda and scope, the Democratic-Conservative legislators still had to admit that enough votes to pass a bill could be secured only if the party's members were bound by a vote in caucus. Although this maneuver produced the required votes, the convention that was eventually elected found itself split evenly between the parties. The worst fears of the convention's proponents seemed to have been realized. They would be denied success at the very last moment. Indeed, the convention might never have met had not a wavering Republican, Edward Ransom, voted against his party's resolution to adjourn *sine die*. Under these circumstances, the Democratic-Conservatives in the convention had little room for maneuver and so the scope of its deliberations was quite restricted.[10]

The pressure for a constitutional convention in North Carolina had emanated overwhelmingly from districts whose local government was still under Republican dominance. Located mainly in the coastal sections and faced with black electoral majorities, they could not obtain control of their local affairs without external aid. Since they were anxious to reassert their declining influence in party councils, the coastal counties pressed tirelessly for a convention to bring relief, rather than wait for the election of a Democratic-Conservative governor. Led by the "Journal clique," as the Republicans called Joseph Engelhard, the Wilmington *Journal* editor, and his supporters, this faction eventually obtained its convention by a deal with the western counties.[11] The arrangement was explained by Richard C. Badger, a former Republican and well-connected politician. He told a Senate committee in 1879 that it was "a direct bargain and trade by which it was understood and agreed, but not put down on paper, that the eastern people would aid in putting forward the West[ern] North Carolina Railroad, and in return have from the legislature the selection of their own magistrates."[12]

As in the white-supremacy campaigns, the white counties had come to the rescue of the black. Accordingly, the convention provided for the assembly to appoint justices of the peace, and they in turn were to select county commissioners. With that secured, Josiah Turner, Jr., the obstreperous editor of the Raleigh *Sentinel*, announced that the convention had done "all we have asked at its hands."[13] And the delegates complied. Although they did deal with some other questions, such as the reduction of the number of judges on the state's supreme and superior courts and the establishment of a bureau of agriculture, they nonetheless refused to grapple with the state debt, which had been a perpetual problem since 1870, and they did not take any initiative towards retrenchment. Actually, the debt issue was raised on several occasions but little headway was made because the Republicans were always joined by a handful of Democrats in voting the question down.

The financial question was, however, so explosive that the Democratic legislature during Governor Vance's administration feared to embark upon it. By the time Thomas Jarvis took over in 1878, it could no longer be ignored, for it burst forth in the legislature of 1879–80, sweeping the party before it and causing contemporaries to use the epithet "Bourbon" to describe the dramatic reversal in priority and tone. During that session, the debt was scaled down drastically, as an outstanding obligation of $20.2 million was reduced to $3.58 million, to be paid over thirty years at 4 percent interest. Furthermore, the special tax bonds were to be declared invalid by means of a constitutional amendment. Nevertheless, there was no outright repudiation and this led the *Charlotte Observer* to claim that "public honesty in North Carolina does not exist in name alone." This comment was in fact merely terminological because, as B. U. Ratchford, the leading authority on American state debts, commented wryly, "It is not clear how the settlement of a debt at about 12 cents in the dollar . . . constituted a noble and honorable vindication of public honesty." [14]

The triumph of virtual repudiation was not, however, sufficient. The lurch of the party in a Bourbon direction was to be compounded by its retrenchment policies. The salaries of state officials, already meager, were slashed by about a quarter and the same cut was inflicted on the state's charitable institutions. In addition, clerical staff would no longer be provided for executive department officials, and the legislative branch was even denied funds to pay for the publication of its laws and proceedings. So ruthless was the impulse for economy that the bureau of agriculture, which had been a major achievement of the farming interest in the constitutional convention, became the target four years later of an almost self-destructive and indiscriminate orgy of retrenchment undertaken by essentially the same element.[15] The cuts went far beyond the necessity of the situation and thereby suggested that retrenchment and repudiation represented not simply a curtailment of Republican excesses and extravagance but a principled and uncompromising protest against the philosophy of government introduced by the Republicans and still countenanced by influential Democrats. The party was being forced to disassociate itself from the governmental system and priorities of the Reconstruction order, and its course in the 1879–80 legislature marked the high tide of the reaction in North Carolina.

This revolt against the temporizing financial policies of the Democratic leadership was occurring throughout the South in the

mid-1870s and after. Its emergence and the course it took were
more visible, however, in those states—unlike Tennessee, Arkansas, and North Carolina—where conventions, rather than the regular legislature process, acted as the arena and catalyst for the fiscal
and political showdown. This occurred in states that held their conventions after Redemption was completed and where there was no
compulsion to move precipitously, thus excluding consideration of
substantive issues. Debate during these conventions revealed more
sharply the existence of a division of forces within the Democratic
party between those who wanted to maintain continuity with the
innovations of Reconstruction and those who demanded a sharp reaction against them. In this contest, the insurgents were frequently
able to seize the initiative. They could do this because, in each convention, there was a small but pivotal delegation of Republicans, so
that party unity often required that the Democrats harmonize their
policy in caucus before the debate and vote. While the caucus produced unity in the party, it also invariably strengthened the hands
of the insurgents. Since a caucus is a strictly party matter, it prevented collusion between the more conservative and fiscally orthodox Democrats and the bulk of the Republican delegation which
would naturally oppose efforts to repudiate debts and disavow policies that they had introduced when in office. Deprived by the caucus
of allies outside the party, the opponents of radical fiscal measures
were outnumbered. Since some kind of preliminary caucusing was
employed in each state, the advantages to the insurgents were significant. During the Alabama convention, so "Francis" of the Mobile *Register* reported, "all questions are first discussed fully in committee, and then each day from nine until one o'clock, a conference
is had among the Democratic members and all propositions are discussed and the will of the majority is ascertained."[16] An exception
was Georgia where the Democrats did not hold a caucus. This was
partly because the small number of Republican delegates made it
unnecessary, but also, no doubt, it was because the Committee of
Revision exerted a good deal of control over what the convention
would discuss and, with Robert Toombs at its head, the radical
position was sure to be promoted. Thus, the insurgents who had
already achieved one victory when the convention for which they
had agitated was called were now on the verge of another, as the
party machinery came under their influence.

The group of states holding conventions that met in the wake of Redemption were Alabama and Texas in 1875, Georgia in 1877, and Louisiana in 1879. The keynote for the Alabama convention that met in September 1875 was set by the former Confederate secretary of war, Leroy Pope Walker, who was later to be chosen president of the convention. In a speech at Flint River Mills in June, he had advised: "Govern as little as possible, and only by general laws is the rule of wisdom, sanctioned by experience."[17] The convention then proceeded to design a governmental system that was lean and frugal. The legislature was severely curtailed. Its sessions were to be biennial, its members' pay was reduced to $4 a day, and its power and jurisdiction were curbed.[18] Also pruned was the executive branch; the pay of all officials was docked by 25 percent and the cabinet posts of lieutenant governor and commissioner of industrial resources were stricken out.

By attacking the post that had been created for the sole purpose of encouraging industrial development and that stood as a symbol of the New South envisaged by both the Republicans and many influential Democrats the convention revealed its animus. Accordingly, severe measures for regulating the railroads were proposed. Although ultimately defeated, they were lost by only narrow margins. Despite this, the convention still prohibited rebates, free passes to public officials, and freight rates that discriminated against short-haul traffic. Furthermore, the legislature was required to enact specific provisions for control over the railroads, which soon resulted in the creation of a railroad commission to be chaired by Walter Bragg. There still remained one final blow for the railroads, and it came with the elimination of aid to internal improvements. State, county, and city governments were all prohibited from lending their credit for this purpose.

Next on the agenda was the debt that had been incurred to aid railroads. A large contingent of agrarians, led by William C. Oates, a future governor of the state, and George P. Harrison, demanded that Alabama return to the purchasers all the railroad bonds that it had underwritten. Although this radical proposition was defeated, the convention did make some degree of repudiation unavoidable by pegging the tax rate at 7.5 mills, which later would drop to 6.5 mills by 1880.[19] Thus, Governor Houston and his chief representative in the convention, Rufus W. Cobb, had been pushed very hard by the repudiators. In fact, on one occasion in mid-October, repudiation had been on the brink of accomplishment, and this had necessitated hasty negotiations with some of the convention's members to keep the radical measure from passing.[20]

With that sort of spirit permeating the convention, Houston must have congratulated himself on his foresight in keeping the initiative on the debt. This he had done by creating a three-member debt commission and instructing it not to report until after the convention had adjourned. Were it not for Houston's maneuver, it is quite likely that significant repudiation would have been achieved. As it was, the convention was able to stipulate only that the state could not be sued in any court of law, thus protecting it in case of repudiation, and that no more than 7.5 mills could be levied for taxes, thereby making repudiation likely. All of this led Malcolm McMillan, the state's constitutional historian, to conclude, "Only on the important question of debt adjustment were the agrarians held in check." Even then Houston had only averted defeat; it was not a victory.[21]

Another casualty of the convention was the educational system. Its appropriation was limited to $100,000; the Board of Education was abolished; and no more than 4 percent of the funds appropriated was to be used to pay for administration. Even the Democratic superintendent of schools, John M. McKleroy, objected to the parsimony and decentralization envisaged in the changes. Meanwhile, the Republicans denounced the convention for halving the school fund, thereby driving "the children of the poor from the school houses."[22] So destructive was the convention's work that, in the legislature of 1876, an attempt was made to raise the appropriation to $180,000 in order to save the schools. But, after acrimonious debate, the radical forces emasculated the proposal.[23]

There was more than just retrenchment in the Alabama convention of 1875. The delegates had attacked the political philosophy that permeated the Reconstruction era and had emasculated the New South program for the promotion of industry and commerce by the public sector. Later in the century, as the state's economy grew, the restrictions and restraints that the constitution of 1875 had imposed became increasingly burdensome. By the 1890s, a new constitution was imperative because, as the Birmingham *Age-Herald* put it, the existing one had "crippled and dwarfed enterprise, education, and progress."[24] Even Governor William Oates, who had been a leading repudiator in 1875, was admitting by 1896 that "the restriction of the right of cities to tax themselves retards their growth and progress."[25] A year later, his successor, Joseph F. Johnston, was pressing for a convention so that "some of the iron bands that have prevented the growth and development of the state should be struck off."[26] By the 1890s, the state tax rate was down to 4 mills; city and county taxation still could not exceed 0.5 percent on assessed valuation; and the ban on state aid had prevented even the building of roads. The Bourbon and agrarian reaction of the late 1870s had constituted a radical disengagement from Republican policies, not the gradual readjustment contemplated by the more cautious and accommodating elements in the party.

Similar forces were unleashed in the Texas convention that was also held in 1875. Senator Samuel B. Maxey told his wife, "The leading idea of the Convention seems to be retrenchment and reform. These are great qualities but may be run into the ground which is the danger."[27] These fears were indeed borne out, with the result that the Democracy was badly split when the convention adjourned. Faced with so much discontent, the governor, Richard Coke, decided not to make the constitution "a party test" in the ratification campaign. He himself felt that the proposed system "will fit too tight for comfort, will have too much legislation in it and I fear will not make government sufficiently vigorous." Consequently, many "orthodox Democrats" would object to it, he feared, and thereby endanger "the unity and harmony of the party."[28] Coke's decision to keep the document nonpartisan was heartily approved by J. F. Camp, a state representative and friend of the governor. In a letter to Oran Roberts, who was currently the chief justice and soon to be governor, he admitted that the defeat of the constitution might even be preferable, since any attempt to force it through would incite the opposition of the more orthodox and conservative elements in the Democracy and so split the party. Its rejection would, however, serve "as a rebuke to that mistatesmanlike [sic] pandering to popular error, which characterized that body of men, or rather a majority of them, that framed the instrument."[29]

The trouble was that the Democratic majority in the convention had been too extreme in its demands for cutting the cost and power of government and in its opposition to public promotion of the New

South. While the convention was sitting, a leading conservative Democrat, Alexander W. Terrell, was complaining, "A spirit of positive hostility to lawyers is prevailing among the ruta-baga element, that promises nothing good. The intilectual [sic] minority, is still more weakened by the time-serving apostasy of some of their own number, who go a-granging on easy pretext."[30] Although Terrell complained mainly about the influence of the agrarians over the convention, he might well, judging by his own abysmal spelling, have worried more about what the convention did to the school system. This was a task taken up by the likes of Ashbel Smith, a leader of the party's New South wing. The schools, Smith grumbled, were "without system, without uniformity, without State control, without any responsibility." Admittedly, the convention had set aside a fund consisting of a quarter of the state's revenue and the proceeds from a $1 poll tax, but there was no apparatus to run the schools, except for a board consisting of the governor, the comptroller, and the secretary of the state, who were given no responsibilities except to divide "the income of the School Fund among the several Counties of the state!"[31]

Smith's criticisms were not confined to the school system, for he also believed that, because of the ban on state and local aid, the constitution's "provisions concerning railroads and other works known as Internal Improvements are calculated to discourage . . . development of the unrivalled resources of Texas." Admittedly, the convention had approved subsidization of railroads through land grants of sixteen sections per mile, but Smith was convinced that economic development required a more active role for government in encouraging and generating capital, something land grants did not do.[32] This same hostility to governmental activism had resulted in the abolition of the bureau of immigration and the accompanying prohibition on state expenditures to encourage settlers. Smith regretted this too. An indictment similar to Smith's came from Webster Flanagan, a prominent Republican and a convention delegate, who felt the constitution "cripples immigration, education, and internal improvements. It gives the legislature too much power over railroads, and ties down corporations which should be regulated by public sentiment, competition, and commerce" rather than by government.[33]

In the convention itself, immigration and internal improvements had been the grounds on which the New South Democrats had decided initially to take their stand, but they were routed and their opponents then swept on to formulate equally distasteful measures of retrenchment. They cut executive and judicial salaries; they instituted a debt ceiling of $200,000; they reduced taxation to 0.5 percent; and they pared the legislators' pay and required biennial legislative sessions. The Democrats could claim that the convention had saved the state $1.5 million per year, but the cuts often went much too far.[34] William Pitt Ballinger, a Galveston lawyer and a member of the convention, told Roberts about one of them, the per diem of the legislature. "By and by," Ballinger confided, "the original proposition was to limit the Legislature to 60 d. [days], and, after that, no pay. Opposed to all such resolutions, I offered the $2 a day intending really to ridicule it—and it passed."[35]

Two other items in the Texas convention should be mentioned in closing. The first was the decision to make offices in the executive and judicial branches popularly elected, yet another indicator of the influence of the insurgent agrarian forces. The second was the defeat of a proposition to introduce a poll-tax voting qualification. This demonstrated the power of the white counties within the party, because the poll tax stipulation would certainly have disfranchised many whites, and it would also have expanded the power within the party and state of those Democrats in the black counties. The latter sought, by means of a poll tax restriction, to solidify their control over the black voting majorities that continually obstructed them. By refusing to enact this measure of disfranchisement, the white counties were demonstrating an unwillingness, unlike their counterparts in North Carolina that same year, to rescue their black-belt colleagues from their difficulties. This provoked from Guy M. Bryan the expostulation that such behavior was "infamous," "a great political sin and, a shame to intelligence and justice."[36] Bryan's annoyance highlighted the shift of the center of gravity in the party as the farmers and the white counties determined the shape of Texas government in the late nineteenth century.

In Texas, the development of the state's natural resources and the construction of a railroad network had hardly begun when the constitution imposed its prohibitions and strictures. The situation in Georgia, however, was quite different. Consequently, in what was virtually the banner state of the New South, those who wanted to trim the government's power to bestow privileges on railroads and other corporations could cite the state's unsatisfactory record in support of their case. "There has never been a single railroad aided by the state of Georgia which has ever paid a dividend," Robert Toombs told the convention of 1877, as he explained that the "burial" of state aid was "one of the main objects of my coming here." For, he continued, railroads "wreck and ruin themselves and then plunder the public treasury."[37] The assault on government aid to corporations was nowhere more vigorous than in Georgia where Toombs led the attack.

After deciding that the state's economy had been distorted immeasurably by the growth of monopolies, the convention proceeded to dismantle the system of government promotion that had been inaugurated in the 1850s and that was widely regarded as the source of all the trouble.[38] To this effect, state aid was abolished and not even permitted on the local level. So hostile were the delegates that, when Joseph Brown tried to retain a minimal form of public support for railroads through the provision of cheap convict labor from the state prisons, even this request was turned down by a 93−50 margin.[39] In addition, the state road, the Western and Atlantic, which had been given liberal aid in 1866 and then had been leased in 1870, was now to be sold.[40] And finally, the convention increased the taxes of the railroads, forcing them to pay the standard rate and depriving them of the favorable status that they had previously enjoyed.[41]

The railroads were to suffer still further at the hands of the convention when it confirmed the legislature's repudiation in 1872 and in 1875−76 of $7.74 million of endorsed railroad bonds and tightened the strictures against their repayment.[42] As a further curb on the railroads, the convention mandated the creation of a regulatory commission to fix freight rates and oversee the operation of the roads. Ridiculing the idea that free trade meant that railroad monopolies could set their own rates, Toombs believed that the convention should try to reestablish "liberty of trade," which is what he believed free trade really meant. Since corporations were simply "the creatures of the law of legislation," they possessed no vested rights that were uninfringeable, and "they have no powers except what the legislature gave them."[43] The convention responded to Toombs's accusations with provisions for a railroad commission which, when it was given statutory form at the legislature's next session, constituted one of the strongest introduced at the state level in the late nineteenth century.[44]

The animus against the commercial and industrial beneficiaries of government support was carried over into other areas. In order to restrict still further the state's ability to incur debts in aid of internal improvements, the convention forbade any increase in the current debt and imposed a ceiling of $200,000 for casual deficits.[45] The exemption from taxation for ten years which had been offered during the early 1870s to manufacturers of iron products and of cotton and woolen goods was eliminated, making it clear that virtually all corporate privileges were to be withdrawn.[46] Beyond the fiscal realm, too, curbs were imposed on these same interests. Government was forbidden to grant irrevocable privileges, such as charters of incorporation, and all existing charters were repealed. Moreover, all matters relating to charters were withdrawn from the legislature, which had in the past enacted bills of incorporation, and, instead, were handed over to the courts for adjudication and settlement.[47] Because it was felt that the legislature had been pressured by railroad and other lobbyists in the past, strict limitations on its power and size were imposed.[48] Such curbs were even applied to the judiciary, which was thought to have been insufficiently independent of these influences. The remedy was to make judges elective so that they would be responsible directly to popular sentiment, but the risks of so democratic a move, where half the electorate consisted of blacks, made the convention reconsider. The result was a compromise whereby the judges were to be elected by the legislature rather than directly by the voters.[49]

As in the other states' conventions, reduction of the scope of government was accompanied by limitation of its size and expense. The extent of the retrenchment in Georgia can be seen very readily in the remarkably low three-mill rate of taxation that was in effect by 1882.[50] In addition, legislative sessions were to be biennial and limited to forty days. Finally, the number of executive officers was reduced and those remaining were given salary cuts, of which the most important and symbolic was that of the governor. After extensive debate, the convention opted to lower his income by a quarter, making it $3,000, rather than sell the executive mansion and increase his salary, as Governor Colquitt had suggested. The straight-

forward cut in salary was believed far preferable because the reduction had to be overt and visible. The leader of the forces of
retrenchment, A. W. Holcombe, made it clear that if these cuts
were not made very apparent and very deep, "there will not be a
vote in all the mountain country for the constitution."[51] Behind the
decision to ignore Colquitt's suggestion, there also lurked considerable hostility toward his administration which soon became manifest in a powerful demand that the convention call new elections, as
had been done in Texas and Arkansas. This was the "new deal"
that Representative Turnbull had referred to, as had Toombs in his
threat to "sweep the deck," but fear that the prospect of new elections would result in all the incumbent officeholders throwing their
energies into defeating the ratification of the constitution forced
even Toombs to reconsider his initial aim.[52] Also not included in the
constitution were the new provisions for reducing by half Georgia's
very large homestead exemption and for retaining the state capital
in Atlanta, for the Bourbons who dominated the convention feared
that there was so much opposition to both items that their inclusion
could drag the entire constitution down to defeat. Consequently,
they were submitted as separate ordinances.[53]

The pressure for new elections was obviously very powerful and
pervasive since it was defeated by only fifteen votes, 85–100. Evidently, forces within the Democratic party, demanding influence
and recognition, had been unloosed by the calling of a convention;
and they sought, through the measures of laissez-faire and economical, minimal government that the convention established, to expand
even farther their influence both within the Democratic party and
on the conduct of public policy in Georgia. New elections were simply a logical step in this process. Since the convention took place
seven years after the ouster of the Republicans, it could not be
explained merely as a response to Republican rule. Instead, the
lengthy struggle for a convention and the eventual triumph of its
proponents marked the resurgence of elements in the Democratic coalition that had been set aside during Reconstruction and the early
1870s. The party was returning to its Democratic roots. The principles of Jacksonianism were ascendent once again and the Whiggish partnership between government and business was being
dismantled.

In Louisiana's convention, the focal point of the proceedings was not the taming of corporations but the repudiation of the debt. The Funding Act of 1874, a Republican measure, scaled the debt down from $24.35 million to $15 million, to be paid at 7 percent interest; and then, in 1875, another $3.19 million was repudiated.[54] This reduction was, however, deemed insufficient by the convention's committee to investigate the debt and its chairman, Captain E. E. Kidd, who were overwhelmingly in favor of more drastic doses of repudiation.[55] But the virulence of the assault was not anticipated. The committee's majority report declared that only $4 million of the debt was valid; the prewar railroad debt, postwar levee bonds, and the funded debt of 1874 were all rejected. This prompted a denunciatory riposte from the minority, led by Donelson Caffrey, Thomas J. Semmes, and Henry C. Warmoth, the former Republican governor, demanding that the state should honor all its outstanding indebtedness. The *Picayune* was also aghast, vainly hoping that the majority "does not express either the sentiment or the purpose of the convention." It certainly did not represent the taxpayers of the state, the *Picayune* decided, because the New Orleans and river parishes from which the minority came paid three-fourths of the taxes and, if they were prepared to pay, it was superfluous, if not absurd, for others to try to force them not to.[56]

The upshot was that the convention rejected both reports, each of them extreme in its own way, and adopted a compromise. After protracted debate and interminable caucuses and conferences throughout June and July, the outstanding debt was to be scaled by 25 percent, less than the 50 percent the repudiators had ultimately wanted, and it would be paid at an overall rate of 4 percent.[57] Although the settlement was not satisfactory to the bondholders who later rejected it and sued the state, it had nevertheless been more favorable than the assumptionists had feared. Initially, they had not been at all sanguine about the success of their attempts at containing the repudiators. Their efforts had been severely circumscribed, first, by their opponents' insistence that decisions be made in party caucus, thereby depriving them of the support of the thirty-two Republicans and, second, by the convention's imposition of a tax limit of five mills, which made some repudiation unavoidable. So, although the settlement was a severe setback to members of the assumptionist faction, they accepted it as the best they could get.

The remainder of the convention's work was anticlimactic, but it did bear the obvious imprint of the agrarian forces from the back-country white parishes who were so eager to prune and retrench. The salaries of state officials were reduced by well over 50 percent, from a total of $70,350 to $24,000.[58] The office of superintendent of public education was abolished, leading the *Picayune* to write an editorial entitled "Schools without a Head," which complained that "the cause of public education in Louisiana" had been "imperilled" by the convention's action.[59] Furthermore, between 1876 and 1880, appropriations for schools, already inadequate, dropped about 50 percent.[60] The tax rate was also ruthlessly pared, as we have seen, from 14.5 mills to 5. And finally, the powers of the legislature were narrowly defined and that body was not allowed to lend the state's credit or grant charters, a development regarded by the *Picayune* as excessive and likely to endanger the state's economic development.[61]

Two other features of the convention indicated precisely what elements had gained control. The first of these was the creation of a department of agriculture and the removal of the capital from New Orleans to Baton Rouge, a clear indication that the agrarian anti–New South elements in the upcountry parishes had become the dominant force. The second aspect was to be found in the convention's decision to leave the Louisiana Lottery Company undisturbed. The company's allies had favored a convention as a way of preserving the institution and outmaneuvering the sizable opposition to it in the legislature. Moreover, in alliance with the agrarians, the lottery forces were also able to cut short Governor Nicholls's term and thereby remove a powerful obstacle to the company's future security. By way of explanation, it should be added that Nicholls had also been critical of any attempts at repudiation. In his place, they obtained Louis Wiltz, a former mayor of New Orleans, president of the constitutional convention and a known supporter of the lottery. This new deal also provided opportunities for the agrarians and repudiators to consolidate their hold through an increased share of the offices. The assumptionists and their allies in the Nicholls wing of the party had suffered a resounding defeat at the hands of the Bourbons of the northern parishes and their allies among the lottery forces.[62] As was true in other southern states, the constitutional convention in Louisiana had been the device through which the suppressed anti–New South forces had been able to regain influence.

Two states omitted so far from the roster of those holding conventions during and after Redemption were Mississippi and South Carolina. Both considered the possibility of calling a convention, and bills for this purpose were introduced into their legislatures in 1876 and 1878 respectively, but nothing resulted. No doubt, the black electoral majorities in each state contributed significantly to the decision not to risk a convention, although this factor had not deterred Louisiana's Democrats. What most probably decided the issue was that in neither state was there a concentration of New South interests sufficient in size to provoke confrontation and assault. As a result, government had not been enlisted in a partnership that had resulted in the siphoning off of a considerable amount of public funds for the purpose of fostering private industrial enterprise. This was quite unlike the situation in Alabama and Georgia, for example, or even Virginia where the Funders and their industrial and commercial allies were so well entrenched that, in the 1880s, the opposition would need to resort to a new political party, not just a constitutional convention, to challenge their hegemony.[63]

In Mississippi, the Republican administrations of Alcorn and Ames had been extremely cautious and frugal in their policies of state aid to internal improvements, so that, by 1877, there was virtual unanimity within the Democratic party and press that a convention was unnecessary. In December, the *Clarion* concluded that a convention would be too expensive a proposition, since all that needed to be done was the introduction of a poll-tax prerequisite for voting, a change in the schedule for elections so that state and congressional elections could be held simultaneously, and a provision for popular election of judges.[64] Moreover, an amendment requiring biennial sessions of the state legislature had just been ratified. Consequently, House bill number one was tabled during January 1878 and a convention was not called.[65]

All the same, the party did manifest tendencies that had been evident elsewhere in more exaggerated form. The Mississippi debt was a mere $1 million, so that repudiation was not advocated either from necessity or from principle.[66] Nevertheless, government expenditures that the Democratic platform of 1877 claimed were just over $1 million were slashed by over 50 percent in the legislatures of 1876 and 1877. Judges' salaries were sharply reduced and judicial districts were consolidated, resulting in a saving of $134,000 per year. In addition, the pay of officers and teachers in the school system was drastically reduced, causing the new Democratic superintendent of education to rebuke the legislature for the irretrievable damage it had done.[67] This retrenchment provided the leeway for a tax cut, by which the state's rate of taxation was lowered to a mere 3.5 mills by 1878, and the county tax, which had been much higher, was reduced to 12.5 mills.[68] A government which was lean and spartan to begin with had been pared even further. In his inaugural of 1878, Governor John M. Stone said that "government should do no more than provide protection of life, liberty and property," and that was just about all Mississippi did.[69]

As in Mississippi, there had been little industrial development and railroad building in South Carolina during Reconstruction. In addition, the Moses administration had already repudiated $5.96 million of the debt and funded the remainder, about $10 million, in the Consolidation Act of 1873. That same year, a constitutional amendment had banned further state aid.[70] The main props of the Reconstruction system had therefore been removed already. Consequently, a constitutional convention was not of pressing concern and a bill to call one was defeated in the 1878 legislative session.[71] But the legislature nevertheless proceeded to slash government expenses, particularly official salaries, and to reduce the tax rate to 5 mills.[72] A year later, the assembly also restrained the railroads through the creation of a commissioner to examine their books and operations; this limited foray into regulation was later expanded considerably in 1882 when the commissioner's powers were increased to include rate setting.[73]

The major challenge to the status quo arose over the state debt. The issue surfaced in 1877 when, despite their party's public endorsement in 1876 of the Consolidation Act, Democrats in the legislature voted against appropriating any money to pay the interest due on the debt in 1877. This precipitated a crisis that endangered party unity and would only be resolved after the Bond Commission was appointed and had reported at the next session of the assembly. When the commission announced its recommendation, it made the situation worse. It proposed that $3.6 million of the consolidated debt should be declared void and repudiated. Because of this, the assumptionists, led by Governor Wade Hampton, found themselves faced with the impossible task of having to marshal enough votes to defeat the report. In order to avoid the danger of relying on the votes of Republicans to ensure assumption, a compromise was produced, the Simonton plan, which submitted the question of the validity of the bonds to a court of three judges selected by the assembly; meanwhile, the interest on the whole debt was to be paid for the coming year.[74] The Democratic caucus agreed to this device, and Francis Dawson of the *News and Courier* breathed again, as he realized that, since Republican support had not been required, the powerful antidebt group, with Martin W. Gary in the lead, could not now accuse its opponents of infidelity to the party. In addition, they would be foiled in their attempt to gain the upper hand at the next election by submitting the debt question "to the people at every Courthouse and Cross-roads in the middle and upper counties" where hostility to the debt was rife.[75]

Mississippi and South Carolina had not been beset by the agitation and turmoil that invariably accompanied the calling and assembling of a constitutional convention. Nevertheless, the Democratic leadership was confronted by the very same issues that were sweeping like a tornado across the South. The demand for sharp reductions in the cost, scope, and power of government amounted to nothing less than an offensive against the activism that had characterized public policy since the war. In those years, government had been a dynamic force intervening in and shaping social and economic development. This it had done mainly through its promotion of internal improvements but also through its assumption of responsibility for schools and welfare institutions. If that kind of approach to government and public policy is aptly described as Whiggish, then the trend in the 1870s was clearly Jacksonian, for its aim was to reverse, even dismantle, the existing framework of governmental intervention. As a result, government's role would be minimal, and its capacity to shape and promote economic development would be severely restricted.

The pressure for these changes arose, to a large extent, from the hard reality of the South's material condition in the mid-1870s. The panic of winter 1873 had had a severe impact on the southern economy; northern investors had called in their loans and credit, while markets for southern products, particularly cotton, had shriveled up. The result was several years of stringency and hardship. In addition, the postwar increase in taxation was beginning to take its toll. Among the owners of small farms, the distress was very evident, and the growing number of defaults and foreclosures bore witness to the problem and its scope. These experiences and complaints gave rise to the mighty demand for tax reductions and retrenchment which erupted throughout the South. Not least of the South's worries was, of course, the manifest failure of some of the costly programs introduced by the Republicans to deliver on their promises. Most notable of these was the railroad policy, for, after immense amounts of expectation and money had been lavished on railroads, there was little to show; a disproportionately small amount of track had been laid, while very little cohesion and articulation had been imposed upon the region's multitude of local lines.[76] The material hardship itself as well as the anger at the Republicans for their role in producing it were very real, and the Democrats took political advantage of the discontent. Powerful though they were, these sentiments among the rank and file cannot, by themselves, account for the bitter tone and extreme form in which the antidotes were pressed upon the Democratic party as it assumed power.

The explanation for the radicalism of the demands lay in the political context that gave them force and form, for the solutions proposed to deal with these problems were part of a struggle to reorient Democratic policy. Therefore, they were not offered simply as practical remedies. At issue was the necessity felt by the Bourbon wing of the party that the leadership's endorsement of, or at least acquiescence in, the activist role of state government following the war had to end. Moreover, the insurgents' own uncompromising and antipathetic stance towards the Republicans was, in this way, contrasted most favorably with the complicity and acquiescence of the current leaders. They presented their case in the form of a challenge. There was to be no gradual phasing out or decrease of Republican programs and policies. Instead, they were to be renounced and rejected entirely. A different approach to the role of government was to be established in its place, not just less of the same. It is significant therefore that debts incurred for these policies were to be repudiated and not merely scaled down or partially unpaid. Another indication of the Bourbons' desire to break completely from

Republicanism and the Whiggish policies it pursued was their insistence on implementing the change by means of a constitutional convention. In that way, public interest would be focused by the calling and meeting of the convention and the break would thus be dramatized and highly visible. Furthermore, by being embodied in a new constitution, rather than in a series of bills, these changes would become part of the fundamental law and so be given permanence as well as a shaping influence over the South's future development. With a new constitution, it was hoped that a new era would emerge in which the state and the Democratic party would be permeated by the doctrines and priorities of the Bourbon insurgents.

When the Bourbons set out to repudiate the Whiggish policies of the Republicans, they were also overturning the priorities and past actions of their own party. In the ensuing fight to repudiate state debts, the incumbents, with their New South orientation and desire for continuity in policy, were quick to impress upon their challengers the seriousness of the ramifications of their demands. The Democrats' reputation for honesty and reliability as well as the incumbents' own position within the party were at stake. So the latter pointed out unceasingly the past commitments they themselves had made on behalf of the party to uphold debts incurred by the Republicans. In South Carolina, on one occasion, "R.E.H." warned repudiators that the taxpayers' convention of 1871 had promised to pay the state debt, which at that stage was only a little smaller than it was by 1878; the resolution had stated that the debt was "valid" and that "the honor and funds of the State are lawfully pledged for the redemption thereof."[77] One of the debt commissioners in Alabama, Levi Lawler, reminded the repudiationist opposition that their policy was bound to run into legal difficulties. As he explained it, "From Nov. '70 to Nov. '72 we had a so-called democratic Governor, and a large majority in the *H.* of *R.* During that period authority was conferred on Gov. Lindsay to borrow money to pay interest on the endorsed bonds of the A[labama] & C[hattanooga] R.R.Co." In addition, the Democratic majority in the Senate from 1872 to 1874 had approved the enactment of a law "authorizing the substitution of bonds of the State for endorsed bonds on the basis of one for four."[78] Also complicit in giving legitimacy to Republican bonds were Louisiana's Democrats. They endorsed the Funding Act of 1874, while their platform in the 1876 canvass pledged the party to honor the existing debt. A leading assumptionist in the state's convention, Donelson Caffrey, described the party's situation very matter-of-factly when he said, "The acts of the Kellogg government have been ratified by the Nicholls government."[79] Caffrey's colleague, Thomas J. Semmes, was rather more emotional. "I shrink from doing an act which would violate solemn pledges," he avowed when confronted by the prospect of repudiation.[80] Nevertheless, these objections were invariably overruled, and the debts were set aside. Indeed, to the repudiators, the substance of the objection was itself cause for repudiation because the termination of all Democratic complicity in Republican policies was their overriding concern.

The Democratic party was not the only entity whose reputation and reliability were at stake in the debate over repudiation. Each state whose bonds were being nullified was also in danger of losing its good name. Thomas Semmes, for one, was quick to point out that, once a state's credit was gone, the money needed to honor the debt was "a mere bagatelle" compared with the likely financial loss involved in the state's failure to lure future investment.[81] All in all, the southern states repudiated $116.3 million by 1890 and avoided paying perhaps another $150 million in interest payments.[82] Had the repudiators got their way completely, the amount would have been even greater. Nevertheless, the effect, as Georgia's financial agent, Hannibal Kimball, explained it, was devastating. "The policy of Repudiation has been a curse to the State," he told Robert Alston in 1874, "and throttles every enterprise that requires outside capital."[83] This observation was actually made before most of the southern states had engaged in widespread repudiation, yet, if it were to prove accurate, the impact on the region would be severe. After all, the public debts that were being renounced had been incurred for the very basic reason that the South did not have any private capital of its own to draw on.[84] With no means of generating capital internally, it would then be forced into utter reliance on outside sources. Yet repudiation reduced drastically even the likelihood of obtaining this, leaving the South to confront the possibility that it would be bereft of investment capital.

In actuality, however, external investment did not dry up, as Kimball had feared. But, all the same, the South was no longer a reliable place to invest after the massive repudiation of the 1870s. Therefore, when capital did venture in, it invariably gravitated toward concerns that were already established and offered little risk. Consequently, its objectives were rarely to develop, enlarge, and diversify the region's economy since those activities would involve risk and innovation. Instead, external capital tended to consolidate and control the southern economy, and the interests and purposes it served were not necessarily those of the region itself. The result was that, because it was fiscally untrustworthy and financially dependent, the South had, in effect, surrendered control over its future economic development.[85]

The abolition of state aid to internal improvements also constituted a setback to the region's industrial development. Because the South's industry was embryonic, it could not rely on just the neutrality and nonintervention of government but required much more. It needed active encouragement and stimulation from the public sector. Moreover, the large amounts of capital that were needed could not be obtained from private sources in the South, thus making it incumbent on government to create those funds through subsidies, loans, or the endorsement of bond issues. Consequently, with the elimination of state aid, an essential instrumentality for the generation of capital and the sponsorship of growth was removed. Few were more aware of this than two of Georgia's best-known promoters, Joseph Brown and Hannibal Kimball. Brown warned the Georgia convention that the abolition of state aid "will do more than any other one thing to cripple the enterprises of the state."[86] Earlier, in 1874, Kimball had told Robert Alston, the editor of the Atlanta *Herald*: "I have been and am still a believer in 'State aid' and a liberal policy toward Railroad enterprises. I do not say that this policy has not been somewhat overdone; but the policy, wisely executed, is *correct*." To illustrate this assertion, Kimball pointed out that the Union Pacific "never could have been built but for the aid of government. But now that it is built the government would be a hundred times better off even if they had to pay every dollar guaranteed, than they would have been with no road and no pay." If public aid was so crucial in the North, Kimball concluded, such a policy was even more vital in the South where "your people are too poor and have not the means to develop your resources."[87]

Of course, Brown and Kimball were interested parties. Nevertheless, they were quite right in pointing out that, with the elimination of state aid, the public sector could no longer be a positive and creative force in the promotion of southern economic development, and that was a distinct loss to the region. Some forms of support were, however, still possible. If aid were unavailable at the state level, it could be provided by county government; and it was, but it was minimal in amount. Also its impact was only local, and, at a time when the South really needed a network of lines, county aid was ineffective. Some states, like Florida and Texas, were able to subsidize railroads through the granting of land. This policy gave railroads in both localities millions of acres and it produced growth, but land grants were not an option open to other states.[88] Therefore, with these few exceptions, state government in the South was, by the mid-1870s, no longer involved in the promotion of railroads.

Even though active support of railroads was no longer possible, states could still encourage industrial development by less direct means. After all, to many who opposed the state-aid schemes, it had been the manner in which the benefits had been given rather than the support itself that had so infuriated them. As Robert Toombs had insisted, a system of favoritism and corruption had resulted, producing "big bonanzas" for particular interests that then had drained away public resources. Consequently, he was proud to announce that the ending of state aid by the Georgia convention "had locked the door to the treasury and put the key in the pocket of the people."[89] In its place, perhaps other devices less open to abuse could be found.

Besides the offering of land grants to railroads, there were two schemes for fostering and encouraging industrial development which southern states considered, but neither amounted to much. The first was the contracting out to railroads and to mining and construction companies of a state's convict population. Convict leasing was carried on by virtually all the southern states under the Democrats. While this constituted a subsidy in the form of extremely cheap labor, its contribution was insubstantial. This was because the supply of convicts was not that large and the number available was generally leased to one or two agents and firms, thus limiting drastically its overall economic impact. Actually, the promotion of industry was only of marginal consideration when the states leased their convicts. Far more important to them was the reduction in prison expenditures which would be achieved by leasing.

Therefore, neither in intention nor result was leasing to be a great boon to southern industrialists.[90]

The intention of aiding industrial development was much more obvious when states considered the second possible form of indirect aid which was the offer of tax exemption to new manufacturing firms. This device would require no outlay of funds and no special legislation and thus would provide no reason for lobbying. Despite its avoidance of the perversions of state aid, tax exemptions were regarded with surprising ambivalence, even disfavor. Few states adopted the measure in the 1870s and those that did often imposed restrictions. Alabama, for example, did not exempt manufacturing establishments from taxation, though it was considered in 1879.[91] Georgia's convention in 1877 withdrew the exemption privilege that the state had granted earlier in the decade.[92] North Carolina's legislature rejected proposals for exempting manufacturing in 1877 and again in 1881.[93] The idea of an exemption was introduced into Arkansas' convention in 1874, but it precipitated the most bitter debate of the entire session. The result was a seven-year privilege limited only to cotton mills, tanneries, mines, and manufacturers of agricultural implements with a capitalization of over $2,000, a concession the *Gazette* regarded as a fair start but limited.[94] Louisiana manufacturers wanted a twenty-five-year exemption but obtained from the convention relief for only a seven-year period.[95] Mississippi, in 1876–77, reconsidered its earlier broad grants of tax exemption and decided that, rather than withdrawing the exemption, it would restrict the relief only to the machinery and stock of the operation.[96]

Thus, tax exemptions for manufacturers were evidently regarded with mixed feelings by the Democrats in the 1870s. Sometimes, those who opposed them did so because they were hostile to industrial and railroad interests and regarded them as in need of discouragement rather than inducement and incentives, but usually the feeling was that government should not side with any particular economic interest. Instead it should be evenhanded towards all, protecting rights but not bestowing privileges and promoting schemes. This was what Jesse Cypert had meant when, in the debate on a tax exemption during the Arkansas convention, he said it was "unjust" to support particular interests; instead, he suggested, "Let every avocation stand upon the legitimate principles of trade."[97] Whether the tax exemption was opposed because it encouraged governmental favoritism on behalf of a particular economic interest or because that interest was industrial rather than agricultural, these two objections were symptomatic of the kind of forces that were rising to the top of the Democratic party and were using constitutional conventions to achieve a redirection of the party's priorities and principles. These elements that were demanding recognition and power were from the Bourbon wing of the party. Most of all, they were insisting on a clean break from the Whiggish, activist policies of the postwar years, but there was also an antiindustrial, anti–New South component to their remonstration. Animated by these Jacksonian and, to some extent, agrarian sentiments, the Democrats ensured that government would no longer be an active force in the life of the region, particularly its economic affairs. Thus, the New South could expect virtually no assistance from the public sector.

In the winter of 1879, after his state had held its convention, George T. Ruby, a prominent black Republican in Louisiana, who had earlier been a leading figure in Texas Republicanism, observed, "Capitalists and businessmen were rather of the opinion that the local party managers of the Democracy had gone not only too far but had given the state a fatal blow in its industrial interests . . . they feel that under the present party in power they cannot get the development, the material development that they need."[98] And that, indeed, was the upshot of the shift in public policy of the mid-1870s. By its renunciation of state aid, the Democratic party had foreclosed the possibility of enlisting the public sector in the generation of capital and the concentration of available resources. Furthermore, by their extensive repudiation, the southern states had gained an unenviable reputation in the financial markets which limited the ability of their governments to obtain credit outside their region. These actions forced the South onto the defensive and sealed off many vital options in its pursuit of the economic development and diversification that it needed so much.

10. The Resurgence of the Agricultural Interest

Agriculture is the groundwork of all else. Let it languish and everything else languishes.
—Governor William D. Simpson of South Carolina, Annual
  Message, 1879

Ever since the end of the war, the interests and needs of southern agriculture had been overlooked, if not actively ignored, by state governments throughout the region. By the mid-1870s, however, agriculturalists were beginning to act decisively to end the disregard and exclusion they had suffered. Meetings of disgruntled farmers erupted across the land and organizations like the Grange emerged to implement demands and satisfy needs. This reassertion of its influence by the agricultural sector contributed significantly, perhaps more than anything else, to the readjustment of the economic forces in southern life which was occurring throughout the decade. This, in turn, fostered the realignment within the Democratic party which was already underway with the rising influence of the Bourbons.

The distress and decline that southern agriculture was experiencing in the 1870s made little sense to the region's planters and farmers. After all, agriculture was "the foundation, the basis of all other employments" as they constantly pointed out, and the South's recognition of agriculture's natural importance before the war had ensured the prosperity of the farming interest as well as of the region as a whole.[1] Since then, however, economic priorities had been altered drastically, and the consequences of this change were disastrous. According to the farmers, what had happened was easy to explain; there was nothing complex or inscrutable about it. Other interests had simply thrust themselves forward, claiming that economic regeneration and development were to be had through the building of railroads as well as through similar schemes of internal improvement and diversification. Furthermore, these claims had been backed by considerable political influence, with the result that aid and encouragement had been secured readily from government. Consequently, the southern economy was out of balance and its system of government had gone awry.

The perception that the agricultural interest was being pushed aside by an assertive and politically influential rival was widespread. As early as 1872, Commodore Matthew Fontaine Maury, the celebrated oceanographer, was complaining, "The manufacturing interest has combined to procure legislation for its exclusive benefit"; as a result, the railroads had "grown to be a huge monopoly." Because the public sector was committed to the active promotion of these kinds of economic development, Maury concluded angrily that agriculture was "left not only to work its way unaided, but is loaded with enormous burdens for the benefit of others."[2] A similar analysis was proffered in December 1876 by a gathering of Mississippi planters, headed by Frank Burkitt and J. B. Yellowley, two of the state's leading farm spokesmen. The meeting was intended to bring pressure on the new Democratic legislature that had been elected in the successful Redemption campaign of 1875. To this end, the delegates explained, first, that the state had "for the last ten years been under the control of politicians, whose legislation has been antagonistic to the interests of the farmers." Then, to rectify this situation, they resolved to cooperate so as to ensure that "the state government shall be hereafter administered *in the main* by men who are directly interested in the agricultural and mechanical interests of the country, and whose slogans shall be *Honesty* and *Reform* in all departments of trade, and Death to rings and monopolies."[3]

Agriculture's problems were evidently political in origin. A group of farmers from Autauga County, Alabama, discovered this for themselves late in 1873 when their request for an inconsequential amount of aid was rejected by the state's Republican governor. Yet, as they informed him, their application was "in striking contrast with those so often made by other interests, whose relation to government is not so vital, while their growth has been so largely encouraged by its aid."[4] Even in Democratic Georgia, agriculture received little sympathy. That same year, Benjamin Hill was telling a gathering of farmers in Jonesboro: "The whole tendency of legislation in this country is to enrich and build up every other interest at the expense of the Agricultural."[5] Hill's observation was confirmed in a survey carried out by the Georgia Grange, which concluded, "The farming interest does eight-tenths of the voting, and yet gets less than one-tenth of the laws. The other nine-tenths relate to corporations, contracts, the code, etc."[6]

These admissions of failure and weakness in the past also served to reveal the potential power of the farming interest now aroused and determined to regain an influence commensurate with its acknowledged importance. The resurgence of this newly awakened and assertive agricultural sector was facilitated by two concurrent developments during the 1870s. The first was the loss of confidence in the schemes of internal improvement whose ability to stimulate the revival and prosperity of the South had once been so enthusiastically propagated. Despite the grand promises, they had produced just a small amount of track and a large public debt. Across the South, epitaphs for the schemes of internal improvement were being offered up. In typical fashion, Robert McKee, the editor of the Selma *Times and Argus*, pronounced: "The people of Alabama have had enough of development. They are threatened with the loss of their houses and homes by those who but the other day were deluding them with plausible schemes for the material regeneration of their State."[7]

The other occurrence likely to benefit agriculture was taking place within the Democratic party. Long frustrated at their inability to garner the electoral support they expected, the Democrats began to see in the farm vote the prospect of relief from their political embarrassment. With the Republicans making only minimal gestures towards agriculture, it might be comparatively easy to win over the farming sector now that it was aroused and seeking redress through political action. The farmers' enthusiasm for the Democrats was stimulated, to some extent, by the emphasis upon race and reduced property taxes in the mid-decade election campaigns, but the party also went out of its way to identify itself with the needs of agriculturalists. All of the major Democratic newspapers, even though published in the cities, ran weekly agricultural sections devoted to the discussion of farm problems and edited by a leading farm spokesman such as Wyatt Aiken in the Charleston *News and Courier*, Charles C. Langdon and J. Parish Stelle in the Mobile *Register*, and Malcolm Johnston in the Atlanta *Constitution*. Furthermore, state Democratic parties became so increasingly identified with policies aimed at dismantling the system of state-sponsored internal improvements and reducing public expenditures and taxation that the beleaguered and spurned agricultural sector began to expect a sympathetic response from the Democrats once they were returned to power. Of course, Democratic candidates were often selected with the farming vote in mind, the most obvious example of this being the choice of Grange leader William L. Hemingway for state treasurer in Mississippi in 1875. This prompted the Republican Jackson *Pilot* to enquire facetiously that, if he "was not nominated because he was the Grand-Master of the Grange, what was he nominated for?"[8]

After the Democrats seized control of the southern states towards the end of the 1870s, it was generally acknowledged that their success had been achieved because they had secured the electoral support of the aroused agricultural sector. Even the Charleston editor and New South promoter, Francis Dawson, admitted the indispensable contribution of the farmers to the Democratic victory. In 1878, he observed, "The remarkable preponderance of the agricultural elements is the fact that most impresses a casual visitor to the Legislature." This was so because "the great uprising that lifted us into the upper air of political life was mainly accomplished by their unanimity and determination."[9] Meanwhile, in Mississippi, a correspondent of the *Clarion* called "Justice" announced, "The Democratic party in this State owes its existence to the energy of the farmers, to the patriotism of the farmers, to the votes of the farmers." Because it had played so vital a role in the Democrats' success, "Justice" demanded that the agricultural interest be rewarded with the gubernatorial nomination in 1877.[10] Similarly, Dawson recognized in 1878 the equity of the farmers' demand for a department of agriculture since, "having accomplished [so much], it is but natural they should endeavor to protect and advance the great interests they represent, and which look to proper legislation for encouragement."[11]

Across the entire region, the farming interest was contributing significantly to the revival of the Democratic party. In states like Mississippi and South Carolina, the votes of white farmers in the backcountry counties had been responsible for eclipsing the Republicans' black electoral majorities. Elsewhere, in states like Georgia, North Carolina, Arkansas, Virginia, and Texas, the Democrats were increasingly aware that landowning farmers in the white counties were the backbone of the party's constituency. When to this element were added the planters and farmers of the black belt who were also aggrieved at the plight of agriculture and becoming increasingly self-conscious as members of an abused group, it was evident that the party was beholden to a numerous and vocal combination. Moreover, this pressure-group, having rallied so successfully behind the Democrats, now demanded the recognition and reward it deserved.

The impact of the agricultural interest on the Democratic party was evident from the kinds of issues and measures that came before the state legislatures in the second half of the decade when the Democrats assumed control. Suddenly there was a rush of proposals relating to agriculture. Agricultural concerns pervaded and dominated the deliberations of the legislative assemblies and usually these proposals were enacted into law. After years of neglect, planters and farmers were evidently determined to produce legislation to benefit and protect themselves.

The most obvious of these measures was the creation of a government department responsible for looking after and encouraging agriculture. The first state department of agriculture in the nation was instituted in Georgia in 1874, and others followed suit soon after.[12] North Carolina created its agriculture department in the legislative session of 1876–77, and, in 1879, South Carolina's legislature and Louisiana's constitutional convention made similar provisions.[13] Curiously enough, despite Alabama's abolition of its commissioner of industrial resources in 1875, the state did not create an agriculture department until 1883, but the department soon made up for its late start by becoming a power in the state government "second only to the governor."[14]

These agencies had been agitated for by such leading farm organizations as the state agricultural societies and the Grange, and their purpose was to further the interests of agriculture by encouraging farmer education, inspecting fertilizers, conducting soil and livestock experiments, and publishing statistics on agricultural production.[15] To complement the work of the department, most state legislatures during the 1870s also established experimental farms and provided funds for conducting geological surveys, both of which were sought by and benefited the farming community.[16] But the promotion of agriculture did not stop there, for legislatures also donated subsidies to their state agricultural societies to enable them to hold an annual state fair and to carry out their programs of social and educational work among the scattered and poorly informed farm population.[17] Perhaps even more important, states founded agricultural and mechanical colleges, notably Mississippi, North Carolina, South Carolina, and Virginia. Furthermore, where these institutions existed already, their operation and maintenance were funded at increased levels.[18]

This array of measures for promoting the interests of the agricultural sector was not too surprising in view of the large numbers of farmers who sat in the elected assemblies of the South in the late 1870s. Their prominence was widely commented upon by contemporaries who would suggest not merely that this was significant but that it was also somewhat unusual. Francis Dawson had noted, as we have already seen, that, by 1878, the South Carolina legislature was dominated by farmers. Two years later, the lower house contained thirty-three lawyers, three merchants, and three manufacturers, but sixty-three other legislators described themselves as planters, another four doubled as merchants and planters, and yet ten more were physicians as well as planters.[19] The legislative session of 1876–77 in Alabama was so thoroughly controlled by the farming interest that it was referred to as the "Grange" legislature, an appropriate epithet confirmed by the body's subsequent passage of extensive agricultural legislation, notably for the regulation of

cotton weighing, the protection of farm animals, the taxation of
commercial drummers, the creation of a commissioner of immigration, and the implementation of a geological survey. That one particular session was not atypical. After the Democrats returned to
power in Alabama, so one historian of the period has written, the
legislature was "dominated largely by Grangers and farmers."[20]
Mississippi's legislature during the late 1870s was also composed of
a continuous majority of farmers, and in Louisiana, they were invariably the largest single group.[21] Concurrently, the constitutional
conventions of the period usually had a heavy preponderance of
tillers of the soil or their representatives.[22]

Their numbers gave planters and farmers the means to introduce
and pass a considerable amount of legislation aimed exclusively at
benefiting the agricultural sector, but the scope of the measures that
were passed at their insistence was even broader than has so far
been suggested. Farming in the second half of the 1870s needed not
only to be promoted but it required protection as well. Consequently, measures intended to aid agriculture directly were complemented by propositions that would limit and restrain pressures
upon it from other quarters. Since, in these instances, farmers were
not the only group or interest that felt aggrieved, they frequently
found themselves working in tandem with others as part of a broad-
based coalition.

A case in point was the campaign to relocate the state capitals of
Georgia and Louisiana in the country towns where they had been
established before the war and where, it was felt, the actions of
government would be more responsive to the needs of the rural
population. Naturally enough, farmers, as rural dwellers, were in
the forefront of this effort. They were acting, however, less as an
occupational interest group, than as part of a larger protest by the
countryside against the urban thrust of postwar society and politics,
epitomized by the increasing size and influence of Atlanta and New
Orleans.[23] In this contest, they were joined by reactionaries in general who lamented the departure from earlier practices that were
simpler and more traditional. Issues like this mobilized support on
a wider front than agriculture alone.

This was also true of the fight for a usury law. Throughout the
1870s, the southern states debated the wisdom of setting a limit on
the legal rate of interest. Although it was frequently argued that re-

strictions on the rate of return that money could earn would only make holders of capital less willing to loan and thus worsen the predicament of those who were in debt or were reliant upon credit, the overwhelming pressure for usury legislation came from debtors who felt oppressed by the high rate of interest they had to pay. Most vociferous among these were, of course, the farmers who customarily operated on credit and always seemed to be in debt.

With the Grange, and sometimes the state agricultural society, heading the call for usury laws, farmers were a major force in the movement, and they were successful on a number of occasions.[24] In its legislative session of 1874–75, North Carolina enacted a 6 percent limit on the rate of interest and made its infringement so serious an offence that it was to be treated as a misdemeanor.[25] In 1873, Georgia repealed its usury law of 1871, but then two years later, in 1875, reinstituted it at 7 percent, raising it a percentage point in 1879, and there it stayed throughout the eighties.[26] Alabama retained its 8 percent usury provision despite considerable pressure to repeal it, particularly in 1875.[27] By the end of the decade, South Carolina belatedly joined the ranks of the opponents of usury when the legislature, at its 1877–78 session, required a maximum rate of 7 percent.[28] Usury restrictions were in fact the norm, and farmers played a major role in the agitation and enactment of them.

Of all the issues in southern politics during the later 1870s, none matched in importance the relentless pressure for retrenchment and the reduction of the costs of government. It overrode all other concerns and shaped the course of the region's political development. State budgets had to be cut and economies were to be achieved by the reduction of expenditures and through the repudiation of large portions of the state debt. This in turn would make possible a significant decrease in taxation. Although these demands for retrenchment were not raised by any particular segment alone, for many interests sought lower taxes and limits on public expenditures, there was nevertheless an unmistakably agrarian thrust and coloration to it.

The debts to be repudiated had been incurred principally to promote internal improvements. Moreover, the interests suggesting them as well as benefiting from them were, for the most part, nonagricultural and urban. Yet, for the funding of these obligations as well as for the support of government services and operations in general, the farming sector provided the bulk of the revenue since the taxes were levied primarily on land. Therefore, it was not surprising that the preponderance of support for these measures, and their most fervent advocates, came from the farming communities, particularly those located in the backcountry where taxes were especially burdensome to small landowning farmers operating on a margin.[29] Indeed, in every state, from Tennessee and Arkansas across the Gulf states to the Atlantic coast, the low taxers and the repudiators were to be found in the white farming areas of the piedmont and the hills.[30]

The zeal for retrenchment was, however, at odds with demands for greater support and services from government. Agrarians who had voted for cuts in expenditures had then to struggle to obtain funding for the state agricultural college or for the geological survey. On occasion, the sentiment for retrenchment was so formidable that it threatened to destroy even the newly created departments of agriculture. Receiving support from interests unsympathetic to agriculture, the retrenchers in Georgia assailed the department in 1876 and at the convention a year later. In the legislative session of 1878–79, the attacks reached a climax, and only by agreeing to an investigation of the department's operation did the farmers manage to repel the opposition, but it was just a temporary respite. In the early eighties, the office was subjected annually to demands for its abolition, and in the ranks of its opponents could be found numerous farmers who preferred to obtain relief from the tax on fertilizers rather than to keep in existence the department that had been set up specifically to aid the farming interest but whose funding was derived exclusively from the tax.[31] The same process was at work in North Carolina where the legislature of 1879 accompanied its drastic measures of repudiation and retrenchment with an attempt to abolish the new agriculture department. North Carolina's farmers were more supportive of their agency, even though, in both states, the fertilizer tax was used to finance it.[32]

The farmers' apparent willingness to harm their own interests can easily be explained, for they were experiencing cross-pressures, wanting both an agriculture department and reduced expenditures. Since the budget cuts generated a broad coalition consisting of more elements than the farmers alone, demands for fiscal restraint often received majority support. Consequently, farmers often found themselves helping to cut appropriations for their own programs and agencies. Nevertheless, for the mass of them, it was quite possible that retrenchment, and the reduced taxation that would ensue, was of primary importance. Since the war, landowners of all descriptions had been shouldering the tax burden, while previously only the more prosperous landowners who owned slaves and paid the slave tax had been required to contribute. With taxes levied more heavily on land, smaller landholders whose profit margin was probably slim anyway were highly incensed by their present predicament. Furthermore, the services that government provided after emancipation had been expanded, partially because the Republicans had a more activist view of government's role but more basically because the black population's wants were no longer taken care of by their owners. They had become consumers of government services and their numbers were considerable. The impact of this on the farmers was that they perceived that they now paid more but received less.[33] Relief from this novel and, to them, absolutely unfair situation was to be found in a drastic reduction of the flat tax rate on landed property.

The Democratic party was fully aware of how important tax reduction was. In Arkansas, the tax rate of 8 mills in 1874 toppled to 4 mills by 1885, while Florida, starting with a millage of 12.5 in 1876, was also down to 4 by 1884.[34] Alabama's rate fell one mill from 7.5 to 6.5 between 1875 and 1880, but the local taxation was so minimal that its per capita tax was only $1.15 on each $100 of property as late as 1890.[35] In Louisiana, a rate of 14.5 mills was reduced to 6 by the convention of 1879.[36] Meanwhile, the first year of Democratic control saw Mississippi lower its property tax by 30 percent.[37] Across the South, taxes on landed property dropped significantly in response to this intense pressure, arising mainly from the farmers of the white counties.

A corollary of this development was a shift in the weight of taxation onto the backs of other interests. Railroads and corporations were frequently deprived of their advantageous rates and required to pay property taxes at the same level as other interests. In addition, privilege and license taxes were increased, both through their stricter collection, as was the case in Mississippi, for example, as well as through their expansion into new areas such as the phosphate royalty South Carolina imposed in 1878 or the tax on commercial drummers which Alabama introduced in 1876.[38] The share of taxes that the landed interest paid thus shrank as the years passed. In Georgia, Judson Ward calculated that by 1890 half the state's revenue came from the cities, compared with a third in 1872. Meanwhile Alabama's revenues were derived not so much from taxes on landed property as from the license taxes that had almost tripled between 1877 and 1887 as well as from the state's leasing of its convicts. In addition, there was a 2 percent tax on the gross receipts of all telephone, electric light, and express companies as well as increased liquor taxes.[39]

A shift in the incidence of taxation was therefore quite perceptible in the post-Reconstruction years. Of course, the net effects of this change were sometimes lessened because tax collection may have been less than efficient or because property was underassessed, but, nevertheless, the intentions of the lawmakers were readily apparent: the tax burden of the agricultural population was to be ameliorated.

It would be quite erroneous, however, to assume that these actions were all intended to harm or punish the mercantile and commercial interests. Sometimes, this did however seem to be so. In the spring of 1874, when the Virginia legislature imposed a tax on the purchases made by merchants, there arose a great outcry from the country merchants in particular. More generally, there was a feeling that the commercial element that was now a "minority in legislation" was being penalized excessively.[40] This prompted the Richmond *Dispatch* to demand a test of the law's constitutionality since it was class legislation. "The representatives elected mainly by the real estate owners, [are] declaring," the *Dispatch* claimed, "that there cannot be an increase of taxes on the land, but the whole increase must be upon the mercantile and manufacturing classes."[41] Far away, in Alabama, the Republican *State Journal* was even more incensed, regarding the Virginia incident as merely one more episode in a developing pattern. "Wherever Democracy has full swing, it seems to realize intense delight in oppressing the mercantile class and relieving landholders."[42]

These reactions were excessively fearful, however. Far from attesting to the existence of an irrepressible conflict between agriculture and commerce, the merchants' tax in Virginia was exceptional in its hostility towards traders. Perhaps that was why it elicited such an outburst of alarm. Instead, the intention of the farming interest in its espousal of retrenchment and lower taxation had been not to transfer the heavy burden of taxation from the farmer to the merchant but to reduce its weight for every interest and then to apportion it more equitably. Naturally enough, those who had enjoyed a favored status would complain. Francis Dawson once commented that, in a legislature in which "the majority are farmers" who "know where their shoes pinch," it was highly likely that the measures they took to repair their fortunes would "impinge, at various points, upon business circles."[43] Nevertheless, it would be erroneous to conclude that there was an animus against commerce and trade and a determination to harm or proscribe them. In fact, at all times, the farmers' representatives disavowed such goals. Instead, their aim was to end the privileges and advantages that government had bestowed on railroads and other interests since the war. The whole purpose was not to gain exclusive and special privileges but to restore balance and equity in the operations of government and thereby in the political economy as a whole.

In this chapter so far, agriculture, or the farming interest, has usually been referred to as an entity seemingly without internal distinctions. Yet, of course, the farming population was not monolithic. Farm operations differed enormously in their size and scale, in their concentration on differing crops, and in their relation to the market. Later, in the 1880s and 1890s, the interests of small-scale farmers who had only limited contact with the market would be articulated through the Farmers' Alliance and Populism. In the 1870s, however, those who spoke and agitated on behalf of agriculture and demanded that its concerns be recognized and satisfied were representatives of planters and commercial farmers. These were the groups that were mobilized in the mid-1870s and that sought to obtain redress from and influence in the Democratic party as it returned to power.

The Grange, or Patrons of Husbandry as it was also called, acted as the organizational focus for the demands of these more substantial and commercial elements of southern agriculture. Rather than insisting upon a reordering of the priorities and structure of the agricultural system as would have been the case if the interests of the smaller, less-advantaged farmers had been at stake, the Grangers were simply insisting that agriculture as an occupation not be overlooked and neglected any longer. Essentially, they wanted inclusion and recognition by the political system. By contrast, they sought neither dominance over the nonagricultural sector nor, alternatively, any major change or reordering within agriculture itself. As a result, the Grange leaders, as spokesmen for this segment of the agricultural interest, assumed that there existed a fundamental harmony among the various elements comprising the southern economy and that this balance had been upset by the temporary difficulties agriculture was experiencing. Consequently, agriculture was not at war with trade, railroads, and manufacturing.

Nevertheless, because farmers were demanding remedial legislation, nonagricultural interests accused them of infringing on their turf and being hostile. Responding to these criticisms, William K. Duglas, Master of the Mississippi State Grange, denied that the organization was either antimerchant or antirailroad. In the first instance, farmers were opposed only to the "wild credit" that had been spawned, not to merchants as a group. The remedy was not that merchants should be forbidden to make advances, but that farmers should make themselves independent of credit by producing most things for themselves. "It will be best always to buy at home and sell at home," he advised. Moreover, because farmers were overly dependent on middlemen for marketing their crops and buying their necessities, Duglas regretted that "too many have the handling of what we buy and what we sell."[44] This same complaint was made in 1876 by Alfred Colquitt, a Granger who was then governor of Georgia: "We know to our cost and the cost of every other cognate interest, that a farmer's labor cannot bear the tariff which unnecessary agencies and a round-about road to market exact."[45] It was the excessive number of intermediaries, not the middlemen themselves, that was the problem.

Duglas's speech also disclaimed any purpose on the Grange's part to mobilize farmers against railroads. Only if railroads charged freight rates that were deemed excessive or if they ran over stock and refused to give more than 50 percent compensation would farmers attack them.[46] Accordingly, the Grange could always be found demanding cheap transportation and regulation of freight rates; in fact regulatory legislation in the Northwest and South came to be known as "Granger Laws." But railroads themselves were vital. W. W. Lang, the Worthy Master of the Grange in Texas, told a statewide meeting in 1874, "Railroads are indispensable auxiliaries to the agricultural prosperity of any country." Railroads were opening up interior farming communities, connecting farms to marketing centers, in a word, they were developing agricultural regions and expanding and facilitating agricultural commerce. Therefore, Lang urged, "Make no war upon railroads."[47]

Manufacturing was another development to which, it was thought, farmers were opposed. After all, the growth of factories and industries was hardly compatible with agriculture, but in the South of the 1870s, the leading farm spokesmen expressed no great fear that they might be overwhelmed by industrialization and the urban culture likely to accompany it. Instead, they were quite confident that agriculture could accommodate to and absorb factories and, better still, derive benefit from manufacturing. Time and again, officials of farm organizations spoke of manufacturing not as a serpent that would destroy the southern Eden but as a complement to agricultural revival and a crucial agent for achieving prosperity. W. C. Irwin, the president of the Madison County Farmers' and Planters' club in north Alabama, told a club meeting in 1873 that when agriculture, "the foundation, the basis of all other employments," prospers, "cotton factories, and woollen factories, and furnaces, and rolling mills, would spring up, and the music of the shuttle and the sound of the hammer would be heard from one end of the cotton-producing states to the other." Indeed, were the South to fail to develop manufactures, it would, in effect, "give this noble heritage over to log cabins, bushes, dogs, and gutters."[48]

Although its language was invariably less insistent than Irwin's, the Grange certainly favored the development of manufacturing in the South, for expressions of approval and encouragement appeared continually in the addresses and programs of the organization. In fact, the development of a manufacturing sector was seen as an essential ingredient in the Grange's efforts to make southern farmers independent as well as prosperous. This notion may seem paradoxical in retrospect, but, to farmers at the time, there was no inconsistency. John T. Jones, the well-known and well-respected Grand Worthy Master of the Arkansas Grange, explained how vital manufacturing was to agricultural revival: "We sell our staple at prime cost and purchase almost all our necessary appliances of comfort from abroad, not at prime cost but burdened with the profits of merchants, the costs of transportation, duties, commissions, exchange and numerous other charges all of which go to enrich others at our expense. This is the true reason the South is growing poorer." If manufacturing were carried out in the South, farmers and southern consumers in general would not have to pay inflated prices for purchases from outside. The gains were so obvious that Jones urged planters to pool their resources and "form associations with sufficient money to start a cotton mill in every important district." [49]

The assumption underlying this enthusiasm for manufacturing was revealed in Jones's last comment, suggesting that planters actively promote and finance cotton factories. For, evidently, mills were perceived not as the advance guard of a wrenching, disruptive industrialization but merely as adjuncts, increasingly needed, to the farm and village. Indeed, the only danger that the Grange seemed to detect in the promotion of manufacturing was that government might intervene to facilitate it. That would be special legislation and a reintroduction of the state-aid formula that had been so pernicious and stultifying when provided for railroad construction. On these grounds, the head of the South Carolina Grange decided to cast his vote against a tax exemption for new manufacturing establishments when, in 1878, a bill to that effect was introduced into the South Carolina House. To vote that way did not imply that J. M. Lipscomb, or the Grange itself, was antagonistic to industry.[50] On the contrary, L. O. Bridewell, the chairman of the Mississippi Grange, explained, "As Patrons [of Husbandry], we have no personal quarrel with the manufacturer; we only ask for equal consideration."[51] Confident that agriculture was the source of all production and wealth and that it could flourish if it were not discriminated against, farm spokesmen believed manufacturing and farming were not antagonistic but that both were essential to the creation of a prosperous South.[52]

Thus, the increasing influence of the agrarians within the echelons of the Democratic party did not necessitate a struggle for control with the New South industrializers. Seemingly, the two interests were not at odds. Manufacturing and farming could prosper together, provided that government did not actively support one to the detriment of the other. Although farmers argued vociferously for governmental inaction and laissez-faire, raising it to a matter of principle in the Jefferson-Jackson tradition, there was one instance in which they sought the intervention of public authority. As the Democrats returned to power, immense pressure was exerted to enlist government and law on the side of the landed interest in its attempts to alter the system of agricultural credit and to discipline and control the labor force on the farms and plantations. The harmony of interests that farmers obviously perceived between the various occupations and estates of the South did not, it seemed, apply to the relations between employer and employee, landlord and tenant. They did not ask government to proffer aid or privileges but they were very exacting in their demand that laws be passed sanctioning certain measures of labor control that they contemplated introducing. If the precise extent of agrarian influence on the Democratic party in the wake of Redemption were not clear so far, the spate of laws passed during the late 1870s to regulate class relations in the fields and villages of the South provided unmistakable evidence that it was now of critical importance.

11. The Agrarian Reaction

The labor is becoming, every year more scarce and difficult to procure. It is also becoming more unreliable, whilst laborers are demanding ruinous prices; and those negroes that are not employed live by theft. The thieving, in this section is becoming so intolerable, that I fear a revival of the much to be deplored Ku Klux. We are waning, in prosperity every year, & unless some beneficial change can be effected our ruin, utter & total, is only a question of time. Fences & houses are falling into decay & our old lands are constantly depreciating in value.
—Herschel V. Johnson to Dr. J. R. Price, 12 November 1872

Herschel Johnson's despair and dejection over the state of southern agriculture at the end of 1872 was not an idiosyncratic or a jaundiced view. On the contrary, few could be found who would deny "the gloomy prospect of the planting interest."[1] Ever since the war, the future of plantation agriculture had been shrouded in uncertainty and pessimism. At the root of this concern was a persistent anxiety about the supply of labor. Planters had been convinced that emancipation was ill-advised and would have disastrous consequences because black laborers would not work without the compulsion of servitude.[2] When that did not happen, planters were still dissatisfied because they regarded the terms of remuneration that labor demanded likely to make farming an uneconomical or insufficiently profitable enterprise. They blamed their disadvantageous bargaining position on what they perceived to be a shortage of labor. They attributed this to abolition because freedom had enabled many blacks to move into the cities to find work while, among those who stayed, freedom gave women the opportunity to stay at home rather than work in the fields.[3]

The planters' inability to command a supply of labor on their own terms was not the only problem they faced, however. More serious were the structural shortcomings and operational defects of the South's agricultural system. These were exposed and criticized with unrelenting persistence in the postemancipation years by a host of agricultural reformers and their associated organizations. Although there were among them differences of emphasis and of strategy, there nevertheless emerged a well-defined and distinctive critique of southern agriculture, along with an agenda for reform that commanded widespread assent. This perspective and program amounted to what was, in effect, a proposal for the renewal and revitalization of the South's agricultural system. As such, it was an agrarian counterpart of the schemes for industrial development most generally associated with the term "New South."

This agricultural New South, which the reformers envisaged and for which they clamored so insistently, necessitated simply that, as J. W. Norwood of North Carolina once put it, the region's "present ruinous mode of production must be changed."[4] In the words of the Atlanta *Constitution* later in the decade, the overriding need was for nothing less than "an agricultural revolution." If the South's agricultural sector were to revive and prosper, its transformation was essential. Things simply could not continue in the same decrepit and harmful way and be expected to flourish.[5]

To shake the South's agriculture out of its stagnation and reverse its decline, the reformers proposed essentially two remedies. The first requirement was for a dramatic improvement in the techniques of farming and in the attitude of farmers towards their occupation. Cultivation had to be more efficient and more up-to-date. What was needed, the *Constitution* suggested, was the introduction of "deep instead of shallow plowing; thorough instead of partial cultivation; economy and skill instead of improvidence and clumsiness."[6] In the same vein, Charles C. Langdon, the Alabama politician and agricultural reformer, concluded, "The true policy is to first make the land very rich; cultivate no more than you can cultivate well and manure heavily." If the land were tilled intensively and efficiently, there would emerge "a system that will make twenty acres yield as much as a hundred do now."[7]

If the advice of Langdon and his fellow reformers were taken, their second injunction, that farmers would need fewer acres than before, followed naturally. In that case, there was every incentive to cut down the amount of land that was being farmed wastefully and to run instead a compact, manageable, and efficient operation more like a family farm than an extensive plantation. Accordingly, reformers called for "small instead of large farms," and they demanded that "the planter must give way to the small proprietor."[8] Although such a change amounted to "a revolution in the manner of holding land," the Atlanta *Constitution*, in uttering such a view, was only saying what it had been urging since 1869 when its editor had asserted: "The fact is that food raising and small farming are far more profitable than large plantations."[9]

To most reformers, the introduction of family farms would also make it possible to attract to the South the immigrants the region so desperately needed. If surplus or uncultivated lands were sold by their owners, not only would the scale of farming change for the better, but the means for attracting homesteading immigrants would be made available. Consequently, reformers like "Granger" in Virginia called unceasingly for excess land to be given up. "The landowners neither improve the land nor will sell it to others who will improve it." Yet, he lamented, "It costs more than the market value of most lands to improve the soil to a paying basis; and high rents and deferred payments will not bring laborers to the vacant fields."[10] So, by selling their surplus, those "who have more land than they can well work" would be increasing the efficiency and profitability of their own operation as well as facilitating the arrival of immigrants. The latter, in turn, could improve the uncultivated acres, once they were made available.[11] Small farming was, therefore, critical to a revived and reformed southern agriculture.

Although the outcome of the reformers' recommendations was the substitution of small-scale for large-scale farming, not all of them were quite so programmatic or specific. Instead, many placed more emphasis on the need for farmers to become independent and self-sufficient. They pointed out how their insatiable preoccupation with growing cotton as a cash crop was forcing farmers into reliance on others for their food, their supplies, and their credit. The "all-cotton policy," so the reformers believed, was disastrous. Planters were urged instead, through slogans such as "Make Cotton Your Surplus Crop" and "Raise Your Own Provisions," to change the crop priorities. To impress them with the gravity of the situation, Benjamin H. Hill was even prepared to invoke the emotive threat that servitude was the alternative, for "a people who depend on other people for food and clothing are, and must be, slaves."[12] A year later, in 1874, D. Wyatt Aiken, the South Carolina Grange leader and perhaps the region's best-known agricultural reformer, laid out the essential ingredients for attaining self-sufficiency. After complaining that his recommendations had been "set forth in these pages again and again; but the desired effect has not been produced," he once more outlined his advice to farmers: "Diversify your crops; avoid debts and liens; buy for cash and, by cooperation in Granges or Clubs, secure the economies of extensive and first-hand purchases; sell your produce with the intervention of as few intermediaries as possible. . . ."[13]

To be prosperous, therefore, farmers must be, first, self-reliant and, second, no longer at the mercy of external forces for their essential services and supplies. Yet there was a third element, not mentioned on this occasion by Aiken, that both he and other reformers regarded as critical. This was to diminish the farmers' dependence on costly labor. In the speech that has already been cited, Charles Langdon concluded with this admonition: "But more important than all, work yourself, and learn your boys to work, and dispense with hired labor as far as possible."[14] If the members of the farmer's family rolled up their sleeves and worked in the fields, they would earn their keep. Simultaneously, they would lessen, or even remove, the need to rely on paid laborers, with the accompanying problems of bargaining with them and paying the wages they were able to command. Of course, by shifting labor priorities, the farmer was likely to be less inclined to take on numerous tenants, thus encouraging him to curtail his landholdings and farm intensively what he retained. "Hold the plow and drive" was the phrase widely employed at the time to admonish farmers to both supervise the farm as well as work it themselves. It was no longer to be considered virtuous not to labor and tend the soil oneself.

Self-reliance and independence for the individual farmer was the hallmark of the agricultural New South portrayed by the reformers. If their recommendation for the improved and diversified cultivation of fewer acres were followed extensively throughout the region, not only the farmers but the entire South would become prosperous and no longer reliant on outsiders for credit, supplies, and expertise. Sensible and attractive though the proposal for a system of small-scale independent farming was, it did not elicit much enthusiasm. In fact, by the late 1870s, the reformers' agenda had been eclipsed and effectively removed from consideration. The region's chance to break out of its existing system of agriculture had been lost. Instead, a very different remedy for the troubles ailing southern agriculture was applied. Rather than changing the system, this course of action tightened and consolidated it, thereby foreclosing the possibility of reform in the future. An idea of the nature of this choice—and of how decisive it was—was revealed rather tellingly in a communication to the Galveston *News* early in 1874 from a planter who signed himself "Fort Bend." Remarking that farming conditions in the lower eastern counties of Texas where he lived were very bad, "Fort Bend" complained that the farmer's predicament was caused by his having to pay "too dearly for labor"—half the crop rather than the quarter paid in 1867—while cotton prices were lower than before. The answer, said "Fort Bend," was not to become independent of hired labor—not, in other words, to "hold the plow and drive"—as the reformers proposed. Rather, he urged, "Let us both hold and drive; hold possession of our soil, not nominal possession but real, and drive the stakes that shall mark the dividing line between employer and employed."[15]

"Fort Bend's" remedy of tightening the employer's control over his labor force rather than reducing his dependence upon it proved far more appealing and far less threatening than reform. It was vigorous and direct, unlike most other recommendations, which were structural and long term. Furthermore, it involved no discomfort or risk for the farmer; the only one who would suffer was the laborer. Finally, of course, the appeal of the "Fort Bend" type of solution was that it paralleled the drive for political control which was under way in the mid-1870s. After years of Republican domination, the

Democratic-Conservatives were regaining power throughout the region. With control over the political apparatus came the capability for restoring order and discipline to the black labor force that had been unsettled and agitated because of Reconstruction and its promises. Consequently, as the Democratic-Conservatives returned to power, a spate of proposals, emanating mainly from the black belt, was introduced into the southern legislatures whose intent was the restriction of labor's mobility and rights. Prior to 1874, such propositions as these had, with the exception of the Black Codes in several states from 1865 to 1866, been scarce, but thereafter they suddenly became widespread and conspicuous. Together with other similar actions introduced at the same time, the labor-restrictive laws of the redeemed South constituted a counteroffensive on the part of the landholders and planters, which ended all possibility of agricultural reform.

The intent of this legislation was to control labor and increase its dependency on the employer, but there were several ways of doing this. Usually, a combination of them was employed, although the exact provisions varied from state to state. One kind of regulation that appeared frequently was the tightening of the law and penalty against petty theft. What legislators had in mind was not just any kind of theft but, specifically, the stealing of agricultural produce or livestock. Farmers had been complaining constantly that their property was not safe; cotton was being stolen while it was growing in the field and so were food crops and animals. As a result, farmers obviously incurred financial loss. They also viewed these losses as evidence that the farm labor population was lawless and had become independent of their employers' control by supplementing their income and food supply in this fashion. To stem this loss and reassert domination, farmers demanded harsher punishment for these offenses, which usually involved recategorizing petty theft as grand larceny that carried penalties of two to five years in the penitentiary. The implications of this change were very clear, and Adelbert Ames, the Republican governor of Mississippi, for one, did not hesitate to register his opposition. He vetoed the new Democratic legislature's stock-stealing bill with this observation, "Should this bill become law, persons convicted of stealing any animal therein mentioned, of not more than one or two dollars in value, may be sent to the penitentiary, perhaps for a term of years." Moreover, "Even if sent for a short time, the person so sentenced is disfranchised," because the crime was now a felony not just a misdemeanor.[16]

The antitheft measure was sufficiently important to the Democrats that, later in the session after Ames had been forced out of office, a new bill was passed which made it grand larceny to steal livestock whatever its value as well as other property if worth more than $10.[17] A year earlier, Alabama's triumphant Democrats amended section 7506 of their Revised Code so that stealing part of a corn or cotton crop, not just stock, was grand larceny with a penalty of two to five years in prison or at hard labor.[18] In its 1874–75 session, the Arkansas legislature required that petty theft of items valued at $2 or more be considered grand larceny, with a penitentiary sentence of one to five years.[19] This law to punish theft became known as the "pig law" as was Mississippi's 1876 act and Georgia's statute of 1875 that specifically made hog-stealing a felony rather than a misdemeanor.[20] The ultimate in virulence was reached by South Carolina where, in an act of 22 March 1878 amending the criminal law, stock stealing was defined as grand larceny punishable with one to ten years at hard labor in the penitentiary, burglary with lifetime imprisonment at hard labor, and arson and rape with the penalty of hanging.[21]

This legislative crackdown on petty thieving in the countryside was not merely a declaration of intent, for the statutes were enforced vigorously. As a result, the number of convicts in southern state prisons increased drastically, Mississippi's rising from 272 in 1874 to 1,072 in 1877, while, in the latter year, Georgia's convicts numbered 1,441 compared with 432 in 1872.[22] Furthermore, these prisoners were overwhelmingly black, which suggests that the subordination of the labor force was a primary concern. The depth of the planters' determination to restore order and control in the agricultural districts was also evident in the array of laws to punish arson and trespassing which the Democrats passed as soon as they regained power. In its first session under Democratic control, the Arkansas assembly tightened the state trespass law, levying fines from $10 to $100 for a misdemeanor, and it passed an act to prevent the firing of woods and prairies with heavy penalties from $5 up to $300.[23] In 1874, Georgia moved decisively against both these offenses, and elsewhere the pattern was virtually the same.[24]

Tough measures to curb theft, arson, and trespass were only part of the offensive to overawe the agricultural population and reverse a situation in which, as the Charleston *News and Courier* once observed, "the law has lost its terrors for . . . our criminal classes."[25] Besides securing a general state of deference and order, the landholders wanted to consolidate their economic control. To this end, they began to press relentlessly for another kind of law. Usually referred to as the "deadfall" bills, they were intended to prevent the sale of produce or cotton before it was harvested and registered with the planter on whose land the seller worked. In these transactions, the buyer was invariably a local storekeeper who operated a small grocery and supply store called pejoratively a "deadfall." Since these sales were, in some respects, illegal, they were usually carried on at night and so the laws banning them were also known as "sunset to sunrise" bills.

The pressure for firm action to stamp out the nighttime trade at the crossroads grocery stores was mounting during the 1870s. "There can be no question," the Mobile *Register* concluded in November 1874, "that the villainous operation of what are known as 'Dead-falls' have [sic] done more to disturb agriculture in this State than lazy negroes, high taxes, misgovernment, and the caterpillar."[26] That verdict was unfortunately excessive, but it did indicate how strongly landowners felt about the need to stop the traffic. Indeed, the planters' own organizations, like the Grange and the state agricultural societies, were already exerting pressure. For example, the Georgia Agricultural Society, which was meeting in November 1874 at the same time as the assembly was debating passage of a "deadfall" bill, passed resolutions applauding this action and urging enactment of the measure. Moreover, in his address as president, Alfred H. Colquitt, the future governor, reiterated its importance particularly in the black-belt areas of middle and southwestern Georgia where a ban on nighttime trading was "greatly needed."[27]

The first "deadfall" law was passed by North Carolina at its legislative session of 1873–74. The act simply prohibited nighttime sales of cotton or other growing crops.[28] Alabama followed suit in 1875, after Republican opposition in that state had earlier prevented passage of a law in 1873. The act specified that selling crops at night was a misdemeanor punishable by a fine of $10–500 or up to a year in jail.[29] A year later, Arkansas, Mississippi, and Georgia followed suit.[30] Finally, in 1877, Louisiana and South Carolina fell in line.[31]

The banning of nighttime sales often proved inadequate. The experience of Alabama and Georgia showed that more stringent and precise regulations were needed. Thus, the Alabama legislature of 1878–79 went so far as to ban the nighttime transportation of seed cotton, not merely its sale; also, in nine black-belt counties, selling cotton in the seed at any time and anywhere was to be treated as a felony.[32] The committee on agriculture in the 1876 Georgia assembly tried to extirpate the traffic completely by a bill that would have required the storekeeper to prove that the cotton or crops he received had not been stolen. This, however, was believed to be both unenforceable and unconstitutional because it presumed prior guilt on the merchant's part. So another proposition, from a leading Democratic senator, W. N. Tumlin, was considered which suggested licensing all merchants who purchased seed cotton with a fee of $500 and a pledge not to receive stolen goods as a prerequisite. What ultimately became law was a bill that made the knowing receipt of stolen goods a felony with a minimum jail term of one year.[33]

The "deadfall" legislation was the device whereby the employers of agricultural labor, the landowners in effect, intended to bring under firm control the farm workers, upon whom they relied for the planting, growing, and harvesting of their crops. With the return of the Democratic party to power, and through their increasing influence within it, the landowners anticipated that the opportunity they had been seeking was at hand and the moment propitious. Thus, the prohibitions on "deadfalls," nighttime trading, and removing growing cotton from the fields, together with the intensification of criminal sanctions through the revision of the penal code, comprised an initiative of great significance aimed at reducing to a minimum the autonomy and mobility of the labor force in the fields and plantations of the post-Reconstruction South.

Since the war, a system of labor had been emerging in the South which consisted of a series of expedients such as the annual contract and payment in shares. These had been adopted piecemeal and in response to immediate necessities, essentially the scarcity of currency and the disruption of labor after emancipation. The result, however, was a situation that was ill-defined and anomalous. As a black Republican from Alabama described it in an 1873 Senate debate on the "deadfall" bill, it was "a sort of cross between free and slave labor, and was neither the one nor the other . . . a system unknown to the laws of any country, and hence we find it bound up in liens of all sorts, the effect of which is to evil and evil only." The remedy that Senator Bruce proposed for rectifying this dangerous ambiguity was for the landlord to pay wages, so any tenant removing crops was obviously guilty of theft. Rather than tilting toward stressing the free element in this imprecise relationship, however, the Democratic legislators chose instead to emphasize its coercive component, thereby forcing tenants and sharecroppers into greater dependence on their landlord.[34] The "deadfall" laws and the criminal sanctions against theft forced the laborer to acknowledge that the crop he was growing—and from which he would pay his rent— was not his until after the settlement at the end of the year. Therefore, he could not use any portion of it as collateral to obtain supplies or food before the entire crop was harvested and his landlord and employer paid. Whether the laborer was a tenant who rented for a fixed amount annually or a cropper who rented for a share of the eventual crop, he could claim none of it until after the division.[35]

The import of these laws, which had been passed by the ascendant Democrats at the instigation of the landowners and landlords, soon became apparent. In February 1875, the Republicans in Alabama noted with alarm the actions of the Democratic legislature. Their response was to draft a petition to President Grant and the state's congressmen, telling them to keep Congress in session and force some kind of revocation of Alabama's antilabor legislation and its belligerent call for a constitutional convention. The Democrats' course in the first legislative session after Redemption had revealed, they believed, a determination to overthrow the political order set up under Reconstruction and also to dismantle the labor arrangements established after emancipation. Since Alabama's attack on labor was to serve as a precedent by offering a pattern for other states to follow, the urgency of a decisive countermove was evident.[36] What most worried the Republicans who memorialized the president was that the assault was not blatant. Slavery was not reintroduced and therefore the dangerous intent of the legislation might be overlooked. Urging the president and Congress to perceive the similarity between the coercion of labor under the recent legislation and the domination of slavery, the memorial pointed out, "The issue [of the civil war] was free-labor institutions and principles against slave-labor institutions and principles" and, although not actually reinstituting slavery, "the drift and tendency of all [this legislation] is to establish a system of compulsory labor and peonage utterly inconsistent with the genius and spirit of free-labor States and institutions." Despite its hostility to those "free-labor" laws and institutions, this system of restraint and coercion was being installed "under color of and under the forms of law." Thus, it was legal and would, therefore, prove most difficult to contest.[37]

Portentous as the "deadfall" legislation and the provisions against agricultural theft were, they were not as important in reducing the options and independence of rural labor as the laws redefining the legal relationship between employer and laborer, and between landlord and tenant. This third feature of the Democrats' drive to control farm labor involved the recasting of the region's lien laws. These laws had been introduced immediately after the war and their purpose was to provide security, in the form of a lien on the future crop, to merchants and others who were advancing supplies to farmers and farm workers. The latter needed tools and fertilizer to enable them to plant and grow their crops as well as clothing and food to sustain them until the crop was harvested and sold. Since cash was so scarce after the war, there was no possibility of a monetary loan; instead, the goods themselves were supplied in advance and the lien on the crop provided a guaranteed collateral. Had this convenience of mortgaging the crop not been available, loans might then have been exorbitant or just not forthcoming.[38] In time, however, this way of advancing credit began to operate to the farmer's disadvantage. While it made advances obtainable, it also encouraged the farmer to overextend himself, driving him into debt; and from this predicament it was almost impossible to escape. As Alfred Colquitt told the Georgia Agricultural Convention in 1874, the credit system offered a royal road into debt, but there was "no royal road out."[39]

Despite the general distress the lien laws caused, one economic interest seemed to benefit from the situation—the local storekeepers and supply merchants who were at the heart of the lien system. It was they who extended the credit and initiated the chain of indebtedness and they who stood to gain most because they were able to charge high rates of interest to credit-starved farmers and tenants whose only asset was a nonexistent crop. The crowning injustice was that the merchant's lien had to be paid before any others that the debtor had incurred. So it was not surprising that the merchants who provided the credit and advanced the supplies became a prime target of the aggrieved landlords. As Senator Parks of Pike County put it in the Alabama debate over lien-law repeal, "All had to give way to the only prosperous pursuit which seems to thrive among us, and to absorb all others."[40]

Some critics of the existing system proposed that the remedy lay in shifting the source of credit from the local storekeepers who were eager for customers, no matter how unreliable they might be, to the large factorage houses in the cities which would be more cautious and responsible about whom they financed.[41] Most critics urged a more radical remedy, the complete abolition of the lien laws and the recklessness they spawned. The main advocates of lien-law repeal were the Grange and the agricultural reformers. For example, in 1873, the head of the Georgia Grange, Dr. T. D. Hutchinson, urged repeal because the laws had made available an endless supply of goods on credit which had "given rise to a spirit of prodigality and reckless speculation."[42] No one, however, was more vocal in denouncing the lien system than South Carolina's leading Granger, D. Wyatt Aiken. "A very curse" was how he described the lien laws. In the first place, they encouraged a population of farmers already ignorant of "practical economy" to "live beyond their means." Consequently, the system was shielded from the pressure to economize and thereby reform itself. Instead, unaware of "the value of time" and keeping "no books," "they grow cotton to buy corn to feed stock and hands to work a crop to make cotton, and so the year goes, a wheel within a wheel with every spoke in the hub loose; and the only wonder is that they have not before this gone all to pieces." The ready availability of credit through the lien laws had also tempted farmers to take on more labor than they needed, and thus prevented economy and reform. "Don't hire these negroes," Aiken urged, "let them go and shuffle for themselves; they are a nuisance to you and your farm. Sell a mule and buy enough bread and meat to feed just such labor as will profit you and refuse positively to give a lien." If this were done, "next year your crop will be your own."[43]

Among agricultural reformers, the ending of the lien system was expected to provide the stimulus for "the enforced prudence and economy" that they had long sought.[44] Also anticipating benefits from repeal of the lien laws were the thousands of farmers who were suffering from declining crop prices in the mid-1870s and who believed repeal could remove their farms from the grasp of supply merchants and from dependence upon insubordinate black tenants. To this pressure, the Democratic party responded, and measures for repeal were introduced in Georgia, Alabama, Mississippi, South Carolina, and Louisiana.

Georgia was the first state to move against the lien laws when it passed an amendment in 1874 forbidding merchants to take a crop lien. So strong was the sentiment in favor of the proposal that, after it passed the Senate, a journalist for the Louisville *Courier-Journal* was convinced it would be "sanctioned by the House and approved by the Governor."[45] Repeal generated intense debate in the Alabama assembly throughout the late 1870s after the Democrats regained control. By the 1876–77 session, the agitation was almost successful; a bill passed the Senate but it then failed in the House.[46] Two years later, and at every biennial session thereafter, repeal was considered until it was finally achieved in 1884.[47]

The South Carolina legislature repealed the state's lien law at its special session in 1877. Twelve months later, however, the repeal was itself repealed. This sudden reversal was explained by the Charleston *News and Courier* as "the result of the generally admitted fact that the simultaneous repeal of the lien law and passage of the usury law has nearly ruined the planters in many sections of the State."[48] The difficulty was, as a correspondent called "Newberry" pointed out, that "many farmers who by this means [the crop lien] were able to get their support are not in a position to claim the credit that is necessary to sustain them."[49] Rather than releasing them from the coils of credit, repeal had denied them supplies and so had plunged them into chaos and despair. South Carolina's repeal was not emulated by Louisiana, however. Repeal was considered there in 1878, but it was indefinitely postponed by the Senate.[50] During that same year, a most interesting debate occurred in the legislative assembly of its neighbor, Mississippi. Outright repeal failed by two votes in the Senate, but, as a compromise and a preliminary to the anticipated repeal at the next biennial session, a measure for partial repeal was passed, prohibiting liens between 1

January and 1 May. This was the time of year when the crops were growing and the eventual yield was therefore totally unknown; it was also when most liens were contracted. Thus repeal would end the dangerous mortgage on the growing crop and prepare farmers for self-support when the merchants' lien was entirely removed.[51]

The record of these five states revealed that, despite the pressure for repeal, legislators were not convinced and, even when they did act, they sometimes repented later by reversing themselves. There was clearly more doubt about repeal and more opposition than had initially surfaced, and the debate in the Mississippi House revealed why this was so. Advocates of repeal may have been convinced that the lien laws encouraged improvidence and bad farming, one legislator even claiming that Mississippi had "suffered more from the lien law than Radical rule," but others were more fearful of the immediate consequences once repeal was enacted.[52] Denied easy access to credit, the fear was that planters and their tenants would be unable to plant a crop, thus leaving the landowners with uncultivated lands. In the economic chaos that ensued, those who had brought on the disaster would be severely castigated, and one Democratic representative feared "a tidal wave in the history of this State" for "the dissatisfied white element would arouse the colored vote, and the Democracy would be defeated."[53]

Another who forecast turmoil in the wake of repeal was W. A. Percy, the House speaker and forebear of that influential Delta family. Percy regarded repeal as "the most important subject before the House" since it affected the future of the state's predominant interest, plantation agriculture. Nonetheless, Percy opposed repeal because he feared that it would prevent tenants and laborers from obtaining their supplies and advances from the merchant, essentially denying them "a part of their credit." Without access to the merchant, tenants would be forced to look elsewhere for credit, and "it must come from the land," Percy concluded. Yet, "if the landholders have not got it, and they are universally poor, they will have to get it on credit [themselves] by mortgaging and deeding their lands." Repeal would harm both landowners and tenants, and the only beneficiaries ultimately would be the bankers and merchants. They alone could extend credit and would, in time, gain control over the land. By contrast, Percy claimed that the lien laws had been advantageous to farmers by providing the credit and supplies, without which they would have been forced to sell about two-thirds of the land in the state.[54]

Although they had decided against repeal and against reorganizing the agricultural credit system, the legislators had still to face the issues that had been behind the pressure for ending the lien laws in the first place. With no action taken, farmers and landlords were no nearer solving their problems with laborers and tenants; the latter would continue to be beholden to the merchants who supplied them, and the landowner's control over his farm operation and its labor force would still elude him. A remedy had to be found and, as the movement for repeal faltered, the alternative quickly emerged. Plagued by none of the uncertainty about its effects that had prevented the accomplishment of repeal, the substitute measure was unmistakable in its operation and impact. There would be no tampering with the existing situation such as repeal contemplated. Instead, ascendancy within it was to be shifted decisively—away from the merchant and into the hands of the planters and landlords. The device for achieving this was a major revision of the lien laws, whereby the landlord's lien for rent became paramount. Accordingly, the merchant's lien for supplies advanced was relegated to a subordinate position in the chain of financial obligations incurred by the tenants and laborers.

The paramountcy of the landlord's lien was often established through revision of the landlord and tenant legislation of a state rather than through changes in the lien laws, but, by whichever means it was introduced, the effect was the same. The landlord's lien, usually for rent but also frequently for supplies advanced as well, was made primary. In addition, the landlord was given undisputed control over the crops growing in fields owned by him. Even though all rental agreements set aside a portion of the crop for the tenant, the latter was forbidden to remove any part of his entitlement until the division at the end of the year. Thus, the tenant had no right to his share until after the landlord had taken his portion. Furthermore, to enforce this, the amended laws made the removal of growing crops a crime, usually a misdemeanor.[55] With these measures implemented, the gains made in the earlier enactment of "deadfall" legislation were extended and confirmed. The landowners, in their capacity as employers of labor and as landlords over tenants, had seized the initiative and gained control over their farming operations. No longer were their farms and plantations decentralized collections of semiautonomous tenants and croppers producing a marginal crop without direction and control. Furthermore, while most of a planter's dependents might still obtain supplies from the local storekeeper, the tenant's primary financial obligation was now to his landlord.

The legislative form that these decisive changes took varied from state to state, as did the timing and sequence of their introduction. Georgia, for example, established the primacy of the landlord's lien not through a single legislative act but by a series of provisions that followed the prohibition of merchant liens enacted, as we saw earlier, in 1874. By 1876, the purchase of growing crops that were under the landlord's lien was defined as a misdemeanor and, three years later, the landlord could foreclose before the lien was due if his tenant tried to remove crops from the field.[56] These enactments secured the dominance of the landlord over the local merchant and over his work force. Meanwhile, North Carolina bowed to landlord pressure in 1875 when the legislature repealed sections 13 and 18 of its 1868 Landlord and Tenant Act. By this measure, the landlord's lien was made paramount, and the tenant was declared guilty of a misdemeanor if he removed any of the growing crop without the landlord's permission. Through these changes, the agricultural labor force was brought under the undisputed control of its employers, and the Republican Wilmington *Post* was aghast. "Than this there never was a more deliberate piece of rascality," the editor exclaimed, since there was no need for these crippling guarantees because the landlord's lien was already secured under the act.[57] A year later, when the Democrats gained control in Mississippi, similar alterations were made through the repeal of the Republicans' lien laws of 1872 and 1873. In their place, a new Agricultural Liens Act was introduced in 1876 which removed all previous ambiguity about which interest was primary in the lien system and eliminated the provisions for securing the laborer's wages which had existed in the earlier laws.[58]

In two states, Louisiana and Texas, the supremacy of the landlord's lien was achieved by indirection, but it was ultimately as secure as elsewhere. In 1874, Louisiana subordinated the merchant's lien for supplies to the landlord's lien for rent and to the laborer's for wages. This seeming parity with the laborer's lien was perhaps explained by the fact that the legislature was still Republican; but soon after the Democrats returned, the ability of the laborer and tenant to act independently was curbed by the passage of laws prohibiting the nighttime sale of unginned cotton.[59] Meanwhile, in Texas the Landlord and Tenant Act was redrafted in 1874 when the Democrats attained power as an act "concerning rents and advances." Although the law seemed to give equal status to the merchant's lien, it proceeded to deny the applicability of the personal property exemption where debts were "due for rents or advances made by a landlord." Thus, the landlord's lien was effectively given preeminence.[60]

Changes in the lien laws favoring the landlords took place throughout the 1870s in Alabama. Beginning in 1871, when the Democrats regained the political initiative and proceeded to enact a law making the landlord's lien superior to all other liens for both rent and advances, and continuing through the legislative sessions from 1874 until 1879, the landlord's power over his tenants was constantly expanded and strengthened. The state's Revised Code was amended regularly to tighten sanctions against the selling of crops by tenants and to forestall any possibility that a landlord might be unable to enforce his lien. In the 1876–77 session, after lien-law repeal failed, a new Landlord and Tenant Act was passed establishing the primacy of the former's lien.[61] By the end of the decade, the landlord's lien was unquestionably paramount and covered goods supplied in advance as well as any property bought with money that had been loaned. Finally, in South Carolina, after the reintroduction of the lien law in 1878, the landlord's lien for rent guaranteed him up to half of the crop without even requiring a written contract. Through further legislation passed later in the year, the landlord's lien was to cover the entire crop, whether for rent or advances, and if the tenant removed any of it without permission, an equivalent amount could be seized by the landlord at settlement time. Finally, in 1881, the disposal of any property under lien was considered a misdemeanor with a penalty of up to two years in jail or a fine of $500.[62]

The effect of these amendments in the legislation relating to liens and to landlord-tenant relations was to make repeal of the lien laws unnecessary, even undesirable. The control of labor and the curbing of the merchants could be accomplished far more convincingly through the landlord's domination of the existing lien system than through its elimination. By seizing the initiative, the landowners, in their capacity as landlords and employers, had in effect achieved preeminence over the local merchants and complete control over the tenants and croppers who worked their farms. The system of land and labor, primarily in respect to the black belt, had been tightened in the landowner's favor so that, whatever alternatives lien-law repeal had offered, now vanished. The repeal issue would continue to be raised well into the 1880s, but the balance of power in the plantation areas among landlord, merchant, and laborer had shifted irrevocably.[63]

The balance of forces among the landowners themselves had also changed dramatically as a result of these same developments. While the agitation against the lien laws and the demand for legislation to deal with the problems of agriculture formed a general complaint on the part of the landowning population as a whole, the response to them marked a signal victory for the planters, particularly the large planters located in the black belt. They stood to gain most from the kind of legislation that was enacted so readily by the newly Democratic legislatures. With their large, predominantly black labor force, they were the ones who called most insistently for the restriction and control of labor. As W. A. Percy noted, the "deadfall" laws and antistealing provisions would have been unthinkable if their intended victims had been white.[64] Furthermore, the call for "deadfall" legislation rarely, if ever, came from white nonplantation areas. Senator Black of Georgia, for example, pleaded for sympathetic support for his bill prohibiting the removal of growing crops with the cry, "You do not suffer from these evils, men of North Georgia." Alfred Colquitt once told his state's agricultural society that a "deadfall" law was "greatly needed in Middle and Southwestern Georgia," but the northern section was opposed because such a law was not so vital there.[65] These changes in the landlord-tenant relationship and the lien system particularly benefited large planters. As landlords who "ran" many tenants and croppers, they would derive from the paramount landlord lien a far more powerful and remunerative weapon than mere repeal of the merchant lien could ever provide. Moreover, with the transfer of the supply lien from the merchant to the landlord, the latter obtained, if he had the financial resources to undertake it, the capacity to operate as supplier to his tenants. All landlords would be benefited by the supremacy of the landlord lien, but, for the owner of many acres with numerous tenants whom he could also supply, the increased leverage he obtained was enviable.

A graphic account of the planters' initiative was provided in early 1875 by a newspaper reporter who had been assigned to cover the state legislature in Georgia. He reported, "The only significant fact apparent in this majority is its subservience to the will of a handful of wealthy planters who have made up their minds to break down the small farmers of Georgia, and who have openly declared war upon the merchants of the State. In the plain and unquestionable condition of our affairs, it is folly to disguise the purpose to strike down the labor system."[66] Vivid though the report was, the picture it painted was overdrawn. There was no coordinated maneuver on the part of the landed grandees to attack the merchants or the small farmers. If there had been, perhaps the countermove anticipated by the correspondent would have emerged relatively quickly. The prediction that "the small farmers and the merchants will enter into a combination" and that there would be "a repetition of the 'wool hat' issues . . . once so conspicuous . . . in Georgia politics" did not materialize.[67] The merchants and small farmers were not arrayed solidly against the large planters in Georgia or anywhere else in the South in the 1870s. Rather, all three groups were vying for advantage. The fact that the planters did, indeed, gain the ascendancy, especially in the black belt, was not because they launched successful attacks on the others but because they took the initiative, and they did so at a vital moment when the merchants and small farmers were unable to.

With the interests of agriculture at a premium in the resurgent Democratic party, it was not surprising that the storekeepers' and merchants' financial influence over farm operations should be circumscribed. After all, the landowners were determined to wrest control over their laborers and tenants from the supply merchants who were furnishing them, but the merchants' influence would have been even more restricted had the lien laws been completely repealed. In fact, the reformers urged repeal in order to end the credit system, to make farmers self-sufficient, and to encourage the sale of surplus land to the land-poor small farmers. Yet repeal had run into difficulties where it was introduced; as a result the way was cleared for the redefinition of the lien system that the planters and landlords wanted. This course preserved the credit system and thus retained a place for the merchant in plantation areas. The chief beneficiaries, however, were the landlords whose hegemony was secured while, at the same time, the threat of dislocation and challenge that had been posed by lien-law repeal was averted. Thus, the planters who had urged this repressive solution outflanked both the reformers and the small farmers who would have been better served by repeal. Because battle lines had never been marked out, while a multiplicity of interests and perspectives jockeyed for position in the swirling currents of post-Redemption Democratic politics, the crucial decision about the South's land and labor system was made without drama and seemingly without a full realization of what it portended.

The solution to the landowner's problem had consisted of two parts—ascendancy over the merchant and control over his labor force. Of these, the impact of the former was to prove far less significant than the latter. Although the merchant's lien was now subordinate, he could still provide supplies to the plantations and farms in his locality, and landlords might even, if they wished, assign him their lien for supplies and advances. The merchant had not been eliminated or drastically curtailed.[68] On the other hand, the labor force was brought under increasing restraint and control by the coercive legislation introduced by the Democrats. Whatever options tenants and croppers had previously possessed were now all but abolished. The repercussions of this choice were even greater still because the formation of a static, dependent labor force reduced the options and maneuverability of the entire region, jeopardizing the possibility of achieving the economic change and development that was so desperately needed.

The momentousness of the decision made by the resurgent Democrats can be gauged by three measures. The first of these was its impact on the perennial southern search for immigrants. Convinced that their work force was now under control, landowners and employers of agricultural labor no longer felt that they were at a disadvantage in determining the terms and conditions under which their farms would be run. Consequently, the earlier lament about the shortage of labor evaporated, and, with it, the necessity of increasing the supply of unskilled workers who would help keep wages down. With the Republicans removed from power, yet another ingredient in the former appeal for immigrants was now less in evidence, namely the political bonus that the Democrats felt they would gain if the immigrants were white.[69] Nevertheless, the South still needed immigration—about that there was no argument—but the kind of immigration and the spirit in which it was sought were quite different after the land and labor question was settled by the resurgent Democrats. Instead of tractable unskilled laborers who would be imported in colonies to work in gangs, the emphasis was increasingly placed upon the desirability of securing settlers who were white and who were skilled cultivators, capable of owning and running their own family farms.[70]

Accordingly, when the Democrats came to power and brought order and control to the land, they established bureaus of immigration in almost every state.[71] An air of expectation and confidence pervaded these activities. One historian of late-nineteenth-century southern immigration captured this when he wrote, "The period 1876–1900 as contrasted with the earlier eleven years illustrates several important changes. The desperate search for laborers was succeeded by a calm and well-organized campaign. New race elements were no longer sought to keep the Negro in his proper place or to bring him to terms." The "frenzy" of the years of Republican ascendancy had dissipated, and "people were now invited to share in the wealth of a coming section by developing it; they were not implored to save it from ruin."[72]

The tone of the appeal and its object may have changed, but, among Grangers and other agricultural reformers, the importance of obtaining skilled white immigrants was undiminished. Wyatt Aiken, for one, was unrelenting. Concurring that now "the South needs no influx of laborers," that is, unskilled farm workers, Aiken nevertheless insisted that the region's agricultural revival necessitated an increase in the number of small farmers. He recommended the active involvement of government in the campaign to attract homesteading settlers through fostering organized immigration agencies and through offering incentives such as a ten-year tax exemption on all property improvements made by immigrants. In addition, he urged landowners to make their surplus acres available for settlers to buy.[73]

Insistent though the promoters of settler immigration were, the very attainment of control over agricultural labor which had cleared

the way for the introduction of the new immigration policy ironically doomed it from the start. Secure in the control of their land
and the labor that worked it, the planters were quite unwilling to
consider making parcels of land available for purchase by immigrants. Moreover, whether as unskilled laborers or small farmers,
immigrants were regarded as a destabilizing intrusion into a system
only recently consolidated and brought under control. As a result,
planters viewed immigration with a good deal of scepticism, even
considerable hostility.[74] Needless to say, their tightened control over
the region's system of land and labor hardly acted as an enticement
to the potential immigrant as he contemplated the prospect of set-
tling and farming in the South. On top of all these obstacles, the
promoters of immigration found their efforts hamstrung by the lack
of public funds, which made an organized drive virtually impossible. In Alabama, for example, the legislature refused to appropriate
funds for the bureau of immigration, and the commissioner was
forced to work through existing organizations such as the Grange
in his efforts to collect information and stimulate action. On other
occasions, the bureau was given some funding but its powers were
often limited.[75] Mississippi's commissioner could do very little besides collect data on the opportunities for settlers and solicit proposals on how to lure them, which he did by writing to county governments and publishing the results in the newspapers.[76] This was,
however, hardly an aggressive or formidable approach. So the policies of limited and economical government that had accompanied
Redemption contributed further to the Democrats' inability to attract white settlers.[77]

The second consequence of the Democrats' solution to the land
and labor question was that, as a complement to their efforts to prevent the introduction of new settlers and laborers, the black-belt
landowners took vigorous action to retain and confine the labor
they already had. No longer did they consider ways of replacing
their black laborers with Chinese coolies or European paupers as
they had done throughout Reconstruction. Instead, now that they
were under a tight rein, blacks were viewed as a labor force highly
suitable for southern needs. They began to be described as "the
best and most reliable, if not the only, class of laborers we shall ever
be able to procure" and as "the best laborers we are likely to get in

the South."[78] Strenuous efforts were now made to prevent their leaving, a striking reversal of priority. In 1878 and 1879, this change was highlighted, and even brought to national attention, when the exodus to Kansas began, causing great consternation among southern landowners. Louisiana was the state most affected by Kansas fever and when, in the spring of 1879, thousands of black laborers from the northern river parishes were rumored to be on the road, steps were taken to prevent their departure. The constitutional convention, whose calling made blacks fear the worst and so had probably precipitated the flight, then tried to dispel these worries by reassuring them that its purpose was not to eliminate their rights or return them to slavery. As a supplement to this resolution, the body dispatched one of its black members, the Reverend David Young, to Vidalia, across the river from Natchez, to urge departing blacks to stay. When Young's mission succeeded in turning the migrants back, he was greeted with applause and relief by the Democratic press as well as by the convention.[79]

Although Louisiana had responded to the exodus with conciliation, that kind of reaction was rare. Far more frequent—in fact, it was pervasive—was a response that was coercive and restrictive. The action taken by North Carolina, Georgia, and Alabama was typical. When confronted by substantial black emigration in the mid-1870s, all three proceeded to enact legislation to intimidate and drive off labor agents rather than encourage blacks to stay.[80] Because the labor system was highly exploitative and rested on a foundation of coercion, it could only be maintained by more of the same whenever its smooth operation was threatened. Paradoxically, it was because the labor system was coercive that control could never be complete, even though control had been the purpose behind the coercion in the first place. Coercion prompted resistance, which then necessitated more coercion. This was what had occurred during the Kansas excitement. Witnesses before the Senate committee investigating the exodus testified that it was the oppressive and intimidating living conditions in the countryside that had driven black laborers to migrate. On those occasions when a causal explanation for the intensified threats and increased bulldozing activities by whites was suggested, it was invariably attributed to the recent changes in the labor system and the penal code. These had enabled the landlords and employers to close in on their vulnerable laborers, who concluded that there was no hope of ever coming out ahead and no recourse available except to leave.[81]

The fact of the matter was that the coercive labor system, to which the southern states committed themselves irrevocably in the late 1870s, required careful supervision if it were to operate effectively. Employers wanted their laborers to have very little independence, yet not be denied autonomy altogether; they wanted to immobilize labor, but not prevent movement entirely. Had they tied labor down to one location and prevented mobility, a system of that sort, involving some kind of peonage or indentured servitude, would almost certainly have provoked federal intervention. In addition, employers would have been constrained in their ability both to dismiss laborers or, alternatively, take on more when occasion, such as harvesting, demanded it.[82] The problem was that the flexibility that they wanted limited their control, so they had to balance the contradictory elements in the system, and that necessitated constant attention and adjustment.

At the core of the labor system in the plantation areas was the labor contract and the landlord's lien for rent and supplies. Surrounding this legal relationship were the provisions of criminal law against removing growing crops, selling cotton, and stealing stock. For a number of years after the Redemption labor settlement, the system did not appear to require reinforcement. Only the occasional need to deter labor agents was the exception. As the eighties progressed and certainly in the 1890s when laborers found conditions unbearable, additional legislation became increasingly necessary. To further compel labor, laws were, therefore, introduced to enforce contracts as well as to penalize vagrancy. In addition, the criminal-justice system was utilized to give employers greater control over existing laborers and to provide access to additional supplies. To these ends, criminal surety laws were passed, enabling employers to obtain the labor of convicted offenders in return for paying their fines. Also, broad construction of the vagrancy statutes at harvest time, when the need for hands was greatest, created additional supplies of coerced labor. Interestingly enough, laborers were not the only ones needing to be restrained in a coercive labor system. Employers as well had to be forced to abide by the rules. As a result, antienticement laws were introduced, forbidding landowners to offer employment to a laborer already under contract to someone else. In addition, as we have seen, license fees were frequently imposed on labor agents, whether they moved labor from one state to another or just between neighboring localities.[83]

In these various efforts to plug holes in the system of control, it is interesting to note that those concerned always resorted to legislation. Indeed, the central role of law in the South's post-Reconstruction labor system has been stressed by its two most recent students. "Law gave the system structure and the appearance of legitimacy," William Cohen has written, and Pete Daniel has concluded that "law was at the center of compulsion.[84] Because law played so critical a role in its creation, two rather significant observations on the system's development can be offered. First of all, employers evidently chose not to rely exclusively on the powerful forces of compulsion that they could enlist from within their neighborhoods—compliant courts and officials, community pressure, racial fear, and violence—to coerce their black croppers and tenants. Instead, they enlisted the law first and applied these other informal resources as support. Since employers looked first to the law and then were able to push their measures through the legislature, they had also revealed the extent of their political influence. Landlords and employers in the black belt had demonstrated their power within the Democratic party and the state government, and they had forced the state to uphold their land tenure and labor system. The subsequent consolidation of the labor system of the 1870s was therefore indicative of the political influence of the planters and landowners, especially those in the black belt.

This oppressive system that the planters had imposed on their labor force had an impact extending beyond the lives of the laborers themselves, for the effect of this dependent and repressed labor force on the agricultural system was decisive. Virtually eliminated now was the possibility for a change of direction in southern agriculture. With their labor force increasingly frozen in place and dependent, there was no incentive for employers to change their ways and to consider diversifying their crops and becoming self-sufficient. Nor was there a need to sell off land and then farm what was retained on a smaller scale with scientific methods. In fact, a labor-efficient remedy was quite inappropriate when labor was readily available and under constraint. The existing system of farming, with all of its well-known and widely lamented deficiencies, was therefore retained. The only difference was that in order to compensate for these weaknesses, as manifested in the low cotton prices of the 1880s and 1890s and the drain of southern capital to pay for imported food and manufactured goods, the labor force had to be exploited even more intensively.

The deleterious impact of the static labor force was not felt in agriculture alone. The third outcome of the Redemption land and labor settlement was that it curbed the development of southern industrialization. Had there been a labor-efficient reform of agriculture, as the New South advocates suggested, a surplus of labor might have been generated which would then have sought work in the cities and provided manpower for the region's embryonic industries. Instead of making that a possibility, however, the Redemption labor settlement held back the agricultural changes that have so often precipitated, or at least accompanied, industrialization. These changes in the agricultural sector and their importance to industrial growth have been described most succinctly by Alexander Gerschenkron when he wrote:

> An agrarian reorganization has come to be regarded as a major prerequisite of modern industrialization. Ideally, it is supposed to increase the productivity of agriculture so that its growing produce will allow shifts of population out of agricultural areas and will support the increasing numbers of men engaged in non-agricultural pursuits. At the same time, it is supposed to eliminate, or at least reduce, the traditional restraints on the mobility of the agrarian population and its freedom to exercise a free choice of occupation.[85]

The South's path in the late 1870s was in the opposite direction. Agricultural reorganization was rejected, as was a more flexible deployment of its labor force. Consequently, rather than facilitating the flow of labor into manufacturing, as was the case in England, for example, the effect of the changes in the labor system of the black belt was to curb such a flow.[86] To a large extent, it was because of this that southern industrialization would develop incrementally and gradually rather than act as a transforming process with repercussions throughout the economy.

The ability of the planters of the black belt to exert such control over their labor force and to stem whatever chances there had existed for agricultural reform meant that options and possibilities looking towards the diversification of southern agriculture and the growth of a significant industrial sector were no longer available, at least in the short run. In addition, the increasing political importance of the agricultural interest as well as the recent changes in the scope and priorities of state government further indicated that a concerted effort to promote the New South with the aid of public energy and financing was not likely to be mounted for the foreseeable future.

At the same time, it should be stressed that these restrictive economic and political developments which accompanied Redemption did not commit southern state governments to actively prohibiting the growth of manufacturing or railroads or any other features of a New South. So abrupt a departure was impossible because no single vision or interest had come to dominate the post-Reconstruction South and therefore could not exert such decisive leverage and power. Rather, several of them, after having been set aside briefly after the war, had reasserted themselves and were contending for a place in the emerging economic and political order. Although there were now more active elements in the situation than before, none was preponderant; instead, each demanded that its priorities and concerns be acknowledged. There was a multiplicity of voices, all insisting on being heard. This was also evident in party politics. With the reemergence of the Bourbons and agrarians as well as of the black-belt landlords and planters, the Democratic party had become the embodiment of the conflict and diversity within the redeemed South. Since no single grouping was dominant within the party, the task of its leadership was to reconcile the components of this volatile and discordant coalition.

12. The Democracy Restored and Readjusted

The wealth and culture of the South is in the Democratic party. In the North these classes more largely predominate in the Republican party. What is to hinder them from coming together?
—H. V. Redfield, Cincinnati *Commercial*, 23 February 1877

The South & West are wretchedly poor and are growing poorer every day. They have a common fiscal interest, their pursuits are similar & the rules which will relieve one will relieve the other.
—L. Q. Washington to Robert M. T. Hunter,
    11 February 1874

While the Democrats were ousting the Republicans from power and consolidating their ascendancy over southern political life, their own party was experiencing something of an internal upheaval. With the rise of the Bourbons during and after Redemption, priorities and interests previously in eclipse were reasserting themselves and demanding recognition and influence. As the preceding chapters have suggested, this shift amounted, in broad terms, to a resurgence of the party's agrarian constituency and of the ideas and men formerly associated with the Democracy.

As they rose, the influence of the previously ascendant industrial and railroad interests and that of the former Whigs accordingly declined.

This development did not mean, however, that one group had replaced the other and forced it into a subordinate position within the party. There was no such decisive reversal in the fortunes of the element that had hitherto been in the ascendancy. In specific terms, the resurgence of the Bourbons and agrarians did not result in the elimination of the Whiggish New South faction. What happened, instead, was that the new groups reasserted their strength and forced the party to acknowledge and include them. As a result, the number of interests to which the Democrats had to respond increased, as did the variety of voices to which they had to listen. The task of the party leadership was, therefore, to reconcile these different groups and perspectives and to hold them together. It did this by refraining from any attempt to assign priority within the party structure. Because this approach was taken, the Democratic party of the second half of the 1870s was not so much a hierarchy of unequal and ranked forces as a broadening coalition of elements that were to be coordinated and balanced.

This perspective on the composition and organization of the southern Democratic party was evidently not shared by Rutherford B. Hayes and his advisers in the winter of 1876–77, when they were trying to detach the former Whigs and the business-oriented element from the southern Democratic party. Casting about for allies outside the Republican party to help secure the presidency for the former governor of Ohio, they assumed that the Whiggish, internal improvement wing of the Democracy was sufficiently dissatisfied and neglected that it was ready to break away and seek political alliances elsewhere. A leading exponent of the overture to the Whigs, Congressman James A. Garfield, reported to Hayes in December 1876 that the "old Whigs" felt they had been "forced, unwillingly, into the Democratic party." By the mid-1870s, their alienation was thought to be virtually complete because the Democracy's northern wing was hostile to federal subsidization of internal improvements, and its southern branch had just dismantled the region's state-aid programs and yielded to the pressure of the planters and former Democrats for an end to governmental activ-

ism.[1] Consequently, if Hayes could offer assurances of federal subsidies and could also adopt a conciliatory policy towards the South,
it was believed that he might be able to win over and detach the
former Whigs.

In order to attract the southern Whigs during the election crisis, the Hayes forces offered the prospect of immediate advantage
through passage of the Texas and Pacific Railroad bill and through
the organization of the House under Garfield rather than the anti-
subsidy Democrat, Samuel J. Randall. This was then to be followed up with commitments to ensure that the South, which had
lost out in the logrolling for federal subsidies during Reconstruction, would be recompensed with its fair share in the future.[2] Although this proposition was discussed widely during the opening
months of 1877, it was probably never agreed to, and it was certainly never implemented.[3] Nevertheless, the idea of drawing off the
southern Whigs and making them "the foundation on which to
build a Southern Republican party" persisted throughout Hayes's
presidency and was in fact the centerpiece of his southern policy.[4] In
November 1877, for instance, the president told the Senate Republican caucus committee that his conciliatory course towards the
South would encourage Whigs to join the Republicans. Indeed, because of the existing dissension within the southern Democratic
party, he anticipated that "it would be possible [in 1880] to carry
for the Republicans North Carolina, Florida, Tennessee, Alabama
and possibly Georgia."[5]

Despite Hayes's tenacity, his scheme did not produce the expected results. In the first place, the southern Democratic leadership resisted it furiously. Although they welcomed Hayes's conciliation, they feared his partisan motives. "I think Hayes intends to be
very kind and liberal to the people of the south with the view of
breaking our ranks—and dividing the white people" was the verdict of Congressman W. H. Forney of Alabama.[6] A similar rebuff
came from Joseph E. Brown, who, although not a former Whig,
had nonetheless been one of the southerners whom Hayes had considered for a cabinet post because he was an industrial promoter
and a former Republican. Brown rejected Hayes's overture, however, declaring angrily, "The South is not in the market. We cannot
be purchased by patronage."[7] In order to thwart Hayes's effort to
siphon off the Whigs, party leaders also began to close ranks and

deny once more that there was any relevance or reality in the distinction between Whig and Democrat. They had done this during the early years of Reconstruction, but, almost a decade later, the grounds for differentiating between the members of the two ante-bellum parties were thought to be even less substantial. "Although redolent with high respectability and noble memories, [Whiggery] has no political significance" pronounced the New Orleans *Picayune*, which was actually a spokesman for the city's commercial, and therefore Whiggish, interests.[8] In similar vein, Congressman Otho Singleton of Mississippi, who had even been involved in the negotiations with Hayes during the electoral crisis, dismissed the overture to the Whigs: "Long since have [the differences between the two antebellum parties] been pronounced dead issues, and no power rests with man to galvanize them into life."[9]

Clearly, the attempt to separate the former Whigs from the rest of the Democratic party was going to be difficult for Hayes to achieve, and there was no good reason for the Whigs themselves to consider it. Although they were not as important to the party as they had been in the late 1860s and early 1870s, they were still a crucial ingredient in the Democratic coalition. In view of this, the Atlanta *Constitution* dismissed Hayes's initiative with the scornful observation that "more fallacious hopes were never harbored in human bosom." Because "it takes two to make a bargain" and because former Whigs were doing so well in the southern Democratic party, they would be unlikely to consider leaving it. After all, both of Georgia's U.S. senators were Whigs and so were five out of eight of its congressmen. Noting the influence that Whigs like Hayes wielded in the North, the paper concluded: "It is plain that the 'old Whigs' in both sections of the country are doing very well."[10]

In addition to valuing the former Whigs and including them in their party councils, southern Democrats were also eager to promote internal improvements. In August 1878, the *Picayune* even went so far as to claim that the Democracy "advocated internal improvements with a zeal which every old Whig must entirely approve."[11] The party's enthusiasm was somewhat qualified on the state level, however, since a powerful segment of it had just recently dismantled the programs of state aid to railroads established during Reconstruction. All the same, the *Picayune* was correct in claiming that Democrats favored economic development; it was just that they were opposed to expensive schemes of subsidization as the means to do it. Instead, the party tended to approve indirect methods that did not create burdens of public indebtedness. More attractive were grants of land or exemptions from taxation that became increasingly available in the 1880s after the initial outcry against railroad subsidies died down.

By contrast with their ambivalence towards subsidies at the state level, Democrats expressed little reluctance to support internal improvements when they were funded by the federal government. This may have been what the *Picayune* had in mind, for Democratic spokesmen constantly reassured industrializers that they did not need to be taken in by Hayes's offers because their own party was committed to the principle of federal aid. Even Bourbon Democrats like John Forsyth went to great lengths to point out that their strict constructionist views did not preclude federal support for "great national undertakings."[12] As long as the projects were not local, Democrats had invariably approved of federal subsidies. Besides, as another Bourbon, the well-connected journalist L. Q. Washington, conceded to R. M. T. Hunter, "The strict construction that we thought right & proper 20 or 30 years ago is not now accepted by one person in ten in America. And he vowed, "For my own part & I know the southern people are the same way, I propose to secure for our section all the benefits we can from this government."[13]

If any Whiggish promoter still believed that he had to forsake the Democracy in order to obtain federal aid, the Jackson *Clarion*, which was at the time an enthusiastic supporter of the Grange in Mississippi, urged him to reconsider. In May 1877, its editor declared that "the man is a dreamer who imagines that it is necessary to abolish the Democratic party . . . in order to reclaim the Mississippi overflowed lands . . . to build a Southern Railway to the Pacific, or to accomplish any other measure of general importance, in which the South is specially concerned."[14] Another politician supportive of the Grange was Congressman John H. Reagan of Texas, yet he told a leading New South advocate in his state that, as a member of the House Committee on Commerce, he was doing all he could "to turn it to good account for our state."[15] With even influential Bourbons and agrarians both advocating federal aid for internal improvements and with some public support still available in the states, there was no need for industrial promoters, who were still eager to avail themselves of Whiggish policies of government aid, to give up on the Democrats. Far from being antiimprovement, there was evidently a substantial amount of support for southern economic development, especially if federal assistance were available for it.

As the Hayes Republicans were endeavoring to detach the Whigs and the New South wing from the southern Democratic party, intense pressure was being exerted against it at the opposite end of the party's spectrum. If the Whigs were thought to be the Democratic party's most respectable and conservative element, then the Greenbackers and inflationists within its ranks were considered its most irresponsible and radical. The emergence of the Greenback party in the late 1870s threatened to draw off large numbers of southern Democrats, mainly farmers, who believed that a considerably inflated currency would bring them economic relief by increasing both the supply of money and credit as well as the price of the crops they produced.[16] With alarm, Alexander W. Terrell of Texas noted in the summer of 1878 that "this Greenback schism is spreading with startling rapidity—all through north Texas it is formidable."[17] The bases of Democratic support among the farmers of the white counties, who had risen to the party's aid in the Redemption campaigns, were under siege. Interestingly enough, it was among these elements—the financially heterodox Greenbackers, as well as the low taxers and debt repudiators who were often closely associated with them—that independence from the Democratic organization was most likely to be found in the late 1870s. Thus, it was here that Hayes would have been more likely to find allies ready to break away from the Democrats, rather than among the Whigs who were actually quite contented and firmly ensconced within the Democratic fold. Had Hayes ignored the Whigs who were undetachable and had he concentrated instead on attracting the dissatisfied inflationists and repudiators, he would have had more chance of success.[18] No wonder L. Q. C. Lamar complained in the spring of 1877 that Hayes was "well-meaning, but is very ignorant of the South." And besides being ill-informed on southern politics, Hayes had enunciated a policy that was itself deficient because it was internally contradictory. As Lamar correctly observed, "He is full of the idea of being a great Pacificator." Yet his aim was, in fact, nothing less than to undermine and ultimately destroy the southern Democratic party—hardly a conciliatory gesture.[19]

Hayes chose to ignore the potential in the Greenback challenge, but the southern Democrats were neither unaware nor oblivious of its potency and menace. They were extremely fearful that it might precipitate large-scale defections from the party so they moved in quickly to defuse it. The Democrats in Louisiana perhaps went farther than in any other state in the attempt to undermine the appeal of the Greenbackers. In their 1878 election platform, they virtually adopted the Greenback stance on currency when they called on the federal government to retire all existing national bank notes and replace them with greenbacks, as the wartime paper money was called. Thus, greenbacks were not to be retired from circulation but actually increased, the platform requiring the government to start printing more. Furthermore, as the Greenbackers demanded, they were not to be pegged either to specie or to the amount of government bonds in circulation. Finally, the Louisiana Democrats demanded that the U.S. debt be payable in greenbacks.[20] Most state Democratic parties stopped short of Louisiana's capitulation, however. In Arkansas, they considered the currency question to be so important that they devoted the first nine planks of their 1878 platform to finance. After opposing any contraction of the currency and demanding the repeal of the Resumption Act, which had established the method and timetable for the withdrawal of the greenbacks and a return to specie, the party then called for the issuance of greenbacks in place of all existing national bank notes and asked for a law making gold, silver, and the paper dollar equal in value.[21]

These stipulations went a long way towards meeting the objections of the Greenbackers, and so did the similar platform proposed by the Democrats of Texas in the same year. They too wanted national bank notes to be retired in favor of greenbacks, which were then to be recognized as the sole form of paper money, but, as one prominent Democrat lamented, "Even after our platform, the Greenbackers cling to the absolute money idea & the payment at once *in paper* of the whole National debt."[22] Although they were prepared to adopt a stance highly favorable to inflation, Texas Democrats could not match the Greenbackers in their stance on the U.S. debt since, in the view of the party's gubernatorial candidate, Oran M. Roberts, the Greenbackers' position was not only unconstitutional but entailed partial repudiation.[23] At any rate, even though their platforms were not interchangeable, the Texas Democrats were still doing all they could to retrieve "erring brethren" who were consorting with the Greenbackers. During the campaign, Governor Richard Coke claimed that Congressman Roger Q. Mills had actually gone too far in his efforts at conciliation. "I was with the main Democratic army marching at quick step," Coke claimed, "while he was out on the skirmish line going at *double quick*, trying to catch 'Democratic Greenbackers by the coat tails, and pull them back into ranks.'"[24] Meanwhile, in North Carolina, such frantic activity was probably unnecessary. Governor Thomas J. Jarvis, for one, was confident that the advocates of greenbackism would not defect from his party because "the chief principle advocated by them is warfare against the bondholders of the country, and the Democratic party has been so much more closely allied to the greenback feeling and interest than the Republican has, that I don't think any very considerable number of its members will desert its ranks."[25]

Jarvis's observation on the kinship between the views of the Democrats and the Greenbackers on financial matters explains, to a considerable extent, how the Democrats were able to steal their thunder. In the 1870s, and even into the 1880s, the southern Democrats were not committed to an orthodox hard-money position, with its attendant emphasis on returning the country to specie as soon as possible. Instead, they were far closer to the Greenbackers than has often been assumed. Because of this, their adoption of an inflationist stance in 1878 was not simply a cynical ploy to deceive their opponents by masking their real beliefs and interests. Of course, the maneuver was opportunistic, but it did not require a complete reversal of their stance on the currency, just a shifting of their current position.

Throughout the 1870s, it was generally agreed in the South that the region's supply of money was desperately deficient. After the war, there had obviously been very little national currency available there, but, later on, the paucity of banks in the South which were members of the national banking system meant that the region obtained far less than its fair share of the nationwide distribution of currency. As a result, southern congressmen pressed unceasingly for an increase in the money supply, and they voted solidly against contraction and specie resumption. This southern concern that the circulating medium be both expanded and redistributed manifested itself as soon as the region was readmitted to Congress. In the debates over the Public Credit bill in 1868 and 1869, southern congressmen, Republican as well as Democratic, voted solidly for efforts to redistribute and increase the nation's bank-note supply. Indeed, the three southerners who voted against the legislation in its final form, all of them Democratic-Conservatives, did so because the proposal was insufficiently expansionist.[26]

Three years later, in the wake of the 1873 panic, the southern demand for additional currency grew more insistent. Even the Charleston *News and Courier*, which later became a leading exponent of "hard money" views, declared in December 1873, "The South is a debtor, and what is meat to [the creditors and bond-holders] is poison to her. A hundred million more legal tenders will not be too much for the South and West."[27] Consequently, when Grant shattered the hopes of currency expansionists by his veto of the "Inflation bill" in April 1874, the South was up in arms. The bill's proposed $400 million ceiling on greenbacks and national bank notes, which amounted to a small increase of between $50 and $60 million was described by the fiscally cautious Atlanta *Constitution* as "the minimum demand of the more currency party." As such, its defeat was likely to provoke political turmoil, "perhaps creating sectional parties," so angered was the South.[28] Furthermore, when the Republican Jackson *Pilot* voiced its opposition to the increase, its rival, the *Clarion*, expressed shock that the *Pilot* not only "does not agree with almost the entire Southern [Democratic-] Conservative representation in Congress, but parts company with all the Southern Republicans as well.[29]

While there was no question that the South's congressmen, irrespective of party, were opposed to a decrease in the existing supply of money, they were nevertheless cautious about expanding it too much. Similarly, although they were skeptical of any proposals to peg greenbacks to specie, they could not countenance the possibility of their not being redeemable at all. At the height of the debate on the "Inflation bill," they therefore favored tying them either to a low interest-rate government bond with which greenbacks would be interchangeable or to the existing supply of national bank notes.[30] The South therefore was neither rigid nor radical in its monetary views; instead it desired a currency system that both produced a sufficient amount of available money and was flexibly organized and fairly allocated. As John B. Gordon, the Georgia senator and a representative southern spokesman on currency issues, put it, what the region wanted was "not an increase of the volume of the currency, but a cessation of the contraction policy." In addition, it favored "a change in the character of the present circulating medium, and a modification at least of the national banking system."[31] According to Gordon, this approach was neither inflationist nor contractionist but simply "anti-contractionist."[32]

After the defeat of the "Inflation bill," northern Republicans produced instead the Specie Resumption Act of 1875. Because the act was certain to reduce the greenback supply, southern Democrats voted solidly against it and, thereafter, were insistent that it be repealed.[33] Along with their advocacy of repeal, southerners and other antiresumptionists then seized on the remonetization of silver as another available weapon with which to counter contraction. By reintroducing silver as a metallic basis for the currency, it would be possible to avoid, at one extreme, the risk of an exclusive reliance on gold and, at the other, the danger of having to resort to an irredeemable paper currency such as the Greenbackers were beginning to demand. Since silver offered flexibility and options in resolving the currency problem, southerners readily supported its remonetization. In the House in 1877, they voted 48 to 4 in favor of the Bland silver coinage bill, and, in the Senate, only two southerners voted against a special order calling up the House bill that had been passed in December 1877.[34] Further evidence of southern support for silver was provided by the vote on the Matthews resolution, a crucial proposal making the public debt payable in silver or gold. On this, the South was overwhelmingly in favor by tallies of 51 to 5 and 14 to 1.[35] In fact, support for remonetization and for the Matthews resolution tying the national debt to silver was so strong that the Mississippi legislature went so far as to invoke its rarely used power to instruct the state's congressional delegation when it demanded that its members vote in favor. Even so, L. Q. C. Lamar refused to yield, and he cast the lone dissenting vote.[36] The truth was that, with the exception of a few commercial centers like New Orleans, the South was overwhelmingly prosilver.[37]

Thus, on the major proposals introduced in Congress on the currency question during the 1870s, the South had adopted a consistent position. Only rarely did its representatives vote with the "hard money" interests of the northeastern states. Instead, while they shunned the Greenbackers' antidote and thus were far from radical on the money question, they were invariably to be found voting alongside the "soft money" westerners, and the trend continued into the 1880s. This pattern meant that when the southern Democrats were confronted with the greenback conflagration of the late 1870s, they approached it from a position that was relatively flexible and by no means as antipathetic as "hard money" contractionism would have been. It also meant that the South's sympathies and interests were more with the West than the Northeast. In the midst of the silver remonetization furor, the financially conservative Charleston *News and Courier* noted with disapproval, "The South is now seen ranged and arrayed alongside of the West, opposing the resumption of specie payment, and seeking to pay, in debased silver dollars, debts contracted for payment in gold or its equivalent."[38]

While the *News and Courier* was displeased at this development, Senator Gordon was delighted. Although cautioning southerners to realize that remonetization was not the cure-all for the region's economic problems, he nevertheless rejoiced that the silver issue will "bury the sectional divisions which have disunited the South and the West too long," for "their commercial interests are identical" and "united politically, they are invincible."[39] With this convergence, the possibility of a South-West alliance, which Gordon had anticipated and wished for since 1873 when he was first elevated to the U.S. Senate, was brought closer to realization. The westerners were "naturally our allies" he had said then, since both regions were producers rather than manufacturers. Besides, the South was immensely important to the West, because "we are the market of the West; we are their mules; we buy their corn; we buy their hay."[40] These views were representative of a broad segment of orthodox, respected opinion in the South which assumed that there existed an identity of economic interest between the two producing regions of the country. On this basis, it was expected that a political alliance could be constructed that would restore the South-West axis that had been the foundation of the Jacksonian coalition of the 1830s and whose revival would catapult the South back to a position of political influence. Consequently, whenever the vote in Congress, particularly on financial issues, revealed this regional alignment, as it so often did in the 1870s, it was greeted with great optimism. For example, after Grant's veto of the "Inflation bill" in the spring of 1874, the *Clarion* announced with glee: "We go with the West" in opposing the veto, for "the South and West united, can control the government."[41] Several years later, after Hayes defied the western and southern silverites with his veto of the Bland-Allison act, Congressman John Ellis of Louisiana rejoiced, "Thus do I see my dream of Democratic empire in the West & South taking shape. It will be a great day . . . when they unite and govern the country and the sceptre depart from the East."[42]

These western sympathies as well as the "soft money" views that invariably accompanied them were well represented in the Democratic party throughout the 1870s. Furthermore, they were to be found within its mainstream, not just on the margins, and they were gathering strength as the decade progressed. This meant that the party's center of gravity on the financial question was sufficiently close to the positions adopted by the inflationists and Greenbackers that it was able to prevent defections. At the same time, the Democrats' stance on internal improvements and economic development was not so restrictive and qualified that New South industrializers would be lured away by the offers from Hayes. On the contentious issues confronting the party after Redemption, southern Democrats were able to adopt policies that were flexible and of broad appeal. They were not wedded to rigid or extreme positions on economic issues, so they were able to reconcile and adjust the various interests that were competing for advantage. There was, however, another important feature in the approach taken by party managers to the problem of keeping the diverse Democratic coalition intact. This was their refusal to give primacy, or to commit the party, to any particular interest. The gravest threat to party unity in the wake of Redemption lay in the possibility that the agrarian-Democratic forces that had exerted such tremendous leverage during the mid-1870s might become an exclusive and aggressive faction determined to dominate the party. This would have forced a confrontation with the New South–Whig element with disastrous consequences. Instead, their respective demands were adjusted, with the result that the party comprised a balance of forces rather than a hierarchy of interests. Thus, a destructive struggle for primacy was avoided.

The Democrats' ability to minimize conflict in this way was facilitated by two political developments that were simultaneous but coincidental. The first was the expansion of the party's boundaries by becoming an electoral majority and in some states, like Georgia, a large electoral majority. This not only provided more room in the party where the increasing number of assertive groups could be fitted, but it also resulted in the greater availability of patronage with which to satisfy these demands for recognition and influence. Put in rather basic terms, the pie that the Democrats were dividing up was itself expanding, making it possible to satisfy the growing volume of claimants. The second fortuitous advantage was that, as a result of the recent constitutional changes invariably introduced by the Democrats, government was no longer actively promoting particular interests, as had occurred during Reconstruction. This obviated the need to make choices between economic groups competing for public favor. Because government was no longer active in the economy, parties were not therefore having to line up for or against specific interests.

In view of this, it became a cardinal tenet of party policy to insist that no favoritism be given. As Augustus S. Merrimon, one of North Carolina's U.S. senators, put it, "A party organization that looks to the promotion of individuals or classes, is not fit to be supported or encouraged."[43] Similarly, after his election to the Georgia governorship in 1876, Alfred H. Colquitt denied immediately that he would be "unduly attentive to the affairs of the farmers, who were his especial friends in the campaign. . . . It is absurd to say that I will use the powers of the office . . . for the advancement of one class, to the oppression of another."[44] That was not the only precaution the Democratic leadership took to protect against the dominance of either its agrarian or its New South wing. To keep the two tendencies balanced, Democrats usually sent a representative of each to the U.S. Senate during the late 1870s and early 1880s—for example, Zebulon B. Vance and Matt W. Ransom from North Carolina and John W. Daniel and James Barbour from Virginia, the latter in each pair being the proponent of the New South.[45] Another balancing device was the practice of offsetting the agrarian propensities of the state legislature with a more business-oriented executive branch.[46] If these mechanisms proved ineffective, there was always available, as a constant reminder of how necessary it was to avoid conflict and disunity, the warning of the dire consequences they might produce. To this end, the rallying cry of white supremacy, along with the specter of the horrors of Reconstruction, was frequently mobilized to ensure that internal differences were buried. By means of these various devices and maneuvers, the Democrats managed to hold together the broad and diverse coalition that they had amassed in the wake of Redemption.

The Democratic party that had seized control of the South in the mid-1870s was therefore in no way a monolith dominated by a single interest or committed to a particular political goal. Instead, it was an expanding, diverse, and disaggregated coalition. Because of this, its all-consuming preoccupation was with keeping itself intact. To this end, it had to develop policies sufficiently flexible to satisfy all of the dissonant elements of which it was composed. Moreover, it had to generate institutional devices to balance and adjust these differences. This meant that it was unable to act forcefully and decisively on any particular front. The Democrats were a party without priority or direction, a political organization whose survival required that balance and equilibrium be its paramount consideration. As a result, they could provide neither stimulus nor focus. Having already saddled the region with a constricted governmental apparatus and a repressive system of land and labor, the Democrats now offered the South a politics of balance, inertia, and drift.

Notes
Bibliography
Index

Notes

Introduction

1. For the postwar southern economy, see Ransom and Sutch, *One Kind of Freedom*; Wright, *The Political Economy of the Cotton South*, chap. 5; Woodman, *King Cotton and His Retainers*, chaps. 21–27; DeCanio, *Agriculture in the Post-Bellum South*; Higgs, *Competition and Coercion*, chaps. 1, 3, 4, 6; and Woodman's assessment, "Sequel to Slavery: The New History Views the Postbellum South."

For class structure in the postbellum South, see Wiener, *Social Origins of the New South*; Mandle, *The Roots of Black Poverty*; Billings, *Planters and the Making of a "New South"*; Wiener, "Class Structure and Economic Development in the American South, 1865–1955."

For land tenure and labor systems, see Ransom and Sutch, *One Kind of Freedom*, chaps. 4, 5; Novak, *The Wheel of Servitude*; Schwartz, *Radical Protest and Social Structure*; Woodman, "Southern Agriculture and the Law"; Daniel, "The Metamorphosis of Slavery, 1865–1900"; Cohen, "Negro Involuntary Servitude in the South: A Preliminary Analysis"; Foner, *Politics and Ideology in the Age of the Civil War*, chap. 6.

For the culture and expectations of the landlords and freedmen, see Roark, *Masters Without Slaves*; Levine, *Black Culture and Black Consciousness*; Powell, *New Masters*; Litwack, *Been in the Storm So Long*.

A general account of the contribution made by these historiographical developments can be found in Degler, "Rethinking Post-Civil War History."

Chapter 1

1. Francis P. Blair, Jr., speech, Omaha, 13 July 1868, and letter to James O. Brodhead, 30 June 1868, in McPherson, *A Hand-Book of Politics for 1868*, pp. 369–70, 380–81.

2. Benjamin H. Hill, speech at the Bush Arbor, Atlanta, 23 July 1868, in Hill, *Senator Benjamin H. Hill of Georgia*, p. 312; Trelease, *White Terror*, chaps. 7–11.

3. The perspective of the southern Democrats prior to 1868 can be found in Perman, *Reunion Without Compromise*. For the northern Democrats, see Gambill, *Conservative Ordeal*; Silbey, *A Respectable Minority*; and Coleman, *The Election of 1868*.

4. U. S. Grant, letter accepting the Republican nomination, in McPherson, *Hand-Book of Politics for 1868*, p. 365.

5. A. H. Garland to Alexander Stephens, Little Rock, 9 November 1868, Stephens Papers, LC. A copy is also in the Graham typescripts, Chapel Hill. In the end, the delegation was not sent, although many southerners did go to Washington independently and made representations to the president-elect.
The delegation did not go, so Garland told William A. Graham, because Stephens "did not approve of the plan, as he thought Grant knew all about affairs in our States,—as much as our leading men could tell him—and he seems to place great confidence in Grant's sense and patriotism, much more I believe, than either you or myself would." Clearly, Stephens interpreted the purpose of the delegation as informational whereas Garland had a rather different aim in mind, for he added: "The main point with me was for our representative men to assure Grant they would give him a cordial and generous support in the Southern States, and to make this impression on him before he was molded or manipulated by the fierce &, I fear, unrelenting spirit of the party whose candidate he was in the late presidential contest," Garland to Graham, Little Rock, 20 January 1869, Graham typescripts.

6. Augustus Garland to Stephens, Little Rock, 9 November 1868, Stephens Papers, LC.

7. Alexander Stephens, interview with a correspondent from the Macon *Telegraph*, reprinted in Augusta *Constitutionalist*, 5 February 1869, located in Stephens Papers, LC.

8. Joseph E. Brown to Stephens, Atlanta, 21 November 1868, Stephens Papers, LC.

9. The National Union initiative and the South's role in it have been treated in my *Reunion Without Compromise*, chap. 6.

10. John H. Reagan to General W. G. Webb, editor of the Houston *Telegraph*, Palestine, Tex., 9 March 1869, Reagan Papers.

11. John H. Reagan to Major W. M. Walton, Palestine, 13 March 1869, Reagan Papers.

12. Major W. M. Walton and John Hancock to Colonel Ashbel Smith, C. C. Gillespie, et al., Austin, 22 February 1869, Ashbel Smith Papers.

13. John H. Reagan to Ashbel Smith, Palestine, 23 February 1869, Ashbel Smith Papers.

14. These maneuvers are treated extensively in Maddex, *Virginia Conservatives*, chap. 6.

15. See Alexander, "Political Reconstruction in Tennessee," pp. 37–39.

16. The Mississippi "new movement" is discussed in Pereyra, *James Lusk Alcorn*, pp. 96–103, and Harris, *Day of the Carpetbagger*, pp. 199–263.

17. Z. P. Landrum, editor of the Columbus *Index*, to Alexander Stephens, Columbus, Miss., 13 October 1869, Stephens Papers, LC.

18. Wiley P. Harris to Alexander Stephens, Jackson, 12 December 1869, Stephens Papers, L. C.

19. Article in Cincinnati *Gazette*, cited by Montgomery *Advertiser*, 6 August 1869. The Chase initiative, following close on his attempt to gain the Democratic nomination in 1868, was the catalyst shaping Republican politics in 1869 and 1870. At first, it forced Grant to a stance more in accord with the party's regulars and then it paved the way for the Liberal-Republican movement after Chase's death. By moving to the middle, Chase was in a position where he could even consider the Democratic nomination, which is what the *Advertiser* assumed he was actually seeking. See Montgomery *Advertiser*, 18 December 1869.

20. Montgomery *Advertiser*, editorial, 21 January 1869.

21. Raleigh *Sentinel*, editorial, 1 September 1869.

22. See Nathans, *Losing the Peace*, for an account of the Republicans' difficulties in that state.

23. Montgomery *Advertiser*, editorial, 26 June 1869.

24. James H. Clanton to Thomas J. Judge, Greenville, Ala., 18 January 1869, in Montgomery *Advertiser*, 26 January 1869.

25. Jackson *Clarion*, editorial, 9 September 1869.

26. W. P. Chilton, Jr., speech to the county convention, Lee County, Ala., in Montgomery *Advertiser*, 17 May 1870.

27. John H. Reagan to gentlemen, 23 February 1869, Ashbel Smith Papers.

28. Atlanta *Constitution*, editorial, 24 August 1869.

29. Campaign address of the Conservative party members of the North Carolina General Assembly, 26 March 1870, in Raleigh *Sentinel*, 28 March 1870.

30. Raleigh *Sentinel*, editorial, 9 September 1869.

31. E. G. Cabaniss to General A. R. Wright, Forsyth, Ga., 24 June 1869, in Atlanta *Constitution*, 10 July 1869.

32. Atlanta *New Era*, editorial, 4 June 1870.

33. Montgomery *Advertiser*, editorials, 6 March 1869 and 24 February 1870.

34. Hendricks's speech was given on 12 February 1870 and discussed in the Montgomery *Advertiser*, 19 February 1870.

35. The address from the Democratic congressmen, dated 24 April 1871, can be found in the Raleigh *Sentinel*, 4 May 1871.

36. Vallandigham announced his change of course when he spoke in favor of the resolutions approved at a congressional district convention held in Dayton, Ohio, on 18 May 1871. He defended the resolutions in terms of their being "not a New Departure; but a Return; the restoration of the Democratic party once more to the ancient platform of Progress and Reform." The political purpose of this move was to promote the presidential chances of Salmon P. Chase, whose failure to obtain the nomination in 1868 Vallandigham regretted greatly. Vallandigham, *A Life of Clement L. Vallandigham*, pp. 438–42, 444.

37. From the address of the Democratic congressmen, 24 April 1871, in Raleigh *Sentinel*, 4 May 1871.

38. Joseph E. Brown to Rufus Bullock, Atlanta, 3 December 1868, Brown typescripts.

39. Alex White to William H. Smith, Selma, Ala., 14 December 1868, William H. Smith Papers.

40. Atlanta *New Era*, editorial, 28 October 1870.

Chapter 2

1. Ranney, *Curing the Mischiefs of Faction*, pp. 134, 139. Recent discussion among political scientists about the goals and strategies of political parties can be found in Downs, *An Economic Theory of Democracy*, and Riker, *The Theory of Political Coalitions*, as well as in the qualifications and criticisms offered by Hirschman, *Exit, Voice, and Loyalty*, chap. 6, and Schlesinger, "The Primary Goals of Political Parties," pp. 840–49.

2. Silbey, *A Respectable Minority*. Unlike the terms used by Ranney, Silbey's "Legitimist," "Purist" dichotomy is historically specific, referring to the divisions within the Democratic party in the northern states during the Civil War and immediately after.

3. See previous chapter and Maddex, *Virginia Conservatives*, chap. 6; Harris, *Day of the Carpetbagger*, chap. 6; and Moneyhon, *Republicanism in Reconstruction Texas*, chap. 6.

4. Russ, "Disfranchisement in Louisiana," pp. 579–80.

5. Wiggins, *Scalawag in Alabama Politics*, pp. 38–39, 42.

6. Morgan C. Hamilton to James P. Newcomb, 1 October 1868, Newcomb Papers.

7. Moneyhon, *Republicanism in Reconstruction Texas*, chap. 6. See also Carrier, "A Political History of Texas during the Reconstruction," chap. 9.

8. For events in Florida during 1868, see Klingman, *Josiah Walls*, chap. 1, esp. pp. 17–19; Shofner, *Nor Is It Over Yet*, chap. 11; Meador, "Florida Political Parties," pp. 90–95.

9. Charles Dyke to Edward M. L'Engle, 16 March 1868, quoted in Meador, "Florida Political Parties," p. 103.

10. Harrison Reed to David L. Yulee, 16 February 1868, quoted in ibid., pp. 93–94.

11. Harrison Reed to Yulee, 22 April 1867, in ibid., p. 130.

12. The course of Georgia's Republican party in 1868 and 1869 has been treated by Nathans, *Losing the Peace*, chaps. 3–7, esp. chaps. 3, 4; Conway, *Reconstruction of Georgia*, pp. 150–56 and chap. 7; Parks, *Joseph E. Brown of Georgia*, chap. 19; Drago, *Black Politicians and Reconstruction in Georgia*, chap. 3; and Mathews, "Negro Republicans in the Reconstruction of Georgia," pp. 145–64.

13. The role of debtor relief as the issue around which a class-oriented Republicanism could have been forged is discussed in Robinson, "Beyond the Realm of Social Consensus," pp. 283–90.

14. See Nathans, *Losing the Peace*, chaps. 5, 6.

15. Morgan C. Hamilton to Newcomb, Washington, D.C., 9 April 1870, Newcomb Papers.

16. M. C. Hamilton to Newcomb, Glen Haven, N.Y., 10 August 1870, Newcomb Papers.

17. Hume, "Negro Delegates," p. 144. I am very grateful to the editor, Howard Rabinowitz, and to Frank Williams of the University of Illinois Press for letting me see this important collection of essays while it was still in galley proofs. Also relevant are Vaughn, *Schools for All*, pp. 56–73, and Rabinowitz, *Race Relations in the Urban South*, p. 165.

18. Hume, "Negro Delegates," pp. 142–43. See also Olsen, *A Carpetbagger's Crusade*, pp. 105–8, for an example of how minimal was discussion of the land issue in an 1868 constitutional convention. The case in question is North Carolina, which had a sizable Radical element.

19. For blacks in South Carolina's constitutional convention on the questions of confiscation and land, see Holt, *Black Over White*, pp. 125–31. Holt finds that blacks were frequently divided on confiscation, with the alignment separating freeborn and mulatto delegates from freedmen, the latter sympathizing with efforts to get land from its current owners.

20. Communication to Governor William W. Holden, 20 August 1868, quoted in Summers, "Radical Reconstruction and the Gospel of Prosperity," p. 191.

21. For discussion of the railroad issue as a unifying one, see ibid., chaps. 3, 4, in particular pp. 113, 127. Support for railroad aid cut across the differences between Radical and Centrist as well as the distinctions between black and white, and native and northerner. The differences that did arise were over local rivalries and preferences for particular lines, not over whether or not railroads should be promoted through government subsidy.

22. *North Carolina Standard*, editorial, 8 December 1869.

23. R. W. Lassiter, speech in the North Carolina Senate, 11 March 1869, in *North Carolina Standard*, 18 March 1869.

24. Report of grand railroad meeting at Cedartown, Ga., 15 October 1870, in Atlanta *New Era*, 18 October 1870.

25. *Texas State Journal*, editorial, 23 July 1870.

26. Jackson *Weekly Pilot*, editorial, 11 May 1871.

27. Governor William H. Smith, proclamation, 14 April 1870, and letter to the sheriff of Greene County, 9 April 1870, published in Montgomery *Advertiser*, 13 April 1870.

28. Governor Robert K. Scott, message to South Carolina legislature, January 1871, reprinted in Raleigh *Sentinel*, 21 January 1871. See also Trelease, *White Terror*, pp. 115–17, 377, for discussion of Scott's earlier role. The Klan in South Carolina in 1871 is treated in chaps. 22, 23.

29. Trelease, *White Terror*, pp. 377–80.

30. Harris, *Day of the Carpetbagger*, p. 391.

31. James L. Alcorn to Ethelbert Barksdale, the paper's editor, published in Jackson *Weekly Clarion*, 30 May 1872; see also Harris, *Day of the Carpetbagger*, pp. 394–96.

32. Hume, "Negro Delegates," p. 141. Hume's dissertation on the southern con-

stitutional conventions is the definitive treatment and it is strange that it has not been published; see Hume, "The 'Black and Tan' Constitutional Conventions of 1867–1869."

33. For evidence that blacks acted this way on the franchise and for discussion about why they did so, see Litwack, *Been in the Storm So Long*, pp. 501–7, 525–26, 531–38; Klingman, *Josiah Walls*, p. 72; Balanoff, "Negro Legislators in North Carolina," pp. 32–33. A paper, entitled "Reconstruction and the Black Experience," which Eric Foner gave at the University of Chicago in October 1981, makes this point very persuasively.

34. James Lynch, interview with the Cincinnati *Commercial*, in Jackson *Weekly Clarion*, 26 August 1869.

35. See, for example, Holt, *Black Over White*, pp. 101–3.

36. Quoted in Litwack, *Been in the Storm So Long*, pp. 549–50.

37. See Moneyhon, "George T. Ruby and the Politics of Expediency," pp. 378–82.

38. Klingman, *Josiah Walls*, p. 19.

39. The practice of ethnic and interest-group politics in the late nineteenth century was becoming widespread outside the South. Blacks too were engaging in it; see, for example, Katzman, *Before the Ghetto*, pp. 196–98.

40. See Klingman, *Josiah Walls*, p. 25, and Reidy, "Aaron A. Bradley," pp. 297–99.

41. Klingman, *Josiah Walls*, p. 99. Klingman, in chap. 6, offers a rare and valuable discussion of the black convention movement of the Reconstruction era.

42. Klingman, "Race and Faction," p. 71.

43. Even the most conservative and accommodationist of black politicians, such as Dr. Benjamin Boseman, Jr., of South Carolina, made sure that the party's electoral prospects were safeguarded and that the black voters upon whom it relied so heavily were not ignored or their ballots undermined. See, for instance, Hine, "Dr. Benjamin A. Boseman, Jr.," pp. 354–55.

44. Holt, *Black over White*, pp. 105–8.

45. Schweninger, *James T. Rapier and Reconstruction*, pp. 75–79.

46. Klingman, *Josiah Walls*, p. 35.

47. Moneyhon, *Republicanism in Reconstruction Texas*, p. 179. At the state level, James G. Tracy had begun to break up the Union League in 1871 as a signal to whites that the party was in earnest for their support. For Mississippi, see Harris, *Day of the Carpetbagger*, pp. 413–23.

48. Moneyhon, *Republicanism in Reconstruction Texas*, p. 196.

49. See Meador, "Florida Political Parties," pp. 97–98, 260–61; Shofner, *Nor Is It Over Yet*, pp. 195–97, 288–89, and passim.

50. This distinction has been made most concisely by Klingman in "Race and Faction," pp. 63–64. See also Kolchin, "Scalawags, Carpetbaggers, and Reconstruction," pp. 63–76, for a perceptive analysis and interpretation of the struggle between natives and newcomers over nomination to congressional office.

51. Elisha M. Pease to James G. Tracy, Austin, 24 May 1869, Elisha M. Pease Papers.

52. Alexander White to William H. Smith, Selma, 2 January 1869, Governor W. H. Smith Papers.

53. Horatio Simrall, speech in Vicksburg, 20 April 1869, in Jackson *Weekly Clarion*, 27 May 1869.

54. William A. Smith, communication, Company Shops, 7 March 1870, in *North Carolina Standard*, 9 March 1870.

55. William B. Rodman to David M. Carter, Raleigh, 23 January 1868, Carter Papers.

56. James L. Alcorn to Robert W. Flournoy, reprinted in Jackson *Weekly Clarion*, 2 February 1871.

57. William H. Smith to President Ulysses S. Grant, Washington, D.C., 13 March 1869, Governor W. H. Smith Papers.

58. Joseph C. Bradley to William H. Smith, Huntsville, Ala., 11 January 1870, McKee Papers.

59. Adelbert Ames to Blanche Ames, Jackson, 14 October 1871, in Ames, *Chronicles from the Nineteenth Century*, 2:332–33.

60. Joseph E. Brown to William D. Kelley, confidential, Atlanta, 18 March 1868, Brown typescripts.

61. William B. Rodman to David M. Carter, Raleigh, 23 January 1868, Carter Papers. Confirmation that Rodman acted for conservative, propertied interests in the convention is provided by Olsen in his *Carpetbagger's Crusade*, p. 106.

62. Governor William H. Smith, speech at Ashland, Ala., reported in Montgomery *Advertiser*, 20 September 1870.

63. Alcorn, "Views of the Honorable J. L. Alcorn," p. 4.

64. Richmond Pearson, "An Appeal to the Calm Judgement of North Carolinians," 20 July 1868, in *North Carolina Standard*, 15 October 1868. The *Standard*, which was Governor Holden's paper, published a portion of this public letter daily during the 1868 canvass in the hope that others like Pearson would follow his lead.

65. Wiggins, *Scalawag in Alabama Politics*, chap. 4, and Cash, "Alabama Republicans during Reconstruction," pp. 275–82.

66. See Sansing, "The Scalawag in Mississippi Reconstruction," and Harris, *Day of the Carpetbagger*, esp. chaps. 7, 12.

67. Joseph E. Brown to Rufus B. Bullock, Atlanta, 3 December 1868, Brown typescripts.

68. See Moneyhon, *Republicanism in Reconstruction Texas*, chaps. 5, 9, and Nathans, *Losing the Peace*.

69. Taylor, *Louisiana Reconstructed*, pp. 209–11; Warmoth, *War, Politics, and Reconstruction*, pp. 91–93. In his "Henry Clay Warmoth, Reconstruction Governor of Louisiana," p. 557, Francis Byers Harris quotes Henry C. Dibble, a contemporary Republican, as saying "all the opposition to governor Warmoth among the republicans of the State began when he refused to sign . . . the first social equality [civil rights] bill," and Oscar Dunn, the black leader, concurred.

70. See Shofner, *Nor Is It Over Yet*, pp. 203, 223; Meador, "Political Parties in Florida," pp. 190–91, 240–41. Reed confirmed his Centrist strategy by taking

little action against the Klan, particularly in Jackson County in 1869; see Shofner, *Nor Is It Over Yet*, pp. 231–32, 234.

71. For Clayton's message about amnesty, see *Arkansas Gazette*, 5 January 1871. The quote is from an editorial in the *Arkansas Gazette* on 10 January 1871. See also Ellenburg, "Reconstruction in Arkansas," chap. 8.

72. See Holt, *Black Over White*, pp. 116–120.

73. Ellenburg, "Reconstruction in Arkansas," chaps. 2, 3.

74. Will C. Scott to Thomas Settle, Greensboro, N.C., 22 December 1871, Settle Papers, Series 2.

75. Adelbert Ames, speech in the U.S. Senate, 20 May 1872, *Congressional Globe*, 42 Cong., 2 Sess., part 6, appendix, pp. 393–95.

76. Ibid., p. 396.

77. Davis's few lapses were still too many for Morgan Hamilton, who felt the governor had given in to the railroad lobby. See Morgan Hamilton to James P. Newcomb, Glen Haven, N.Y., 8 September 1870, James P. Newcomb Papers, and Moneyhon, *Republicanism in Reconstruction Texas*, pp. 140–43.

78. See Summers, "Radical Reconstruction and the Gospel of Prosperity," chaps. 5, 16. When Brooks decided to challenge Clayton, he attacked the governor's entire record on railroad aid, not his preference for the Little Rock and Fort Smith.

Chapter 3

1. Samuel Phillips, speech at Concord, Cabarrus County, N.C., in July 1870, reprinted in *North Carolina Standard*, 13 July 1870.

2. *North Carolina Standard*, editorial, 20 May 1870.

3. "A Voter," reporting Phillips's speech at Graham, Alamance County, *North Carolina Standard*, 17 June 1870.

4. There was a precedent for this policy, although fleeting. Several opponents of Reconstruction had urged the endorsement of black suffrage immediately after the passage of the Reconstruction Act of March 1867. But their effort to attract black votes was quickly countered and, in the elections for a constitutional convention, a policy of resistance and abstention won out instead. See Perman, *Reunion Without Compromise*, pp. 269–85.

5. *North Carolina Standard*, editorial, 24 March 1870.

6. James H. Clanton to Robert McKee, Montgomery, Ala., 22 March 1870, McKee Papers.

7. Montgomery *Advertiser*, editorial, 10 August 1870.

8. Quoted in ibid.

9. James B. Kershaw to R. M. Brown, editor of the Mississippi *Central*, Camden, S.C., 19 July 1870, in Jackson *Weekly Clarion*, 4 August 1870.

10. Trenholm, "Local Reform in South Carolina," pamphlet, 1872.

11. Albert Elmore to John W. A. Sanford, Mobile, 13 June 1870, Sanford Papers.

12. Joseph E. Brown to Rufus B. Bullock, Atlanta, 3 December 1868, Brown typescripts.

13. Democratic-Conservative Central Executive Committee, address, in Raleigh *Sentinel*, 8 August 1870.

14. Robert B. Lindsay, testimony, 16, 17 June, report of Ku Klux Klan Investigation Committee, *House Reports*, 42 Cong., 2 Sess., no. 22, part 8, p. 183.

15. Zebulon B. Vance, speech, Augusta, Ga., reported in Raleigh *Sentinel*, 4 October 1870.

16. Raleigh *Sentinel*, editorial, 29 March 1872.

17. W. H. Avera to Daniel M. Barringer, Selma, N.C., 9 August 1872, Barringer Papers.

18. David H. Hemphill to R. R. Hemphill, Chester, S.C., 27 October 1870, Hemphill Family Papers.

19. Charles Hays, testimony, June 1871, in the Ku Klux Klan Investigation Committee, *House Reports*, 42 Cong., 2 Sess., no. 22, part 8, p. 216. Perhaps the best explanation of the relationship between the Klan and the Democratic-Conservative party at the local level is to be found in Olsen, "The Ku Klux Klan," esp. pp. 352–59.

20. John G. Pierce, testimony, 21 June 1871, in Ku Klux Klan Investigation Committee, *House Reports*, 42 Cong., 2 Sess., no. 22, part 8, p. 304.

21. J. J. Jolly, testimony, 20 June 1871, in ibid., p. 295.

22. Benjamin H. Hill, testimony, 30 October 1871, report of Ku Klux Klan Investigation Committee, *House Reports*, 42 Cong., 2 Sess., part 7, p. 773. See also Harris, *Day of the Carpetbagger*, pp. 388–90.

23. Albert Elmore to J. W. A. Sanford, Mobile, 3 May 1871, Sanford Papers.

24. The curtailment of the Klan and its operations is treated in Trelease, *White Terror*, pp. 383–419, and, more specifically in Harris, *Day of the Carpetbagger*, pp. 390–405. For the Klan in general, see also Olsen, "The Ku Klux Klan," pp. 340–62; Shapiro, "The Ku Klux Klan During Reconstruction," pp. 34–55; Stagg, "The Problem of Klan Violence," pp. 303–18.

25. For discussion of fusion, see the various state Reconstruction studies, but, for those where it was practiced extensively, see Harris, *Day of the Carpetbagger*, pp. 410–13, 471–76, 680–81; Taylor, *Louisiana Reconstructed, 1863–1877*, pp. 227–40; Williamson, *After Slavery*, pp. 353–54, 396–99. Also see chap. 5 where the 1872 state election campaigns and the Liberal-Republican fusion are analyzed.

26. Raleigh *Sentinel*, editorial, 7 November 1868.

27. Benjamin H. Hill, "Notes on the Situation," new series, in Augusta *Chronicle*, cited in Montgomery *Advertiser*, 24 December 1869.

28. *North Carolina Standard*, editorial, 12 November 1868. In a later editorial on 20 November 1868, the party's philosophy of economic development was laid out.

29. Jackson *Weekly Clarion*, editorials, 25 March and 1 April 1869.

30. Atlanta *Constitution*, editorial, 7 May 1869.

31. Editorial from Huntsville *Democrat*, reprinted in Montgomery *Advertiser*, 7 April 1869.

32. The *News and Courier* was reiterating these slogans from 1873 onwards, see especially editorials on 16 July and 1 August 1873; Montgomery *Advertiser*, 31 October 1869.

33. Montgomery *Advertiser*, editorial, 20 January 1869.

34. Ibid., 23 January 1870.

35. Ibid., 11 March 1870.

36. Edwin Belcher, motion in Georgia House of Representatives, 31 August 1870, in Atlanta *New Era*, 1 September 1870.

37. Atlanta *New Era*, editorial, 28 October 1870.

38. For a detailed discussion of the intentions and calculations behind the Republicans' railroad policies, see Summers, "Radical Reconstruction and the Gospel of Prosperity," chaps. 1, 2.

39. Quoted in the Natchez *Weekly Democrat*, 7 December 1870, and cited in Harris, *Day of the Carpetbagger*, p. 541.

40. M. C. Hamilton to Elisha Pease, Washington, D.C., 20 May 1871, Pease Papers.

41. Thomas P. Conner, speech, Mississippi House of Representatives, in Jackson *Weekly Clarion*, 30 June 1870.

42. Jackson *Weekly Pilot*, editorial, 18 June 1870. The *Pilot*, a Republican paper, was actually supporting Governor Alcorn's veto of the bill because it agreed that the bill was poorly drafted and gave too much unqualified power to a small group of promoters, in Jackson *Weekly Pilot*, editorial, 25 June 1870.

43. See, for example, Heath, *Constructive Liberalism*, esp. chap. 11, and Thornton, *Politics and Power in a Slave Society*, pp. 268–80, 321–31.

44. Ellenburg, "Reconstruction in Arkansas," pp. 108–10; Thompson, *Arkansas and Reconstruction*, pp. 200–201, 147–48. In 1868, the Republicans expanded the scope of the aid and set up a supervisory board to decide which roads were to be the beneficiaries.

45. *Arkansas Gazette*, editorial, 3 July 1868.

46. Levi W. Lawler to Robert McKee, Mobile, 18 December 1873, McKee Papers.

47. Price, "Railroads and Reconstruction in North Carolina," p. 372. See also Goodrich, *Government Promotion of American Canals and Railroads*, chap. 6, which contains a discussion of southern railroad aid policies during Reconstruction.

48. Goodrich, *Government Promotion of American Canals and Railroads*, pp. 209–10; Wallenstein, "From Slave South to New South," pp. 294–98.

49. Carrier, "A Political History of Texas During the Reconstruction," chap. 2.

50. *North Carolina Standard*, editorial, 18 June 1870.

51. Ibid., editorial, 29 November 1869; in its 18 June 1870 editorial, an explanation for the disarray in the railroad program was offered. It was essentially that "the error lay in uttering too many bonds at once, and in placing them into too many hands for sale." Charles Price later concurred, adding also that the problem was exacerbated by the failure of the legislature to levy taxes to finance the state bonds, see "Railroads and Reconstruction in North Carolina," pp. 384–94.

52. *North Carolina Standard*, editorial, 8 February 1870. The many letters from George W. Swepson, the North Carolina railroad promoter, in the Matt W. Ran-

som Papers are very revealing of the degree of Democratic-Conservative involvement. See also Jonathan Daniels's biography of Milton S. Littlefield, *Prince of Carpetbaggers*, chaps. 9–12.

53. Trelease, "Republican Reconstruction in North Carolina," pp. 319–44. Trelease's argument, derived from statistical analysis of roll-call voting, is that there was considerable partisan divergence on the propositions that the Republican-dominated House considered. While he is correct in suggesting that the Democrats were voting for internal improvements to a lesser degree than Republicans, it is most significant that they were not utterly opposed. In fact, they were probably more favorable to railroad construction with state aid than the vote, considered at its face-value, would indicate.

54. Price, "Railroads and Reconstruction in North Carolina," pp. 384–92.

55. William A. Graham to William A. Graham, Jr., Hillsboro, N.C., 16 April 1870, Graham typescripts.

56. Henry C. Warmoth, speech in the Louisiana Constitutional Convention, reported in New Orleans *Picayune*, 12 June 1879.

57. After the state programs had been dismantled, public aid in the form of subsidies could still be obtained in many instances at the county and local level. At the state level, railroads later secured support through the more indirect means of tax exemption or favorable valuation and assessment. This was not widely practiced until the 1880s, however. Meanwhile, Texas and Florida gave aid but it was in the form of grants of land. These were often extensive. Texas handed out over 32 million acres from 1873 to 1882, and Florida 22 million from 1880 to 1884. Although unredeemable and, in the long run, an immense loss to those states, land grants were thought to be far preferable to financial subsidies. See Goodrich, *Government Promotion of Canals and Railroads*, chap. 6, and Summers, "Radical Reconstruction and the Gospel of Prosperity," p. 984.

58. "A Review of the Resolutions of the Press Conference, Held in Charleston," S.C., 1870, p. 6, Reconstruction Broadsides, Duke University Library.

59. Mobile *Register*, editorial, 1 April 1871.

60. Ibid., editorial, 13 January 1871.

61. Ibid., 15 January 1871.

62. John A. Winston to Charles Scott, editor, Wilcox *News and Vindicator*, Mobile, 20 April 1870, in Mobile *Register*, 3 June 1874.

63. Mobile *Register*, editorial, 26 March 1871.

64. Ibid., 14 March 1871.

65. An idea of the constellation of values and principles that comprised the ideology of the Democratic party in the 1850s and 1860s can be gleaned from Collins, "The Ideology of the Antebellum Northern Democrats," pp. 103–21, and from Joel Silbey, *A Respectable Minority*, esp. pp. 23–26. On page 234, Silbey states very succinctly, although in negative terms, the essentials of the Democratic philosophy when he says that, in 1868, "they still resisted the power of the central government and the puritan interventionism they believed inherent in Whig and Republican thought." For a recent discussion of Democratic beliefs in a southern state, see Thornton, *Politics and Power in a Slave Society*, pp. 42–58.

66. Alexander Stephens to Herschel Johnson, Crawfordville, Ga., 15 August 1870, Johnson Papers.

67. Mobile *Register*, editorial, 14 March 1871.

68. Dudley M. DuBose to Stephens, House of Representatives, Washington, D.C., 16 March 1871, Stephens Papers, Emory University.

69. John W. A. Sanford to an unidentified correspondent, Montgomery, 30 August 1870, Sanford Papers.

70. Ibid.

71. H. M. Somerville to Robert McKee, Tuscaloosa, Ala., 8 July 1873, McKee Papers.

72. James R. Randall to Alexander Stephens, Augusta, 20 February 1870, Stephens Papers, L.C.

73. Richard H. Clark to Alexander Stephens, Atlanta, 29 October 1870, Stephens Papers, L.C.

74. Alexander Stephens to Herschel Johnson, Crawfordville, Ga., 15 August 1870, Johnson Papers.

75. Communication from the editor, I. W. Avery, Dalton, Ga., 23 November 1870, in Atlanta *Constitution*, 25 November 1870.

76. John W. A. Sanford to unknown, Montgomery, 30 August 1870, Sanford Papers.

77. Alexander Stephens to Herschel Johnson, Crawfordville, Ga., 15 August 1870, Johnson Papers.

78. John A. Winston to Charles Scott, Mobile, 20 April 1870, in Mobile *Register*, 3 June 1874.

Chapter 4

1. Jackson *Weekly Pilot*, editorial, 26 November 1870. The details and background of the Whig meeting are described in Harris, *Day of the Carpetbagger*, pp. 407–10.

2. Woodward, *Reunion and Reaction* (1951) and *Origins of the New South* (1951). Alexander's thesis was most cogently and expansively presented in "Persistent Whiggery in the Confederate South," in August 1961, but the argument had been broached earlier (August 1950) in "Whiggery and Reconstruction in Tennessee." More specific state studies of "Persistent Whiggery" appeared in the *Alabama Review*, January 1959, and the *Journal of Mississippi History*, August 1961. Woodward and Alexander have been the most forceful and persuasive proponents of an enduring Whiggery, but most of the historians writing on the postwar period in recent years have endorsed their observations about Whiggery's existence and significance. In fact the historiography of the era has been permeated by the Whiggery theme. See also Mering's evaluation of the "Persistent Whiggery" thesis in "Persistent Whiggery in the Confederate South," pp. 124–43.

3. See, for example, Van Deusen, *William Henry Seward*, p. 426; Stampp, *Era of Reconstruction*, chap. 2.

4. See Woodward, *Reunion and Reaction*, passim, and Gillette, *Retreat from Reconstruction, 1869–1879*, chap. 14.

5. Atlanta *Constitution*, editorial, 18 August 1871.

6. The Whig vote in 1852 in the states that formed the Confederacy was 43%, see Alexander, "Persistent Whiggery in the Confederate South," p. 306 (n. 3).

7. Montgomery *Advertiser*, editorial, 19 August 1869.

8. Ibid., 28 and 31 January 1869 and 5 August 1869.

9. Zebulon B. Vance, speech to the Iredell County Democratic-Conservative convention at Statesville, N.C., 2 April 1872, in Raleigh *Sentinel*, 10 April 1872.

10. Jackson *Weekly Clarion*, editorial, 2 June 1870.

11. "Old Line Whig," communication to the editor, Jackson *Weekly Clarion*, 7 July 1870.

12. Vance, speech at the Iredell County convention, in Raleigh *Sentinel*, 10 April 1872.

13. Horn's editorial was reprinted in the Jackson *Weekly Clarion*, 3 March 1870.

14. Raleigh *Sentinel*, editorial, 13 July 1872.

15. Jackson *Weekly Clarion*, editorial, 2 June 1870.

16. Atlanta *Constitution*, 22 and 25 June 1871.

17. Joseph E. Brown, speech to "Fellow Citizens," given in Atlanta, 19 August 1868, Brown typescripts.

18. The New York *Herald* comment is rebutted in the Jackson *Weekly Clarion*, 23 May 1872; the *Courier-Journal* observation was occasioned by Benjamin Hill's recent speech avowing his support for the Democrats, Atlanta *Constitution*, 13 March 1872.

19. Quoted in Alexander, "Persistent Whiggery in the Confederate South," pp. 311, 314.

20. Ibid., pp. 311–13; see also Perman, *Reunion Without Compromise*, pp. 164–66 and passim.

21. Major William A. Hearne's influential communication was first published in the Wilmington *Journal* and then reprinted in the Raleigh *Sentinel*, 13 September 1871.

22. See, for instance, details about Whig influence in the Jackson *Weekly Clarion*, editorial, 1 March 1872. Interestingly, the *Clarion*'s editor was Ethelbert Barksdale, who had been a secession Democrat. But, with a few exceptions like Albert Gallatin Brown and L. Q. C. Lamar, the party's leadership was thoroughly permeated by Whigs.

For indications of the extent of Whig influence in Alabama, Virginia, and Arkansas, see respectively Levi Lawler, speech at Talladega, printed in Montgomery *Advertiser*, 20 August 1870; Philip P. Dandridge to R. M. T. Hunter, Winchester, Va., 18 December 1872, R. M. T. Hunter Papers; and *Arkansas Gazette*, editorial, 31 December 1869 and 11 April 1871.

23. Joseph E. Brown, address to "Fellow Citizens," Atlanta, 19 August 1868, Brown typescripts.

24. Benjamin H. Hill, address explaining his recent political course, in Atlanta *Constitution*, 24 February 1872.

25. Ibid.

26. Joseph E. Brown to Alexander Stephens, Atlanta, 27 December 1873, Stephens Papers, L.C.

27. Governor James L. Alcorn, inaugural address, 10 March 1870, in Jackson *Weekly Pilot*, 11 March 1870.

28. *North Carolina Standard*, editorial, 25 June 1870.

29. Entry for 25 June 1870 in David Schenck's diary, typescript, volumes 5 and 6, p. 170, in Southern Historical Collection.

30. William A. Graham to William A. Graham, Jr., Hillsboro, 1 July 1870, Graham typescripts.

31. John Kirkwood, communication to *Arkansas Gazette*, Little Rock, 23 September 1870, in *Arkansas Gazette*, 25 September 1870.

32. Tuscumbia *Times and Alabamian*, quoted in Montgomery *Advertiser*, 20 April 1870.

33. "Henry Clay Whig" to C. C. Langdon, Camden, Ala., 27 August 1872, reprinted in *Alabama State Journal*, 1 September 1872.

34. Mobile *Register*, editorial, 10 February 1874, concurring with a similar viewpoint expressed by Charles Scott's Wilcox *Farmer's Vindicator*.

35. J. Clark Swayze to Benjamin Conley, Macon, Ga., 8 March 1872, Conley Papers.

36. Wilmington *Post*, editorial, 24 March 1876.

37. Lancaster, "The Scalawags of North Carolina, 1850–1868," p. 361.

38. Cash, "Alabama Republicans during Reconstruction," p. 183.

39. Ellem, "Who Were the Mississippi Scalawags?" p. 240. David Donald's "The Scalawag in Mississippi Reconstruction" appeared in the *Journal of Southern History* in November 1944. See also Harris, "A Reconsideration of the Mississippi Scalawag," and Sansing, "The Role of the Scalawag in Mississippi Reconstruction," for further discussion of native white Republicanism in Mississippi.

40. Lancaster, "The Scalawags of North Carolina," p. 359. Democratic supporters of Stephen Douglas in 1860 were even more inclined to support the Republicans. Of Lancaster's sample of twenty-five, 92 percent of them sided with the Republicans.

41. Cash, "Alabama Republicans during Reconstruction," p. 186; Lancaster, "The Scalawags of North Carolina," p. 360.

42. Lancaster, "The Scalawags of North Carolina," p. 360.

43. Ibid., pp. 362–63. Because Cash does not use the opposition as a control-group, he describes the characteristics of the native white Republicans in Alabama but does not realize that these same qualities and antecedents were very much to the fore and highly valued in the Democratic-Conservative party. See Cash, "Alabama Republicans during Reconstruction," pp. 383, 161.

44. Charleston *Daily Republican*, editorial, 28 July 1870, cited in Foner, *Politics and Ideology in the Age of the Civil War*, p. 116.

45. Columbia *Daily Union*, editorials, 24 January and 21 March 1872.

46. *North Carolina Standard*, editorial, 4 August 1870.

47. The high point of Republican radicalism occurred in the constitutional conventions that were held under the Reconstruction Acts in 1868 and 1869. Debtor

legislation, the establishment of public schools and democratization of the political system were discussed and, with the frequent exception of debtor relief, enacted. Laborers' lien provisions were introduced a little later in the state legislatures.

48. Joseph E. Brown to Schuyler Colfax, the Republican vice-presidential nominee, Atlanta, 9 June 1868, Brown typescripts. Brown was telling Colfax that Congress should not consider removing the debtor relief provision in the new Georgia constitution. "Without the very measure they propose to strike out, we could not have carried the State in the last election," he warned.

49. Moneyhon, *Republicanism in Reconstruction Texas*, p. 174.

50. The failure of the Republicans "to raise the stake" and offer inducements to the less well-off is discussed by Brock in his perceptive essay, "Reconstruction and the American Party System." Eric Foner has recently depicted the debate over whether or not to appeal to the poorer classes as a contrast of approach between "Modernizers" and "Redistributionists" within the party; see Foner, *Politics and Ideology in the Age of the Civil War*, p. 117. This categorization rests on ideological differences, when in fact distinctive bases of electoral support were probably more influential in determining the composition of the contending factions. Moreover, these priorities cut across the ideological categories that Foner adduces.

51. Simon Newcomb to his son, James P., El Paso, 24 June 1873, Newcomb Papers.

Chapter 5

1. John S. Mosby to Captain A. G. Babcock, Warrenton, Va., 13 May 1872, in Columbia *Daily Union*, 23 May 1872.

2. Alexander Stephens to Thomas Hardeman, Crawfordville, Ga., 15 September 1872, Stephens Papers, Ga. Dept. of Arch. The Liberal-Republican platform can be found in Johnson and Porter, *National Party Platforms, 1840–1972*, pp. 44–45.

3. The debate in South Carolina over whether to call a convention and to send delegates to Baltimore was presented in full detail in the Mobile *Register*, 30 May 1872. The committee's statement can be found in this article, entitled "South Carolina and Baltimore."

4. Mobile *Register*, editorial, 26 May 1872.

5. Gordon's observation is quoted in Maddex, *Virginia Conservatives*, p. 135.

6. Thomas M. Hardeman, public address, 26 August 1872, in Atlanta *Constitution*, 28 August 1872.

7. Raleigh *Sentinel*, editorial caption, 29 July 1872; in the same issue, the paper published the "Letter to the People of North Carolina" from Daniel M. Barringer, the party chairman.

8. Lyman Trumbull to Horace White, U.S. Senate, 24 April 1872, Davis Papers.

9. The report was dispatched from New York on 20 May 1872 and printed in the Mobile *Register*, 26 May 1872.

10. Raleigh *Sentinel*, 30 March 1872, and H. H. Helper, letter to the editor,

regarding problems likely to emerge at Cincinnati, in Raleigh *Sentinel*, 2 April 1872.

11. Daniel R. Goodloe to Benjamin S. Hedrick, Raleigh, 6 February 1870, Hedrick Papers.

12. The proceedings of the executive committee and its membership were reported in the Raleigh *Sentinel*, 20 July 1872.

13. W. W. Wofford to David B. Davis, Corinth, 28 April 1872, Davis Papers. Wofford handpicked the delegation and told Davis it would support him for president. He was so confident that he even assured Davis that Governor Alcorn "will be compelled to come with us."

14. The Liberals' meeting in Jackson to coordinate the alliance with the Democratic-Conservatives was reported in the Jackson *Weekly Clarion*, 15 August 1872. See also Harris, *Day of the Carpetbagger*, pp. 456–57.

15. Correspondence from Atlanta, 1 August 1871, in Mobile *Register*, 10 August 1871; Forsyth concurred, it is interesting to note, in the reporter's analysis of the southern Republicans' conservatism.

16. *Alabama State Journal*, editorials, 31 July, 1 and 2 August 1872.

17. Ibid., 31 July 1872. When accepting the Republican gubernatorial nomination, David P. Lewis expressed his pleasure that the party had broadened its base "by its generous recognition of the Douglas and Bell men in 1860, in the choice of its leaders in this canvass." Lewis to D. C. Whiting, the party chairman, 23 August 1872, in *Alabama State Journal*, 29 August 1872.

18. See Wiggins, *Scalawag in Alabama Politics*, pp. 79–83. Bradley and Rice did not embrace the Liberals fully, voting for Greeley while supporting the state ticket of the Republicans.

19. Atlanta *Constitution*, editorial, 28 May 1872.

20. Editorial Correspondence, 10 August 1872, in Mobile *Register*, 14 August 1872.

21. See Moneyhon, "The Republican Party and Texas Politics," pp. 335–36.

22. Jackson *Weekly Clarion*, 15 August 1872.

23. Report of the proceedings of the Democratic-Conservative convention, in Atlanta *Constitution*, 24 July 1872.

24. Huntsville *Democrat*, editorial, 2 August 1872.

25. The leading lights in this party were Christian Roselius, Isaac N. Marks, and George Williamson, and it had emerged from the formation of the Committee of Fifty-one, which met in November 1871 to consider ways of improving the governance and condition of New Orleans. Marks and some others in this group were to initiate a similar nonpartisan and interracial movement a year later, see Williams "The Louisiana Unification Movement of 1873," pp. 349–69.

26. See Taylor, *Louisiana Reconstructed*, chap. 6.

27. William P. Kellogg to Stephen B. Packard, Washington, D.C., 7 December 1871, Warmoth Papers.

28. Taylor, *Louisiana Reconstructed*, p. 234; Haskins, *P. B. S. Pinchback*, pp. 129–57.

29. In the account of his Reconstruction experience, *War, Politics, and Reconstruction*, p. 161, Warmoth wrote: "I was forced to sympathize with this move-

ment. General Grant had violated his understanding with me; he had taken sides with his brother-in-law, Collector Casey, Marshal Packard, Postmaster Lowell, and the other Federal officials who had so grossly abused their positions in their efforts to outrage me, Lieutenant-Governor Pinchback and the people who supported me in my efforts to build up a Republican party in which the conservative and honest white people of the state should have a share." Grant had also, so Warmoth claimed, sided with "the attempts of the Federal officials to Africanize Louisiana."

30. P. A. Morse and William M. Levy to Thomas J. Semmes, Natchitoches, La., 5 November 1871, in Warmoth Papers.

31. John Ellis to his brother, Tom, New Orleans, 22 May 1872, Ellis Family Papers.

32. Taylor, *Louisiana Reconstructed*, pp. 235–37.

33. For details of the schism, see Ellenberg, "Reconstruction in Arkansas," chap. 8.

34. Report in *Arkansas Gazette*, 23 and 24 May 1872.

35. The breadth and variety of Brooks's support was attributable not simply to his own appeal and organizational talent but also to his own record. A northerner, he was prominent in the Freedmen's Bureau and then played a leading role as a Radical Republican in the 1868 constitutional convention. When he locked horns with Clayton, he contested the latter's reliance on federal patronage and criticized his sympathy toward northerners in Arkansas, while concurrently he sought support from native whites and offered them amnesty and good government. The platform and the membership of the Liberal-Republicans' central committee were reported in the *Arkansas Gazette*, 9 March 1872. As was usually the case, the initiators of Liberal-Republicanism at the state level were marginal men of limited influence within either major party.

36. Brooks made his offer in an interview he gave immediately after the Liberal-Republican convention adjourned on 19 June. This happened to be the evening before the Democratic-Conservatives met on 20 June. His political purposes were therefore obvious. *Arkansas Gazette*, 19 June 1872.

37. "Proctor," report on the Democratic-Conservative convention, in *Arkansas Gazette*, 9 July 1872. A discussion of the range of strategies espoused by the Democratic-Conservatives, especially Augustus Garland, Harris Flanagin, and David Walker, can be found in Thompson, *Arkansas and Reconstruction*, pp. 91–101.

38. *Arkansas Gazette*, 22 June 1872.

39. Editor of Fort Smith *New Era*, quoted in *Arkansas Gazette*, 29 June 1872.

40. Quote from Arkadelphia *Standard*, in *Arkansas Gazette*, 4 July 1872.

41. Report of the joint agreement, with critical editorial comment, in *Arkansas Gazette*, 28 August 1872. Three members of each party had comprised the committee.

42. *Arkansas Gazette*, 1 October 1872.

43. Ibid., 2 October 1872.

44. This was in the committee's official statement advocating support of Hunter, *Arkansas Gazette*, 2 October 1872. In the end, the committee reendorsed Brooks.

298 Notes to Pages 121–26

45. H. V. Johnson to Alexander Stephens, Sandy Grove, Ga., 14 November 1872, Johnson Papers.

46. J. W. Throckmorton to Ashbel Smith, McKinney, Tex., 11 November 1872, Ashbel Smith Papers.

47. Burnham, *Presidential Ballots*, pp. 252–55. Also, see Gillette, *Retreat from Reconstruction*, pp. 390–91 (n. 40).

48. Atlanta *Constitution*, 24 November 1872; Moneyhon, "The Republican Party and Texas Politics," pp. 341–42.

49. Burnham, *Presidential Ballots*, p. 252.

50. Virginia's vote was 91,647 to 93,463 and Mississippi's was 47,288 to 82,176, in Burnham, *Presidential Ballots*, p. 252. There was no state race in Texas, yet Greeley won by 67,675 to 47,910. The Democratic-Conservatives mounted a vigorous local campaign to capture the legislature which they did overwhelmingly. This local effort probably accounted for the size of the Greeley vote, although, as was noted, it was still less, on a statewide basis, than the year before. Moneyhon, "Republican Party and Texas Politics," pp. 341–42.

51. *Alabama State Journal*, editorial, 8 November 1872; Raleigh *Sentinel*, 10 August 1872.

52. *Appleton's Annual Cyclopedia for 1870*, p. 682, and Simkins and Woody, *South Carolina During Reconstruction*, p. 468. The vote in 1872 for Tomlinson was 36,533, compared with 51,537 for R. B. Carpenter in 1870. The Republicans' vote was also down by a similar amount, but their margin of victory was still considerable, in fact proportionally greater than in 1870 because of the smaller total vote cast.

53. Atlanta *Constitution*, 19 September and 1 October 1872.

54. Raleigh *Sentinel*, editorial, 9 October 1872.

55. Raleigh *Sentinel*, 10 August 1872.

56. Ibid., 16 November 1872.

57. Jackson *Weekly Clarion*, editorial, 15 November 1872.

58. Robert E. Withers to James L. Kemper, 7 December 1872, quoted in Maddex, *Virginia Conservatives*, p. 134.

59. James W. Throckmorton to Ashbel Smith, McKinney, Tex., 11 November 1872, Ashbel Smith Papers.

60. Column from "William," 9 November 1872, in Jackson *Weekly Clarion*, 21 November 1872.

61. Speech of Langdon, Mobile, 1 November 1872, reported in Mobile *Register*, 2 November 1872.

62. Herschel V. Johnson to A. H. Stephens, Sandy Grove, 8 June 1872, Johnson Papers.

63. The comment was made by the Lumberton *Robesonian*, which concurred in the Salisbury *Watchman*'s estimation of the Democratic-Conservative loss, quoted in Columbia *Daily Union*, 21 September 1872.

64. Selma *Times* report, quoted in *Alabama State Journal*, 19 September 1872.

65. I. G. Harris to Robert McKee, Livingston, Ala., 31 May 1872, McKee Papers.

66. The occurrence of independency was naturally most likely in states where a formal alliance with the Liberals had not been negotiated, leaving the latter's votes uncommitted and available for a rejected nominee who felt he was more able to attract them than the nominee. Independency was therefore more likely in Alabama and Georgia where there was no coalition at the state level. Independency was also prone to occur at the county and local level, either where the Democratic-Conservatives were seriously divided and disorganized or else where fusion had not been formalized and a reasonable bloc of Liberal votes was therefore thought to be available.

67. Atlanta *Constitution*, 17 September 1872.

68. Mobile *Register*, 21 September 1872.

69. Alexander Stephens to Herschel V. Johnson, Crawfordville, Ga., 21 October 1872, Johnson Papers.

70. Thomas Hardeman, address to the Democratic-Conservative voters of Georgia, Macon, 26 August 1872, in Atlanta *Constitution*, 28 August 1872.

71. Daniel M. Barringer and W. S. Mason, chairmen of the Democratic and Liberal-Republican parties, address, Raleigh, 18 October 1872, in Raleigh *Sentinel*, 29 October 1872.

72. Hardeman's address was published in the Atlanta *Constitution*, 28 August 1872.

73. New York *Tribune*, 28 October 1872, reprinted in Mobile *Register*, 2 November 1872. The editorialist cited a fifteen thousand white majority in the state to show that only lethargy could account for a Republican victory. A New York *Herald* correspondent in Richmond provided an interesting account of how the black vote was organized and cast, when he wrote: "The negroes are the most thoroughly disciplined voters that ever cast ballots. By holding small and apparently indifferent meetings at various points where their opponents are strong they lull their apprehensions and produce an impression of weakness; but on the day of election every mother's son of a darky will be as promptly at the polls as if his very existence depended upon it." The extract was reprinted in the Richmond *Dispatch*, 2 October 1873.

74. The nature of the political system during the 1870s and 1880s can best be discovered in Keller, *Affairs of State*, especially chaps. 7 and 14, entitled respectively "The Triumph of Organizational Politics" and "The Politics of an Industrial Society"; Kleppner, *The Third Electoral System*; and Jensen, *The Winning of the Middle West*, esp. chap. 6, called "From Battlefield to Marketplace: The Transition in Electioneering Style."

Common to all these approaches to the politics of the era is the tendency to see the decades between the sectional crisis and the 1890s as a distinctive period in American political history. The characteristics they focus on as distinguishing it are: (1) the emergence of highly organized political parties, more concerned with organizing and turning out their own vote than with appealing ideologically to broad sections of the electorate (Keller); (2) the stability of the electoral coalitions composing the parties, resulting in a politics of equilibrium rather than of shifting, realigning party formations (Kleppner); and (3) electioneering conducted with military fanfare and with drilling of the party's cadres to rally the voters to the polls. This style gives way after 1896 to an approach intended to be inclusive and to proselytize voters, in effect to sell them the party's wares (Jensen).

The politics of the southern states was evidently entering the same phase. In this regard, it is worth pointing out how much the South was a part of the course and development of American politics rather than something sui generis and separate. Cf. Kleppner, who, in his description of America's third electoral system, virtually excludes the South, except for a brief section, pp. 97–120, about the return of the Democrats to power in the middle of the 1870s.

75. Raleigh *Sentinel*, editorials, 31 October and 16 September 1872.

76. Mobile *Register*, editorial, 29 August 1872.

77. Robert J. Powell to David F. Caldwell, Washington, D.C., 9 October 1872, David F. Caldwell Papers. Powell had been the state agent in Washington after the war.

78. The change in campaign organization had been adopted earlier and more readily by the Republicans in the South, for they, after all, had had to get down to the beat level in order to inform black voters of their suffrage rights and make sure they registered. Thereafter, institutional devices like the black churches, the Freedmen's Bureau, and the Union League, as well as Republican political clubs, had ensured that black voters were involved. Increasing awareness of how successful Republican organization at the local level was probably contributed significantly to the Democratic-Conservatives' realization that they needed to emulate it.

79. Columbia *Daily Union*, editorial, 5 June 1872.

80. Atlanta *Constitution*, editorial, 26 November 1872.

81. Samuel B. Maxey to his wife, Washington, D.C., 26 June 1876, Samuel Bell Maxey Papers. Maxey was promoting Bayard for the Democratic presidential nomination in 1876 rather than a candidate acceptable to swing voters.

82. Raleigh *Sentinel*, editorial, 9 November 1872.

83. Atlanta *Constitution*, editorial, 9 November 1872; also Jackson *Weekly Clarion*, editorial, 15 November 1872.

Chapter 6

1. *Alabama State Journal*, 4 January 1873.

2. Columbia *Daily Union*, 22 November 1872.

3. Raleigh *Sentinel*, 10 August 1872.

4. Taylor, *Louisiana Reconstructed*, pp. 248–49; Gillette, *Retreat from Reconstruction*, pp. 110–16, 137; Wiggins, *Scalawag in Alabama Politics*, pp. 82–86.

5. In *Black Over White*, pp. 99–100, Thomas Holt discusses most perceptively the problem of determining how much power black politicians wielded.

6. Holt, *Black Over White*, pp. 107–8.

7. Ibid., pp. 109–10.

8. P. B. S. Pinchback to Henry C. Warmoth, Boston, 11 September 1875, Warmoth Papers.

9. Vincent, *Black Legislators in Louisiana During Reconstruction*, pp. 153–57.

10. Moneyhon, *Republicanism in Reconstruction Texas*, pp. 178–79; see also Jackson *Weekly Clarion*, 27 July 1871.

11. *Arkansas Gazette*, 21 January 1873.

12. Harris, *Day of the Carpetbagger*, pp. 420–24, 427–28.

13. Governor Adelbert Ames, inaugural address, 22 January 1874, in Jackson *Weekly Clarion*, 29 January 1874.

14. Adelbert Ames to James W. Garner, Lowell, 17 January 1900, Garner Papers.

15. Harris, *Day of the Carpetbagger*, pp. 437–50. The bill passed the House in January 1873 by a vote of 61 to 41, with only 3 white Republicans opposing, p. 446.

16. Vincent, *Black Legislators in Louisiana*, p. 166; *Arkansas Gazette*, 21 March 1873; Shofner, *Nor Is It Over Yet*, p. 291.

17. Wiggins, *Scalawag in Alabama Politics*, pp. 86–88. The bill failed in the House, mainly because the opposition Democratic-Conservatives prevented the introduction of amendments that would have moderated the bill's terms. As a result, Republicans in white districts were opposed to the measure in its undiluted form. Ironically, therefore, the bill passed the Democratic Senate and failed in the Republican House—a far from satisfactory outcome for the Republicans.

18. Ulysses Grant, interview with Charles Hays, James Rapier, George Spencer, 14 September 1874, reprinted in Mobile *Register*, 22 September 1874.

19. The federal Civil Rights bill is discussed at length by William Gillette in chaps. 8–11 of his *Retreat from Reconstruction*. While he exaggerates the bill's significance in reversing the Republicans' electoral position, it certainly did not revive their prospects. Neither did it reestablish the party's commitment to equal rights and the well-being of its black supporters nor restore the influence of its radical wing.

20. "A White Republican," communication, *Alabama State Journal*, 8 July 1874.

21. H. V. Redfield's report was reprinted in the Mobile *Register* on 10 October 1874.

22. Oliver H. Dockery to "My Dear Russell," Mangum, N.C., 7 June 1874, Daniel L. Russell Papers.

23. Gillette, *Retreat from Reconstruction*, pp. 220–25.

24. See Shofner, *Nor Is It Over Yet*, chap. 11.

25. See Taylor, *Louisiana Reconstructed*, pp. 233, 481–82.

26. See Harris, *Day of the Carpetbagger*, pp. 461–80 and chap. 11, and Lynch, *The Facts of Reconstruction*, pp. 70–76.

27. Lamson, *The Glorious Failure*, pp. 198–206.

28. Columbia *Daily Union*, 26 August 1872. Five of the platform's eight sections were devoted to financial reforms, and the *Daily Union* complained that so conservative a manifesto (it was written by the conservative Thomas J. Mackey) ignored both "the fundamental principles of the party as respects the great and vital question of human rights" and the party's constituency "almost entirely composed of the laboring poor."

29. Robert B. Elliott, speech to both houses of the South Carolina assembly, Columbia, 19 February 1874, quoted in Lamson, *The Glorious Failure*, pp. 185–87.

30. Republican State Executive Committee, address to Republican voters of South Carolina, 22 July 1874, in Charleston *News and Courier*, 24 July 1874.

31. Allen, *Governor Chamberlain's Administration in South Carolina*, pp. 10–29. See also Charleston *News and Courier*, 9 February 1875.

32. Jackson *Weekly Clarion*, 29 January and 26 February 1874. See also Harris, *Day of the Carpetbagger*, pp. 432–37, 603–5.

33. Charleston *News and Courier*, editorial, 11 December 1874.

34. Jackson *Weekly Clarion*, editorial, 26 February 1874; Harris, *Day of the Carpetbagger*, p. 604.

35. Daniel Chamberlain to Francis Dawson, 18 February 1875, Dawson Papers.

36. Allen, *Governor Chamberlain's Administration*, pp. 304–6. From 5 to 18 July 1876, the *News and Courier* published a series of detailed articles describing the financial record of the Chamberlain administration. The purpose of this summary was to impress upon Democratic-Conservatives the wisdom of supporting Chamberlain's candidacy rather than nominating a separate gubernatorial choice of their own which the straight-outs were urging.

37. William P. Kellogg to J. A. J. Cresswell, New Orleans, 29 January 1874, Kellogg Papers. As Kellogg pointed out to Cresswell, the bondholders obtained "sixty cents on the dollar in seven % bonds while the Chamber of Commerce & the Committee of citizens urged fifty cents in six % bonds."

38. Taylor, *Louisiana Reconstructed*, pp. 260–65.

39. An editorial from the Republican Vicksburg *Times* criticizing Ames's record was printed in the Jackson *Weekly Clarion*, 14 April 1875. See also Harris, *Day of the Carpetbagger*, pp. 608–10.

40. Vicksburg *Times*, in Jackson *Weekly Clarion*, 4 February 1875. Compare this with Ames's sanguine analysis of state finance in his 1876 message.

41. This entente is evident from Dawson's letters to Chamberlain in the Dawson Papers. In his *Black Over White*, Thomas Holt devotes chap. 8 to a discussion of Chamberlain's motives and plans.

42. *Arkansas Gazette*, 22 and 27 April 1873.

43. Governor Franklin Moses, annual message, 14 January 1873, in Columbia *Daily Union*, 15 January 1873. Under Chamberlain, the planter's lien on the crop for advances made to tenants was strengthened, see Holt, *Black Over White*, pp. 169–70.

44. Governor Adelbert Ames, inaugural address, 22 January 1874, in Jackson *Weekly Clarion*, 29 January 1874. See Harris, *Day of the Carpetbagger*, pp. 611–12.

Chapter 7

A shorter version of this chapter was presented to the second annual symposium on Emancipation and Its Aftermath at the Graduate Center, City University of New York on 22 May 1981.

1. Circular address of the chairman of the Democratic-Conservative party of Texas, 12 September 1873, in *Texas State Gazette*, 11 October 1873.

2. Charleston *Daily News*, editorial, 18 April 1873.

3. Albert G. Brown, speech at the Mississippi taxpayers' convention, Jackson, 4 January 1875, in Jackson *Weekly Clarion*, 21 January 1875.

4. James Chesnut, speech at the South Carolina taxpayers' convention, in Charleston *News and Courier*, 19 February 1874.

5. New York *Tribune* editorial, cited in Jackson *Weekly Clarion*, 4 June 1874; New York *Herald* editorial, in Mobile *Register*, 4 January 1874.

6. *Arkansas Gazette*, editorial entitled "Party Platforms," 14 August 1874.

7. Atlanta *Constitution*, editorial, 23 November 1873. The observation about the significance of the electoral shift was from the Lynchburg (Va.) *Republican*.

8. Charleston *News and Courier*, editorial, 14 November 1873.

9. Horn's remarks were in an editorial for the Meridian *Mercury*, cited and discussed in the Jackson *Weekly Clarion*, 19 November 1874.

10. L. Q. C. Lamar, in an interview with Henry Grady of the Atlanta *Constitution*, March 1875, cited in Mayes, *Lucius Q. C. Lamar*, p. 226.

11. Letter to the editor from a prominent but unnamed north Mississippi politician, Jackson *Weekly Clarion*, 10 September 1874.

12. Williams, "The Louisiana Unification Movement of 1873," pp. 349–69; see also the report in *Alabama State Journal*, 29 June 1873, and P. G. T. Beauregard, "The Unification Question," an address to the people of Louisiana, New Orleans, 1 July 1873, broadside in Farrow Papers.

13. Beauregard to Lee Crandall, 21 June 1873, published in *Alabama State Journal*, 1 July 1873.

14. For reactions, see Jackson *Weekly Clarion*, editorial, 17 July 1873; Atlanta *Constitution*, editorial, 13 July 1873; and Charleston *News and Courier*, editorial, 28 July 1873.

15. Democratic-Conservative meeting, 17 September 1873 in Meridian, reported in Jackson *Weekly Clarion*, 25 September 1873; see also discussion of the debate over policy in *Weekly Clarion*, 21 and 28 August 1873. The episode is covered in Harris, *Day of the Carpetbagger*, pp. 470–71.

16. Hiram Cassedy, Sr., to the *Clarion*, Summit, 23 August 1873, in Jackson *Weekly Clarion*, 4 September 1873.

17. See Moneyhon, *Republicanism in Reconstruction Texas*, chap. 10.

18. Nathaniel B. Meade to Philip Dandridge, Richmond, 28 April 1873, Hunter Papers.

19. Ben L. Herr to Robert McKee, Livingston, Ala., 6 August 1873, McKee Papers.

20. A listing of the black-belt newspapers opposed to race as the campaign issue

was provided by the *Alabama State Journal*, 20 August 1873. The debate in the black belt and within the party generally was reported in detail by the *Alabama State Journal* throughout the winter and spring of 1873–74. Also full of discussion of these issues are the McKee Papers.

21. C. C. Langdon to McKee, Mobile, 16 May 1874, McKee Papers.

22. Rufus K. Boyd to McKee, confidential, Guntersville, Ala., 24 April 1874, McKee Papers.

23. B. B. Lewis to McKee, Helena, Ala., 14 May 1874, and Langdon to McKee, Mobile, 16 May 1874, both in McKee Papers.

24. The proceedings of the party's state convention were reported fully in the Mobile *Register* and the *State Journal* in the last days of July. The McKee forces were also placated by the elimination of "Conservative" from the party's title.

25. See Taylor, *Louisiana Reconstructed*, pp. 279–84; H. Oscar Lestage, Jr., "White League in Louisiana," pp. 628–49.

26. Taylor, *Louisiana Reconstructed*, pp. 285–86; Lestage, "White League in Louisiana," pp. 649–90.

27. Taylor, *Louisiana Reconstructed*, pp. 287–96; Rable, "And There Was No Peace," chap. 8; Lestage, "White League in Louisiana," pp. 671–90.

28. E. John Ellis to Tom, his brother, At home, 3 August 1874, Ellis Family Papers; Taylor, *Louisiana Reconstructed*, p. 297, however, interpreted the Baton Rouge convention as having been controlled by the White League rather than removed from its clutches.

29. The New Orleans *Picayune*, a responsible New Departurist paper, urged "*Patience!*" in a remarkably candid editorial of 18 February 1876: "It would be easy enough for [the Democratic-Conservatives] to overthrow the present Government in a few hours throughout the limits of the State. But if they should do so their triumph would be but short-lived. In a few days their work would be undone by the Federal soldiery . . . we have one hope: it is to carry the next Presidential election."

30. New Orleans *Picayune*, editorial, 27 June 1876.

31. "Ascension" to the *Picayune*, in New Orleans *Picayune*, 15 June 1876.

32. See discussion at the beginning of chap. 1.

33. Although the negotiations from 1874 to 1875 for a "third term" were of considerable concern to Grant and even influenced the course of his southern policy, they are surprisingly overlooked in William McFeely's fine *Grant: A Biography*.

34. The president's widely reported remarks, which were made to a group of prominent Republicans visiting the White House, can be found in the New York *Herald*, 18 January 1874.

35. In the 1872 election, Stephens himself had been active in the Charles O'Connor Straight Democratic campaign, while Mosby had actually voted for Grant, the Republican nominee.

36. Stephens's negotiations with the Republicans in his district can be followed through letters from leading party officials there; see J. S. Fannin to Stephens, Augusta, 27 January and February 1873, the latter a very revealing and specific communication marked "confidential"; William Boyle to Stephens, Augusta, 22 Febru-

ary 1873, and James Atkins to Stephens, Savannah, 18 October 1873, all in Stephens Papers, LC.

In an interview with the Chicago *Tribune* on 15 May 1873, Mosby explained what his relationship with the Grant administration had been and what he had derived from it, in Atlanta *Constitution*, 25 May 1873.

37. Governor James L. Kemper, inaugural address, 1 January 1874, in Richmond *Dispatch*, 2 January 1874.

38. Alexander Stephens, speech on the Civil Rights bill, in the U.S. House of Representatives, 5 January 1874, reported in Atlanta *Constitution*, 6 January 1874. Also Stephens to Kemper, Washington, D.C., 15 March 1874, Kemper Papers, congratulating Kemper on his inaugural and on the political principles it contained. Kemper's reply, dated 17 March 1874, is in the Stephens Papers, LC.

39. Lafayette McLaws to Stephens, Savannah, 6 August 1874, Stephens Papers, LC.

40. Jackson *Weekly Clarion*, 2 July 1874.

41. Charleston *Daily News*, 19 March 1873; W. W. Mills to Elisha M. Pease, Washington, D.C., 11 October 1874, Pease Papers.

42. "Buell," dispatch from Nashville to the St. Louis *Republican*, 18 February 1875, reprinted in Charleston *News and Courier*, 2 March 1875. See also Gillette, *Retreat from Reconstruction*, pp. 139–41, for Grant's role in Arkansas.

43. Interview with Senator Robertson, in Charleston *News and Courier*, 11 July 1874.

44. Adelbert Ames to Blanche, his wife, Jackson, 31 July 1874, in Ames, comp., *Chronicles from the Nineteenth Century*, 1:693.

45. For details about the failure of the "third term" negotiation, see "Buell" letter, reprinted in Charleston *News and Courier*, 2 March 1875. "Buell," a political correspondent of the St. Louis *Republican*, felt it was Grant's betrayal by the Arkansas Democrats when they rejected Baxter and called a constitutional convention which had provoked the president into giving up his southern negotiations.

46. Charleston *News and Courier*, editorial, 19 November 1875.

47. Ibid., editorial, 9 May 1876.

48. Harris, *Day of the Carpetbagger*, pp. 389, 639–40. For their white-line opponents, see ibid., pp. 389–90, 410–13.

49. For the tax union in Texas, see Moneyhon, *Republicanism in Reconstruction Texas*, pp. 160–62, and for South Carolina, see Proceedings of the Tax Payers' Convention of South Carolina, held in Columbia, 9–12 May 1871.

50. James B. Kershaw to William H. Trescot, Camden, 26 August 1874, Trescot Papers.

51. Harris, *Day of the Carpetbagger*, p. 625.

52. Charleston *News and Courier*, editorial, 15 October 1874. See also South Carolina taxpayers' convention, "Address to the People," February 1874, in Trescot Papers.

53. Charleston *News and Courier*, 29 June 1874.

54. South Carolina taxpayers' convention, "Address to the People," February 1874, in Trescot Papers.

55. See, for example, Sproat, "*The Best Men*"; Blodgett, "Reform Thought and

the Genteel Tradition"; and Hoogenboom, "Civil Service Reform and Public Morality," the last two in Morgan, ed., *The Gilded Age*.

56. Reported in Jackson *Weekly Clarion*, 10 December 1874.

57. Jackson *Weekly Clarion*, 11 March 1875; Jackson *Weekly Pilot*, 22 May 1875; Harris, *Day of the Carpetbagger*, p. 654.

58. L. Q. C. Lamar to Charles Reemelin, 25 August 1875, in Mayes, *L. Q. C. Lamar*, p. 258.

59. Adelbert Ames to Blanche, Jackson, 4 August 1875, in Ames, comp., *Chronicles from the Nineteenth Century*, 2:124.

60. Jackson *Weekly Pilot*, editorial, 14 August 1875.

61. See Lamson, *The Glorious Failure*, pp. 212–25.

62. Chamberlain's comments were made in an interview with Francis Dawson, editor of the *News and Courier*, on 19 December 1875, in Allen, *Governor Chamberlain's Administration in South Carolina*, p. 195.

63. Charleston *News and Courier*, editorial, 18 December 1875.

64. Charleston *News and Courier*, 6 May, 21 July 1876.

65. Ibid., 21 July 1876.

66. C. Richardson Miles to Bro. William, Charleston, 26 August 1876, Miles Papers.

67. Ibid.

68. Jackson *Weekly Pilot*, editorial, 23 September 1875.

69. "One Who Knows" to the editor, *Alabama State Journal*, 26 September 1874.

70. "Liberty, Tolerance and Peace," campaign address of the Republican State Executive Committee of Alabama, p. 8, in *Alabama State Journal*, 1 October 1874.

71. New York *Herald*, 3 August 1876, reprinted in Charleston *News and Courier*, 5 August 1876.

72. Columbia *Union-Herald*, editorial, 6 December 1876.

73. Alexander White, speech on Civil Rights bill, U.S. House of Representatives, 4 February 1875, *Congressional Record*, 43 Cong., 2nd Sess., vol. 3, part 3, appendix, p. 23; also in *Alabama State Journal*, 17 March 1875.

74. New York *Times* reports of the Arkansas convention, reprinted in Columbia *Union-Herald*, 2, 3 October 1876.

75. Wilmington *Post*, editorial, 3 September 1875.

76. James W. Sloss, testimony, "Alabama Elections, 1874–76," *Senate Reports*, No. 704, 44 Cong., 2 Sess., vol. 1, p. 139.

77. Because the term "secessionist" was so emotive, Republicans tended to use it rather loosely and often in an attempt to draw attention to the dangers that the determined white-line campaigns posed to the survival of southern Republicanism. In this sense, "secessionist" was something of a southern equivalent of the "bloody shirt" as a rallying-cry in the North. All the same, even if it did not describe *precisely* the political record of those who were in the forefront of the white-line insurgency, there was no doubt that extremists and former Democrats, two political categories connoted by the term "secessionist," did reenter the upper echelons of the Democratic party and become reinstated.

78. Alexander White, speech on Civil Rights bill, U.S. House of Representatives, 4 February 1875, *Congressional Record*, 43 Cong., 2nd Sess., vol. 3, part 3, appendix, p. 23; also in *Alabama State Journal*, 17 March 1875.

79. Alexander White, speech, U.S. House of Representatives, 27 February 1875, *Congressional Record*, 43 Cong., 2nd Sess., vol. 3, part 3, p. 1928.

80. Mobile *Register*, editorial, 10 November 1874.

81. Texas Democratic campaign platform, 1875, in *Appleton's Cyclopedia for 1875*, p. 729.

82. Report of proceedings in the state Democratic convention, 29 July 1874, in Huntsville *Democrat*, 6 August 1874; see also report in *Alabama State Journal*, 30 July 1874.

83. Report of the state Democratic convention, *Alabama State Journal*, 30 July 1874.

84. "Marshall County" to the editor, in Jackson *Weekly Clarion*, 24 November 1875.

85. W. A. Vinnwell to Alexander Stephens, Louisville, 14 April 1875, Stephens Papers, LC.

86. "Democrat" to the editor, *Arkansas Gazette*, 1 April 1874.

87. See Keller, *Affairs of State*, pp. 238–68, 530–44, 552–64; Marcus, *Grand Old Party*, pp. 5–8; Hansen, *The Making of the Third Party System*, chap. 9 and conclusion.

Chapter 8

1. New Orleans *Picayune*, 29 July 1876.

2. These remarks were made by Robert Toombs in the course of an interview concerning his views on the policy southern Democrats should adopt towards the new president, Rutherford B. Hayes, in Atlanta *Constitution*, 14 March 1877.

3. See Key, *Southern Politics in State and Nation*, and Kousser, *The Shaping of Southern Politics*.

4. DuBois, "Reconstruction and Its Benefits," p. 799. Subsequent historians have followed DuBois's lead and accepted his judgment.

5. One exception to this is Otto Olsen's extensive discussion of the 1875 convention in North Carolina in *Carpetbagger's Crusade*, pp. 183–94.

6. In 1871, a convention bill was enacted in North Carolina and a referendum held. But the call was defeated by popular vote, a severe setback for the Democrats and an indication of the basic strength of the Republicans. See John Pool, article on the background and purpose of North Carolina's constitutional convention, in Wilmington *Post*, 14 May 1875.

7. Mobile *Register*, 16 April, and editorial, 18 May 1875. Houston's speech at Athens, in Limestone County, containing his views on a convention had been delivered on 3 May 1875.

8. Mobile *Register*, 28 January 1875.

9. McMillan, *Constitutional Development in Alabama*, p. 181.

10. New Orleans *Picayune*, editorial, 11 January 1879. Caddo and Natchito-

ches were in the northwestern corner of the state and were centers of convention sentiment.

11. Atlanta *Constitution*, editorial, 11 December 1873.

12. See Brandon, "Calling the Georgia Constitutional Convention of 1877," pp. 189–203.

13. Gainesville *Eagle* editorial, in Atlanta *Constitution*, 11 January 1874.

14. Joseph C. Abbott to Thomas Settle, Wilmington, N.C., 6 August 1875, Settle Papers, Series 2.

15. David Schenck, diary, January 1875, bound typescript, vol. 7, p. 138, Schenck Diaries.

16. Debate in Georgia House on a convention bill, Atlanta *Constitution*, 28, 29, 30 January 1876.

17. Richard Coke, governor's message, in Mobile *Register*, 19 January 1875.

18. Richard Coke to Samuel B. Maxey, Austin, 7 September 1874, Maxey Papers.

19. Mobile *Register*, editorial, 27 January 1875.

20. Governor Coke, message, in Mobile *Register*, 19 January 1875.

21. Atlanta *Constitution*, editorial, 30 January 1876.

22. John Pool, article on the background and prospects for a convention, Wilmington *Post*, 14 May 1875.

23. Report of the Cincinnati *Gazette*'s Washington correspondent, in *Alabama State Journal*, 19 February 1875.

24. Atlanta *Constitution*, editorial, 25 December 1873.

25. D. B. Hamilton, speech in the debate on the convention bill, Atlanta *Constitution*, 28, 29, 30 January 1876.

26. Atlanta *Constitution*, 14 July 1877.

27. Letter to the Birmingham *Iron Age*, reprinted in Mobile *Register*, 17 January 1875. This outcome had been predicted approvingly by John Forsyth who reported in the Mobile *Register*, 19 January 1875, that "the people of North Alabama will have control of the convention."

28. New Orleans *Picayune*, 5 August 1878.

29. Address of Democratic State Executive Committee, announcing the constitutional convention, in Huntsville *Democrat*, 26 March 1874.

30. Jackson *Weekly Clarion*, 13 June 1872.

31. Atlanta *Constitution*, 23 January 1876.

32. Harris, *Day of the Carpetbagger*, pp. 675–76.

33. Remarks of Representative Foster, during discussion of the convention bill in the committee of the whole, reported in Atlanta *Constitution*, 28 January 1874.

34. Debate in Georgia House, 23 January 1877, in Atlanta *Constitution*, 24 January 1877.

35. The turnout in Louisiana was less than 50 percent, according to the *Picayune*, 24 March 1879. The vote polled was under 70,000, compared to the 74,769 for Wiltz and 40,760 for Beattie in the gubernatorial election of 1879, in *Appleton's Annual Cyclopedia for 1879*, pp. 565, 572. The voting statistics for Georgia and Alabama further corroborate this trend. Georgia polled 48,181 to 39,057 in the convention vote, while in the state election of 1876, the vote was

111,297 to 33,444. Alabama's convention vote was 77,763 to 59,928, again a close vote as well as a small one, whereas the Houston–Lewis vote in 1874 was 107,118 to 93,928. The figures are all from *Appleton's Annual Cyclopedia* for the relevant years.

36. New Orleans *Picayune*, 24 March 1879.

37. Atlanta *Constitution*, editorial, 14 January 1876.

38. Hair, *Bourbonism and Agrarian Protest*, pp. 99–102. A similar analysis of the convention can be found in a speech by the Republican gubernatorial candidate, Taylor Beattie, which was reported in the New Orleans *Picayune*, 30 November 1879.

39. Debate in the Georgia House on the convention bill, 24 January 1877, in Atlanta *Constitution*, 25 January 1877.

40. Interview with Robert Toombs, Atlanta *Constitution*, 14 March 1877.

41. Robert Toombs, speech in Georgia House of Representatives' Chamber, 25 January 1876, in Atlanta *Constitution*, 26 January 1876.

42. Amos Akerman, speech, Atlanta, 4 February 1876, in Atlanta *Constitution*, 5 February 1876.

43. McMillan, *Constitutional Development in Alabama*, p. 210.

44. Barr, *From Reconstruction to Reform*, p. 9.

45. McKay, *Making the Texas Constitution of 1875*, pp. 74, 185.

46. Ward, "Georgia under the Bourbon Democrats," chap. 5.

The Atlanta *Constitution* conducted an analysis of the delegates in its issue of 1 August 1877. The paper found that the members' occupations broke down into the following categories: there were 51 lawyers, of whom many were also planters and farmers, 44 farmers, 15 doctors, 13 merchants, 5 manufacturers; 6 others were either editors, teachers, or ministers, while 4 were professional politicians. The membership also possessed a good deal of experience in public affairs. Sixty-six had held office in the Confederate military and many others had held civilian public office; 22 had sat in previous constitutional conventions, while there were 17 state senators, 22 state representatives, 4 Confederate congressmen, 5 U.S. congressmen, 1 Confederate senator, 2 U.S. senators, 1 governor, and 1 Supreme Court judge.

47. New Orleans *Picayune*, editorials, 25 March and 23 April 1879. See also Hair, *Bourbonism and Agrarian Protest*, p. 99.

48. "Confederate" to the editor, Columbus, Ga., 10 April 1877, in Atlanta *Constitution*, 13 April 1877.

Chapter 9

1. Hart, *Redeemers, Bourbons, and Populists*, pp. 4–7; Kousser, *Shaping of Southern Politics*, pp. 114–15; Curry, *Radicalism, Racism, and Realignment*, p. 76.

2. Ratchford, *American State Debts*, pp. 183–90; Hart, *Redeemers, Bourbons, and Populists*, chaps. 2–3; Jones, *Tennessee at the Crossroads*, chap. 8. See also Ball, "The Public Career of Colonel A. S. Colyar," passim.

3. *Arkansas Gazette*, editorial, 1 May 1874.

4. These details were reported by a Republican member of the convention, S. M. Barnes, in a speech to the party's state convention, *Arkansas Gazette*, 16 September 1874.

5. Convention debate on 26 August 1874, reported in *Arkansas Gazette*, 27 August 1874.

6. William M. Fishback to R. T. Kerr, 8 January 1875, in *Arkansas Gazette*, 13 January 1875.

7. The amendment, known as the Fishback amendment, prohibited the state from paying any bonds declared invalid by the Supreme Court. See Evans, "The Public Debt," 1:370. The invalid bonds consisted of the railroad, levee, and Holford bonds.

8. Thompson, *Arkansas and Reconstruction*, pp. 233–39; Ratchford, *American State Debts*, p. 189; Bayliss, "Post-Reconstruction Repudiation," pp. 243–59; Woodward, *Origins of the New South*, p. 90.

9. Staples, "Arkansas, 1865–1930," 1:170–71.

10. For information on the history of the North Carolina convention of 1875, see U.S. Senator John Pool, article about the precursors of the 1875 convention, in the Wilmington *Post*, 14 May 1875; report of the Democratic caucus in Wilmington *Post*, 26 March 1875; Raleigh *Sentinel*, 2 April 1875, citing the stipulations on the scope of the convention's activity.

11. Wilmington *Post*, editorial, 3 September 1875.

12. Raleigh *Sentinel*, 14 January 1876, for 1876 Democratic party platform; Richard C. Badger, testimony, "The Negro Exodus from the Southern States," *Senate Reports*, 46 Cong., 1 & 2 Sess., part I, p. 405. The accuracy of Badger's account is unquestioned.

13. Raleigh *Sentinel*, 11 October 1875.

14. Ratchford, "The Adjustment of the North Carolina Public Debt," pp. 158–67. The *Observer* quote can be found on page 161.

15. Bromberg, "'Pure Democracy and White Supremacy,'" pp. 40–45.

16. "Francis," reporting the convention's proceedings for 17 September 1875, in Mobile *Register*, 19 September 1875.

17. Reprinted in Mobile *Register*, 24 June 1875.

18. Alabama Constitutional Convention, address to the people, in Mobile *Register*, 8 October 1875.

19. McMillan, *Constitutional Development in Alabama*, pp. 203–5.

20. By 16 October 1875, the convention was on the verge of complete repudiation. See Bond, *Negro Education in Alabama*, p. 60.

21. McMillan, *Constitutional Development in Alabama*, p. 210.

22. Ibid., pp. 206, 207 (n. 118), 213.

23. Mobile *Register*, 18 February 1876.

24. Birmingham *Age-Herald*, editorial, 20 January 1901, cited in McMillan, *Constitutional Development in Alabama*, p. 235.

25. Governor William Oates, annual message, 1896, quoted in ibid., p. 235.

26. Governor Joseph Johnston, annual message, 1897, quoted in ibid., p. 236.

27. Samuel B. Maxey to his wife, Austin, 26 September 1875, Maxey Papers.

28. Richard Coke to Oran M. Roberts, Austin, 8 and 26 November 1875, Roberts Papers.

29. J. F. Camp to Roberts, Palestine, Tex., 14 January 1876, Roberts Papers.

30. A. W. Terrell to Roberts, Austin, 28 October 1875, Roberts Papers.

31. Ashbel Smith to Horace Cone, Evergreen, Tex., 15 November 1875, Ashbel Smith Papers. Incidentally, Smith had run for the convention but had been defeated, an indication of the strength of the insurgents in the state.

32. Ibid. Land was given away extremely generously and this resulted in long-term loss to the state. At the time, it was thought to be a more painless way of encouraging railroad development than giving financial subsidies and endorsements that would have to be paid for in taxes.

33. Webster Flanagan, interview with a reporter from the Galveston *News*, 19 December 1875, in McKay, *Making the Texas Constitution*, pp. 169–70.

34. McKay, *Making the Texas Constitution*, p. 167.

35. William P. Ballinger to Oran Roberts, Galveston, 19 August 1878, Roberts Papers. Numerous attempts were made in the 1880s and 1890s to raise the legislators' pay but they were beaten back, see McKay, *Making the Texas Constitution*, p. 186.

36. Guy M. Bryan to John H. Reagan, Galveston, 17 October 1875, Reagan Papers.

37. Robert Toombs, speech in Georgia's constitutional convention, in Small, *Proceedings of the Constitutional Convention*, p. 298.

38. The Atlanta *Constitution* had noted on 14 July the strength of the sentiment in the convention against state aid. For prewar state aid policies, see Heath, *Constructive Liberalism*.

39. Small, *Proceedings of the Constitutional Convention*, pp. 296–97, 300.

40. Ibid., p. 490. The sale is prescribed in article 7, section 13, paragraph 1, of the constitution.

41. See Ward, "Georgia under the Bourbon Democrats," chap. 5.

42. Ratchford, *American State Debts*, p. 185; Ward, "Georgia under the Bourbon Democrats," p. 309.

43. Small, *Proceedings of the Constitutional Convention*, pp. 405, 409.

44. Ward, "Georgia under the Bourbon Democrats," pp. 367–68.

45. Ratchford, *American State Debts*, pp. 192–93.

46. Ward, "Georgia under the Bourbon Democrats," p. 327.

47. Ibid., p. 235.

48. Ibid., p. 241. Lobbying was also made a crime. The fear that the legislature's size made it vulnerable to influence precipitated one of the biggest debates in the convention; Small, *Proceedings of the Constitutional Convention*, pp. 150–62.

49. Ibid., pp. 215–29.

50. Ward, "Georgia under the Bourbon Democrats," p. 315.

51. A. W. Holcombe, speech on governor's salary proposal, in Small, *Proceedings of the Constitutional Convention*, p. 128.

52. Ibid., pp. 135–38.

53. Both of these ordinances were in fact approved; Atlanta *Constitution*, 6 December 1877.

54. Ratchford, *American State Debts*, p. 188.

55. Kidd had actually been responsible for introducing the convention bill into the assembly, New Orleans *Picayune*, 5 February 1878.

56. New Orleans *Picayune*, editorials, 31 May, 3, 5 June 1879.

57. Ratchford, *American State Debts*, p. 188. The rates were actually pegged to a sliding scale of 2 percent for the first five years, 3 percent for the next fifteen, and 4 percent thereafter.

58. McGinty, *Louisiana Redeemed*, p. 167.

59. New Orleans *Picayune*, editorial, 30 May 1879.

60. Taylor, *Louisiana Reconstructed*, p. 479.

61. New Orleans *Picayune*, editorial, 7 May 1879. A ban on the loaning of the state's credit had already been enacted as part of the Republican administration's tax measures in 1874.

62. McGinty, *Louisiana Redeemed*, pp. 169–76, chap. 7; Hair, *Bourbonism and Agrarian Protest*, pp. 101–5.

63. Governor James L. Kemper had proposed a commission of five or six appointed members to write a new constitution; see his special message to that effect in the Richmond *Dispatch*, 24 April 1874. The General Assembly rejected this notion and instead discussed a number of amendments, many of which were implemented with Kemper's support. To these were added more, which regulated the practices and privileges of corporations in 1875 and pruned government expenditures in 1876. Maddex, *Virginia Conservatives*, pp. 117–20.

64. The trend during this period was usually in the opposite direction, towards separating the federal and state elections. The motive was to deprive the federal government of the occasion and need for intervening in local elections, whereas Mississippi's contrasting course was dictated by economic stringency, not politics.

65. Jackson *Weekly Clarion*, editorial, 23 January 1878. An attempt to abolish the office of lieutenant governor had failed a month earlier.

66. Texas alone had a smaller debt than Mississippi; see Ratchford, *American State Debts*, p. 183, and Harris, *Day of the Carpetbagger*, p. 704.

67. Harris, *Day of the Carpetbagger*, p. 703 (n. 36) and p. 704.

68. Jackson *Weekly Clarion*, 10 April 1878.

69. The Jackson *Weekly Clarion* printed Governor Stone's inaugural of 10 January 1878 in its 16 January 1878 edition; Harris, *Day of the Carpetbagger*, pp. 704–5.

70. Ratchford, *American State Debts*, pp. 185–86. The funding had been carried out under the Consolidation Act of 1873; see Goodrich, *Government Promotion of American Canals and Railroads*, chap. 6, for details of the reversal of policy on state aid.

71. Charleston *News and Courier*, 16 December 1878.

72. Ibid., 11 January 1879.

73. Cooper, *Conservative Regime*, pp. 126–33.

74. Ibid., pp. 45–48; Charleston *News and Courier*, throughout May and June 1877.

75. Charleston *News and Courier*, 5–11 March, and editorial, 11 March 1878.

76. The collapse of the railroad program is discussed in Summers, "Radical Reconstruction and the Gospel of Prosperity," chaps. 17, 18.

77. "R. E. H." to Charleston *News and Courier*, 15 January 1878, in *News and Courier*, 18 January 1878.

78. Levi Lawler to Robert McKee, New York City, 12 June 1875, McKee Papers.

79. Donelson Caffrey, speech in the constitutional convention, reported in New Orleans *Picayune*, 13 June 1879; Taylor, *Louisiana Reconstructed*, p. 483.

80. Semmes's remarks were delivered in the convention and were reported in the New Orleans *Picayune*, 10 June 1879.

81. Ibid.

82. Ratchford, *American State Debts*, pp. 190–93.

83. Hannibal I. Kimball to Robert Alston, Newton, Mass., 7 March 1874, and Joseph E. Brown to Kimball, Marietta, Ga., 21 April 1874, Brown typescripts.

84. The South's lack of capital after the war is regarded as basic to its economic difficulties by Harold Woodman. See his *King Cotton and His Retainers*, chap. 27, and also Summers, "Radical Reconstruction and the Gospel of Prosperity," chap. 4, especially pp. 179–82.

85. Woodward, *Origins of the New South*, chap. 11, entitled "The Colonial Economy"; Summers, "Radical Reconstruction and the Gospel of Prosperity," pp. 983–85.

86. Joseph E. Brown, speech in the Georgia convention, reported in Small, *Proceedings of the Constitutional Convention*, pp. 295–97.

87. Hannibal Kimball to Robert Alston, Newton, Mass., 7 March 1874, Brown typescripts.

88. Moneyhon, *Republicanism in Reconstruction Texas*, pp. 184–85; Barr, *From Reconstruction to Reform*, p. 111; Williamson, *Florida Politics in the Gilded Age*, pp. 72–79.

89. Robert Toombs, speech at Cartersville, Ga., reported in the Atlanta *Constitution*, 21 November 1877; the speech about locking the treasury door was delivered in the convention on 16 August 1877, in Small, *Proceedings of the Constitutional Convention*, p. 407.

90. Green, "The Convict Lease System in the Southern States," pp. 271–87. Green regarded the budgetary motive as preeminent, p. 281. See also, for example, Harris, *Day of the Carpetbagger*, p. 710; Kirwan, *Revolt of the Rednecks*, pp. 167–69; Hair, *Bourbonism and Agrarian Protest*, pp. 129–32; Williamson, *Florida Politics in the Gilded Age*, pp. 28–30; Going, *Bourbon Democracy in Alabama*, chap. 11.

91. Mobile *Register*, 23 January 1879.

92. Ward, "Georgia under the Bourbon Democrats," p. 327.

93. Bromberg, "'Pure Democracy and White Supremacy,'" p. 365.

94. *Arkansas Gazette*, 4 February 1874.

95. New Orleans *Picayune*, 27 May 1879.

96. Jackson *Weekly Clarion*, editorial, 9 February 1876; James Wesson to the editor, Jackson *Weekly Clarion*, 9 February 1876.

97. Jesse Cypert, speech at the Arkansas convention, 26 August 1874, in *Arkansas Gazette*, 27 August 1874.

98. George Ruby, testimony, "The Negro Exodus from the Southern States," *Senate Reports*, 46 Cong., 1 & 2 Sess., part 2, p. 95.

Chapter 10

1. W. C. Irwin, president of the Farmers' and Planters' Club of Madison County, speech, 15 March 1873, in Huntsville *Democrat*, 20 March 1873.

2. Commodore Matthew Fontaine Maury, speech at the St. Louis Fair, cited in the Jackson *Weekly Clarion*, 28 November 1872.

3. Assembly of farmers meeting at the state capitol, Jackson, Miss., 15 December 1876, reported by Jackson *Weekly Clarion*, 20 December 1876.

4. Charles M. Howard, Thomas Underwood, et al., committee of the Mulberry Agricultural Club, to Governor David P. Lewis, Mulberry, Autauga County, Ala., 4 October 1873, in Governor Lewis Papers.

5. Benjamin H. Hill, speech to a gathering of farmers in Jonesboro, Ga., 8 August 1873, in Atlanta *Constitution*, 16 August 1873.

6. Atlanta *Constitution*, editorial, 23 June 1873.

7. From an editorial in the Selma *Times and Argus*, cited by the Mobile *Register*, 14 May 1874.

8. Jackson *Weekly Pilot*, editorial, 16 October 1875.

9. Charleston *News and Courier*, editorial, 29 January 1878.

10. "Justice," communication, in Jackson *Weekly Clarion*, 9 May 1877.

11. Charleston *News and Courier*, 29 January 1878.

12. Ward, "Georgia under the Bourbon Democrats," pp. 252–55.

13. Bromberg, "'Pure Democracy and White Supremacy,'" p. 13; Cooper, *Conservative Regime*, pp. 139–40; Louisiana, *Session Laws,* 1880, pp. 40–41.

14. Rogers, *One-Gallused Rebellion*, p. 110.

15. Cooper, *Conservative Regime*, pp. 139–40; Bromberg, "'Pure Democracy and White Supremacy,'" p. 260; Rogers, *One-Gallused Rebellion*, pp. 114–15.

16. Moore, "Redeemers Reconsidered," pp. 374–75; Rogers, *One-Gallused Rebellion*, pp. 76, 113. Moore notes that North Carolina pioneered the idea of experimental farms, and other states followed later in the decade, p. 374.

17. Moore, "Redeemers Reconsidered," pp. 374–75.

18. Ibid., p. 374. See also Cooper, *Conservative Regime*, p. 166; Mississippi, *Acts*, 1878, pp. 118–23; Maddex, *Virginia Conservatives*, p. 215.

19. South Carolina, *House Journal*, Extra Session, February 1880, appendix.

20. Going, *Bourbon Democracy in Alabama*, p. 208. See also ibid., p. 112, and Rogers, *One-Gallused Rebellion*, p. 76.

21. See Jackson *Weekly Clarion*, 19 April 1876, for an occupational breakdown of the state legislature that year. In 1880, the *Senate Journal* printed an analysis in which lawyers numbered 32 in the House and 14 in the Senate, while "planter/farmer" accounted for 58 and 19 respectively, exclusive of combinations with physician, teacher, minister, lawyer, in Mississippi, *Senate Journal*, 1880, pp. 580–

85. There were 41 "farmer/planters" in Louisiana's House in 1880, compared with 17 "lawyers," 15 "tradesmen," 14 "professionals," and 4 "merchants."

22. Of the Texas convention, its historian, Seth S. McKay, wrote that it "contained forty-one farmers, twenty-nine lawyers, and a few merchants, editors, stockmen and physicians. Many of the farmers and several of the lawyers were known to be members of the State Grange. . . . About one-half of the delegates elected were Grangers," McKay, *Making the Texas Constitution of 1876*, p. 74. This estimate has been revised downward by J. E. Ericson in his "The Delegates to the Convention of 1875," pp. 22–27, but the preponderance of the agricultural element and the Grange is still undeniable.

Another convention whose occupational composition is known was Georgia's. According to an analysis published in the Jackson *Weekly Clarion* on 1 August 1877, there were 51 lawyers, 15 physicians, 13 merchants, 5 manufacturers, and 44 farmers. Of course, many of those lawyers were farmers themselves or sympathetic to agricultural interests and concerns.

23. Georgia and Louisiana submitted the question of relocating their capitals when their new constitutions were to be ratified. Both electorates rejected the change.

24. A regional meeting of the Granges from all the southern states on 25, 26 November 1873 urged a ceiling of 7 percent on interest-rates, in Atlanta *Constitution*, 27 November 1873.

25. Raleigh *Sentinel*, 1 February 1875; Bromberg, "'Pure Democracy and White Supremacy,'" p. 403. The misdemeanor penalty was removed in 1877; there was also considerable pressure at the time to lower the rate even further, to 6 percent.

26. Ward, "Georgia under the Bourbon Democrats," p. 290.

27. See editorial urging repeal in Mobile *Register*, 7 January 1875, and legislative report in *Register*, 19 February 1875.

28. South Carolina, *Acts*, 1877–78, p. 325. Virginia also kept its interest rates down to 6 percent throughout most of the 1870s, see Maddex, *Virginia Conservatives*, p. 169.

29. Thornton, "Fiscal Policy and the Failure of Radical Reconstruction in the Lower South," in *Region, Race, and Reconstruction*, pp. 349–94. Thornton's careful analysis, comparing state taxation and budgetary policy before and after the war, reveals how drastic was the change introduced by the Republicans. Moreover, it also explains why tax reduction was so important to landowners, in particular to small-scale farmers outside the plantation areas who provided the backbone of the movement.

30. The policies of these groups, and their impact, were discussed in the previous chapter.

31. Ward, "Georgia under the Bourbon Democrats," pp. 262–64, 267–70. The geological survey was abolished in 1880, p. 274.

32. Bromberg, "'Pure Democracy and White Supremacy,'" pp. 13, 41–42.

33. Thornton, "Fiscal Policy and the Failure of Radical Reconstruction," passim.

34. Moore, "Redeemers Reconsidered," p. 374 (n. 46). For Arkansas, see also Scott, *The Repudiation of State Debts*, p. 123.

35. Going, *Bourbon Democracy in Alabama*, pp. 85–87.

36. Garnie W. McGinty, *Louisiana Redeemed*, pp. 199–200; Hair, *Bourbonism and Agrarian Protest*, pp. 100–101.

37. Harris, *Day of the Carpetbagger*, p. 704.

38. Ibid., pp. 704–5; Cooper, *Conservative Regime*, p. 125; Going, *Bourbon Democracy in Alabama*, p. 112.

39. Ward, "Georgia under the Bourbon Democrats," p. 295; Going, *Bourbon Democracy in Alabama*, p. 86.

40. Richmond *Dispatch*, 18 April 1874; the conflict was also commented upon in subsequent issues of the paper, see 23, 24, 25 April 1874.

41. Ibid., 1 May 1874.

42. *Alabama State Journal*, editorial, 5 May 1874.

43. Charleston *News and Courier*, editorial, 13 June 1877.

44. William K. Duglas, speech, Dry Grove, Miss., 6 July 1877, in Jackson *Weekly Clarion*, 15 August 1877.

45. Alfred H. Colquitt to James Randall, editor of the Augusta *Constitutionalist*, 29 May 1876, in Atlanta *Constitution*, 11 June 1876.

46. Duglas speech, in Jackson *Weekly Clarion*, 15 August 1877.

47. W. W. Lang, speech to the annual assembly of the Texas State Grange, 17 April 1874, in Galveston *News*, 18 April 1874.

48. W. C. Irwin, president, address to the Farmers and Planters Club of Madison County, Alabama, 15 March 1873, reported in Huntsville *Democrat*, 20 March 1873.

49. John T. Jones, speech to the Arkansas State Grange, reprinted in *Arkansas Gazette*, 9 February 1875. Wyatt Aiken, the leading South Carolina Granger and agricultural spokesman, chided the planters of his state in 1878 for failure to buy and manage a phosphate factory four years earlier, in the agricultural section of the Charleston *News and Courier*, 1 February 1878.

50. Legislative report, Charleston *News and Courier*, 30 January 1878.

51. L. O. Bridewell, president's annual address to the Mississippi Grange, in Jackson *Weekly Clarion*, 1 October 1874.

52. For corroboration of this point, see Billings, *Planters and the Making of a "New South,"* and Hearden, *Independence and Empire*.

Chapter 11

1. Herschel Johnson to Dr. J. R. Price, Sandy Grove, 12 November 1872, Johnson Papers.

2. See Roark, *Masters Without Slaves*, pp. 156–57; Litwack, *Been in the Storm So Long*, chaps. 7, 8.

3. See Ransom and Sutch, *One Kind of Freedom*, chap. 3.

4. J. W. Norwood, president of the North Carolina Agricultural and Industrial Convention, address to the people, Hillsboro, 19 September 1872, in Raleigh *Sentinel*, 24 September 1872.

5. Atlanta *Constitution*, editorial, 27 May 1877.

6. Ibid.

7. C. C. Langdon, speech, "Southern Agriculture," given at the fair of the Agricultural and Mechanical Association of West Alabama, Eutaw, 28 October 1872, in Mobile *Register*, 17 November 1872.

8. Atlanta *Constitution*, editorial, 27 May 1877. See also Wiener, *Social Origins of the New South*, pp. 189–90, for the role of small farms in the New South agenda.

9. Atlanta *Constitution*, editorial, 24 March 1869.

10. Communication from "Granger," in Richmond *Dispatch*, 16 April 1874.

11. Speech of P. J. Malone, corresponding secretary, Colleton Agricultural and Mechanical Society, Waterboro, 12 April 1870, in *Rural Carolinian*, June 1870, p. 538.

12. Benjamin H. Hill, speech at Jonesboro County fair, Georgia, in Austin *Texas State Gazette*, 11 October 1873.

13. D. Wyatt Aiken, editorial column, *Rural Carolinian*, September 1874, p. 621.

14. C. C. Langdon, speech at Eutaw, Mobile *Register*, 17 November 1872.

15. Communication from "Fort Bend," in Galveston *News*, 4 March 1874. For the alternative interpretation, see editorial in the Jackson *Pilot*, 28 July 1875, suggesting that "Southern *Planters* should more generally imitate the Northern *Farmers* and hold the plow as well as drive."

16. Adelbert Ames, veto message, 2 March 1876, in *Journal of the Mississippi House of Representatives*, 1876, p. 359.

17. *Journal of the Mississippi Senate*, 1876, p. 485; Jackson *Weekly Clarion*, 19 April 1876.

18. *Acts of Alabama, 1874–75*, pp. 259–60.

19. *Acts of Arkansas, 1874–75*, p. 112.

20. *Acts of Georgia, 1875*, p. 26.

21. *Statutes of South Carolina, 1877–78*, p. 631.

22. The effect of the "pig" laws is assessed in Woodward, *Origins of the New South, 1877–1913*, p. 213; Wharton, *Negro in Mississippi*, pp. 237–38; McWhiney, "The Revolution in Nineteenth-Century Alabama Agriculture," pp. 24, 27.

23. *Acts of Arkansas, 1874–75*, pp. 90, 128.

24. *Acts of Georgia, 1874*, pp. 21–22.

25. Charleston *News and Courier*, editorial, 12 May 1877.

26. Mobile *Register*, editorial, 26 November 1874.

27. Colquitt's address was reported in the Atlanta *Constitution*, 13 February 1874.

28. The act was slightly modified in the following session; *Laws of North Carolina, 1874–75*, p. 63.

29. Going, *Bourbon Democracy in Alabama*, p. 98; *Acts of Alabama, 1874–75*, p. 241.

30. *Acts of Arkansas, 1875–76*, pp. 139–40; *Journal of the Mississippi Senate*, 1876, p. 464; Atlanta *Constitution*, 6 February 1876.

31. *Acts of Louisiana, 1877,* p. 23; *Statutes of South Carolina,* 1877, pp. 318–20.

32. Going, *Bourbon Democracy in Alabama,* p. 98; *Acts of Alabama, 1878–79,* pp. 206–7.

33. Debate in the Georgia Senate, reported in Atlanta *Constitution,* 22, 28 January 1876.

34. Report of the Senate debate in the *Alabama State Journal,* 26 November 1873.

35. For discussion and definition of southern tenure arrangements on the land, see Woodman's perceptive "Southern Agriculture and the Law." Also insightful is W. E. B. DuBois's little-known report, "The Negro Farmer," pp. 511–540, esp. pp. 522–23.

36. The significance of Alabama as the initiator of the labor-repressive trend was stressed by James T. Rapier, a former black Republican congressman from Alabama, and by W. E. Harne, a Texas Republican, in testimony to the Senate Committee Investigating the Exodus of 1879. See "Negro Exodus from the Southern States," *Senate Reports,* 1879–80, 46 Cong., 1 & 2 Sess., vols. 7 & 8, parts 1–3. Rapier's remarks are in part 2, p. 466, and Harne's are in part 3, p. 459.

37. Address from Alabama Republican state legislators to President Grant and the Alabama members of Congress, 15 February 1875, in *Alabama State Journal,* 9 March 1875. Similar observations about the Democrats' intention of reducing the status of black labor were made by John Pool of North Carolina; see his opinion about the upcoming constitutional convention in North Carolina, Wilmington *Post,* 14 May 1875.

38. Woodman, "Southern Agriculture and the Law," p. 327. See also his *King Cotton and His Retainers,* chap. 24, and Ransom and Sutch, *One Kind of Freedom,* chap. 6, for further discussion of the merchant and his financial role after emancipation.

39. Alfred Colquitt, presidential address to the convention of the Georgia Agricultural Society, Atlanta, in Atlanta *Constitution,* 14 February 1874.

40. Debate on repeal of the cotton lien law in the Alabama Senate, reported in *Alabama State Journal,* 15 January 1875.

41. Harold Woodman has pointed out how the local supply-merchant took over the furnishing system from the large city factors who used to dominate it before the war, with the local merchant functioning simply as an adjunct to the factor's operation. Mainly this shift was attributable to the postwar changes in farm practices, namely the emergence of a large number of tenants engaged in small-scale and semi-independent farming and the concentration on growing a cash crop, cotton. Woodman, *King Cotton and His Retainers,* chap. 24. Ransom and Sutch go so far as to claim that the local merchants had a monopoly; *One Kind of Freedom,* chap. 7.

42. Dr. T. D. Hutchinson, speech on the lien laws, to the Grange of Cherokee Corner, Ga., 13 December 1873, in Atlanta *Constitution,* 16 January 1874.

43. D. Wyatt Aiken, agricultural column, Charleston *News and Courier,* 18 January 1878.

44. Mobile *Register,* editorial, 15 February 1876.

45. J. Henly Smith to Alexander Stephens, Atlanta, 22 January 1874, Stephens Papers, LC.

46. Rogers, *One-Gallused Rebellion*, p. 15; Going, *Bourbon Democracy in Alabama*, pp. 93–94; Wiener, *Social Origins of the New South*, p. 102 (n. 48).

47. Going, *Bourbon Democracy in Alabama*, p. 94. Even then, the repeal did not extend to twenty-three counties in the extreme northwest and southeast of the state, outside the black belt.

48. Charleston *News and Courier*, editorial, 30 January 1878.

49. Communication from "Newberry," Marion, 26 January 1878, in Charleston *News and Courier*, 29 January 1878.

50. New Orleans *Picayune*, 7 March 1878.

51. Jackson *Weekly Clarion*, 13 February 1878. The entire 1867 law was not repealed, just its eleventh section that permitted liens on growing crops.

52. Representative Shands in the House debate on the lien law, reported in Jackson *Weekly Clarion*, 13 February 1878.

53. Representative Pegram, in ibid.

54. Representative W. A. Percy, in ibid.

55. Sometimes, this was introduced in separate legislation, as in Alabama, 1874–75, South Carolina, 1878, and Florida, 1877.

56. Ward, "Georgia under the Bourbon Democrats," pp. 291–92.

57. *Laws of North Carolina, 1874–75*, pp. 281–83; Wilmington *Post*, editorial, 25 June 1875.

58. Jackson *Weekly Clarion*, 24 November 1875, 26 April 1876; *Journal of the Mississippi Senate*, 1876, p. 636.

59. *Acts of Louisiana, 1874*, pp. 114–15; *1877*, p. 23.

60. Galveston *News*, 8 April 1874; Woodman, "Southern Agriculture and the Law," p. 333.

61. Wiener, *Social Origins of the New South*, pp. 84–94; *Acts of Alabama, 1870–71*, p. 19; *1874–75*, pp. 259–60, 254–55; *1875–76*, p. 189; *1876–77*, pp. 74–77.

62. *Statutes of South Carolina, 1878*, pp. 410–11, 744–45; *1881–82*, pp. 560–61. Also Florida and Arkansas gave primacy to the landlord's lien in 1879 (*Acts of Florida, 1879*, pp. 72–74) and in 1874–75 (*Acts of Arkansas, 1874–75*, pp. 230–32) respectively. These statutes also prohibited the removal of growing crops.

63. For example, repeal was proposed in the Alabama legislature in 1876–77 and again in the next session 1878–79; see Wiener, "Planter-Merchant Conflict in Reconstruction Alabama," p. 91.

64. W. A. Percy, speech in the House debate on lien-law repeal, reported in Jackson *Weekly Clarion*, 13 February 1878.

65. Senator Black's speech was reported in the Atlanta *Constitution* on 9 February 1876, while Alfred H. Colquitt's had appeared in the same paper on 13 February 1874. For a discussion of the rather different dimensions and outcome of the contest over the lien law and of the lesser importance attached to controlling the labor force outside the black belt, see Hahn, "Roots of Southern Populism," chap. 5.

66. Unidentified newspaper clipping, early 1875, in scrapbook #1, Felton Scrapbooks.

67. Ibid.

68. For a somewhat different interpretation, see Wiener, *Social Origins of the New South*, part 2.

69. See Woody, "The Labor and Immigration Problem," p. 206.

70. For this distinction, see Berthoff, "Southern Attitudes Toward Immigration," pp. 328–50; Rogers, *One-Gallused Rebellion*, chap. 4; Futrell, "Efforts of Mississippians to Encourage Immigration," pp. 59–76; and Foner, *Politics and Ideology in the Age of the Civil War*, pp. 110–11.

71. For example, Alabama, 1875; Florida, 1877; Georgia, 1878; Louisiana, 1877; Mississippi, 1878; North Carolina, 1877. Very often, the responsibility for immigration was assumed by the department of agriculture, as was the case in North Carolina and Louisiana; or else it was removed from the jurisdiction of the commissioner of industrial resources where, as in Alabama, it had been placed previously.

72. Loewenberg, "Efforts of the South to Encourage Immigration," pp. 377, 380.

73. Aiken's perspective is derived from two of his columns in the Charleston *News and Courier*, 19 January 1877 and 15 March 1878.

74. See, for example, the negative reaction of Alabama's black-belt planters in Rogers, *One-Gallused Rebellion*, p. 87.

75. Ibid., pp. 85–88.

76. See Jackson *Weekly Clarion*, June & July 1878. This flurry of activity soon after the commissioner was appointed did not last.

77. By 1910, the South's foreign-born population had actually declined as a proportion of the total population from its level in 1865. In 1910, it numbered less than half a million and represented 2 percent compared with a 20 percent figure for the non-South. See Berthoff, "Southern Attitudes Toward Immigration," p. 342.

78. Speech of Dr. T. D. Hutchinson to the Cherokee Corner Grange, 13 December 1873, in Atlanta *Constitution*, 16 January 1874; Zebulon B. Vance, speech to a council of North Carolina farmers, reported in Mobile *Register*, 2 October 1875.

79. Interview with Reverend David Young in New Orleans *Picayune*, 17 May 1879; resolution in the convention urging migrants to reconsider, proposed by a delegate named Stephenson of Iberville Parish in *Picayune*, 24 April 1879. See also Hair, *Bourbonism and Agrarian Protest*, pp. 83–98, especially pp. 94–96, for Democratic planters' views; and Painter, *Exodusters*, chap. 14.

80. Cohen, "Negro Involuntary Servitude in the South," p. 39. Also see Taylor, "Great Migration from North Carolina," pp. 18–33, esp. p. 31; Bromberg, "'Pure Democracy and White Supremacy,'" p. 261.

81. The address of the committee on business of the Louisiana Colored Convention of 21 April 1879 reporting on the causes of the exodus argued that it was "the avowed disposition of the men now in power . . . to reduce the laborer and his interests to the minimum of advantages as freemen, and to absolutely none as citi-

zens, [which] has produced so absolute a fear that in many cases it has become a panic." Reported in New Orleans *Picayune*, 22 April 1879.

82. A chapter entitled "Sharecroppers Are Always Moving," in the autobiography of the twentieth-century black activist, Hosea Hudson, acknowledges the seeming paradox of spatial mobility in a system intended to restrict the laborer's ability to move. "Like other Negro sharecroppers," he writes, "we were always moving, always in the hope of finding a landlord who would not take advantage of us. But we hardly ever succeeded in bettering our condition." Hudson, *Black Worker in the Deep South*, p. 13. This extensive amount of movement did not mean that labor was not coerced and constrained, because, as Hudson says, it was virtually impossible to improve one's lot by moving. The system locked in the labor-force as a whole and prevented upward economic mobility, even though individuals could move about in the hope of improving their situation. Mobility did not therefore provide opportunity. The significance of this question of mobility is raised by Harold Woodman in Wiener, "Class Structure and Economic Development in the American South." In his *White Supremacy*, George Fredrickson concludes that the existence of considerable mobility did not alter the labor system's fundamentally coercive nature and intent, pp. 212–16, 220.

83. Cohen, "Negro Involuntary Servitude," passim. See also Novak, *Wheel of Servitude*, chaps. 3, 4, 5.

84. Cohen, "Negro Involuntary Servitude, p. 59; Daniel, "The Metamorphosis of Slavery," p. 99.

85. Gerschenkron, "Agrarian Policies and Industrialization," p. 712. The importance of a revolution in agriculture as a precipitant of industrialization, a "prerequisite," is generally conceded by students of the problem; see, for example, Gerschenkron, *Economic Backwardness in Historical Perspective*, pp. 31–51; Cole and Deane, "The Growth of National Incomes," pp. 1–59; and Kuznets, *Six Lectures on Economic Growth*. The need for an increase in the supply of cheap labor to facilitate industrialization in the towns is also stressed in Marxist analysis; see, for example, Dobb, *Studies in the Development of Capitalism*, pp. 273–77.

86. Two interpretations of how the planters influenced the course of southern industrialization have been suggested recently by Wiener, *Social Origins of the New South*, and Billings, *Planters and the Making of a "New South."* Wiener argues that the planters were staunchly opposed to industrialization and prevented its emergence. By contrast, Billings asserts that, in North Carolina at least, planters were investors who were in the forefront of the promotion of industrial development, albeit an industrialization permeated by paternalistic labor relations and conservative patterns of growth, harmonizing with rather than threatening agricultural interests.

Chapter 12

1. James A. Garfield to Rutherford B. Hayes, 12 December 1876, quoted in Woodward, *Reunion and Reaction*, p. 22.

2. See ibid., esp. chap. 3.

3. For discussion of how real the bargain between Hayes and the South was, see Peskin, "Was There a Compromise of 1877?" pp. 63–75; Benedict, "Southern Democrats in the Crisis of 1876–1877," pp. 489–524; and Rable, "Southern Interests and the Election of 1876," pp. 347–61.

4. Remarks attributed to Congressman James A. Garfield in a report from the Washington correspondent of the Baltimore *Sun*, 19 February 1877, reprinted in Charleston *News and Courier*, 23 February 1877.

5. Report of President Hayes's remarks to the Republican Senate caucus committee in Jackson *Weekly Clarion*, 28 November 1877. See also Gillette, *Retreat from Reconstruction*, chap. 14.

6. W. H. Forney to John H. Reagan, Jacksonville, Ala., 7 April 1877, Reagan Papers.

7. Joseph E. Brown, open letter to the editor, Atlanta *Constitution*, 1 April 1877.

8. New Orleans *Picayune*, editorial, 21 August 1878.

9. Otho R. Singleton, speech at Carthage, Miss., 3 September 1877, in Jackson *Weekly Clarion*, 5 September 1877.

10. Atlanta *Constitution*, editorial, 15 March 1877.

11. New Orleans *Picayune*, editorial, 11 January 1878.

12. Mobile *Register*, editorial, 16 January 1878.

13. L. Q. Washington to Robert M. T. Hunter, Washington, D.C., 8 June 1873, Hunter Papers.

14. Jackson *Weekly Clarion*, editorial, 2 May 1877.

15. John H. Reagan to Ashbel Smith, Washington, D.C., 13 February 1876, Ashbel Smith Papers.

16. See Woodward, *Origins of the New South*, pp. 81–85; Unger, *Greenback Era*, pp. 68–119, passim; and Montgomery, *Beyond Equality*, pp. 340–56.

17. A. W. Terrell to Oran Roberts, Austin, 31 July 1878, Roberts Papers.

18. Of course, an alliance with monetary heretics like the Greenbackers and advocates of irresponsible fiscal policies like the repudiators would not have been congenial to Hayes's financial conservatism and "hard money" views. As a result, the president had to recognize, though it is doubtful if he did, that the two possibilities available to him were either unattainable or else inconceivable.

19. L. Q. C. Lamar to E. D. Clark, Washington, D.C., 30 March 1877, Lamar-Mayes Papers.

20. Hair, *Bourbonism and Agrarian Protest*, pp. 64–65. On the other hand, even the responsible New Orleans *Picayune* approved the platform, see *Picayune*, 7 August 1878.

21. Platform of Arkansas Democratic party, in Jackson *Weekly Clarion*, 10 July 1878.

22. A. W. Terrell to Oran Roberts, Austin, 31 July 1878, Roberts Papers.

23. Oran Roberts, speech during 1878 campaign, no location cited, in Roberts Papers.

24. Richard Coke to Oran Roberts, Waco, Texas, 15 August 1878, Roberts Papers.

25. Interview with Governor Jarvis, by P. H. Wilson of Raleigh *Observer*, 18 July 1878, reprinted in Yearns, *Papers of Thomas Jordan Jarvis*, 1:25.

26. Seip, "Southern Representatives and Economic Measures during Reconstruction," pp. 105–15, 133–55.

27. Charleston *News and Courier*, editorial, 17 December 1873.

28. Atlanta *Constitution*, editorial, 25 April 1874.

29. Jackson *Weekly Clarion*, editorial, 5 March 1874; Seip, "Southern Representatives and Economic Measures," pp. 228–42, 246–52. See also Harris, "Right Fork or Left Fork?" pp. 478–80, and p. 482, roll call 1.

30. Seip, "Southern Representatives and Economic Measures during Reconstruction," pp. 230–36, 242.

31. Senator John B. Gordon, interview with reporter from the Atlanta *Herald* in which Gordon rebutted Carl Schurz's recent Cincinnati speech on the financial question, in Charleston *News and Courier*, 12 October 1875.

32. Gordon, speech on southern politics before the Georgia legislature, in Charleston *News and Courier*, 22 February 1876.

33. Harris, "Right Fork or Left Fork?" p. 481.

34. Weinstein, *Prelude to Populism*, pp. 239, 309.

35. Ibid., pp. 313, 315.

36. Senators M. C. Butler of South Carolina and Benjamin Hill of Georgia were also opposed, but they must presumably have either paired or not voted.

37. Weinstein, *Prelude to Populism*, pp. 270–71, 292.

38. Charleston *News and Courier*, editorial, 14 January 1878.

39. John B. Gordon, Senate speech on the Matthews resolution, reported in Jackson *Weekly Clarion*, 6 February 1878.

40. John B. Gordon, speech to the Georgia legislature as a candidate for the U.S. Senate, in Atlanta *Constitution*, 21 January 1873.

41. Jackson *Weekly Clarion*, editorial, 2 April 1874.

42. E. John Ellis to Tom Ellis, Washington, D.C., 28 February 1878, Ellis Family Papers.

43. Augustus S. Merrimon to David F. Caldwell, Washington, D.C., 8 April 1876, David F. Caldwell Papers.

44. Alfred H. Colquitt, interview with the Atlanta *Constitution*, in Atlanta *Constitution*, 19 October 1876. See also James Z. George, speech to the Democratic state convention, in Jackson *Weekly Clarion*, 1 August 1877.

45. See Rothman, *Politics and Power*, pp. 170–71.

46. For this observation, I am grateful to Professor J. Mills Thornton of the University of Michigan.

Bibliography

A. Manuscript Collections

Alabama Department of Archives, Montgomery, Ala.
  Charles W. Dustan Papers
  Governor David P. Lewis Papers
  Governor Robert B. Lindsay Papers
  Robert McKee Papers
  Edward H. Moren Papers
  Lewis E. Parsons Papers
  John W. A. Sanford Papers
  Governor William H. Smith Papers
Atlanta Historical Society, Atlanta, Ga.
  Benjamin Conley Papers
Austin Public Library, Austin, Tex.
  Elisha M. Pease Papers
Chicago Historical Society, Chicago, Ill.
  David B. Davis Papers
Duke University Manuscripts Collection, Durham, N.C.
  John E. Bryant Papers
  Tod R. Caldwell Papers
  John W. Daniel Papers
  Francis W. Dawson Papers
  Benjamin S. Hedrick Papers
  Hemphill Family Papers
  Herschel V. Johnson Papers (Letterpress volumes)
  William D. Simpson Papers
  Alexander H. Stephens Papers
  Ellen Clanton Thomas Diary
  Henry Watson, Jr., Papers

Emory University Manuscript Collection, Atlanta, Ga.
  Alexander H. Stephens Papers
  Leander N. Trammell Papers
Georgia Department of Archives, Atlanta, Ga.
  Alexander H. Stephens Papers
Library of Congress, Division of Manuscripts, Washington, D.C.
  President Ulysses S. Grant Papers (microfilm)
  Alexander H. Stephens Papers (microfilm)
Louisiana State University, Department of Archives, Baton Rouge, La.
  Donelson Caffrey Papers
  Ellis Family Papers
  Benjamin Flanders Papers
  William P. Kellogg Papers
  James G. Taliaferro Papers
Mississippi Department of Archives and History, Jackson, Miss.
  James L. Alcorn Papers
  Governor Adelbert Ames Papers
  James W. Garner Papers
  L. Q. C. Lamar–Edward Mayes Papers (microfilm)
  William Walthall Papers
South Carolina Department of Archives, Columbia, S.C.
  Governor Daniel Chamberlain Papers
  Governor Franklin Moses Papers
  Governor Robert Scott Papers
South Caroliniana Library, Columbia, S.C.
  A. P. Aldrich Papers
  Milledge Bonham Papers
  Martin W. Gary Papers
  William H. Trescot Papers
  Alexander S. Wallace Papers
Southern Historical Collection, Chapel Hill, N.C.
  Daniel M. Barringer Papers
  Battle Family Papers
  David F. Caldwell Papers
  Tod R. Caldwell Papers
  David M. Carter Papers
  Joseph S. Fowler Papers
  William A. Graham Papers (typed transcripts)
  Daniel H. Hill Papers
  William Porcher Miles Papers
  Richmond M. Pearson Papers
  Matt W. Ransom Papers
  Daniel L. Russell Papers
  David Schenck Diaries
  Thomas Settle Papers, Series 2
  Tucker Family Papers

Henry C. Warmoth Papers (microfilm)
Benjamin C. Yancey Papers (microfilm)
Texas State Archives Department, Austin, Tex.
Samuel B. Maxey Papers
John H. Reagan Papers
University of Georgia, Manuscript Collection, Athens, Ga.
Foster Blodgett Papers
Joseph E. Brown Papers, typescripts in the Felix Hargrett Collection
Alfred H. Colquitt Papers
Henry P. Farrow Papers
Rebeccah L. Felton Scrapbooks
William H. and Rebeccah L. Felton Papers
Nelson Tift Papers
Robert Toombs Papers
University of Texas, Archives, Austin, Tex.
William P. Ballinger Papers
Benjamin Epperson Papers
James P. Newcomb Papers
Oran Roberts Papers
Ashbel Smith Papers
James W. Throckmorton Papers
University of Virginia, Alderman Library, Charlottesville, Va.
Robert M. T. Hunter Papers (microfilm)
James L. Kemper Papers

B. Newspapers

All the listed newspapers were read on microfilm. The dates cited do not
necessarily refer to the extant run of a paper but to those segments of it actually
consulted. Sometimes, however, what was read was all that was available.
Alabama State Journal, 1873–75
Arkansas Gazette, 1869–75
Atlanta *Constitution*, 1869–77
Atlanta *New Era*, 1869–70
Charleston *News and Courier*, 1873–78
Columbia *Daily Union/Herald-Union*, January 1872 to March 1877
Galveston *News*, 1873–74
Huntsville *Weekly Democrat*, August 1873 to June 1874
Jackson *Daily Pilot*, July 1875 to November 1875
Jackson *Weekly Clarion*, March 1869 to October 1878
Jackson *Weekly Pilot*, November 1869 to December 1870; December 1874 to
November 1875
Mobile *Register*, 1869–80
Montgomery *Advertiser*, 1869–70
New Orleans *Picayune*, 1876–79

North Carolina Standard, September 1868 to December 1870
Raleigh *Sentinel*, January 1869 to December 1876
Richmond *Dispatch*, July 1873 to July 1874
Texas State Gazette, 1869–70, scattered
Texas State Journal, February 1870 to April 1874, scattered
Wilmington *Post*, 1872–75, incomplete

C. Government Documents

I. UNITED STATES
U.S. Congress. Report of the Joint Select Committee to investigate the Ku Klux
   Klan, *House Reports*, 42 Cong., 2 Sess., no. 41, parts 1–13, 1872.
———. Report of the Select Committee to inquire into the Mississippi Election
   of 1875, *Senate Reports*, 44 Cong., 1 Sess., no. 527, 1876.
———. Report on the Alabama Elections of 1874, 1875, and 1876, *Senate
   Reports*, 44 Cong., 2 Sess., no. 704, parts 1 & 2, 1877.
———. Report of the Select Committee to investigate the Causes of the Removal
   of Negroes from the Southern States, *Senate Reports*, 46 Cong., 2 Sess.,
   no. 693, parts 1–3, 1880.
U.S. Census Office, *Twelfth Census of the United States: 1900*. W. E. B. DuBois,
   "The Negro Farmer" in *Special Reports, Supplementary Analysis and
   Derivative Tables*, 1906.

II. SOUTHERN STATES
Sessional laws of the states of Alabama, Arkansas, Florida, Georgia, Louisiana,
   Mississippi, North Carolina, South Carolina, and Texas.
Journals of the House and Senate in the above states.
These documents were consulted in three locations: the Library of the Harvard
   Law School; the Library of the Massachusetts State House, Boston; and
   the Harper Library of the University of Chicago.

D. Primary Sources

I. BOOKS
Ames, Blanche Butler, comp. *Chronicles of the Nineteenth Century: Family Letters
   of Blanche Butler and Adelbert Ames*. 2 vols. Clinton, Mass.: Colonial
   Press, 1957.
Appleton's Annual Cyclopedia and Register of Important Events. New York:
   D. Appleton, [1869–80].
Lynch, John R. *The Facts of Reconstruction*. New York: Neale Publishing Co.,
   1913.
McPherson, Edward. *A Hand-Book of Politics for 1868*. Washington, D.C.:
   Philip and Solomons, 1868.

Small, Samuel W. *A Stenographic Report of the Proceedings of the Constitutional Convention Held in Atlanta, Ga., 1877.* Atlanta: Constitution Publishing Co., 1877.

Warmoth, Henry Clay. *War, Politics, and Reconstruction: Stormy Days in Louisiana.* New York: Macmillan & Co., 1930.

Yearns, W. Buck, ed. *The Papers of Thomas Jordan Jarvis.* Vol. I. Raleigh: N.C. Department of Archives and History, 1969.

II. PAMPHLETS

Alcorn, James L. "Views of the Honorable J. L. Alcorn on the Political Situation of Mississippi." Friars Point, Miss.: n.p., 1867.

"Proceedings of the Taxpayers' Convention of South Carolina, Held in Columbia, 9–12 May 1871." Charleston: Edward Perry, Printer, 1871. Caroliniana Library, Columbia, S.C.

"A Review of the Resolutions of the Press Conference, Held in Charleston," 1870. Reconstruction Broadsides, Duke University Library.

Trenholm, William L. "Local Reform in South Carolina," 1872. Reconstruction Broadsides, Duke University Library.

E. Secondary Sources

I. BOOKS

Allen, Walter. *Governor Chamberlain's Administration in South Carolina: A Chapter of Reconstruction in the Southern States.* New York: G. P. Putnam's Sons, 1888.

Barr, Alwyn. *From Reconstruction to Reform: Texas Politics, 1876–1906.* Austin: University of Texas Press, 1971.

Billings, Dwight B., Jr. *Planters and the Making of a "New South": Class, Politics, and Development in North Carolina, 1865–1900.* Chapel Hill: University of North Carolina Press, 1979.

Blake, Nelson M. *William Mahone of Virginia: Soldier and Political Insurgent.* Richmond: Garrett & Massie, 1935.

Bleser, Carol. *The Promised Land: The History of the South Carolina Land Commission, 1869–1890.* Columbia, S.C.: University of South Carolina Press, 1969.

Bond, Horace Mann. *Negro Education in Alabama: A Study in Cotton and Steel.* Washington, D.C.: Associated Publishers, 1939.

Brandfon, Robert L. *Cotton Kingdom of the New South: A History of the Yazoo-Mississippi Delta from Reconstruction to the Twentieth Century.* Cambridge: Harvard University Press, 1967.

Burnham, W. Dean. *Presidential Ballots, 1836–1892.* Baltimore: Johns Hopkins University Press, 1955.

Clark, E. Culpepper. *Francis Warrington Dawson and the Politics of Restoration: South Carolina, 1874–1889.* University: University of Alabama Press, 1980.

Coleman, Charles. *The Election of 1868: The Democratic Effort to Regain Control.* New York: Columbia University Press, 1933.

Conway, Alan. *The Reconstruction of Georgia.* Minneapolis: University of Minnesota Press, 1966.

Cooper, William J., Jr. *The Conservative Regime: South Carolina, 1877–1890.* Baltimore: Johns Hopkins University Press, 1968.

Copeland, C. Isaac, ed. *Democracy in the Old South: Essays by Fletcher Green.* Nashville: Vanderbilt University Press, 1969.

Cox, LaWanda, and John H. Cox. *Politics, Principle, and Prejudice, 1865–1866: Dilemma of Reconstruction America.* Glencoe, Ill.: The Free Press, 1963.

Curry, Richard O., ed. *Radicalism, Racism, and Reconstruction.* Baltimore: Johns Hopkins University Press, 1969.

Daniels, Jonathan. *Prince of Carpetbaggers.* New York: J. P. Lippincott, 1958.

DeCanio, Stephen. *Agriculture in the Post-Bellum South: The Economics of Production and Supply.* Cambridge: M.I.T. Press, 1974.

Degler, Carl. *The Other South: Southern Dissenters in the Nineteenth Century.* New York: Harper & Row, 1974.

Dobb, Maurice. *Studies in the Development of Capitalism.* New York: International Publishers, 1947.

Downs, Anthony. *An Economic Theory of Democracy.* New York: Harper & Row, 1957.

Drago, Edmund L. *Black Politicians and Reconstruction in Georgia: A Splendid Failure.* Baton Rouge: Louisiana State University Press, 1982.

Foner, Eric. *Politics and Ideology in the Age of the Civil War.* New York: Oxford University Press, 1980.

Fredrickson, George M. *White Supremacy: A Comparative Study in American and South African History.* New York: Oxford University Press, 1981.

———, ed. *A Nation Divided: Problems and Issues of the Civil War and Reconstruction.* Minneapolis: Burgess Publishing Company, 1975.

Gambill, Edward. *Conservative Ordeal: Northern Democrats and Reconstruction, 1865–1868.* Ames: Iowa State University Press, 1981.

Gillette, William. *Retreat from Reconstruction, 1869–1879.* Baton Rouge: Louisiana State University Press, 1979.

Going, Allan J. *Bourbon Democracy in Alabama, 1874–1890.* University: University of Alabama Press, 1951.

Goodrich, Carter. *Government Promotion of American Canals and Railroads, 1800–1890.* New York: Columbia University Press, 1960.

Hair, William I. *Bourbonism and Agrarian Protest: Louisiana Politics, 1877–1900.* Baton Rouge: Louisiana State University Press, 1969.

Hansen, Stephen L. *The Making of the Third Party System: Voters and Parties in Illinois, 1850–1876.* Ann Arbor: University Microfilms International Press, 1980.

Harris, William C. *The Day of the Carpetbagger: Republican Reconstruction in Mississippi.* Baton Rouge: Louisiana State University Press, 1979.

Hart, Roger L. *Redeemers, Bourbons, and Populists: Tennessee, 1870–1896.* Baton Rouge: Louisiana State University Press, 1975.

Haskins, James. *P. B. S. Pinchback.* New York: Macmillan, 1973.

Hearden, Patrick J. *Independence and Empire: The New South's Cotton Mill Campaign, 1865–1901.* DeKalb, Ill.: Northern Illinois University Press, 1982.

Heath, Milton S. *Constructive Liberalism: The Role of the State in Economic Development in Georgia to 1860.* Cambridge: Harvard University Press, 1954.

Higgs, Robert. *Competition and Coercion: Blacks in the American Economy, 1865–1914.* New York: Cambridge University Press, 1977.

Hill, B. H., Jr. *Senator Benjamin H. Hill of Georgia: His Life, Speeches, and Writings.* Atlanta: T. H. P. Bloodworth, 1873.

Hirschman, Albert O. *Exit, Voice, and Loyalty: Responses to Decline in Firms, Organizations, and States.* Cambridge: Harvard University Press, 1970.

Holt, Thomas. *Black Over White: Negro Political Leadership in South Carolina During Reconstruction.* Urbana: University of Illinois Press, 1977.

Hudson, Hosea. *Black Worker in the Deep South: A Personal Record.* New York: International Publishers, 1972.

Jensen, Richard J. *The Winning of the Middle West: Social and Political Conflict, 1880–1896.* Chicago: University of Chicago Press, 1971.

Johnson, Bruce, and Kirk H. Porter. *National Party Platforms, 1840–1972.* Urbana: University of Illinois Press, 1973.

Jones, Robert B. *Tennessee at the Crossroads: The State Debt Controversy, 1870–1883.* Knoxville: University of Tennessee Press, 1977.

Katzman, David M. *Before the Ghetto: Black Detroit in the Nineteenth Century.* Urbana: University of Illinois Press, 1973.

Keller, Morton. *Affairs of State: Public Life in Late Nineteenth-Century America.* Cambridge: Harvard University Press, 1977.

Key, V. O., Jr. *Southern Politics in State and Nation.* New York: Alfred A. Knopf, 1949.

Kirwan, Albert. *Revolt of the Rednecks: Mississippi Politics, 1876–1925.* Lexington: University Press of Kentucky, 1951.

Kleppner, Paul. *The Third Electoral System, 1853–1892: Parties, Voters, and Political Culture.* Chapel Hill: University of North Carolina Press, 1979.

Klingman, Peter D. *Josiah Walls: Florida's Black Congressman of Reconstruction.* Gainesville: University Presses of Florida, 1976.

Kousser, J. Morgan. *The Shaping of Southern Politics: Suffrage Restriction and the Establishment of the One-Party South, 1880–1910.* New Haven: Yale University Press, 1974.

Kuznets, Simon. *Six Lectures on Economic Growth.* Glencoe, Ill.: Free Press, 1957.

Lamson, Peggy. *The Glorious Failure: Black Congressman Robert Brown Elliott and the Reconstruction in South Carolina.* New York: W. W. Norton, 1973.

Levine, Lawrence W. *Black Culture and Black Consciousness: Afro-American Folk Thought from Slavery to Freedom.* New York: Oxford University Press, 1977.

Litwack, Leon. *Been in the Storm So Long: The Aftermath of Slavery.* New York: Alfred A. Knopf, 1979.

Maddex, Jack P., Jr. *The Virginia Conservatives, 1867–1879: A Study in Reconstruction Politics.* Chapel Hill: University of North Carolina Press, 1970.

Mandle, Jay. *The Roots of Black Poverty: The Southern Plantation Economy After the Civil War.* Durham, N.C.: Duke University Press, 1978.

Marcus, Robert D. *Grand Old Party: Political Structure in the Gilded Age, 1880–1896.* New York: Oxford University Press, 1971.

Mayes, Edward. *L. Q. C. Lamar: His Life, Times, and Speeches.* Nashville: Methodist Episcopal Church, South, 1896.

McFeely, William S. *Grant: A Biography.* New York: W. W. Norton, 1981.

McGinty, Garnie. *Louisiana Redeemed: The Overthrow of Carpetbag Rule, 1876–1880.* New Orleans: Pelican Publishing Co., 1941.

McKay, Seth S. *Making the Texas Constitution of 1876.* Philadelphia: privately printed, 1924.

McMillan, Malcolm C. *Constitutional Development in Alabama, 1798–1901: A Study in Politics, the Negro, and Sectionalism.* The James Sprunt Studies in History and Political Science, vol. 37. Chapel Hill: University of North Carolina Press, 1955.

Moneyhon, Carl. *Republicanism in Reconstruction Texas.* Austin: University of Texas Press, 1980.

Montgomery, David. *Beyond Equality: Labor and the Radical Republicans, 1862–1872.* New York: Random House, 1967.

Moore, James T. *Two Paths to the New South: The Virginia Debt Controversy, 1870–1883.* Lexington: University Press of Kentucky, 1974.

Morgan, H. Wayne, ed. *The Gilded Age.* Syracuse: Syracuse University Press, 1970.

Nathans, Elizabeth S. *Losing the Peace: Georgia Republicans and Reconstruction.* Baton Rouge: Louisiana State University Press, 1968.

Novak, Daniel A. *The Wheel of Servitude: Black Forced Labor After Slavery.* Lexington: University Press of Kentucky, 1978.

Olsen, Otto H. *A Carpetbagger's Crusade: The Life of Albion Winegar Tourgée.* Baltimore: Johns Hopkins University Press, 1965.

———, ed. *Reconstruction and Redemption in the South.* Baton Rouge: Louisiana State University Press, 1980.

Painter, Nell. *Exodusters: Black Migration to Kansas After Reconstruction.* New York: Alfred A. Knopf, 1977.

Parks, Joseph H. *Joseph E. Brown of Georgia.* Baton Rouge: Louisiana State University Press, 1977.

Pereyra, Lillian A. *James Lusk Alcorn: Persistent Whig.* Baton Rouge: Louisiana State University Press, 1966.

Perman, Michael. *Reunion Without Compromise: The South and Reconstruction, 1865–1868*. New York: Cambridge University Press, 1973.

Rabinowitz, Howard N. *Race Relations in the Urban South, 1865–1890*. New York: Oxford University Press, 1978.

———, ed. *Southern Black Leaders of the Reconstruction Era*. Urbana: University of Illinois Press, 1982.

Ranney, Austin. *Curing the Mischief of Faction: Party Reform in America*. Berkeley: University of California Press, 1975.

Ransom, Roger, and Richard Sutch. *One Kind of Freedom: The Economic Consequences of Emancipation*. New York: Cambridge University Press, 1977.

Ratchford, Benjamin U. *American State Debts*. Durham: Duke University Press, 1941.

Riker, William. *The Theory of Political Coalitions*. New Haven: Yale University Press, 1962.

Roark, James L. *Masters Without Slaves: Southern Planters in the Civil War and Reconstruction*. New York: W. W. Norton, 1977.

Rogers, William W. *The One-Gallused Rebellion: Agrarianism in Alabama, 1865–1896*. Baton Rouge: Louisiana State University Press, 1970.

Rothman, David. *Politics and Power: The United States Senate, 1869–1901*. Cambridge, Mass.: Harvard University Press, 1966.

Saloutos, Theodore. *Farmer Movements in the South, 1865–1933*. Berkeley: University of California Press, 1960.

Schwartz, Michael. *Radical Protest and Social Structure: The Southern Farmers' Alliance and Cotton Tenancy, 1880–1890*. New York: Academic Press, 1976.

Schweninger, Loren. *James T. Rapier and Reconstruction.* Chicago: University of Chicago Press, 1978.

Scott, William A. *The Repudiation of State Debts: A Study in the Financial History of Mississippi, Louisiana, etc.* In the Library of Economics and Politics. Edited by Richard T. Ely. New York: Thomas Y. Crowell, 1893.

Shofner, Jerrell H. *Nor Is It Over Yet: Florida in the Era of Reconstruction*. Gainesville: University Presses of Florida, 1974.

Silbey, Joel. *A Respectable Minority: The Democratic Party in the Civil War Era, 1860–1868*. New York: W. W. Norton, 1977.

Simkins, Francis B., and Robert H. Woody. *South Carolina During Reconstruction*. Chapel Hill: University of North Carolina Press, 1932.

Sproat, John G. *"The Best Men": Liberal Reformers in the Gilded Age*. New York: Oxford University Press, 1968.

Stampp, Kenneth M. *The Era of Reconstruction, 1865–1877*. New York: Random House, 1965.

Taylor, Joe Gray. *Louisiana Reconstructed, 1863–1877*. Baton Rouge: Louisiana State University Press, 1974.

Thomas, David Y., ed. *Arkansas and Its People: A History, 1541–1930*, Vol. 1. New York: American Historical Society, 1930.

Thompson, George H. *Arkansas and Reconstruction: The Influence of Geography, Economics, and Personality*. Port Washington, N.Y.: Kennikat Press, 1976.

Thornton, J. Mills, III. *Politics and Power in a Slave Society: Alabama, 1800–1860*. Baton Rouge: Louisiana State University Press, 1978.

Trelease, Allen W. *White Terror: The Ku Klux Klan Conspiracy and Reconstruction*. New York: Harper & Row, 1971.

Unger, Irwin. *The Greenback Era: A Social and Political History of American Finance, 1865–1879*. Princeton: Princeton University Press, 1964.

Vallandigham, James. *A Life of Clement L. Vallandigham*. Baltimore: Turnbull Brothers, 1872.

Van Deusen, Glyndon. *William Henry Seward*. New York: Oxford University Press, 1962.

Vaughn, William P. *Schools for All: Blacks and Public Education in the South, 1865–1877*. Lexington: University Press of Kentucky, 1974.

Vincent, Charles. *Black Legislators in Louisiana During Reconstruction*. Baton Rouge: Louisiana State University Press, 1976.

Weinstein, Allen. *Prelude to Populism: Origins of the Silver Issue, 1867–1878*. New Haven: Yale University Press, 1970.

Wharton, Vernon L. *The Negro in Mississippi, 1865–1890*. New York: Harper & Row, 1965.

Wiener, Jonathan M. *Social Origins of the New South: Alabama, 1860–1885*. Baton Rouge: Louisiana State University Press, 1978.

Wiggins, Sarah W. *The Scalawag in Alabama Politics, 1865–1881*. University: University of Alabama Press, 1977.

Williamson, Edward. *Florida Politics in the Gilded Age, 1877–1893*. Gainesville: University Presses of Florida, 1976.

Williamson, Joel. *After Slavery: The Negro in South Carolina During Reconstruction, 1861–1877*. Chapel Hill: University of North Carolina Press, 1965.

Woodman, Harold. *King Cotton and his Retainers: Financing and Marketing the Cotton Crop of the South, 1800–1925*. Lexington: University Press of Kentucky, 1968.

Woodward, C. Vann. *Reunion and Reaction: The Compromise of 1877 and the End of Reconstruction*. Boston: Little Brown, 1951.

———. *Origins of the New South, 1877–1913*. Baton Rouge: Louisiana State University Press, 1951.

Wright, Gavin. *The Political Economy of the South: Households, Markets, and Wealth in the Nineteenth Century*. New York: W. W. Norton, 1978.

II. ARTICLES AND CHAPTERS FROM BOOKS

Alexander, Thomas B. "Persistent Whiggery in the Confederate South, 1860–1877." *Journal of Southern History* 27 (August 1961): 305–29.

———. "Political Reconstruction in Tennessee, 1865–1870." In *Radicalism, Racism, and Party Realignment*. Edited by Richard O. Curry, pp. 37–39. Baltimore: Johns Hopkins University Press, 1969.

———. "Whiggery and Reconstruction in Tennessee." *Journal of Southern History* 16 (August 1950): 291–305.

Balanoff, Elizabeth. "Negro Legislators in the North Carolina General Assembly, July 1868—February 1872." *North Carolina Historical Review* 49 (Winter 1972): 2–55.

Ball, Clyde C. "The Public Career of Colonel A. S. Colyar, 1870–1877." *Tennessee Historical Quarterly* 12 (March 1953): 23–67; (June 1953): 106–28; (September 1953): 213–38.

Bayliss, Garland E. "Post-Reconstruction Repudiation: Evil Blot or Financial Necessity?" *Arkansas Historical Quarterly* 23 (Autumn 1964): 243–59.

Benedict, M. Les. "Southern Democrats in the Crisis of 1876–1877: A Reconsideration of *Reunion and Reaction*." *Journal of Southern History* 46 (November 1980): 489–524.

Berthoff, Rowland. "Southern Attitudes Towards Immigration, 1865–1914." *Journal of Southern History* 17 (August 1951): 328–50.

Brandon, William P. "Calling the Georgia Constitutional Convention of 1877." *Georgia Historical Quarterly* 17 (September 1933): 189–203.

Brock, William R. "Reconstruction and the American Party System." In *A Nation Divided: Problems and Issues of the Civil War and Reconstruction*. Edited by George M. Fredrickson, pp. 81–112. Minneapolis: Burgess Publishing Company, 1975.

Cohen, William. "Negro Involuntary Servitude in the South: A Preliminary Analysis." *Journal of Southern History* 42 (February 1976): 31–60.

Cole, W. A., and Phyllis Deane. "The Growth of National Incomes." In *The Cambridge Economic History of Europe*, edited by H. J. Habakkuk and M. Postan, vol. 6, part 1, pp. 1–59. Cambridge: Cambridge University Press, 1965.

Collins, Bruce. "The Ideology of the Antebellum Northern Democrats." *Journal of American Studies* 11 (April 1971): 103–21.

Dailey, Douglas C. "The Elections of 1872 in North Carolina." *North Carolina Historical Review* 40 (Summer 1963): 338–60.

Daniel, Pete. "The Metamorphosis of Slavery, 1865–1900." *Journal of American History* 66 (June 1979): 88–99.

Degler, Carl. "Rethinking Post-Civil War History." *Virginia Quarterly Review* 57 (Spring 1981): 250–67.

Donald, David. "The Scalawag in Mississippi Reconstruction." *Journal of Southern History* 10 (November 1944): 447–60.

DuBois, W. E. B. "Reconstruction and Its Benefits." *American Historical Review* 15 (July 1910): 781–99.

Ellem, Warren A. "Who Were the Mississippi Scalawags?" *Journal of Southern History* 38 (May 1972): 217–40.

Ericson, J. E. "The Delegates to the Convention of 1875: A Reappraisal." *Southwestern Historical Quarterly* 67 (1963): 22–27.

Evans, W. C. "The Public Debt." In *Arkansas and Its People: A History, 1541–1930*, edited by David Y. Thomas, vol. 1, pp. 355–77. New York: American Historical Society, 1930.

Futrell, Robert F. "Efforts of Mississippians to Encourage Immigration, 1865–1880." *Journal of Mississippi History* 20 (April 1958): 59–76.

Gerschenkron, Alexander. "Agrarian Policies and Industrialization: Russia, 1861–1917." In *The Cambridge Economic History of Europe*, edited by H. J. Habakkuk and M. Postan, vol. 6, part 2, pp. 706–800. Cambridge: Cambridge University Press, 1965.

———. "Reflections on the Concept of 'Prerequisites' for Modern Industrialization." In *Economic Backwardness in Historical Perspective*, edited by Alexander Gerschenkron, pp. 31–51. Cambridge, Mass.: Harvard University Press, 1962.

Green, Fletcher M. "Some Aspects of the Convict Lease System in the Southern States." In *Democracy in the Old South: Essays by Fletcher M. Green*, edited by C. Isaac Copeland, pp. 271–87. Nashville: Vanderbilt University Press, 1969.

Harris, Carl V. "Right Fork or Left Fork? The Section-Party Alignments of Southern Democrats in Congress, 1873–1897." *Journal of Southern History* 42 (November 1976): 471–506.

Harris, Francis B. "Henry Clay Warmoth, Reconstruction Governor of Louisiana." *Louisiana Historical Quarterly* 30 (April 1947): 523–653.

Harris, William C. "James Lynch: Black Leader in Southern Reconstruction." *The Historian* 34 (November 1971): 40–61.

———. "A Reconsideration of the Mississippi Scalawag." *Journal of Mississippi History* 32 (February 1970): 3–42.

Hine, William C. "Dr. Benjamin A. Boseman, Jr.: Charleston's Black Physician-Politician." In *Southern Black Leaders of the Reconstruction Era*, edited by Howard N. Rabinowitz, pp. 335–62. Urbana: University of Illinois Press, 1982.

Hume, Richard L. "Membership of the Florida Constitutional Convention of 1868: A Case Study of Republican Factionalism in the Reconstruction South." *Florida Historical Quarterly* 51 (July 1972): 1–21.

———. "Negro Delegates to the State Constitutional Conventions of 1867–69." In *Southern Black Leaders of the Reconstruction Era*, edited by Howard N. Rabinowitz, pp. 129–54. Urbana: University of Illinois Press, 1982.

Klingman, Peter D. "Race and Faction in the Public Career of Florida's Josiah H. Walls." In *Southern Black Leaders of the Reconstruction Era*, edited by Howard N. Rabinowitz, pp. 59–78. Urbana: University of Illinois Press, 1982.

Kolchin, Peter. "Scalawags, Carpetbaggers, and Reconstruction: A Quantitative Look at Southern Congressional Politics, 1868–1872." *Journal of Southern History* 45 (February 1979): 63–76.

Lestage, H. Oscar, Jr. "The White League in Louisiana and Its Participation in Reconstruction." *Louisiana Historical Quarterly* 18 (July 1935): 617–95.

Loewenberg, Bert J. "Efforts of the South to Encourage Immigration, 1865–1900." *South Atlantic Quarterly* 33 (October 1936): 363–85.

Mathews, John M. "Negro Republicans in the Reconstruction of Georgia." *Georgia Historical Quarterly* 60 (Summer 1976): 145–64.

McWhiney, Grady. "The Revolution in Nineteenth-Century Alabama Agriculture." *Alabama Review* 31 (January 1978): 3–32.

Mering, John V. "Persistent Whiggery in the Confederate South: A Reconsideration." *South Atlantic Quarterly* 69 (Winter 1970): 124–43.

Moneyhon, Carl. "George T. Ruby and the Politics of Expediency." In *Southern Black Leaders of the Reconstruction Era*, edited by Howard N. Rabinowitz, pp. 363–92. Urbana: University of Illinois Press, 1982.

Moore, James T. "Redeemers Reconsidered: Change and Continuity in the Democratic South, 1870–1900." *Journal of Southern History* 44 (August 1978): 357–78.

Olsen, Otto H. "The Ku Klux Klan: A Story of Reconstruction Politics and Propaganda." *North Carolina Historical Review* 39 (July 1962): 340–62.

———. "Reconsidering the Scalawags." *Civil War History* 12 (December 1966): 301–20.

Peskin, Allen. "Was There a Compromise of 1877?" *Journal of American History* 60 (June 1973): 63–75.

Powell, Lawrence N. "The Politics of Livelihood: Carpetbaggers in the Deep South." In *Race, Region, and Reconstruction: Essays in Honor of C. Vann Woodward*, edited by J. Morgan Kousser and James M. McPherson, pp. 315–48. New York: Oxford University Press, 1982.

Rable, George C. "Southern Interests and the Election of 1876: A Reappraisal." *Civil War History* 26 (December 1980): 347–61.

Ratchford, Benjamin U. "The Adjustment of the North Carolina Public Debt, 1879–1883." *North Carolina Historical Review* 10 (July 1933): 157–67.

Reidy, Joseph P. "Aaron A. Bradley: Voice of Black Labor in the Georgia Lowcountry." In *Southern Black Leaders of the Reconstruction Era*, edited by Howard N. Rabinowitz, pp. 281–308. Urbana: University of Illinois Press, 1982.

Riddleberger, Patrick. "The Break in the Republican Ranks: Liberal vs. Stalwarts in the Election of 1872." *Journal of Negro History* 45 (April 1960): 88–102.

Robinson, Armstead, "Beyond the Realm of Social Consensus: New Meanings of Reconstruction for American History." *Journal of American History* 68 (May 1981): 276–97.

Russ, William A., Jr. "Disfranchisement in Louisiana, 1862–1870." *Louisiana Historical Quarterly* 18 (July 1935): 557–80.

Schlesinger, Joseph A. "The Primary Goals of Political Parties: A Clarification of Positive Theory." *American Political Science Review* 49 (September 1975): 840–49.

Shapiro, Herbert. "The Ku Klux Klan During Reconstruction: The South Carolina Episode." *Journal of Negro History* 49 (January 1964): 34–55.

Stagg, J. C. A. "The Problem of Klan Violence: The South Carolina Up-Country, 1868–1871." *Journal of American Studies* 8 (December 1974): 303–18.

Staples, Thomas S. "Arkansas, 1865–1930." In *Arkansas and Its People: A History, 1541–1930*, edited by David Y. Thomas, vol. 1, pp. 135–316. New York: American Historical Society, 1930.

Taylor, Joseph H. "The Great Migration from North Carolina, 1879." *North Carolina Historical Review* 31 (January 1954): 3–32.

Thornton, J. Mills, III. "Fiscal Policy and the Failure of Reconstruction in the Lower South." In *Race, Region, and Reconstruction: Essays in Honor of C. Vann Woodward*, edited by J. Morgan Kousser and James M. McPherson, pp. 349–94. New York: Oxford University Press, 1982.

Trelease, Allen W. "Republican Reconstruction in North Carolina: A Roll-Call Analysis of the State House of Representatives." *Journal of Southern History* 42 (August 1976): 319–44.

Wiener, Jonathan M. "Planter-Merchant Conflict in Reconstruction Alabama." *Past and Present* 68 (August 1975): 73–94.

———, et al. "Class Structure and Economic Development in the American South, 1865–1955." *American Historical Review* 84 (October 1979): 970–1006.

Williams, T. Harry. "The Louisiana Unification Movement of 1873." *Journal of Southern History* 11 (August 1945): 349–69.

Woodman, Harold. "Post-Civil War Southern Agriculture and the Law." *Agricultural History* 53 (January 1979): 319–37.

———. "Sequel to Slavery: The New History Views the Post-Bellum South." *Journal of Southern History* 43 (November 1977): 523–54.

Woody, Robert H. "The Labor and Immigration Problem of South Carolina during Reconstruction." *Mississippi Valley Historical Review* 18 (September 1931): 195–212.

F. Dissertations

Bromberg, Alan B. "'Pure Democracy and White Supremacy': The Redeemer Period in North Carolina, 1876–1894." Ph.D. dissertation, University of Virginia, 1977.

Carrier, John P. "A Political History of Texas During the Reconstruction." Ph.D. dissertation, Vanderbilt University, 1973.

Cash, William M. "Alabama Republicans During Reconstruction: Personal Characteristics, Motivations, and Political Attitudes of Party Activists, 1867–1880." Ph.D. dissertation, University of Alabama, 1973.

Ellenberg, Martha A. "Reconstruction in Arkansas." Ph.D. dissertation, University of Missouri at Columbia, 1967.

Gerber, Richard. "The Liberal Republican Alliance of 1872." Ph.D. dissertation, University of Michigan, 1967.

Hahn, Steven H. "The Roots of Southern Populism: Yeomen Farmers and the Transformation of Georgia's Upper Piedmont, 1850–1890." Ph.D. dissertation, Yale University, 1979.

Hume, Richard L. "The 'Black and Tan' Constitutional Conventions in the Ten Former Confederate States: A Study of their Membership." Ph.D. dissertation, University of Washington, 1969.

Lancaster, James L. "The Scalawags of North Carolina, 1850–1868." Ph.D. dissertation, Princeton University, 1974.

McGee, Edward H. "North Carolina Conservatives and Reconstruction." Ph.D. dissertation, University of North Carolina at Chapel Hill, 1972.

Meador, John A. "Florida Political Parties, 1865–1877." Ph.D. dissertation, University of Florida, 1964.

Moneyhon, Carl. "The Republican Party and Texas Politics, 1865–1874." Ph.D. dissertation, University of Chicago, 1973.

Price, Charles. "Railroads and Reconstruction in North Carolina, 1865–1871." Ph.D. dissertation, University of North Carolina at Chapel Hill, 1959.

Rable, George C. "And There Was No Peace: Violence and Reconstruction Politics." Ph.D. dissertation, Louisiana State University, 1978.

Sansing, David G. "The Role of the Scalawag in Mississippi Reconstruction." Ph.D. dissertation, University of Southern Mississippi, 1969.

Scroggs, Jack B. "Carpetbagger Influence in the Political Reconstruction of the South Atlantic States, 1865–1876." Ph.D. dissertation, University of North Carolina at Chapel Hill, 1951.

Seip, Terry L. "Southern Representatives and Economic Measures during Reconstruction: A Quantitative and Analytical Study." Ph.D. dissertation, Louisiana State University, 1974.

Silverman, Catherine. "'Of Wealth, Virtue, and Intelligence': The Redeemers and Their Triumph in Virginia and North Carolina, 1865–1877." Ph.D. dissertation, City University of New York, 1972.

Summers, Mark W. "Radical Reconstruction and the Gospel of Prosperity: Railroad Aid under the Southern Republicans." Ph.D. dissertation, University of California at Berkeley, 1980.

Wallenstein, Peter R. "From Slave South to New South: Taxes and Spending in Georgia from 1850 Through Reconstruction." Ph.D. dissertation, Johns Hopkins University, 1973.

Ward, Judson C. "Georgia under the Bourbon Democrats, 1872–1890." Ph.D. dissertation, University of North Carolina at Chapel Hill, 1947.

Index

Abbott, Joseph C., 185
Adams County, Miss., 41, 138
Agrarians, 228, 235–36, 263–65, 268, 275–77; in 1870s constitutional conventions, 191–92, 197, 201–5, 210, 214, 220. *See also* Internal improvements: opposition to
Agricultural Reform. *See* Agriculture: reform of
Agriculture, 68; lien laws and, 105, 147–48, 247–56; ignored during Reconstruction, 221–23; legislation favoring, 198–99, 221–36; and merchants, 231, 233, 247–56, 318 (n.41); and industry, 232–35, 316 (n.49), 321 (n.86); reform of, 238–41, 248–49, 256–57, 263; labor control in, 242–56; impact of labor settlement on, 256–63, 321 (nn.82,85). *See also* individual states: agriculture in; individual states: labor control in
Agriculture, Departments of, 198–99, 225–26, 229
Aiken, D. Wyatt, 224, 240, 248, 257, 316 (n.49)
Aiken, Warren, 98
Akerman, Amos, 29, 49, 191
Alabama, 4, 178; and "new movement," 15–16; and New Departure, 16–17, 19, 58, 61–64, 66, 69–70, 73, 77–79, 82, 85; Republicans in, 20–21, 26, 34, 36, 40, 45–48, 51–53, 139–41, 143, 301 (n.17); ex-Whigs in, 92–93, 98, 101–4, 266; and 1872 election, 109, 111–15, 122, 124–28, 136, 178; and white-line, 151, 156–58, 164–65, 169–73, 175–76; and 1875 constitutional convention, 173, 182–83, 188–89, 191, 200–203, 211, 215, 219, 308 (n.35); and agriculture, 222–23, 226–27, 230–31, 234; and labor system, 239, 243–47, 249, 252–53, 258–59, 318 (n.36)
Alabama and Chattanooga Railroad, 85, 215
Alabama State Journal: quoted, 113, 125, 136, 176, 231
Alaska, 70
Alcorn, James L., 13, 166, 211, 296 (n.13); as leading Centrist, 35, 38, 45–48, 54–55, 94, 142, 155
Alcorn, Robert, 112
Alexander, P. W., 98
Alexander, Thomas B., 89–90, 97
Alexandria, La., 159
Alston, Robert, 216–17

Repudiation of debts. *See* Debt: state
Retrenchment, 143–47, 180–81,
191, 214, 218, 228–29, 258; in
Miss., 144–45, 166–67, 211–12;
in S.C., 143–45, 166–67, 212; in
La., 145, 160, 210; in Ark., 146; in
Ala., 183, 201; in N.C., 199; in
Tex., 203–5; in Ga., 207
Rhett, Robert B., 170
Rice, Benjamin F., 51
Rice, Samuel, 48, 93, 114
Richards, Daniel, 27
Richmond *Dispatch*, 231
Richmond *Whig*, 92
Ridding, A. W., 83
Riker, William, 23–24
Roberts, Oran M., 193, 203, 205, 270
Robertson, Thomas, 163
Rodman, William B., 45–46
Rose, U. M., 197
Roudanez, Louis, 154
Ruby, George T., 27, 38, 220
Russell, Daniel, 140–41

Sanford, John W. A., 61, 82, 84, 171
Saunders, William, 27, 39
Savannah, Ga., 39, 42
Sawyer, Frederick, 50, 163
Sayre, P. Tucker, 93
Scalawags (or natives), 29, 35–37,
42–43, 46, 93, 103–4, 113, 137.
See also Centrists
Schenck, David, 100, 125
Scott, Robert K., 34, 50–51
Scott, Winfield, 7
Screws, W. W., 93
Secession, 6n, 8, 96–98, 101–2, 158;
secessionists, 8, 97, 101–4, 113,
171–73, 175, 306 (n.77)
Selma *Times and Argus*, 223; quoted,
58, 77, 156
Semmes, Thomas J., 209, 216
Senate, U.S., 10, 30, 42, 54, 83, 139,
259, 273–74; senators, 13, 42,
50–52, 84, 110, 113, 130, 138, 142

Senter, DeWitt, 12, 14, 194
Settle, Thomas, 185
Seward, William H., 91
Seymour, Horatio, 4, 121–22, 135
Sharkey, William L., 165
Silbey, Joel, 24–25, 291 (n.65)
Silver, remonetization of, 273–74
Simonton Plan, 213
Simpson, William D., 221
Simrall, Horatio, 45, 48
Singleton, Otho R., 171, 267
Sloss, James W., 173
Smith, Ashbel, 121, 204
Smith, W. N. H., 95
Smith, William A., 45, 95
Smith, William H., 26, 34–35, 46–
48, 113
Somerville, Henderson M., 82
South Carolina, 7, 22, 60, 97, 160,
163, 221; Republicans in, 24, 31,
34–36, 40, 50–52, 137, 141–47;
New Departure in, 59–60, 62–63,
66, 69; and 1872 election, 109,
113, 115, 122, 130, 136; and labor
system, 147–48, 240, 243, 245,
249, 253; and white-line, 151–53,
155–56, 164–76, 178; and consti-
tutional revision, 194, 211–12,
215; and agriculture, 224–26, 228,
231, 235
Sparrow, Thomas, 95
Specie Resumption Act, 270, 273
Spencer, George E., 52, 113
State aid for internal improvements.
See Internal improvements; New
South
State rights. *see* Democratic party (of
the South): doctrines of
Stay laws, 31, 105
Stearns, Marcellus, 142
Stephens, Alexander H., 7–8, 56, 99;
and Grant, 8, 160–64, 282 (n.5);
and New Departure, 76, 80–85,
109, 126, 176
Stelle, J. Parish, 224